Choosing Death

Habent sua fata libelli

choosing death

suicide

and

calvinism

in early

modern

geneva

jeffrey r. watt

Copyright © 2001 Jeffrey R. Watt
Published by Truman State University Press
Kirksville, MO 63501
www2.truman.edu/tsup
All rights reserved.

Library of Congress Cataloging-in-Publication Data

Watt, Jeffrey R. (Jeffrey Rodgers), 1958–
Choosing death : suicide and Calvinism in early modern Geneva / Jeffrey
    R. Watt. p. cm. — (Sixteenth century essays & studies)
Includes bibliographical references and index.
ISBN 0-943549-87-6 (pbk. : alk. paper) — ISBN 0-943549-81-7 (case-
bound : alk. paper)
    1. Suicide—Switzerland—History. 2. Calvinism—Switzerland—His-
tory—16th century. I. Title. II. Series.

HV6548.S9 W37 2001
362.28'09494—dc21

Cover design: Teresa Wheeler, Truman State University designer
Text is set in Adobe Garamond 11/14
Printed in the United States of America

To my parents

Contents

Map and Tables

Map

Tables

Acknowledgments

Since beginning work on this book in the summer of 1990, I have received invaluable assistance, encouragement, and criticism from many different sources. In Geneva I had the privilege of working in what must be Europe's best-organized archives for Old Regime sources. I thank the staff of the Archives d'Etat for their diligence and indulgence in accommodating my requests to consult incredible numbers of documents. My greatest debt in Geneva is surely to Dr. Barbara Roth-Lochner, associate archivist, who conscientiously directed me to pertinent documents and patiently answered my countless queries about Genevan sources and historiography. Although her assiduous assistance in the archives was crucially important, Barbara went the extra mile by reading in minute detail the entire book manuscript, making some valuable suggestions for changes. Even more, though, I thank Barbara and Professor Robert Roth for their very warm friendship and hospitality.

During my various stays in Switzerland, I befriended other Genevan historians, who also generously shared with me their knowledge of Genevan sources and history. With fond memories, I thank Drs. Michel Porret, Frédéric Sardet, Dominique Zumkeller, Bernard Lescaze, and the late Gabriella Cahier-Buccelli. Very special thanks go to Dr. Liliane Mottu-Weber, who helped me on so many occasions, kindly sharing with me her time and expertise in the social and economic history of Geneva. I also am most grateful to Dr. Antoinette Emch-Dériaz, a native of Geneva, who read the manuscript in meticulous detail and suggested many useful changes, particularly with respect to the history of medicine.

While the bulk of research was conducted in the state archives, I also consulted some sources at the Institut d'Histoire de la Réformation at the Université de Genève. For helping me identify pertinent literary and theological sources on early modern suicide, I am most grateful to Drs. Francis Higman, Alain Dufour, Reinhard Bodenmann, and especially Max Engammare—my heartfelt thanks to Max and Dr. Isabelle Engammare-Malaise for their generosity in sharing ideas and for their warm hospitality.

My summer research stays in Geneva fortunately often coincided with those of my mentor, Professor Robert Kingdon, who on countless occasions shared his ideas with me, offering invaluable constructive criticism on this project. Thanks also to Dr. Thomas Lambert, friend, colleague, and paleographer extraordinaire, who gave me some useful tips while I was in Geneva, and to Karen Spierling, who checked on some details in the archives when I could not be in the city of Calvin.

On this side of the Atlantic, I received important guidance from Professor Michael MacDonald, whose work on suicide I greatly admire, and from Professors Barbara Diefendorf and James Farr. Here at the University of Mississippi, I am grateful for encouragement and suggestions from my colleagues Professors Lester Field, Kees Gispen, Robert Haws, and Winthrop Jordan. Many thanks are also due to Paul Thayer, who graciously shared his linguistic skills and encyclopedic knowledge of the history of ideas, and to the industrious staff of the H. Henry Meeter Center at Calvin Seminary for their assistance in identifying works by Calvin that are germane to the subject under study. Professor David Greenberg kindly directed me to the most pertinent recent sociological literature on suicide.

Highest commendations go to Professor Raymond Mentzer, general editor of the Sixteenth-Century Essays and Studies monograph series, and to Paula Presley, director of Truman State University Press, for the very professional and efficient manner in which they have handled the evaluation of the manuscript and the publication of this book.

I gratefully acknowledge the generous support I received from the National Endowment for the Humanities and from the University of Mississippi's College of Liberal Arts and Office of Research, which helped make my sojourns in Geneva possible.

More personally, my biggest debt, as always, is to my wife, Isabella. During our stays in Geneva, she often set aside her own work to go to the archives and peruse with me the haunting accounts of untimely deaths among early modern Genevans. She has not only served as my computer guru but has cheerfully endured over the past decade many a conversation about the morbid subject of suicide. Though not with us when this project began, Julia and Erica have made two happy people even happier. Finally, I thank my parents, Jim and Joan Watt, for their continued moral support and interest in my scholarly pursuit—though it has now been twenty years, I am still thankful that they did not object when I chose graduate studies in history over law school!

I have incorporated into this book material that has appeared in different form in the *Archive for Reformation History* 89 (1998): 227–46; *Church History* 66 (1997): 463–76; the *Journal of Family History* 21 (1996): 63–86; and *The Identity of Geneva: The Christian Commonwealth, 1564–1864*, edited by John B. Roney and Martin Klauber, 111–18, published by Greenwood. I thank the various editors for their permission to reuse material here.

Abbreviations

AEG   Archives d'Etat de Genève
CO   Ioannis Calvini Opera Quae Supersunt Omnia
EC   Registres d'Etat Civil
LM   Livres des Morts
PC   Procès Criminels
RC   Registres du Conseil
SC   Supplementa Calviniana

Introduction

THROUGHOUT HISTORY many great minds have pondered the issue of suicide. In the ancient Greco-Roman world, suicide caught the attention of the great philosophers, playwrights, and statesmen. Pythagoras, Plato, Aristotle, Cicero, and Seneca, among others, all considered whether it was licit to end one's life voluntarily. With the appearance of Christianity, theologians discussed the legitimacy of "self-murder" (one can hardly say "debated," given the lack of disagreement on the issue). In their respective eras, Augustine, Aquinas, and, as we shall see, John Calvin, all considered whether suicide was right or wrong. From ancient Rome into the modern era, jurists and legal scholars argued about what, if any, penalties should be inflicted upon the estates or bodies of suicides. The philosophes of the eighteenth century discussed at length whether suicide was ever permissible and whether legal traditions toward it were just.

Modern scholarship has shifted away from the ethics of taking one's life, concentrating on the causes of suicide. In the nineteenth and twentieth centuries, the work on suicide that has garnered the most attention has largely been the scholarship of two sorts of researchers: psychiatrists and psychologists, on the one hand; sociologists, on the other. Of the former, one of the first scholars to examine suicide from the point of view of physiology was Etienne Esquirol, who believed that all suicides were mentally ill, a belief that grew out of the views on suicide of the eighteenth-century philosophes. In 1838 Esquirol wrote in his *Maladies mentales* that people attempt to take their lives only when delirious and that all suicides are "alienated."[1] The

---

[1] Etienne Esquirol, *Des maladies mentales: Considerées sous les rapports médical, hygiénique, et médico-légal,* 3 vols. (Paris: J. S. Chaude, 1838). See also Henry Romilly Fedden, *Suicide: A Social and Historical Study* (New York: Benjamin Blom, 1972), 309; Georges Minois, *Histoire du suicide: La société occidentale face à la mort volontaire* (Paris: Fayard, 1995), 369.

German psychiatrist Emil Kraepelin (1856–1926) stressed the physiological causes of suicide. Most notably, he observed that organic imbalances underlie depressive disorders; consequently, manic depressives by their very constitution are more prone to suicide than others.[2]

For Sigmund Freud (1856–1939) and other psychoanalysts, suicide results not from physiology but from intrapsychic conflicts. According to one hypothesis based on Freudian thought, suicide can result when people concentrate their libido entirely on one object. If, for example, a man invests all his romantic and sexual interests in one woman and that relationship fails—be it through unrequited love or the departure or death of the woman—life for him may no longer seem worth living, and suicide may follow. Psychologists also talk about the desire for tranquility, shared to varying degrees by all humans, which is associated with the desire to return to the stillness of the womb. Since people can never realize this infantile wish, they may feel frustrated in life and melancholic and ultimately may be pushed to kill themselves by this unfulfilled wish for tranquility.[3] Whether they stress biological imbalances or psychic conflicts, both psychological and psychiatric approaches to suicide stress the inner causes that push a person to take his or her life.[4]

By contrast, sociologists have argued that societal forces, external impetuses, are fundamentally important in the etiology of suicide. Many have insisted that suicide has been endemic to modernization and industrialization. In 1879 Enrico Morselli, for example, argued that with industrialization (modernization or urbanization would probably be better terms) the traditional villages of rural Europe gradually disappeared. The rural societies of premodern Europe, Morselli avowed, provided an unquestioned culture based on seemingly timeless traditions. The urban environment that supplanted rural society was characterized by constant cultural change. People increasingly expressed doubts about and criticisms of the ways of the past

[2]Howard I. Kushner, *American Suicide: A Psychocultural Exploration* (New Brunswick, N.J. and London, 1991), 6–7.

[3]Henry Romilly Fedden, *Suicide: A Social and Historical Study* (New York: Benjamin Blom, 1972), 322–23; Kushner, *American Suicide*, 3–6.

[4]Such researchers have tended to modify the connection between suicide and mental illness: rather than insist that all suicides are psychologically disturbed, they tend to look for varying degrees of risk for suicide among different diagnostic groups; David Lester, *Why People Kill Themselves: A Summary of Research Findings on Suicidal Behavior* (Springfield, Ill.: Charles C. Thomas, 1972), 193.

and offered a wide range of alternatives, leading to "normative confusion." This cultural confusion allegedly could lead to despair and, consequently, to growing numbers of suicides.[5]

The figure who towers above the rest in sociological research on suicide is Emile Durkheim (1858–1917), a contemporary of Freud and Kraepelin. Though it has been highly praised and roundly criticized, Durkheim's *Suicide: A Study in Sociology* has undeniably served as a matrix for the sociological study of self-inflicted deaths. There is no work on suicide in psychology or psychiatry that has had anywhere near the impact on those disciplines that Durkheim's *Suicide* has had on sociology. Durkheim's work and that of many followers is based on the assumption that society, or "collective reality," exists external to individuals. Durkheim believed that the suicide rate of a given society is a most effective gauge with which to measure that society's overall cultural or moral health. Struck with the regularity of suicide rates in societies, Durkheim and his followers have interpreted these statistics and endeavored to explain why suicide rates are higher for some societies than for others. Durkheim dismissed the importance of climatic, ethnic, and organic factors behind the widely varying rates at which different populations take their lives, insisting rather that variations in suicide rates reflect differences in social organization. For Durkheim, suicide rates varied inversely to the degree of religious, domestic, and political integration of a particular society: the stronger the support one receives from one's religion, family, and state, the less likely a person is to commit suicide.[6]

In his work on suicide in the late nineteenth and early twentieth centuries, Maurice Halbwachs attributed virtually all suicides to social isolation: a variety of setbacks—job loss, financial reversal, poverty, family sorrow, unhappy love affair, physical or mental illness, drunkenness—can all result in the cutting off of the individual from collective society, increasing the propensity for suicide.[7] Social isolation, or the lack of social integration, has become the one factor that sociologists most often cite as predisposing individuals to commit suicide: the more integrated individuals are in a society,

[5]Enrico Morselli, *Il Suicidio: Saggio di statistica morale comparata* (Milan: Dumolard, 1879). See also Steven Stack, "Suicide and Religion: A Comparative Analysis," *Sociological Focus* 14 (1981): 207–20.

[6]Emile Durkheim, *Suicide: A Study in Sociology*, trans. John A. Spaulding and George Simpson, ed. George Simpson (New York: Free Press, 1951).

[7]Maurice Halbwachs, *Les causes du suicide* (Paris: Félix Alcan, 1930), 512–13.

the fewer suicides are likely to occur; the more people are isolated, the more likely they are to take their lives.[8] In dealing with this issue, the sociologists Jack Gibbs and Walter Martin provided a nuanced explanation, suggesting that the key to variations in suicide rates is status integration. Each person occupies a number of roles or statuses in society, based on age, sex, race, religion, and so forth. They argue that suicide rates vary directly with the degree to which individuals' different statuses conflict in a given society; the more closely people follow the roles society prescribes for them, the lower society's suicide rate will be.[9] There are also some important sociological schools of thought that reject Durkheimian methodology. Among the most important critics is Jack Douglas, who along with others, rejects entirely the use of official statistics, deeming them highly idiosyncratic and unreliable.[10]

While more than five thousand articles and books have been written about suicide from the point of view of sociology, psychology, and medicine, relatively little has been published on the history of suicide. Those works that have been written generally are of two types: studies in intellectual and legal history, and attempts to reconstruct the suicide rates of particular societies. Of the former type, the most ambitious and impressive work remains Albert Bayet's *Le suicide et la morale*, which traces the attitudes toward suicide of philosophers, jurists, theologians, and creative writers from Greco-Roman antiquity through the nineteenth century.[11] Georges Minois has made a fresh contribution to the history of changes in the attitudes toward and the judicial treatment of suicide with his broad synthesis, which concentrates on the early modern era.[12] While an understanding of the views on suicide of intellectual and judicial leaders is important, it does not tell us all we want to know about self-inflicted deaths.

A number of other historical works, basing their research on official statistics, have endeavored to establish the frequency with which members of a given society took their lives. Historians who pursue such research have been

---

[8]Steve Taylor, *Durkheim and the Study of Suicide* (New York: St. Martin's Press, 1982), 27.

[9]Jack Gibbs and Walter T. Martin, *Status Integration and Suicide: A Sociological Study* (Eugene: University of Oregon Books, 1964).

[10]Jack D. Douglas, *The Social Meanings of Suicide* (Princeton: Princeton University Press, 1967). See also Taylor, *Durkheim*.

[11]Albert Bayet, *Le suicide et la morale* (Paris: Félix Alcan, 1922; reprint, New York: Arno Press, 1975).

[12]Minois, *Histoire du suicide*.

inspired, to varying degrees, by Durkheim's pioneering work. Like Durkheim, they stress the importance of social forces in determining the levels of suicide in a society, viewing the suicide rate as an effective barometer for measuring its overall health. A superb example of this type of historical work is Olive Anderson's study of suicide in Victorian and Edwardian England. Effectively using official statistics, supplemented by a host of other sources, Anderson finds important differences in suicide rates based on gender and on region, comparing areas that were industrialized and urbanized with others that remained largely rural.[13]

For most areas of early modern Europe, legal records and death registers are generally too spotty and inconsistent to do much beyond outlining the judicial treatment of suicide.[14] An outstanding work on early modern suicide is, however, Michael MacDonald and Terence Murphy's *Sleepless Souls: Suicide in Early Modern England*. Because a large number of records are lost, the authors eschew trying to make broad conclusions based on statistics or speculating on what "caused" people to take their lives. Rather, they analyze the "meaning of suicide" by looking at suicide as a cultural phenomenon. Examining a wide range of sources, including coroners' reports, selected parish registers, newspapers, and a host of other published sources, Mac-Donald and Murphy trace changing attitudes—both "popular" and "elite"— toward suicide. They persuasively argue that the early modern era in England witnessed revolutionary changes in myriad areas which were readily reflected in the changing views on and treatment of suicide. The increased centralization of royal power under the Tudors, the Reformation of the Church, the Civil War, the Enlightenment reaction against religious fanaticism, and the birth of the popular press all influenced the changing cultural meaning of

---

[13]Olive Anderson, *Suicide in Victorian and Edwardian England* (Oxford: Clarendon Press, 1987).

[14]See, for example, Alain Joblin, "Le suicide à l'époque moderne: Un exemple dans la France du Nord-Ouest, à Boulogne-sur-Mer," *Revue historique* 589 (1994): 85–119; Alfred Schnegg, "Justice et suicide sous l'Ancien Régime," *Musée Neuchâtelois* (1982): 73–94. Even certain statistical works tell us more about changes in the judicial treatment of suicide than in the frequency of self-inflicted deaths. S. J. Stevenson believes that the recorded increase in suicide verdicts in the late sixteenth century was most likely simply the result of more systematic investigations; "The Rise of Suicide Verdicts in South-East England, 1530–1590: The Legal Process," *Continuity and Change* 2 (1987): 37–75; see also idem, "Social and Economic Contributions to the Pattern of 'Suicide' in South-East England, 1530–1590," *Continuity and Change* 2 (1987): 225–62.

suicide in England between 1500 and 1800.[15]

This book includes elements of all the methodologies employed thus far in research on the history of suicide. Like the work of Bayet and Minois, this study considers both the views on suicide of early modern intellectual leaders and judicial customs pertaining to self-inflicted deaths. Research on the testimony of witnesses also provides palpable evidence concerning the cultural meanings of suicide for both Geneva's ruling elite and the rank and file. Moreover, this is the first examination of suicide in a given area, based on consistent documentation, to cover the entire early modern period. It is also the first study that will provide reliable evidence on suicide rates for premodern Europe. Thus, while they are both studies of long *durée*, this examination of suicide has a more important statistical element than does MacDonald and Murphy's work. This study concentrates on one small state, the Republic of Geneva, whose archival sources are incredibly rich and, even more important, most accessible thanks to a vast series of indices and inventories that provide a unique opportunity to study early modern suicide.

Because these sources exist, this book, like Anderson's, examines the sociology of suicide in unusually close detail. It includes precise analyses of information pertaining to the age, gender, occupation, class, marital, and parental status of those who took their lives. Unlike Anderson's study, this work is based not on official statistics but rather on a direct examination of death records and inquests following unnatural deaths. I therefore avoid inconsistencies that might result from different authorities who apply widely different standards to determine whether a death was self-inflicted. (As we shall see, in classifying deaths as suicides, I do not always reach the same conclusions as the early modern Genevan magistrates.) The quantity of suicide cases is large enough to provide some meaningful statistical analyses, but small enough to allow a very close examination of all the individual cases.

Apart from the rich documentation available, why is Geneva an appropriate venue for studying early modern suicide? Geneva served as a vitally important arena for both the Protestant Reformation and the Enlightenment, two radically different cultural movements which inform the traditional belief that early modern Europe witnessed developments toward secularism, ratio-

---

[15]Michael MacDonald and Terence R. Murphy, *Sleepless Souls: Suicide in Early Modern England* (Oxford: Clarendon Press, 1990).

nalism, and industrial capitalism. Changes in these areas appeared first in cities, and Geneva was representative of wider European trends.

Geneva's importance as a center of Protestantism was directly related to its political history. For centuries Geneva had been dominated by a prince-bishop who was associated with the ruling house of Savoy. Under great pressure from the inhabitants of the city, the prince-bishop fled in 1533, enabling Genevans to establish an independent state in 1536. Inspired by the proselytizing of various pastors, Genevans decided in May of that year to convert to Protestantism. Their distrust of the former prince-bishop certainly did nothing to discourage Genevans from rejecting Roman Catholicism. John Calvin (1509–64), the great theologian from Picardy, just happened to be passing through Geneva that year when his fellow Frenchman, the reformer William Farel, convinced the young man that he ought to stay to direct the Reformation in Geneva. Though asked to leave two years later, Calvin returned in 1541 at the request of the Genevan government. Calvin spent the rest of his life in Geneva, where he built his church and established the center of Reformed Protestantism. Calvin was able to succeed in building a strong independent church structure to a large extent because he lived in a newly formed small republic in which political power was not yet firmly entrenched. With spiritual leadership centered in Geneva, Reformed Christianity demonstrated the most dynamic growth of Protestant groups in the second half of the sixteenth century. Drawing ideas on church structure and theology from Geneva, Reformed Protestants promoted their faith in France, the Holy Roman Empire, the Netherlands, Scotland, and elsewhere.

Like ancient Athens or Renaissance Florence, Geneva was a small city-state whose cultural influence far surpassed its political importance. After the overthrow of the prince-bishop, Geneva was in effect a free imperial city, though from the beginning the influence of the Holy Roman Empire in Geneva was virtually nonexistent and eventually disappeared entirely. Interestingly, though a republic in fact from 1536, official documents do not use the title of "Republic" until the mid-seventeenth century.[16] Geneva, which did not become part of Switzerland until 1815, remained independent

---

[16]Lucien Fulpius, "Les institutions politiques de Genève dès origines à la fin de l'ancienne république," *Actes de l'Institut National Genevois, nouvelle série* 3 (1965): 17.

thanks to the rivalries of its three more powerful neighbors: Catholic Savoy and France and Protestant Bern. Though larger than any Swiss community throughout the early modern period, Geneva was never among the largest European cities. In 1500, Geneva numbered probably ten to twelve thousand souls, while Paris had between 210,000 and 240,000 inhabitants and Milan, Naples, and Venice all had more than a hundred thousand. The highest population rank that Geneva ever enjoyed among cities in Europe (excluding Russia) was probably 115 to 130 in the mid-eighteenth century, when it was home to 22,700 people.[17] In overthrowing its bishop, Genevans acquired suzerainty over not only the city but also the lands in the surrounding countryside that had belonged either to the bishop or to Roman Catholic religious orders. In addition to the "Franchises," or lands immediately surrounding the city, Geneva attained political control over the parishes of Jussy, Peney, Dardagny, Malval, Genthod, Céligny, and Thiez, though this last was ceded to Savoy in 1639. For the most part, these scattered holdings were enclaves in foreign territory, surrounded by land belonging to Bern or Savoy (see map). The population of these territories that were subject to Genevan rule was significant vis-à-vis that of the city. At the very end of the period under study (1797–98) the city numbered 21,327 people, while the rural population, including Geneva's suburbs, was 9,264.[18]

While its political influence extended little beyond the city's walls, the cultural impact of Calvin's city was felt far and wide. As such, Geneva is a most important site for studying the history of suicide. An examination of suicide in Geneva enables one to gauge the impact of Reformed Protestantism on attitudes toward and the frequency of self-inflicted deaths. More broadly, it serves as a window to its impact on popular religiosity. Certain seminal studies on the history of suicide suggest that Protestants held a special abhorrence for suicide, unmatched by Catholics. MacDonald and Murphy maintain that in England, the Reformation initiated an era of severity with regard to suicide.[19]

---

[17]Paul Baric, "Genève dans le contexte des villes suisses et européennes de 1500 à 1800," in *Mélanges d'histoire économique offerts au Professeur Anne-Marie Piuz*, ed. Liliane Mottu-Weber and Dominique Zumkeller (Geneva: Istec, 1989), 17–33; Alfred Perrenoud, *La population de Genève XVIe–XIXe siècles* (Geneva: Société d'histoire et d'archéologie de Genève, 1979), 37.

[18]Dominique Zumkeller, *Le paysan et la terre: Agriculture et structure agraire à Genève au XVIIIe siècle* (Geneva: Editions Passé Présent, 1992), 16, 25–26.

[19]MacDonald and Murphy, *Sleepless Souls*, 15–106.

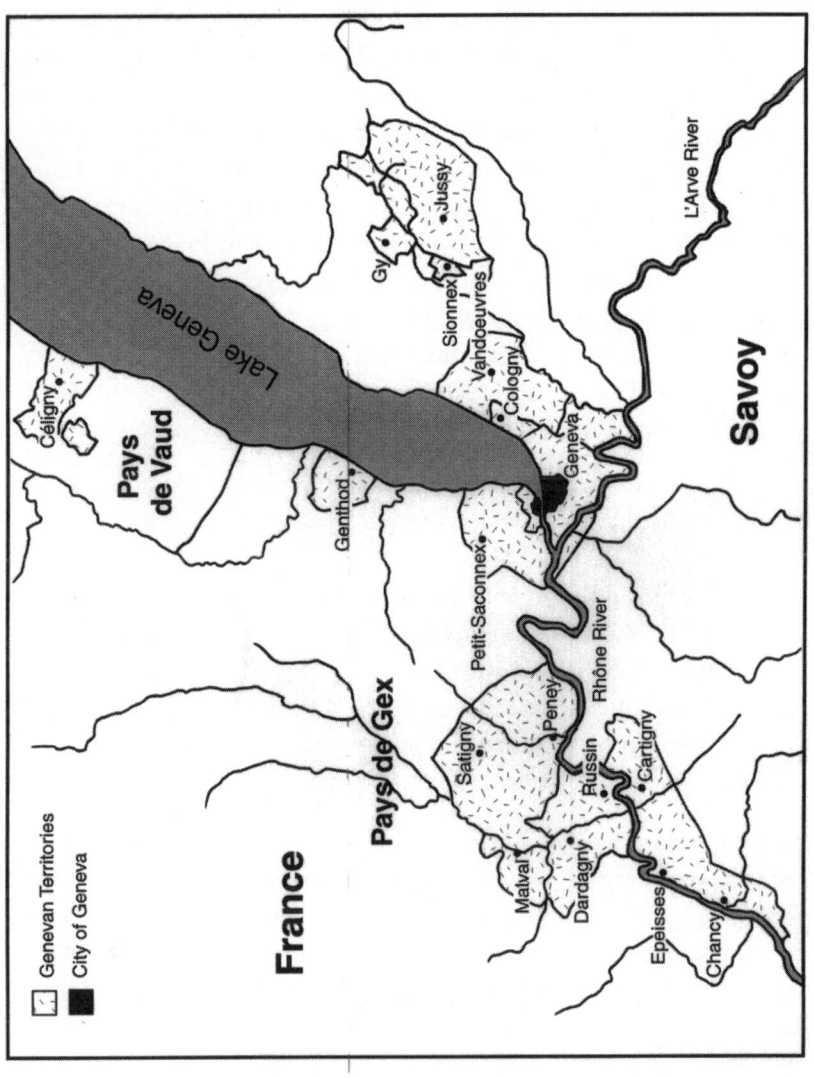

GENEVA AND ITS TERRITORIES IN THE MID-EIGHTEENTH CENTURY
(Based on map in Paul Guichonnet, ed., *Histoire de Genève*, 237.)

Paradoxically, various studies indicate that Protestants had a penchant for suicide. Asserting that suicide is the result of social forces, Durkheim suggested that Protestant societies were more individualistic and less strongly integrated than Catholic societies. Accordingly, Protestants were more likely to commit "egoistic" suicides, occurring when an individual is not adequately integrated into society.[20] Halbwachs argued that this was more an urban-rural than a Protestant-Catholic distinction, but even he found higher suicide rates among rural Protestants than among urban Catholics.[21] Another sociologist, George Simpson, agrees with Durkheim that Protestants, especially Calvinists, kill themselves more often than Catholics, but disagrees as to the cause. Instead of seeing Protestants as less integrated, he sees them as repressed because of certain theological tenets typical of Calvinism:

> Protestant sects [sic] give no sublimatory outlet for infantile repression and frustration, through poetry, art, and ritual, and there is a rampaging of the sense of guilt which cannot be expiated through the confessional but which faces God and his elders' wrath in all its individual nakedness. Calvinism, and to no small degree, Lutheranism, deal with sin repressively and individualistically. In early Protestantism, the unconscious is thrown back upon itself, and later only exclusively non-religious social sanctions hold it in check.[22]

In the Reformation era itself, Luther viewed despair, which might lead to suicide, as a normal part of the spiritual development of the Christian. Acknowledging the difficulty of conforming to God's Law, Luther observed that one could easily despair over one's ability to fulfill what God demands. Luther warned against worrying about one's fate, attributing to diabolical temptation the desire to penetrate the secrets of predestination. Luther ultimately believed that an element of despair was a necessary part of spiritual life and conceded that such fears might lead some to take their lives. Moreover, in sixteenth-century Germany, both Protestants and Catholics were convinced that Lutherans were more likely to suffer from melancholy that

[20]Durkheim, *Suicide*, 152–64.
[21]Halbwachs, *Causes du suicide*, 261–83.
[22]George Simpson, introduction to Durkheim, *Suicide*, 28–29.

was religiously motivated and succumb to suicidal inclinations.[23]

Calvin's theology has been depicted as particularly prone to fostering suicidal inclinations. The Calvinist theory of double predestination has been described as a "destructive weapon" that nurtured melancholy and feelings of despair. According to Calvin, the believer can do nothing to be saved, since one is not saved by merit or works. It has been argued that some believers felt utterly helpless, hopeless, and insignificant vis-à-vis this judgmental and seemingly inaccessible God. As believers were plagued by doubts about whether they were among the saved, melancholy and suicide were supposedly endemic among Calvinists.[24] Markus Schär holds the Reformed faith fundamentally responsible for the significant number of suicides that plagued the area around Zurich from the late seventeenth through the late eighteenth century. He describes the typical suicides as extremely pious Christians who held themselves up to unrealistically high religious norms. The melancholy that affected them was the result of spiritual unrest, based on intense feelings of guilt for sins that could not be forgiven. According to Schär, the growing numbers of suicides around Zurich stemmed from the increasing assimilation of strict Reformed piety.[25]

In England, contemporaries blamed the Puritans for nurturing "religious melancholy," a psychological state characterized by despair over one's salvation, which allegedly stemmed from Calvinistic predestinarian views. In the early seventeenth century, for example, the Anglican parson Robert Burton wrote that one of the most important causes of suicide was religious despair. He accused the Puritans of contributing to religious despair through their frightening apocalyptical sermons and their emphasis on the doctrine of predestination, which inspired terror among many. A few historians have found

---

[23]H. C. Erik Midelfort, *A History of Madness in Sixteenth-Century Germany* (Stanford: Stanford University Press, 1999), 80–139; idem, "Religious Melancholy and Suicide: On the Reformation Origins of a Sociological Stereotype," in *Madness, Melancholy, and the Limits of the Self*, ed. Andrew D. Weiner and Leonard V. Kaplan, vol. 3 of *Graven Images: Studies in Culture, Law, and the Sacred* (Madison: University of Wisconsin Law School, 1996), 41–42.

[24]Fedden, *Suicide*, 157–58.

[25]Markus Schär, *Seelennöte der Untertanen: Selbstmord, Melancholie und Religion im Alten Zürich 1500–1800* (Zurich: Chronos, 1985). By contrast, Werner Blesch, "'Sich selbsten leibloß gemacht und aus Verzweiflung erhenkt': Selbsttötungen im 16. Jahrhundert im Raum Mosbach-Eberbach-Sinsheim," *Beiträge zur Volkskunde in Baden-Württemberg* 5 (1993): 311–31, found that suicide was extremely rare near Heidelberg during the years 1514–94. Although he does not blame Protestantism, he too finds that some of those who took their lives despaired over God's power and mercy.

evidence that seems to corroborate the view that Puritanism did nurture despair and suicidal proclivities.[26] Obsessed with his sinfulness, Nehemiah Wallington, a Puritan artisan in London, suffered from melancholy and despair and attempted suicide several times as a young man in the early seventeenth century. He also collected stories of suicides of "godly" people who suffered anxiety over their salvation.[27] Not surprisingly, Calvinism has been blamed for the epidemic of suicides which allegedly occurred in seventeenth-century England.[28]

As the most Calvinistic state ever, the Republic of Geneva is an ideal case study for examining the possible link between the Reformed movement and suicide. By contrast, Geneva of the late eighteenth century was one of the most important centers of the Enlightenment and, as such, was viewed less as the Protestant Rome than as a "little Paris." Geneva was of course the birthplace of Jean-Jacques Rousseau, and Voltaire lived just outside Geneva for decades. This study will therefore help clarify whether the Enlightenment did indeed effect a certain secularization of mentality and, if so, whether this might have removed some restraints on suicidal proclivities. Moreover, though it did not witness the development of a steam-powered factory system typical of the Industrial Revolution in England, by the late eighteenth century Geneva was a very important site for the manufacture of *indiennes*, colorfully printed cotton fabrics. These factories employed thousands, almost all of whom were unskilled workers who formed a type of nascent proletariat. Their experiences can shed light on whether early industrialization nurtured anomie and thus contributed to an increasing resort to suicide. In short, this small state is most suitable for evaluating whether the early modern era was a period of decisive change in European history. If the alleged trends toward secularism, rationalism, and industrial capitalism had a major impact on popular mentality, one would expect to see changes in

---

[26]MacDonald and Murphy, *Sleepless Souls*, 64–67; Samuel Ernest Sprott, *The English Debate on Suicide from Donne to Hume* (La Salle, Ill.: Open Court, 1961), 29–54. See also Midelfort, "Religious Melancholy and Suicide," 41–56.

[27]Paul S. Seaver, *Wallington's World: A Puritan Artisan in Seventeenth-Century London* (Stanford: Stanford University Press, 1985), 16–24, 31, 60. The seventeenth-century physician Richard Napier, himself hostile to Puritanism, had many patients who suffered suicidal compulsions that were based on their fear of damnation. The bulk of these patients, however, apparently were not related to Puritanism; see Michael MacDonald, *Mystical Bedlam: Madness, Anxiety, and Healing in Seventeenth-Century England* (Cambridge: Cambridge University Press, 1981), 220–21.

[28]Sprott, *English Debate on Suicide*, 29–54.

opinions concerning suicide and in the numbers of people who took their lives.

Chapter 1 outlines the data concerning unnatural deaths, be they suicides, homicides, or accidents. A thorough examination of the data demonstrates that there was a dramatic increase in suicide in the eighteenth century, particularly after 1750, an increase that cannot be dismissed as the result of lost records or lax investigations for one era and complete registers and strict inquests for another. The remainder of the book endeavors to discover what was behind Genevans' growing willingness to choose death. The second chapter therefore looks at the intellectual and legal dimensions. It takes a broad look at the views on suicide of early modern intellectual leaders, including those of Geneva's most famous residents: Calvin for the Reformation era, and Rousseau and Voltaire for the eighteenth century. This chapter includes an examination of the penalties imposed against suicide in Geneva, comparing them with practices elsewhere and outlining the antecedents for such sentences. It shows that there were very significant changes in opinions about suicide over the course of the early modern era, which were reflected in important alterations in the judicial treatment of self-inflicted deaths in Geneva.

The remaining chapters examine the suicides themselves in an effort to establish how suicide was popularly perceived, who killed themselves, what drove them to take their lives, and what factors accounted for the huge increase in suicide in the late eighteenth century. Chapter 3 looks at the economic and political dimensions of suicide. Examining the political and economic statuses of suicides, this chapter evaluates the occupations and the level of wealth of people who were most and least likely to take their lives. It outlines Geneva's economic fluctuations and political conflicts throughout the early modern period in order to discern whether these vicissitudes had a direct impact on the number of Genevan men and women who committed suicide. Popular attitudes toward material wealth are also studied to see if such changing mores might have influenced the risk of suicide.

From a variety of perspectives, chapter 4 looks at the impact of the family on suicide. It investigates the family situation of suicides, identifying the marital and parental statuses of those who took their lives and comparing them with those of the population at large. It inquires into the possible transformations over these two and a half centuries in the area of sentiment:

was romantic love becoming more important in the selection of spouses and the sustaining of marriage, and were the affective ties within the nuclear family becoming stronger? If so, did these sentimental changes play a role in Geneva's increase in suicide toward the end of the early modern period?

The last chapter deals with several aspects of the cultural dimension of suicide. It looks at the popular views on suicide throughout these two hundred fifty years in an effort to see if there was a significant change in mentality. Most notably, it asks whether suicide was associated more with sin, religion, and magic in one era and with illness, medicine, and insanity in another. These popular attitudes toward suicide can provide a valuable window to the mentality of an entire society. This chapter also investigates whether Geneva experienced a secularization of mentality in the eighteenth century: did Genevans of the Enlightenment period believe that the supernatural played a lesser role in affairs on earth than their ancestors of the Reformation had believed? Did the religious values of the clergy and the rank and file change at all during these centuries? Could a secularization of mentality or a modification of popular piety have contributed to the growing number of self-inflicted deaths?

This study of long *durée* affirms that the early modern period was indeed a pivotal epoch in European history. Combining elements of social, cultural, intellectual, legal, and economic history, this work shows that the significant variations in suicide rates over these two and a half centuries reflect most important social and cultural changes. Far from contradicting each other, the theories of Kraepelin, Freud, Durkheim, and their respective successors complement each other in uncovering the complex causes of suicide.[29]

---

[29]For a fine interdisciplinary study, see Kushner, *American Suicide*.

1

Suicides, Homicides, and Accidents: The Data

SOURCES AND METHODOLOGY

THE GENEVAN STATE ARCHIVES have a series of source collections that are exceptionally well preserved and precisely catalogued, providing a unique opportunity to study early modern suicide. With Calvinistic precision, authorities in Geneva consistently investigated and recorded unnatural deaths. Among the most valuable sources are inquests following unnatural deaths, which are contained in the criminal proceedings. These registers are quite voluminous, numbering about twenty thousand for all early modern cases, and include investigations of theft, battery, fraud, and many other types of crimes and misadventures. Close to two thousand of these are inquests concerning sudden or unnatural deaths, providing valuable detailed information about events surrounding these untimely deaths. Upon learning of an unnatural death, one of Geneva's six Auditeurs, a type of police officer created in the sixteenth century, went to the scene of the death to investigate.[1] A physician examined the body, wrote a description of the state of the

---

[1]Michel Porret, *Le crime et ses circonstances: De l'esprit de l'arbitraire au siècle des Lumières selon les réquisitoires des procureurs généraux de Genève* (Geneva: Droz, 1995), 54. The office of Auditeur predated Genevan independence: an edict of November 1529 called for the establishment of four (later increased to six) Auditeurs; E. William Monter, *Studies in Genevan Government (1536–1605)* (Geneva: Droz, 1964), 61. For an outline of the responsibilities of the Auditeurs, see Barbara Roth-Lochner, *Messieurs de la Justice et leur greffe: Aspects de la législation, de l'administration de la justice civile genevoise et du monde de la pratique sous l'Ancien Régime* (Geneva: Société d'histoire et d'archéologie de Genève, 1992), 91.

corpse, and postulated on the probable cause of demise. The Auditeur wrote a detailed description of the circumstances in which the body was found and made a minute inventory of the clothing and other personal effects found on or near the body. Pending a criminal sentence, the Auditeur placed seals on the personal assets of the deceased to prevent anyone, including close relatives, from absconding with them. The Auditeur also carefully interrogated all persons who might be able to shed light on the circumstances leading up to the death.[2] While the Auditeurs investigated crimes and questionable deaths in the city, the Republic created in 1536 six Châtelains (later reduced to five), who inquired into similar affairs in surrounding territories which, following the overthrow of the prince-bishop, were subject to the city of Geneva.[3] The goal of these investigations, which resembled police inquiries in some neighboring areas of early modern Europe, was of course to distinguish among suicides, homicides, and accidental deaths.[4] Though fully extant from the late 1600s, some criminal proceedings have been lost for the sixteenth and seventeenth centuries.

Death records are also most important, effectively filling gaps and complementing the criminal proceedings. For every death in the city of Geneva, a surgeon examined the body and recorded the name, age, profession, and political status of the deceased; the date, hour, and place of death; and, most important for this study, a brief description of the cause of death. I have read all these documents from 1549, the date of the first extant record, through 1798. Recording well more than a hundred thousand deaths in 250 years, these *Livres des Morts* have few lacunae—none after 1616—and provide

---

[2]There are cases, however, where the Auditeurs showed some indulgence for the grieving close relatives of the deceased, refraining from interrogating them. This was particularly true in the eighteenth century.

[3]André-Luc Poncet, *Les châtelains et l'administration de la justice dans les mandements genevois sous l'Ancien Régime (1536–1792)* (Geneva: Presses Universitaires Romandes, 1973), 11, 29, 140.

[4]In the seventeenth and eighteenth centuries, procedures virtually identical to Geneva's were employed in Lyonnais and Beaujolais, northwestern France, the principality of Neuchâtel, and the canton of Bern and its dependent territories; see Françoise Bayard, "Régions et morts subites en Lyonnais et Beaujolais aux XVIIe et XVIIIe siècles," in *Du provincialisme au régionalisme XVIIIe–XXe siècles* (Montbrison: Ville de Montbrison, 1989), 211–22; Alain Joblin, "Le suicide à l'époque moderne: Un exemple dans la France du Nord-Ouest: À Boulogne-sur-Mer," *Revue historique* 589 (1994): 87–93; Alfred Schnegg, "Justice et suicide sous l'Ancien Régime," *Musée Neuchâtelois* (1982): 75–77.

most reliable evidence on the total number of unnatural deaths.[5] Authorities in early modern Geneva, like suicidologists today, consider the following criteria in determining whether a person died by his or her own hand: the direct cause of and circumstances surrounding the death and the personal history of the deceased.[6] With detailed information on the causes of death, death records are thus an essential part of this study.

Also important are the registers of the Small Council, comprised of twenty-five members, four of whom were elected annually as Syndics, the chiefs of state. Although theoretically the General Council, composed of all Citizens, was ultimately the sovereign body in Geneva, this Protestant Republic was no democracy. The Political Edicts of 1543, strongly influenced by Calvin who favored aristocracy and feared democracy, ensured that the Small Council would reign supreme in Geneva. True, the General Council had the right to elect the Syndics, the Small Council, and the Council of Two Hundred. The smaller councils, however, determined the list of eligible candidates for these offices. Moreover, though the General Council had the power to vote on the Small Council's recommendations, it could not initiate legislation. Simply put, throughout the life of the Republic, Geneva was governed by an oligarchy: power was concentrated in the Small Council, which ran the day-to-day affairs of government.[7] The Small Council served not only as the chief legislative body but also as the principal tribunal for civil and criminal matters. Consequently it heard the Auditeurs' reports and passed sentences on all crimes including suicide, which was not officially decriminalized until the end of the eighteenth century. I have consulted the Council's records, fully extant for the life of the Republic, for every death

---

[5]Authorities called for the recording of all deaths in November 1547, though they clearly were not always systematic about registering deaths in the sixteenth century; see *Les sources du droit du canton de Genève*, ed. Emile Rivoire and Victor Van Berchem (Aarau, Switzerland: Sauerländer, 1930), 2:514.

[6]See Steve Taylor, *Durkheim and the Study of Suicide* (New York: St. Martin's Press, 1982), 65–94.

[7]The Council of Two Hundred, which included the twenty-five members of the Small Council, was originally viewed as an intermediary between the Small and General Councils. Though it occasionally tried to assert itself, the Council of Two Hundred eventually lost all independence, including the right to propose legislation. For the most part, members of the Council of Two Hundred deferred and dutifully elected to office the candidates proposed by the Small Council; Lucien Fulpius, "Les institutions politiques de Genève dès origines à la fin de l'ancienne république," *Actes de l'Institut National Genevois*, nouvelle série 3 (1965): 18–19; Robert M. Kingdon, "Calvin and the Government of Geneva," in *Calvinus Ecclesiae Genevensis Custos*, ed. W. H. Neuser (Frankfurt: Lang, 1984), 167–80. See also Kingdon, "Calvinism and Democracy: Some Political Implications and Debates on French Reformed Church Government, 1562–1572," *American Historical Review* 69 (1964): 393–401.

that could possibly have been self-inflicted.

Combined, these various sources provide the unusual opportunity to include statistical analysis in the study of early modern suicide. These various Genevan sources reveal 3,668 unnatural deaths in Geneva from the birth of the Republic in 1536 until its demise in 1798. I have determined that 404 of these deaths, involving 275 men and 129 women, were beyond a reasonable doubt self-inflicted.[8] Filled with rich evidence concerning the individuals and their untimely deaths, the criminal proceedings are easily the most valuable and the most fascinating sources. Of the 404 definite suicides, criminal proceedings have survived for all but seventeen, only two of which date from the eighteenth century. In most cases, the criminal proceedings provide the most important evidence in determining whether a death was self-inflicted.

The sentences passed by the Small Council are, however, also quite useful. Of the 404 certain suicides, 351 are discussed in the registers of the Small Council. Of the 53 that are not, 21 occurred from late 1794 on and 20 of the other 32 suicides occurred before the eighteenth century. (Shortly after the Revolution of December 1792, the Council ceased to function as a court.) In a number of these cases, the Council did not deal with the suicides because the body was never found. The most commonly imposed sentences against suicides pertained to burial, which was obviously a moot point if there was no body. Moreover, the Council ordinarily did not pass judgment regarding a person's estate (including the confiscation of it) unless there was abundant proof that the person was dead. Magistrates usually deemed finding the body as essential to passing such sentences.

---

[8]Previous work has been done on suicide in early modern Geneva. See Laurent Haeberli, "Le suicide à Genève au XVIIIe siècle," in *Pour une histoire qualitative: Etudes offertes à Sven Stelling-Michaud* (Geneva: Presses Universitaires Romandes, 1975), 115–29, a Durkheimian study which attempts to trace changes in suicide rates in the 1700s. Haeberli studied only criminal proceedings, relying heavily on the archives' handwritten *inventaires* to identify self-inflicted deaths. He therefore missed several suicides for which there is no criminal proceeding. More important, he also missed a large number of self-inflicted deaths that were investigated but whose dossiers were labeled simply as "morts" or "levées de corps" rather than "suicides." More recently, Michel Porret has authored several articles on suicide such as "'Je ne suis déjà plus de ce monde': Le suicide des vieillards à Genève aux XVIIe et XVIIIe siècles," in *Le poids des ans: Une histoire de la vieillesse en Suisse Romande,* ed. Geneviève Heller (Lausanne, Switzerland: Editions d'en Bas et Société d'histoire de la Suisse Romande, 1994), 67–94; and "Solitude, mélancolie, souffrance: Le suicide à Genève durant l'Ancien Régime (XVIIe–XVIIIe siècles)," *Cahiers Psychiatriques Genevois* 16 (1994): 9–21. Though of some value from the juridic-medical point of view, these studies are based on selected sources and make little attempt to analyze suicide as a social phenomenon.

Among those suicides that are discussed in the Small Council registers, the amount of information provided varied. At times the registers indicate unambiguously that the members concluded that a death was self-inflicted and passed judgment accordingly. It is thanks to these sentences, together with the death records, that I have been able to uncover eighteen suicides for which there are no extant criminal proceedings. When the Council records do not actually declare that a death was self-inflicted, decisions concerning burial give ample information to infer that the magistrates concluded the death was a suicide. Even if the registers do not specifically deny funerary honors, they may stipulate a variety of conditions that precluded a burial with honors. Funerals that must take place in the early morning or after sundown or burials outside the normal cemetery, for example, were by definition interments without honors. Regardless of the form, the denial of burial honors indicated that Council members were convinced or at least strongly suspected that a death was self-inflicted.[9] I have found no cases in which the Small Council denied funerary honors unless there was considerable evidence that the death was self-inflicted.

It is important to note that this study is not based on official statistics on suicide similar to those examined by Durkheim. Critics avow that official statistics are unreliable, insisting that some coroners are much more likely than others to declare certain deaths self-inflicted, a view that Genevan records tend to corroborate. Jack Douglas, among other sociologists, argues that statistics simply reflect officials' preconceived notions of what drives people to take their lives. For Douglas, suicide is not the result of external social forces. Insisting that external forces have widely varying effects on different individuals, Douglas studies the "social meanings" of suicide; that is, he examines the purported motives for taking one's life, placing them in the context of the social relations in which the suicide was committed. Rejecting official statistics, Douglas calls for a case-study approach by which one

---

[9]Apart from suicides, the only people who were denied funerary rites because of the manner in which they died were people killed in duels. I have not listed as a suicide any death that could conceivably have resulted from a duel. Deaths from duels, however, were not numerous and became rarer during the course of the early modern period. For two and a half centuries, I found only fourteen men who perished as a result of losing a duel, all of whom died from sword wounds. Nine of these died in the seventeenth century, as opposed to only five in the eighteenth.

reaches generalizations through the detailed study of individual suicides.[10]

In pursuing this study, I have borrowed elements both from the Durkheimian and the anti-Durkheimian traditions. On the one hand, I firmly believe that economic fluctuations, political upheavals, marriage patterns, and other social forces can strongly influence suicide rates among different groups. On the other hand, I am basing my conclusions on the detailed analyses of individual cases. I pay close attention to the reports of witnesses to untimely deaths, including comments about possible motives for suicide, although my conclusions are not necessarily those of early modern Genevan officials. Durkheim and other scholars have warned against paying credence to the motives for suicide that witnesses, coroners, and judicial officials put forward. The motives that are assigned to these deaths reputedly do not represent what really drove people to take their lives but merely reflect popular beliefs about why people commit suicide. While it is true that one cannot have direct knowledge of the motives of the deceased, I am nonetheless convinced that explanations for suicides offered by contemporaries generally bore some relation to the causes of suicide. The explanations proffered were shaped by contemporary shared values, an understanding of the social changes then at work, and familiarity with the personality and mental and physical health of those who chose death.[11]

In labeling certain deaths as self-inflicted, I am guided by Durkheim's definition: "The term suicide is applied to all cases of death resulting directly or indirectly from a positive or negative act of the victim himself, which he knows will produce this result."[12] The major difficulty of course is determining whether an individual knew that his or her actions would cause death. Ordinarily a person realizes that leaping off a high cliff will certainly result in death on the rocks below. People who are hallucinating, however, may take that leap believing they can fly; under such circumstances, their deaths

---

[10]Jack Douglas, *The Social Meanings of Suicide* (Princeton: Princeton University Press, 1967), 163–231. Among sociologists who distrust official statistics without going so far as to throw them out altogether is J. Maxwell Atkinson, *Discovering Suicide: Studies in the Social Organization of Sudden Death* (Pittsburgh: University of Pittsburgh Press, 1978).

[11]My methodology has much in common with that of Victor Bailey who studied suicide in a town in nineteenth-century Yorkshire; see *"This Rash Act": Suicide Across the Life Cycle in the Victorian City* (Stanford: Stanford University Press, 1998).

[12]Emile Durkheim, *Suicide: A Study in Sociology*, trans. John A. Spaulding and George Simpson, edited and with an introduction by George Simpson (New York: Free Press, 1951), 44. Shooting oneself would be an example of a positive act, while refraining from eating represents a negative act.

would certainly be involuntary. Genevan magistrates were not always consistent in deciding whether individuals who took their lives were legally culpable. Members of prominent Genevan families were much more apt to be absolved of responsibility for taking their lives than were lesser personages.

André Caille, for example, was a wealthy, thirty-year-old Citizen and merchant who suffered from melancholy prior to shooting himself in his room in 1614. Though not disputing the fact that he died by his own hand, Caille's family begged for mercy, insisting that his mental illness had been the cause of this act. In response to this request, the Small Council decided that Caille could indeed be buried with honors.[13]

In striking contrast was the sentence passed for Jean Bovard, thirty-six, a vinegar maker who committed suicide in June 1645. Having demonstrated extremely bizarre and often violent behavior, Bovard had been treated for several months by various medical professionals, including the surgeon Jean Danel. Immediately before the suicide, Danel and his journeyman surgeon called on Bovard who was in a most agitated state. Bovard was hallucinating, saying he saw two men sleeping with his wife. He repeatedly stabbed the bed and sheets with a knife, thinking that the men were still there, and ran wildly around the bed as if chased by someone else. When the journeyman tried to disarm Bovard, the latter kicked him and tried to stab a soldier who had come to calm him down. The soldier quickly fled the house, but Bovard pursued him and shortly thereafter jumped in the Rhône. Bovard's widow and mother requested to bury Bovard with the traditional honors in light of his blatant "alienation of spirit." The Small Council, however, denied him funerary honors, ordered that he be buried behind the shooting range, and imposed a fine upon Bovard's estate of 5,000 florins.[14] While the hallucinating Bovard was deprived of burial honors and thus deemed culpable, the merely "melancholic" Caille was considered not responsible for his actions and allowed to be buried with full honors, his memory left unsullied.

Over a century later, in October 1774, Anne Judith Bogueret, the daughter of an affluent Citizen merchant, ended her life after suffering from a fever and convulsions for two weeks. Although family members had carefully

---

[13]AEG, EC, LM 24: 190, 28 September 1614; PC 2e série 2071; RC 112: 289.

[14]AEG, EC, LM 34: 72v, 26 June 1645; PC 2e série 2485. Later, his heirs requested that the fine be reduced to 800 florins since Bovard had accumulated a number of debts. The Small Council agreed to reduce the fine to 1,200 florins, provided that they pay it in three days; RC 144: 66v–67, 122v.

looked after the ailing Bogueret, she took advantage of a brief moment of solitude at night to jump to her death from a window of her parents' fourth-floor abode. Though acknowledging that Bogueret clearly jumped to her death, the Small Council ruled that since this "accident was caused by delirium or by high fever," Bogueret could be buried in the customary fashion.[15]

Notwithstanding the judgment of the Small Council, I have included all three of these deaths among suicides. Magistrates were not consistent in distinguishing those guilty of "self-murder" from those who were allegedly unable to perceive the consequences of their actions. As these cases help show, magistrates were blatantly guilty of a class bias—eleven of the twenty-one people who obviously killed themselves but were allowed full funerary honors were wealthy. Although it appears quite plausible that Bovard and a handful of others were not intentionally killing themselves, I have for the sake of consistency included among suicides all those who died as a result of an apparently deliberate action, of which death was the predictable result.

In determining whether a particular death was self-inflicted, I thus tend to give more credence to the evidence from the investigation than to the sentence passed by the Small Council. During these two hundred and fifty years, some magistrates were quite reticent, in spite of overwhelming evidence, to declare a death self-inflicted, especially when it involved a member of a prestigious family. One of the most blatant cases involved the death in June 1663 of the very wealthy Marc de Loriol, thirty-three, the seigneur of Collonges in Bresse, who was staying in Geneva at the home of his sister. Although insisting that Loriol was a good-natured fellow, several servants conceded that he had been extremely sad because a thigh injury had kept him confined indoors. After hearing a shot, household members found Loriol's body in his room. Dressed only in his night shirt, Loriol had suffered a gunshot wound to his right temple, and his pistols were next to his body. Not one of the seven servants saw any strangers entering the house or had suspicions against any members of the household. Despite the very strong evidence of a self-inflicted gunshot wound, the Small Council ruled this death was "caused by an accident."[16] I nonetheless have included de Loriol among the suicides; it seems unlikely that a depressed, ailing man just hap-

---

[15]AEG, EC, LM 64: 361, 31 October 1774; PC 12658; RC 275: 538.
[16]AEG, EC, LM 39: 5, 4 June 1663; PC 2e série 2661; RC 163: 115.

pened to be waving his loaded pistol in the vicinity of his temple when it unexpectedly went off.

The most extreme case of avoiding a ruling of suicide involved, however, not a member of a wealthy, influential family, but rather a humble apprentice weaver living in the village of Landecy outside Geneva. On 25 April 1704 Antoine Charbonnier's mother found his body hanging inside his master's second-floor workshop. As the shop door was locked from the inside, a fifteen-year-old girl, with the assistance of Charbonnier's mother, climbed in a window and unlocked the door. Upon seeing the body, Charbonnier's mother cut the body down and forbade the girl to tell the truth, hoping to pass this off as a natural death. Nonetheless, rumor quickly spread that Charbonnier had hanged himself. Consequently, the investigator interrogated various witnesses. Charbonnier's mother persisted in saying that she found the body on the floor, although she refused to make that statement under oath. Pressed under oath, the girl, however, revealed the truth. Moreover, a surgeon examined the body and concluded that Charbonnier had died by strangulation. As for a motive, several witnesses testified that Charbonnier had been badly mistreated by his mother, often subjected to harsh verbal abuse. A fellow weaver further reported that Charbonnier had been most upset because his mother had alienated some property against his wishes. In spite of this overwhelming evidence, magistrates eventually decided that there was insufficient evidence to determine this was a suicide.[17] Conversely, I maintain that when a body is found hanging in a second-story room that was locked from the inside and in which there was no sign of a struggle, we can safely assume that was a suicide.

It is with such common-sense criteria that I have found 404 deaths that were beyond a reasonable doubt suicides (see table 1). The most striking feature concerning suicides is their heavy concentration in the late eighteenth century. Almost three-fourths of the early modern Genevans who took their lives did so after 1750. This increase in suicide, which far outpaced population growth, was not simply a reflection of lost sources from earlier periods. There are no lacunae in any sources from the late seventeenth century. Be that as it may, as table 2 indicates, through the mid-eighteenth century the suicide rate remained quite low. By contrast, the number of people we know

---

[17]AEG, Juridiction Pénale Lc No. 59, Landecy.

Table 1: Total Suicides, 1542–1798[a]

PERIOD	TOTALS
1542–1600	14
1601–50	26
1651–1700	22
1701–50	54
1751–98	288
Total	404

a. Source: Etat Civil, Livres des Morts; Procès Criminels; Registres du Conseil.

Table 2: Suicide Rates per 100,000
in Early Modern Geneva[a]

PERIOD	RATE
1616–50	3.5
1651–1700	2.9
1701–50	5.2
1751–98	23.3
1781–98	34.4

a. Etat Civil, Livres des Morts; Procès Criminels; Registres du Conseil; population estimates from Perrenoud, *Population de Genève*, 37.

killed themselves during the 1780s and 1790s amounted to an annual suicide rate of 34.4 suicides per 100,000, over six times that of the first half of the eighteenth century.[18] The proportional increase in Genevan suicides from the first to the second half of the eighteenth century was much greater than the dramatic increases that several European countries experienced in the nineteenth century (increases that incited Thomas Masaryk and

[18]It would be dangerous to attempt a suicide rate for the years preceding 1616 because there were lacunae in both the criminal proceedings and the death records. From 1 March 1616, from which date there are no lacunae in the death records, through 1650 there were sixteen suicides recorded, amounting to an annual suicide rate of 3.5 per 100,000 people, based on an average population of 13,200. Population estimates from Alfred Perrenoud, *La population de Genève XVIe–XIXe siècles* (Geneva: Société d'histoire et d'archéologie de Genève, 1979), 37.

Durkheim to bemoan the social malaise that plagued their times).[19]

The year that witnessed the most suicides in early modern Geneva was 1793, immediately following Geneva's democratic revolution. During those twelve months, Geneva witnessed seventeen suicides—all separate cases involving people who apparently were not associated with one another. Moreover, all these suicides involved people who were living in the city of Geneva at the time (the figure does not include any deaths from the Genevan countryside). These seventeen deaths amounted to a very high suicide rate of over 60 per 100,000.[20] During this same year, there were 702 total deaths recorded in the city of Geneva, meaning that suicides represented an extraordinary 2.4 percent of all deaths in Geneva in 1793. Although still showing a considerable penchant for suicide, Genevans of the early nineteenth century did not kill themselves at the same pace that they did in 1781 through 1798.[21] To put these figures in perspective, in 1990 official figures put the suicide rate at 12.6 per 100,000 inhabitants for the United States, 21 per 100,000 in France (the highest rate among the seven largest industrialized powers), and only 7.4 per 100,000 in the United Kingdom. The highest suicide rate in the world in 1990 belonged to Hungary: 40.5 per 100,000.[22] In light of the fact that children made up a much larger percentage of the

[19]Maurice Halbwachs, *Les causes du suicide* (Paris: Félix Alcan, 1930), 481, reports that the suicide rate increased 140 percent in Prussia for the years 1826–1900, 355 percent in France in 1827–88, 92 percent in Saxony in 1841–75, and 78 percent in Italy in 1870–88. See also Thomas Masaryk, *Suicide and the Meaning of Civilization*, trans. William B. Weist and Robert G. Batson (Chicago: University of Chicago Press, 1970).

[20]The population of Geneva declined sharply after the revolution. Perrenoud estimates Geneva's population in 1790 at 29,000, and a census shows that Geneva was home to only 24,331 in 1798. Geneva's population in 1793 would have been between these two figures as the exodus of members of the old Bourgeoisie was already well under way. The suicide rate for 1793 would be 58.6 per 100,000 based on the population of 1790 but 69.9 based on the population of 1798; Perrenoud, *Population de Genève*, 37.

[21]In 1835 Guillaume Prevost, a judge and *Conseiller d'Etat* in Geneva, published a brief treatise on suicide. He found that for the decade 1825–34, there were 133 suicides in the canton of Geneva. According to Prevost, during these ten years there was one suicide for every 90.125 deaths; that is, suicide represented 1.1 percent of all deaths. If Prevost's figures are correct, the canton of Geneva, with a population of about 53,000, experienced an annual suicide rate of about 25.1 per 100,000 people. This figure is still high, though noticeably lower than the rate for the 1780s and 1790s. According to Prevost, the peak year for suicides in his study was 1833 when 24 people took their lives, corresponding to a rate of 45.3 per 100,000; "Extrait d'une note statistique sur le suicide," *Bibliothèque universelle* (June 1835): 13–14.

[22]Jean-Claude Chesnais, "Géographie du suicide," *L'Histoire* 189 (1995): 30. The official rate for the United States in 1995 was 11.8 per 100,000; U.S. Bureau of the Census, *Statistical Abstract of the United States: 1997*, 117th edition (Washington, D.C., 1997), 94.

population in early modern Europe than today and that suicide is almost exclusively an adult phenomenon, the high levels of suicide in Geneva of the late eighteenth century were really quite remarkable. These suicide rates of course should not be taken to indicate the absolute frequency with which Genevans took their lives. They reveal rather the minimum numbers of self-inflicted deaths and serve a comparative purpose, highlighting the dramatic upswing in suicides in the late 1700s.

Contemporaries certainly perceived that suicide was becoming more common after 1750. Members of the Small Council expressed alarm already in 1758, as did the Consistory, a type of morals court, in 1774.[23] Voltaire, who lived at nearby Ferney for over twenty years, wrote in a letter in 1767 that Genevans were more melancholic than the English, and he believed that there were proportionally more suicides in Geneva than in London.[24] In May 1773, Pierre-Michel Hennin, the French Resident in Geneva, wrote to his compatriot, the duke of Aiguillon, that suicide was admired in Geneva and that there were more suicides in that city than anywhere else. In a reply, Aiguillon concurred, blaming Genevans' penchant for suicide on their pride and idleness.[25]

One may wonder, however, if for earlier periods the friends or relatives of suicides successfully covered up many cases of self-murder or if magistrates were less efficient in their investigations than their late-eighteenth-century counterparts. The death records, fully extant from the early seventeenth century, offer a most reliable control mechanism to complement the criminal proceedings, providing a window to all unnatural deaths.[26] With this information, I have been able to uncover the total numbers of people who died from drownings, gunshot wounds, falls from precipices, and the like. There was a sizeable number of deaths for which the evidence was inconclu-

---

[23]AEG, RC 259: 57; Registres du Consistoire 89: 452; the former cited in Haeberli, "Suicide à Genève," 116, n. 6.

[24]Voltaire, *Correspondence and Related Documents*, ed. Theodore Besterman, definitive edition, 51 vols. (Banbury, England, 1968–77), D 13995; see also Haeberli, "Suicide à Genève," 116. This and all subsequent references to Voltaire's correspondence were cited in Robert Favre, *La mort dans la littérature et la pensée françaises au siècle des Lumières* (Lyon: Presses Universitaires de Lyon, 1978). Favre, however, used Besterman's earlier edition of the *Correspondence*.

[25]Voltaire, *Correspondence*, D 18376, n. 1.

[26]In discussing unnatural deaths, I have been guided by Douglas's definition: "Any sudden death for which no organic cause is immediately observable as the basic underlying cause"; *Social Meanings of Suicide*, 228, n. 73.

Table 3: Questionable Unnatural Deaths, 1542–1798[a]

Period	Totals
1542–1600	80
1601–50	125
1651–1700	162
1701–50	155
1751–98	239
Total	761

a. Source: Etat Civil, Livres des Morts; Procès Criminels; Registres du Conseil. Evidence is insufficient to determine beyond a reasonable doubt whether these deaths resulted from suicide or, more likely, from homicide or accident.

sive as to whether the death was intentional and self-inflicted (see table 3).

Included among these questionable deaths was that of Pierre Trembley, thirty, a member of a wealthy and powerful Genevan family, who died of a gunshot wound to the abdomen in July 1706. According to witnesses, Trembley, alone in his room, was preparing to go hunting when this "accident" occurred.[27] Similarly, in July 1781 Gabrielle Picot, thirty-four, drowned in the Arve River. No one witnessed her falling in, and the Auditeur concluded that this may well have been an accident.[28] These questionable deaths also include some for which the evidence is very fragmentary. For example, the death records indicate that Jean-Baptiste Lambert, a shoemaker from Lyon, died of a fractured skull 4 February 1782. There was no criminal investigation for this death, which almost certainly was an accident. Nonetheless, since it is conceivable that Lambert's fractured skull might have resulted from his throwing himself headfirst off a balcony, I have included this among the questionable deaths.[29]

It is quite likely that the increase in Genevan suicides after 1750 may have been greater than the above figures indicate. As table 3 indicates, during these two and a half centuries, there were 761 deaths by gunshots, drownings, falls from precipices, and so on for which the evidence is insufficient to

[27] AEG, EC, LM 52: 143, 30 July 1706; PC 5730; RC 207: 313–14.
[28] AEG, EC, LM 66: 86, 10 July 1781; PC 13737; RC 282: 422.
[29] AEG, EC, LM 66: 111, 4 February 1782.

determine whether they were homicides, accidents, or suicides. Significantly, 239 of these questionable deaths occurred in the period 1751–98, an increase of 54.2 percent over such deaths for the first half of the eighteenth century. Consequently, if some of these questionable deaths were self-inflicted ones that family members successfully covered up, probably more occurred in the eighteenth century than at any other time. True, if we look at the definite suicides and questionable deaths together, late-eighteenth-century magistrates (and I) concluded that a significantly higher percentage of these unnatural deaths were suicides than during the previous two centuries. But even if we make the unlikely assumption that the same proportion of these unnatural deaths were suicides for the period up to 1750 as for the last two decades of the eighteenth century, the suicide rates for earlier periods would still have been less than half that of the late 1700s.[30] The late eighteenth century witnessed an increase not only in suicides but also in homicides, accidents, and questionable deaths.

Causes of Death and Methods of Suicide

Why then the increase in self-inflicted deaths? The explosion of suicides in the late 1700s definitely was related to the choice of methods of killing oneself. Although Durkheim paid scant attention to the methods of committing suicide, Halbwachs believed that the choice of method is an essential part of the decision to take one's life. He argued that one cannot determine whether a decision to end one's life was firm until it has been accomplished, and that depends to a considerable extent on the method chosen.[31] In Geneva the growing popularity of firearms as the weapon of choice for taking one's life clearly had an important impact on the unprecedented numbers of suicides

---

[30]From March 1616 through 1650, I uncovered 16 definite suicides and 108 other unnatural deaths for which, based on the available evidence, we cannot be absolutely certain the death was not self-inflicted. If 62.7 percent of these 124 deaths were actually suicides—the percentage of such deaths that were clearly suicides in the 1780s and 1790s—then 77.7 Genevans would have taken their lives during these 34.83 years. This would translate to an annual suicide rate of 16.9 per 100,000 people. For the period 1651–1700, records reveal 22 definite suicides and 162 questionable deaths. If 62.7 percent of these 184 deaths were suicides, the annual suicide rate would have been 15.4 per 100,000 people. For the years 1701–50, in addition to the 54 confirmed suicides, there were 155 other deaths that could conceivably have been suicides. If 62.7 percent of these 209 deaths were self-inflicted, then the annual suicide rate would have been 12.7 per 100,000, assuming a constant population of 20,600; population estimates from Perrenoud, *Population de Genève*, 37.

[31]Halbwachs, *Causes du suicide*, 43.

in the late 1700s. Although more people committed suicide by drowning themselves for the entire early modern period, shooting oneself was the most common means of taking one's life in the late eighteenth century (see table 4). Death records and criminal proceedings reveal that four hundred people died from gunshot wounds in Geneva during times of peace from the sixteenth century to 1798 (see table 5).[32] Of these, 180 (45 percent) died after

Table 4: Suicide Methods, 1542–1798[a]

PERIOD	DROWNING	FIREARM	HANGING	FALL	POISON	STABBING	TOTAL
1542–1600	5	0	5	0	0	4	14
1601–50	12	3	5	6	0	0	26
1651–1700	9	4	3	3	1	2	22
1701–50	26	7	10	11[b]	0	1[b]	54[b]
1751–98	87	112	38	31	15	5	288
(1781–98)	(44)	(64)	(24)	(16)	(9)	(3)	(160)
Total	139	126	61	51	16	12	404

a. Source: Etat Civil, Livres des Morts; Procès Criminels; Registres du Conseil.
b. In 1722 a man took his life by first stabbing himself and then jumping out an upper-story window.

Table 5: Deaths by Firearms, 1542–1798[a]

PERIOD	TOTAL
1542–1600	20
1601–50	52
1651–1700	85
1701–50	63
1751–98	180
(1791–98)	(105)
Total	400

a. Source: Etat Civil, Livres des Morts;
Procès Criminels; Registres du Conseil.

[32] I am thus not including the ninety-nine inhabitants of Geneva who were killed by gunfire during military conflicts with Savoy in 1589–93 and in 1602–3. Altogether, the *Livres des Morts* reveal that 245 Genevans were killed in these skirmishes, including seventy-four who died from sword, bayonet, or knife wounds. The rest were simply described as "killed by the enemy." The figures for deaths by gunshot also do not include sixteen people who were executed by firing squad, having been condemned by revolutionary tribunals in the period 25 July–31 August 1794.

1750, 112 of whom (almost two-thirds) were clearly suicides. By comparison, only 148 people had died in Geneva from gunshot wounds—be they the victims of murders, accidents, or suicides—during the previous hundred years (1651–1750), a period for which there are absolutely no lacunae in the death records.

Firearms were almost certainly more available in the late eighteenth century than ever before. Men who enjoyed the rights of citizenship were required to be armed in order to ensure the security of the Republic. Postmortem inventories regularly indicate that men possessed muskets or rifles, which they passed on to their sons. While the old arms were inherited, newer, more efficient weapons were also being made. Genevans' demand for arms was sufficient to support seven full-time gunsmiths in 1788, a time when the city and dependent territories numbered fewer than thirty thousand souls.[33] Genevan authorities made serious efforts to control the ownership of weapons, largely because they experienced several armed uprisings during the eighteenth century. About forty edicts were issued against the unauthorized possession of firearms, swords, sabers, and daggers. A great number of these were passed after 1782, when many took up arms to suppress the Genevan oligarchy in favor of democracy. The illicit possession of a hunting rifle could result in a criminal investigation, and those guilty of possession of illegal weapons could be subject to censures, confiscation of the weapon, and prison sentences of up to thirty days.[34] The fact that authorities of the late eighteenth century repeatedly issued these edicts suggests that arms were more of a problem and, presumably, more numerous than ever before. More important, the large number of deaths by gunshot in the late 1700s, especially those that were self-inflicted, indicates that magistrates had very limited success in keeping arms out of the hands of the residents of Geneva.

In most cases, it is relatively easy to determine which deaths by firearms were self-inflicted. Although some individuals shot themselves in the presence of others, the large majority did so privately, most often locked in their own rooms. Under such circumstances, I have labeled as suicides only those deaths for which evidence strongly suggests that they were intentionally self-

---

[33]Perrenoud, *Population de Genève*, 35, 544.
[34]Porret, *Crime et ses circonstances*, 157–60.

inflicted and not the result of accidents.

In several cases, almost all from the late eighteenth century, the deceased left no doubt by leaving suicide notes. Just before shooting himself in the chest in his room in September 1770, the twenty-one-year-old Citizen and perfumer Pierre Jacob Bourget wrote a note, spelling phonetically, in which he bitterly complained about his harsh and negligent father. Hearing the shot, neighbors broke into his room and found the body lying on the bed, his shirt smoking from the gunshot. Putting out the fire, they immediately sent for an Auditeur, who confiscated the note.[35]

More often, however, the evidence for suicide is not so direct. When considering the deaths of people who shot themselves while alone, I labeled as suicides the deaths of individuals who had manifested suicidal behavior or had substantial motives to end their lives. Jacques Cantered, forty-eight and a goldsmith, was lying on his bed with the bed curtains closed when he shot himself in the head in October 1772. According to his sister and brother-in-law, with whom he lived, and to the physician who had treated him, Cantered had suffered from serious physical and mental illness for the past ten months. For the past several days, he had been "deranged" and had eaten nothing.[36] Similarly, Amy Bouvier, sixty-two, a Citizen and watchmaker, committed suicide in April 1782 after suffering from melancholy for about a month. According to his brother, the day before he took his life, Bouvier, who had suffered previous bouts of melancholy, had complained bitterly about some debts he had incurred, even though he was really quite secure financially. The next morning, Bouvier took a rifle and blew his head off in his country house, his body found later by a female employee.[37] Although there were no witnesses to either shooting, no one, including close relatives, doubted that these men intentionally shot themselves. Even though the Small Council did not mention any restrictions on funerary rites, apparently believing that the deceased were not responsible for the shootings, I have included these deaths among the suicides.

I have not listed as suicides, however, any shooting deaths for which there is a reasonable indication that they might have been accidents. In March 1724 the tailor Pierre Durant, thirty-two, was supposedly cleaning

---

[35]AEG, EC, LM 64: 143, 14 September 1770; Juridiction Civile F 100; PC 12052.
[36]AEG, EC, LM 64: 254, 7 October 1772; Juridiction Civile F 690; PC 12386; RC 273: 571.
[37]AEG, EC, LM 66: 126, 22 April 1782; Juridiction Civile F 689; PC 13885; RC 283 bis: 260.

his rifle in his small apartment when it went off, fatally wounding him in the abdomen. Durant's landlord testified that Durant and his wife, who was about to give birth to their fourth child, seemed to get along well together, although they were poor and had trouble making ends meet.[38] Similarly, when Bartholomaei Bonnet, thirty-six, a setter of watchcasings, shot himself in the chest in his workshop in March 1767, the Auditeur's investigation revealed that this could have been either suicide or an accident while cleaning his gun.[39] In October 1769 the body of the Citizen pastor Jean Françoise Bellamy was found in a wooded area near the village of Petit Saconnex, the victim of a gunshot wound to the throat from his own rifle. Although there were no witnesses to this death, magistrates concluded that Bellamy probably accidentally shot himself while hunting alone.[40]

Like modern investigators of unnatural deaths, Auditeurs sought information from witnesses about the state of mind of the deceased, their medical history, and problems they may have faced.[41] This information has been quite important in my designation of deaths as suicide. If, before their untimely deaths, individuals like Durant, Bonnet, and Bellamy had reportedly suffered from "black melancholy" or complained bitterly about their plight, I would have included them among the suicides. In other words, I have embraced the very important "meaning" of suicide, based on common sense, that "something is fundamentally wrong with the situation" of those who take their lives, that suicide is "directly dependent upon the situation in which the individual existed at the time of the action."[42] Of course people suffering from depression can accidentally shoot themselves while cleaning their guns or hunting. Any danger of inappropriately listing a death as a suicide, however, is more than offset by the likelihood of omitting actual suicides. Gun owners surely knew that it is not a good idea to clean a loaded gun or to point the gun at oneself at any time. Nonetheless, barring evidence that the victims of such clandestine shootings had shown suicidal tendencies or a weariness of life, I have not included them among suicides. By so doing, I have undoubtedly excluded some deaths from the list of suicides that were

[38]AEG, EC, LM 56: 222, 29 March 1724; PC 7154; RC 223: 161.
[39]AEG, EC, LM 63: 340, 20 March 1767; PC 11588; RC 268: 119–20.
[40]AEG, EC, LM 64: 99, 24 October 1769; PC 11934; RC 270: 594.
[41]See Taylor, *Durkheim*, 84–85.
[42]Douglas, *Social Meanings of Suicide*, 275.

intentionally self-inflicted. In determining which deaths by firearms were voluntary, I have thus been rather conservative; for these two-and-a-half centuries, the 126 suicides by gunshot should be considered a minimum.

The method chosen to take one's life has often been cited as a major factor between the differences in suicide rates for men and women. Studies of modern Western societies have consistently shown that suicide, which has been characterized as a "masculine type of behavior,"[43] is much more common among men than women.[44] Among the explanations for such differences is that men tend to select more lethal methods, such as firearms, while women use methods that are more apt to fail, such as poisoning or drowning.[45] Beyond a lack of familiarity with firearms, women's traditional reluctance to shoot themselves may suggest that women have a greater concern than men for the appearance of their bodies after death.[46] This also may involve a desire to spare survivors the gruesome scenes so often associated with gunshot wounds.

The findings from Geneva on the gender of suicides is in accord with research on modern Western societies, as men comprised the sizeable majority of those who took their lives (see table 6). Evidence further shows that firearms definitely played a role in the gap between the number of male and

[43]Louis I. Dublin, *Suicide: A Sociological and Statistical Study* (New York: Ronald Press, 1963), 23.

[44]Statistics show men outnumbering women among self-inflicted deaths in all Western countries. In 1990, for example, these countries recorded the following suicide rates (per 100,000 people) for men and women, respectively: Austria, 34.8 and 13.4; United Kingdom, 12.6 and 3.8; Switzerland, 31.5 and 12.7; U.S.A., 20.1 and 5.0; see Silvia Sara Canetto and David Lester, "The Epidemiology of Women's Suicidal Behavior," in *Women and Suicidal Behavior*, ed. Silvia Sara Canetto and David Lester (New York: Springer Publishing, 1996), 44–45.

[45]Halbwachs, *Causes du suicide*, 75. Dublin, *Suicide*, 40–41, shows among white suicides in the United States in the years 1955–58, 53.3 percent of males, as opposed to only 24.9 percent of females, shot themselves. By contrast, 34.6 percent of female suicides did so by poisoning and asphyxiation (employing solid, liquid, or gaseous substances), while only 17.3 percent of white male suicides chose those methods. Several scholars have suggested that modern official statistics may underreport the self-inflicted deaths of women more than those of men. Among possible reasons for such a disparity are: the methods women are more prone to use (e.g. poison) lend themselves more readily to misclassification than those employed by men; because they may equate suicide with male behavior, some coroners may be less inclined to conclude that a female's death was self-inflicted; since many believe that female suicides are most often motivated by family problems, family members may have a stronger incentive to conceal a woman's suicide than a man's; see Canetto and Lester, "Epidemiology of Women's Suicidal Behavior," in *Women and Suicidal Behavior*, ed. Canetto and Lester, 37.

[46]David Lester, *Why People Kill Themselves: A Summary of Research Findings on Suicidal Behavior* (Springfield, Ill.: Charles C. Thomas, 1972), 39–40.

Table 6: Suicides by Gender, 1542–1798[a]

PERIOD	MALES	FEMALES	TOTAL
1542–1600	10	4	14
1601–50	12	14	26
1651–1700	15	7	22
1701–50	28	26	54
1751–98	210	78	288
(1791–98)	(122)	(38)	(160)
Total	275	129	404

a. Source: Etat Civil, Livres des Morts; Procès Criminels; Registres du Conseil.

Table 7: Suicide Method and Gender, 1542–1798[a]

METHOD	MALES	FEMALES	TOTAL
Drowning	72	67	139
Firearm	125	1	126
Hanging	42	19	61
Fall	21	30	51[b]
Poison	6	10	16
Stabbing	10	2	12[b]
Total	275	129	404

a. Source: Etat Civil, Livres des Morts; Procès Criminels; Registres du Conseil.
b. In 1722 a man took his life by first stabbing himself and then jumping out an upper-story window.

female suicides; during the entire 250-year period, only one woman shot herself to death (see table 7).[47] The ratio of males to females among suicides, however, was not constant throughout these two and a half centuries. While men outnumbered women among suicides by over two to one for the entire early modern period, males comprised only 56 percent of suicides in the two centuries up to 1750 and outnumbered females by only 28 to 26 among sui-

[47]Similarly, for Paris of the late 1700s, Jeffrey Merrick, "Patterns and Prosecution of Suicide in Eighteenth-Century Paris," *Historical Reflections* 16 (1989): 10, found that gunshot was the most common method used (31 percent of all suicides), but only one woman shot herself.

cides in the first half of the eighteenth century.[48] After 1750, by contrast, men comprised about three-fourths of the suicides (210 of 288). When the suicide rate reached its peak in the 1780s and 1790s, years that were plagued by economic and political crises, 122 of 160 self-inflicted deaths involved men. The explosion in suicides in the late eighteenth century thus coincided with the appearance of the gender gap that is so typical of modern Western societies.[49]

Firearms alone can explain neither the explosion nor the widening gender gap in suicides. After 1750, 176 individuals ended their lives using some method other than firearms, a figure that easily surpasses the total number of recorded suicides (116), including those involving firearms, for the previous two centuries. Moreover, after 1750 men still outnumbered women among suicides by a substantial margin (98 to 78), even if we exclude all suicides by firearms. Indeed, the data suggest that the increase in deaths by firearms in the late eighteenth century was more a reflection of the increase in suicides than the possibility that guns had simply become more available. If the availability of guns were the key factor, then one would expect concomitant increases in murders and accidents involving firearms. That, however, was not the case (see table 8.) Excluding suicides, we find that sixty-eight people died from gunshot wounds in Geneva from 1751 to the end of the period under study, while the figure for the half century 1651–1700 was a surprising eighty-one. (Significantly, the population of Geneva averaged about fifteen thousand for the second half of the seventeenth century and more than twenty-five thousand in the latter half of the eighteenth.)[50] If we exclude suicides, Genevans of the late eighteenth century were dying from gunshot wounds at a much lower frequency than in the last fifty years of the seventeenth century. More important than the availability of firearms was simply the fact that late-eighteenth-century Genevans had become more willing to use them against themselves. The growing number of Genevans who died from gunshot wounds in the late eighteenth century was entirely the result of the increase in suicides.

---

[48]Studying the seventeenth and eighteenth centuries, Bayard, "Régions et morts subites," 211–22, found that men and women killed themselves in roughly equal numbers (men 51.16 percent, women 48.84 percent).

[49]For more analysis on suicide and gender, see chapters 3 and 4.

[50]Perrenoud, *Population de Genève*, 37.

Table 8: Firearm Deaths, Excluding Suicides, 1542–1798[a]

Period	Total
1542–1600	20[b]
1601–50	49[b]
1651–1700	81
1701–50	56
1751–98	68
(1781–98)	(41)
Total	274

a. Source: Etat Civil, Livres des Morts; Procès Criminels; Registres du Conseil.
b. These figures do not include ninety-nine shooting deaths that occurred in military conflicts with Savoy in 1589–93 and in 1602–3.

Statistics on drownings, by contrast, show that there was a dramatic increase in both intentional and accidental drownings in the second half of the eighteenth century. From the 1540s through the end of the Genevan Republic, records reveal a large number of drownings which represented about a fourth of all unnatural deaths during these two and a half centuries (see table 9).[51] These frequent drownings are predictable, given the proximity of Lake Geneva and the Arve and Rhône Rivers. As with deaths by firearms, in the vast majority of cases we can determine with confidence whether a drowning was a suicide rather than an accident, or more rarely, homicide. In some of these cases, witnesses saw the suicide victims jump in the water. In November 1614, for example, two men tried in vain to prevent Jeanne Maudry, deranged since the birth of a child, from jumping in the Rhône.[52] Likewise, in December 1729, a woman saw a poor man named Greloz, upset because he was rejected for military service, wade into the lake up to his chest. She cried to him that it was a terrible thing to kill himself.

[51]The 849 drownings comprised 23.1 percent of the total 3,668 unnatural deaths recorded for Geneva and its environs from May 1536 through the end of April 1798. I have not included among these drownings any cases of infanticides. The bodies of at least 27 victims of infanticide were found submerged in water, most often in the Rhône. I have not included these deaths among the drownings because several of the infants appeared to have been smothered before being thrown in the water. In such cases, the river or lake was viewed more as a place for disposing the body than as a means of killing the child.
[52]AEG, EC, LM 24: 194, 26 November 1614; PC 2e série 2076; RC 113: 35v.

Table 9: Deaths by Drowning, 1542–1798[a]

PERIOD	MALES	FEMALES	TOTAL
1542–1600	41	20	65[b]
1601–50	64	22	86
1651–1700	100	44	151[b]
1701–50	143	52	196[b]
1751–98	282	69	351
(1781–98)	(123)	(29)	(152)
Total	630	207	849[b]

a. Source: Etat Civil, Livres des Morts; Procès Criminels; Registres du Conseil.
b. The sex could not be identified for four drowning victims for 1542–1600, seven for 1651–1700, and one for 1701–50.

Not responding, he plunged in and was taken away by the current.[53] In a few other cases, the evidence of suicide was manifest even though no one saw the victim jump in the water. In June 1797, a passerby found the clothes of Jean Marc Dupontet on the banks of the Arve River. Attached to the clothes was a suicide note in which Dupontet bitterly complained about his wife.[54]

As with deaths by firearms, more frequent were cases in which the evidence for suicide was less direct. There were a number of individuals who, after suffering from mental or physical illnesses, disappeared, often in the middle of the night, and were found drowned later. For example, wearing only his night shirt, the "alienated" Daniel Nardon, age twenty-two, slipped out of his boarding house at 3:00 A.M. and drowned himself in June 1688. His body was found twelve hours later.[55] I have also listed as suicides the drownings of people who had expressed a desire to end their lives. In July 1733, Marie Jenny, age twenty, from the principality of Neuchâtel, had a bitter argument with another woman, who threatened to have Jenny banished from Geneva. Insulted, Jenny declared she was going to throw herself in the Rhône, to which the other woman sarcastically replied, "Go ahead and do it, you crazy woman. You're afraid of your own skin." Jenny immedi-

[53]AEG, PC 7692; RC 228: 347.
[54]AEG, PC 18563.
[55]AEG, PC 4764. Authorities allowed his uncle to have him buried honorably (though with few mourners) in light of the fact that Nardon's "alienation in spirit was notorious"; RC 188: 222.

ately ran away and was not seen alive again. Two weeks later, her decomposing body was found in the Rhône near the village of Russin.[56] Although in cases such as these there remains a modicum of doubt as to how the drowning occurred, the evidence for suicide is quite convincing.

Using such criteria, I have determined that of the 849 total drownings, 139 were beyond a reasonable doubt suicides. Significantly, 87 of these suicides occurred after 1750. Once again, one may think that the abundance of suicides by drowning may reflect a greater willingness on the part of eighteenth-century authorities to declare deaths to have been self-inflicted. But, if we look at the total number of drownings, we find a heavy concentration in the late eighteenth century. While 351 Genevans drowned between 1750 and 1798 (152 after 1780), only 196 drowned in the first half of the eighteenth century. Although the population of Geneva grew by a fourth from the first to the second half of the eighteenth century, drownings increased by three-fourths in the same period.[57]

Again, the discrepancy in the number of drownings in the early and late eighteenth century was not a case of more accurate record-keeping. As previously explained, the death records are fully extant from the early seventeenth century, noting the demise and its likely cause for every person in the city of Geneva. Drownings were documented and well investigated. The increase in the number of drownings was in part due to the increase in suicides. If we exclude suicides from the calculations, however, the number of drownings increased by 55.3 percent, from 170 drownings before midcentury to 264 thereafter (see table 10). To be sure, since this is still more than twice the rate of population growth, definite suicides alone did not account for the growing numbers of drownings.

The increase in total drownings was also the result of the growing numbers of accidents. Although the death records at times indicate only that a person drowned, they more often give some information on the setting in which the drowning occurred. The death records reveal 497 drownings that were almost certainly accidental (including the victims of boating accidents). Of these, 192 occurred after 1750, as compared to 115 in the first half of the eighteenth century. During the course of two hundred fifty years, sixty-nine

---

[56]AEG, PC 8080; RC 232: 309.
[57]Perrenoud, *Population de Genève*, 37.

Table 10: Deaths by Drowning, Excluding Suicides, 1542–1798[a]

Period	Total
1542–1600	60
1601–50	74
1651–1700	142
1701–50	170
1751–98	264
(1781–98)	125
Total	710

a. Source: Etat Civil, Livres des Morts; Procès Criminels; Registres du Conseil.

people perished in boating accidents, thirty of whom died after 1750 (up from only nine in the first fifty years of the eighteenth century).[58] This increase in boating accidents can be attributed to the growth in trade and the concomitant increase in transport on the lake. Throughout the early modern period, thirty-two of those who died in boating accidents were sailors, two-thirds of whom (22) perished in the second half of the eighteenth century. There were also a few more drownings involving children in the late eighteenth century. Throughout the early modern period, 169 children (defined as aged 13 and under) drowned accidentally. Forty-six young Genevans drowned after 1750, as opposed to thirty-seven for the years 1701–50.[59]

The growing popularity of recreational swimming also appears to have influenced modestly the increase in drownings. For the entire period, records reveal that 114 individuals drowned while swimming. Forty-one of these deaths occurred after 1750, as opposed to thirty-one in the first half of the

[58]The previous half-century high occurred in 1651–1700 when twenty-four people drowned in boating accidents. The figure is large, however, because fifteen people drowned in a single accident in 1690, the most deadly boating accident in early modern Geneva; AEG, EC, LM 48: 50, 10 November 1690.

[59]On a per capita basis, however, the peak in child drownings was in the second half of the seventeenth century, when forty-two people under the age of fourteen drowned. I am not including in these figures fifteen cases of infanticide by drowning. Only one child under fourteen committed suicide by drowning in early modern Geneva. In August 1638 Pierre Voan, twelve, was seen jumping in the water and drowning himself at the port of Molard. The ill Voan was described as suffering from "une frénésie"; AEG, EC, LM 33: 5, 7 August 1638.

eighteenth century. Surely there were others who drowned while swimming who were not identified as such.[60] Other examples of accidental drownings were women who fell off piers while washing clothes, men who fell in the water while working on levies, and people who fell into wells or through trapdoors in buildings that hung over the Rhône. In this wide variety of cases, the evidence points strongly to a post-1750 increase in drownings that were entirely accidental.

An interesting aspect of death by drownings is the breakdown by sex. Of people who drowned, men outnumbered women by three to one. Indeed, men made up the vast majority of all sorts of drownings except for those that were clearly suicides. Genevan men and women committed suicide by drowning in almost equal numbers (72 to 67, respectively). By contrast, among adult drownings that were almost certainly accidental, men outnumbered women by over six to one for the entire period and over twelve to one after 1750 (see table 11). Men all but had a monopoly on recreational swimming: only one of the 114 swimmers who drowned was a woman. Of the

Table 11: Accidental Drownings Involving Adults, 1542–1798[a]

Period	Males	Females	Total
1542–1600	7	2	13[b]
1601–50	22	4	26
1651–1700	43	16	65[b]
1701–50	67	11	78
1751–98	135	11	146
(1781–98)	(54)	(3)	(57)
Total	274	44	328[b]

a. Source: Etat Civil, Livres des Morts; Procès Criminels; Registres du Conseil.

b. The sex could not be identified for four drowning victims for 1542–1600 and six for 1651–1700.

[60]The term used was drowned "en se baignant." That could be translated as drowned while swimming or while bathing. Chances are, many of them were indulging both in recreational swimming and in bathing for reasons of personal hygiene. All but one of these accidents occurred between mid-May and the end of August—indeed all but four were in June, July, or August. There were a number of other deaths that probably involved swimming without mentioning that someone had drowned "en se baignant." If people drowned at Eaux-Vives or Pâquis in the summer months, for example, they most likely had gone swimming.

drownings that could have been either accidents or suicides (or, in a few cases, even homicides), men outnumbered women by over three to one (155 to 46; see table 12). Even among the children who drowned accidentally, boys outnumbered girls by well over two to one (122 to 48).

Table 12: Questionable Drownings, 1542–1798[a]

PERIOD	MALES	FEMALES	TOTAL
1542–1600	19	5	26[b]
1601–50	19	6	25
1651–1700	20	13	34[b]
1701–50	39	12	52[b]
1751–98	58	10	68
(1781–98)	(26)	(7)	(33)
Total	155	46	205[b]

a. Source: Etat Civil, Livres des Morts; Procès Criminels; Registres du Conseil. Evidence for these drownings is insufficient to determine beyond a reasonable doubt whether these deaths were the result of suicide, homicide, or, most likely, accident.

b. The sex could not be identified for two drowning victims for 1542–1600, one for 1651–1700, and one for 1701–50.

Males drowned in greater numbers because they, much more than women, were drawn to the water for work and leisure. Apart from washing clothes or drawing water from wells, women faced few occupational risks of drowning. Women did not work as sailors or as construction workers on projects that were on the waterfront. There were no female soldiers who ran the risk of falling in the water because they fell asleep while on guard duty at night. Not one female was reported as having drowned while fishing, and, as noted above, women apparently had little interest in swimming.

Alcohol abuse also played a minor role in the disproportionate number of men who drowned. The criminal proceedings provide far more examples of drunken men than drunken women. Moreover, when women overindulged in alcohol, they generally did so at home. When men got drunk, they most often did so in taverns which, apart from female servers, were the exclusive domain of men. When they left the taverns, inebriated men had to find their way back to their abodes. Several intoxicated men met their deaths by tumbling down stairs and by drowning after falling off piers or into wells.

There were even a few cases of drunken men drowning because they fell into a river while urinating. The fact that inebriated men had to walk home after the taverns closed helped inflate the number of males who drowned.[61]

But why then did women commit suicide by drowning in roughly equal numbers to men? This proportion of female to male suicides by drowning was not a fluke. Although neither work nor leisure brought women to the rivers or lake as often as men, women viewed drowning as the most attractive method for suicide. They had neither the familiarity with nor the access to firearms that men had. While virtually all women surely had kitchen knives at their disposal, jumping into a river must have seemed a much easier method than slitting one's wrist. The death offered by drowning was much quicker and involved much less suffering than poison, which was, after all, not nearly as accessible as the bodies of water. Jumping in a river was more likely to result in a successful suicide than hanging oneself—when one hanged oneself from a hook on a wall, the rope could break or one could be discovered and cut down before expiring. Upon jumping into the strong currents of the Rhône River, even if observed, one was virtually assured of successfully ending one's life. For women who truly wanted to end their lives, drowning seemed the most viable method. Over half the women who took their lives chose drowning, while only a fourth of the male suicides drowned themselves.[62]

An obvious advantage of drowning for both male and female suicides was that it might appear to be an accidental death. For the entire early modern period, there were 205 drownings for which the evidence is not sufficiently clear to determine whether the death was accidental or self-inflicted (see table 12).[63] Undoubtedly there were some suicides that went undetected among these drownings. There may even have been some suicides among those drownings for which evidence strongly suggests they were accidents. A sailor could, after all, cause a boating accident in order to kill himself. The 139 suicides by drowning thus represent the minimum.

---

[61]On the nightlife that Genevan taverns and *cercles* offered, see Corinne Walker, "Esquisse pour une histoire de la vie nocturne: Genève au XVIIIe siècle," *Revue de Vieux Genève* 19 (1989): 81–82.

[62]More specifically, 26.1 percent of the male suicides drowned themselves; for women the figure was 51.9 percent.

[63]There were ten adults found drowned who appeared to be the victims of homicides. As with infanticides, it is difficult to determine whether they were thrown in the water dead or alive. Most of these corpses bore wounds that were apparently caused by the blows of assassins.

Although the exact number of suicides by drowning cannot be known, there is good reason to believe that the number of definite suicides accurately reflected the overall number of suicides by drowning. As it stands, the male/female ratio among definite suicides differs strikingly from those of accidental and questionable drownings. That women intentionally drowned themselves in virtually equal numbers to men—as opposed to being outnumbered by over three to one among other drownings and among suicides by all other methods combined—reflects the penchant for drowning among suicidal women. If the breakdown by gender for definite suicides had paralleled that for other drownings, there would be more reason to suspect that the former did not in any way correspond to the actual number of suicides by drowning. Rather, they were simply those drownings that by chance had been discovered to have been intentional. But the inequality between the sexes among the other drownings can be explained by work and leisure patterns, while the equality of the sexes among definite suicides shows that for women, drowning was the method of choice for taking one's life. The number of suicides by drowning that were discovered thus appears a reliable barometer to the actual frequency of cases of intentional drowning.

In any event, an unavoidable conclusion from the death records and the criminal proceedings is the reality of the increase in suicides by drowning in the late eighteenth century. The fact that the overall number of drownings was drastically higher after 1750 than in the first half of the century—including the more than doubling of apparent accidents—militates against any theory that the increase in suicidal drownings was simply the result of more thorough investigation in the late eighteenth century. The increase in suicidal drownings went hand in hand with the increase in accidental drownings.

A similar analysis applies to deaths from falls. The death records reveal that during the course of this two-hundred-fifty-year period, 670 people died from some sort of fall (see table 13). These included carpenters who fell off roofs, painters who tumbled with their scaffolding, drunks who fell and hit their heads, elderly folk who stumbled down stairs, and a wide variety of other fatal falls. Although the vast majority of such deaths were accidental, jumping out of buildings and off other precipices was the fourth most common method of taking one's life. As with other methods, I have included among suicides only those deaths from falls for which there is ample evi-

Table 13: Deaths from Falls, 1542–1798[a]

Period	Males	Females	Total
1542–1600	32	10	42
1601–50	72	46	118
1651–1700	79	54	133
1701–50	93	33	127[b]
1751–98	180	70	250
(1781–98)	(60)	(31)	(91)
Total	456	213	670[b]

a. Source: Etat Civil, Livres des Morts; Procès Criminels; Registres du Conseil.

b. The sex could not be identified for one fall victim for the period 1701–50.

dence that a person wished to end his or her life. In September 1672 Jacquemine Davounay, the wife of the farmworker Rolet Moret, jumped to her death from a fourth-floor window. Davounay was described as having been deranged for several years. Two years before she had made an attempt on her life by jumping from a second-floor balcony, an action that only broke her leg. Following that incident, she had been incarcerated for a period, and thereafter her husband often felt compelled to tie her to the column of a bed to keep her from jumping out a window. Although there were no witnesses to the jump, no one doubted for a moment that the death of this "troubled" woman was self-inflicted.[64] The case of Jean Trembley, eighty-one, who fell from a window to his death in July 1785, was less obvious. Trembley was a member of Geneva's elite and had held the position of Syndic, the most powerful office in the Republic. Immediately prior to his death, Trembley had been quite ill and melancholic, suffering from "black vapors." Relatives and his personal physician tried to claim that, as a result of this illness, Trembley may have suffered from vertigo, which could conceivably have caused him to lose his balance and fall out the window. Notwithstanding the prestige of Trembley's family, authorities did not buy this argument. Without explicitly declaring this death a suicide, they ordered that Trembley be buried at 5:00 P.M.; such late afternoon interments amounted to burial without full hon-

[64]AEG, PC 4227; RC 172: 328.

ors.[65] Beyond any reasonable doubt, the elderly Trembley deliberately jumped to his death to put an end to his mental and physical misery.

As with drownings, there was a discrepancy in the breakdown by sex between total deaths from falls and those which were clearly suicides. Among all falls, men outnumbered women by more than two to one. Even among children, boys died more frequently than girls from accidental falls (see table 14). Yet women outnumbered men among those who clearly deliberately jumped from precipices, 30 to 21. Indeed, jumping to one's death was the

Table 14: Deaths from Falls Involving Children, 1542–1798[a]

Period	Males	Females	Total
1542–1600	9	6	15
1601–50	10	9	19
1651–1700	10	10	20
1701–50	6	7	14[b]
1751–98	16	7	23
(1781–98)	(2)	(4)	(6)
Total	51	39	91[b]

a. Source: Etat Civil, Livres des Morts; Procès Criminels; Registres du Conseil. These deaths involved people under the age of fourteen.

b. The gender could not be identified for a child who died from a fall in the period 1701–50.

only suicide method other than poisoning for which women outnumbered men. Why were women less likely to die from an accidental fall but more likely to throw themselves out of upper-story windows? On the one hand, the question of accessibility is again a key factor in the number of women who took their lives in this manner. Jumping to one's death merely required having access to an upper-story window, which virtually all Genevans had. Leaping from an upper-story window also generally assured a quick death without drawn-out suffering. On the other hand, as with drownings, women did not face the same occupational dangers of accidental falls that so many men faced. Throughout the early modern period, there were 128 men who

[65]AEG, EC, LM 66: 343, 27 July 1785; PC 14675; RC 289: 785–87.

worked in construction—carpenters, masons, painters, roofers, and so on—
who were killed from falls from precipices, almost all of which were surely
accidents.[66] There were also 35 soldiers who died in similar falls, a large
number of which occurred at night during guard duty. By contrast, no occupational pattern is evident for women—of the more than two hundred
women who died from falls, we know the professions of only fifteen, all of
which involved little risk of falling.[67]

Table 13 shows that, as with drownings, there was a dramatic increase in
deaths from falls, be they accidents or suicides, in the late eighteenth century. While suicides by jumping off precipices increased almost threefold
from the first to the second half of the eighteenth century, total deaths from
falls doubled for the same periods, again far outpacing population growth.[68]
A small part of this increase in these unnatural deaths can be attributed to a
boom in the construction industry. Indeed the "vieille ville" of Geneva today
is for the most part a product of the eighteenth century, when there were two
important construction booms. The first, in 1715–40, witnessed the construction of many elegant palaces and buildings especially in the upper city
to house Geneva's elite. A second and larger expansion in construction
occurred during the years 1750–80. As the city's population expanded
during these prosperous years, residents of Geneva had to deal with acute
housing shortages. Construction was most intense outside the old city walls,
in areas such as Eaux-Vives, Pré l'Evêque, Pâquis, and Châtelaine to accommodate the growing number of residents. Ambitious public works were also

---

[66]There were 51 carpenters, 25 masons, 4 painters, 2 window installers, 2 roofers, 2 chimney
sweeps, and 3 men who applied gypsum to walls. Also victims of falls were 39 laborers ("laboureurs" or
"manoeuvres"), most of whom appeared to have been involved in construction. Only one of these falls
was definitely a suicide. The carpenter Jean Louis Definot, seventy-five, jumped out his upper-story
window hours after his wife's death from natural causes; AEG, LM 62: 87, 13 July 1755; PC 10241; RC
255: 365.

[67]The fifteen included nine domestic servants, three seamstresses, a lacemaker, a *tireuse d'or* (maker
of gold thread), and a maker of golden watch hands. Domestic servants predominate because records
identified that occupation far more frequently than any other for women.

[68]The death records do not always reveal what caused certain injuries. During the course of the
early modern period, the *Livres des Morts* record the deaths of 65 people (54 men and 11 women) from
"fractures" and another 59 (45 men and 14 women) from "wounds," without indicating what caused
these injuries. Quite likely, falls were behind some of these injuries. Even so, that cannot begin to explain
the great difference between the numbers of deaths from falls for the first and second halves of the eighteenth century; those dying from wounds and fractures of unspecified origins numbered 44 for 1701–50
and 33 for 1751–98.

undertaken at this time. To ensure an adequate supply of water, the Genevan government ordered the installation of a system of pumps, completed in 1791, to take water to six public fountains. The land around the port was diked, old streets were repaired, and new ones were built. The gates of Rive and Cornavin were constructed, and a host of other landscaping and construction projects were completed.[69] After 1750, forty-seven carpenters, masons, and other construction workers died from falls, as opposed to thirty such men for the period 1701–50. Likewise, accidental deaths involving children increased from fourteen in the first half century to twenty-two in the second half.[70] Even combined, however, these factors alone cannot explain the late-eighteenth-century increase in the number of deaths from falls.

As with drownings, the evidence from falls supports the reality of the increase in suicides in the late eighteenth century. If the total number of falls had remained more or less constant during the eighteenth century, there would be reason to suspect that the increase in suicides after 1750 was simply the result of more aggressive investigations of suicides. Since definite suicides and the total deaths from falls increased contemporaneously, the late-eighteenth-century increase in suicide is undeniable. Undoubtedly, the thirty-one cases I have declared suicides were not the only people who intentionally jumped off precipices after 1750. As with other methods, that figure represents a minimum.

In early modern Geneva, poisoning was the only method of suicide that could possibly have gone undetected. Deaths by gunshot wounds, drownings, hangings, and falls from precipices could not have been mistaken for natural deaths. To be sure, death from taking arsenic left telltale signs that competent physicians and surgeons could have easily detected. Nonetheless, during the course of two and a half centuries, there were probably some Genevans who died from poisonings whose deaths were attributed to natural causes. During two hundred and fifty years, only sixteen people, ten women

---

[69]Anne-Marie Piuz, "La Genève des Lumières," in *Histoire de Genève*, ed. Paul Guichonnet (Toulouse: Edouard Privat, 1974), 229–30.

[70]Of these thirty-five children, there were two ten-year-olds, both of whom died in the second half of the eighteenth century; all others were younger. Eleven were three years old or younger, including a ten-week-old baby, the youngest victim of a fall in early modern Geneva. According to the death records, this child, the daughter of Isaac Pictet, the Châtelain of Jussy, died after being dropped by her wet nurse, apparently unintentionally; AEG, EC, LM 58: 349, 17 October 1733.

and six men, clearly died of self-inflicted poisonings.

Since fifteen of the sixteen clear cases of suicide occurred after 1750, one may think, at first glance, that authorities must have become more effective in identifying deaths by poisoning. But medical experts and judicial authorities had plenty of experience in identifying poisonings prior to 1750 (see table 15). If we exclude those poisonings that were obviously suicides, 28 of 36 occurred before the mid-eighteenth century. There were 26 fatal poisonings (including one suicide) before 1700 and in spite of lacunae, records reveal a dozen deaths by poisoning prior to 1600. When we take into account the lacunae and the rather sketchy nature of some sixteenth-century death records, instances of poisonings were probably much more common before 1600 than after 1750.[71] Moreover, of the fatal poisonings that were not definite suicides, thirteen involved small children aged six or under, only four of whom died after 1750. While some of these may have been cases of infanticide—four certainly were—they definitely were not suicides. Although three accidental poisonings of adults occurred after 1750, all eight poisonings that were clearly murders (including the infanticides) took place before that date. In short, since Genevan authorities had ample experience in identifying deaths by poisoning long before 1750, the increase in poisonings in the late eighteenth century must largely be attributed to the increase in suicides.

Among the methods of committing suicide, poisoning stands out for the youthfulness of its suicides. While the average age of suicides of all other

---

[71]The twelve sixteenth-century poisonings included eleven during the years 1584–91, the most intense period of poisonings in early modern Geneva. A criminal proceeding is extant for only one sixteenth-century poisoning; all the others are recorded only in the *Livres des Morts*. Death records began indicating the cause of death only in 1560. In the remaining four decades there were lacunae for two and a half years and several periods where the cause of death was not indicated. The sixth volume (1 January 1565–9 September 1566) does not indicate the causes of death until 7 May 1565. The following volume (14 September 1566–9 February 1568) rarely mentions the cause of death, especially after April 1567; likewise, few causes of death were recorded during the decade stretching from December 1569 to September 1579. During certain periods of extremely high mortality, authorities were mainly concerned with determining whether a person had died of a contagious disease. For example, Geneva suffered a bout of the plague in 1568 (roughly 1 July–21 September). Under these circumstances, the *Livres des Morts* generally indicated only if a person died of the plague. All those dying of something other than the plague were simply described as having died "sans danger" or "non de contagion." When we consider this information along with the fact that Geneva's average population was 16,300 for 1551–1600 as compared to 25,580 for 1751–98, then the twelve deaths by poisoning of the late sixteenth century were indeed more impressive than the twenty-four of the late 1700s. Population estimates from Perrenoud, *Population de Genève*, 37.

methods ranged from the early to mid-forties, those who poisoned themselves were on the average 30.9 years (see table 16). Records reveal only three

Table 15: Deaths from Poisoning, 1542–1798[a]

Period	Males	Females	Total
1542–1600	6	6	12
1601–50	2	3	5
1651–1700	6	2	9[b]
1701–50	2	1	3
1751–98	10	13	23
(1781–98)	(5)	(5)	(10)
Total	26	25	52[b]

a. Source: Etat Civil, Livres des Morts; Procès Criminels; Registres du Conseil.
b. The sex could not be identified for one fall victim for the
period 1651–1700.

Table 16: Average Age of Suicides According to Gender and Method,
1542–1798[a]

Method	Males	Females	Overall Average
Poison	28.7	32.4	30.9
Firearm	41.0	22.0[b]	40.9
Drowning	45.6	37.1	41.6
Stabbing	43.4	43.0[b]	43.3
Hanging	44.5	45.8	45.0
Fall	46.9	46.7	46.8
Overall Average	42.9	40.6	42.2

a. Source: Etat Civil, Livres des Morts; Procès Criminels; Registres du Conseil.
b. Only one woman committed suicide by shooting herself, and only two stabbed themselves to death.

people over forty who took their lives through poison, while nine were under
thirty. The youthfulness by poisoning may be partially skewed. Authorities
would understandably have been more suspicious of deaths from sudden,
violent illnesses when they involved young people. Quite possibly, some similar deaths of older people were recorded as natural.

In other ways, however, the youthfulness of suicides by poison does not appear to have been simply a question of successful identification. More than any other method, suicide by poison was linked to a particular motive. People most likely to poison themselves were far and away those who were suffering from family problems, primarily those who had experienced romantic misadventures. Of the sixteen suicides by poison, investigations revealed that family problems were primary motivating factors for eleven of them.[72] All but one of these involved individuals whose love lives had taken a turn for the worse. Although three cases involved marital breakdown, the other seven, all in the late eighteenth century, involved young people who were devastated because love affairs had not ended in marriage. Significantly, poison was the only method used more often by single people than by married people.[73] Although men who had been jilted by their fiancées were known to poison themselves, suicide by poison was particularly appealing to brokenhearted women, including three women whose suitors had gotten them pregnant but had refused to marry them. Men whose love stories went awry were much more likely to shoot themselves, like Goethe's Werther, than to take poison. Women clearly viewed poison as a more "ladylike" method of ending one's life, and one that was especially appropriate for unhappy lovers. The increase in suicides through poison in the late eighteenth century was thus directly related to the contemporary growth in the importance of romantic love.[74]

Be that as it may, the fact remains that taking poison was not a very popular method for ending one's life. To be sure, it was relatively easy to acquire arsenic, the most frequently cited substance in cases of poisoning, which all but guaranteed death (records reveal only three unsuccessful suicide attempts by poisoning).[75] But taking poison was the slowest, most painful method; suicides by poison always suffered excruciating pain for hours and even days before dying.

Hanging, the third most popular method of committing suicide, after drowning and gunshot, was that which was least likely to be confused with accidental deaths or murder. More than any other method, we can be confident that the number of recorded suicides by hanging was extremely

---

[72]No motive was cited for one suicide by poison.

[73]Of the sixteen, nine were single, five married, and two widowed.

[74]For a fuller discussion of the impact of the family and romantic love on suicide, see chapter 4.

[75]AEG, PC 10999, 12904*, and 15776, in the years 1762, 1776, and 1789, respectively.

close to the actual number of suicides by this method. During the course of two and a half centuries, sixty-three people died from hangings. Fully sixty-one of them were clearly suicides.[76] Throughout the early modern period, men consistently outnumbered women by two to one among those who hanged themselves, and the concentration of suicides by hanging in the late eighteenth century was very pronounced.

Hangings show more emphatically than all other methods the reality of the explosion in suicides in the late eighteenth century. From the early seventeenth century, the death records consistently identified deaths caused by hangings, and magistrates virtually always investigated these unnatural deaths. Close to half the suicides by hanging (27 of 61) involved people who were incarcerated in the prison or the hospital. Of the sixty-one suicides by hanging, there are extant criminal proceedings for all but four—the first two hangings from the 1540s and the last two from 1797–98. The Small Council adjudicated on all but seven of these suicides—three from the sixteenth century, three from the years 1796–98, and one from 1704.[77] In spite of the consistent references to and investigations of hangings, almost two-thirds of the suicidal hangings occurred after 1750, twenty-four of them after 1780.[78] This abundance of suicides by hanging at the end of the eighteenth century can mean only that there was an increase in the number of people who wanted to end their lives.

Evidence on deaths from knife and sword wounds, however, shows that Genevans strongly preferred stabbing other people to stabbing themselves. Although many early modern Genevans lost their lives due to stab wounds, stabbing was the least popular means of ending one's own life. During the two hundred and fifty years of this study, 239 people died in Geneva from stab wounds. Of these, seventy-four (seventy men and four women) were killed in action in military conflicts with Savoy in 1589–93 and in 1602–3.

---

[76]Of the remaining two, one was a murder and the other was apparently a freak accident. On Sunday, 15 August 1618, the sixteen-year-old Joseph Saget was in the tower of the church of St. Gervais, ringing the bell to call young people to come to catechism. As he rang the big bell, the bell's rope looped around his neck, pulling him off the platform and strangling him; AEG, EC, LM 28: 156, 15 August 1619.

[77]The case from 1704 was a suicide from the village of Landecy. Its absence from the registers of the Small Council is simply an aberration; AEG, Juridiction Pénale Lc 59, Landecy.

[78]The ratio of men to women persisted throughout the early modern period. For the half century after 1750, men outnumbered women by 24 to 13. For the 1780s and 1790s, there were sixteen men and eight women who hanged themselves.

Apart from these victims of war, 165 people in Geneva—154 men and only 11 women—perished from stab wounds (see table 17). Of these, 139 were clearly cases of homicide, including fourteen men who lost duels, four victims of infanticide, and six killings in self-defense. From the mid-sixteenth century to 1798, however, there were apparently only twelve people—ten men and two women—who committed suicide by stabbing themselves.[79] People wanting to end their lives found it less difficult to pull a trigger, jump off a balcony or into a river, tie a rope around their neck, or swallow arsenic than to plunge a knife into their throat or chest. A major problem with committing suicide by stabbing oneself had to do with the prospect of failing. Stabbing was the only method for which reported unsuccessful attempts outnumbered suicides (15 to 12). Regardless of how badly they wanted to put an end to their days, many people could not bring themselves to plunge the dagger deep enough to make a fatal wound.[80]

Data on stabbing deaths help show that while late-eighteenth-century Geneva witnessed an explosion in suicides, it did not experience very dra-

Table 17: Deaths by Stabbing, 1536–1798[a]

Period	Males	Females	Total
1536–1600	24	0	24
1601–50	44	4	48
1651–1700	30	2	32
1701–50	25	0	25
1751–98	31	5	36
(1781–98)	(17)	(2)	(19)
Total	154	11	165

a. Source: Etat Civil, Livres des Morts; Procès Criminels; Registres du Conseil. Records exist for murders by stabbing between 1536 and 1542, the date of the first recorded suicide.

[79]In addition, there were three cases of apparently accidental stabbings; for eleven stabbing deaths (all but one from the sixteenth and seventeenth centuries), the evidence is insufficient to determine if they were cases of suicide or, more likely, murder.

[80]The male bias for stabbing is further reflected by the fact that of the fifteen people who unsuccessfully attempted suicide by stabbing themselves, only one was a woman. In March 1644, a sixteen-year-old domestic servant, upset because her master accused her of theft, stabbed herself in an unsuccessful suicide attempt; AEG, PC 3251.

matic growth in homicides. As table 17 indicates, Geneva witnessed only a slight increase in the number of stabbing deaths from the first to the second half of the eighteenth centuries. The number of Genevans who died from stab wounds after 1750 is much lower on a per capita basis than the number of stabbing deaths for the period 1651–1700 and is lower in absolute terms than the number of people stabbed to death in the period 1601–50, even excluding casualties of war.

SUICIDES AND HOMICIDES

These findings bring to mind the relationship between suicide and homicide. Social scientists have tended to view a society's propensity for suicide as inversely related to its proclivity for homicide. Many believe that murder and suicide appear as related, but very different, even opposite phenomena. Durkheim asserted that as a general rule, "where homicide is very common it confers a sort of immunity against suicide."[81] In studying homicide and suicide, Andrew Henry and James Short joined psychology and sociology, arguing that aggression is often the result of frustration. If people are subject to considerable "external restraint" from social superiors and strong social relationships, they are likely to blame their frustration on others. They are more likely to externalize aggression and commit homicide. As a result of cultural norms, other people, especially those who have few social superiors, are allegedly subject to weak external restraint but very strong "internal restraint." They are more likely to blame themselves for any frustration they may experience, perhaps resulting in acts of aggression against themselves, including suicide.[82] There is considerable evidence to suggest that contemporary Western societies generally experience far more suicides but far fewer homicides than their premodern counterparts. Among the factors most often cited as responsible for the decline in homicides was the state's growing control of behavior in modern Western societies. According to some theorists, these same modern societies have undergone a process of the "civilization" of manners, particularly in the eighteenth and nineteenth centuries, which promotes self-control and discourages violence against others. While this may

[81]Durkheim, *Suicide*, 351.
[82]Andrew F. Henry and James F. Short, *Suicide and Homicide: Some Economic, Sociological, and Psychological Aspects of Aggression* (Glencoe, Ill.: Free Press, 1954).

effect a drop in the homicide rate, the confluence of many other variables may cause more people to choose death than in past centuries.[83]

A number of modern studies suggest that suicide varies directly but homicide inversely with urban and industrial development.[84] City dwellers have tended to be better educated than their rural counterparts, and highly educated people allegedly are less likely to commit homicide but more likely to take their own lives. Their refinement of manners will lead many to renounce violence and view bloodshed with a certain horror, resulting in a decrease in murders. By the same token, educated urban folk are less sheltered by the traditional support groups offered by kin and community and more prone to isolation, purportedly a key factor in suicide.[85] Similarly, while suicide is higher in Protestant areas, Catholic regions tend to have larger numbers of homicides. While the suicide rate tends to increase with age, the likelihood of being the victim of a homicide diminishes after the age of thirty or thirty-five. War tends to cause an increase in homicides but a decrease in suicides. In short, a host of sociological studies suggest that suicide and homicide are "polar opposites."[86]

Not all sociologists or criminologists agree, however, that suicide and homicide are so diametrically opposed and that the frequencies of each tend to move in opposite directions. Some scholars maintain that suicide and homicide rates are not polar opposites and may indeed experience parallel rather than contrary changes.[87]

---

[83]Jean-Claude Chesnais, "The History of Violence: Homicide and Suicide Through the Ages," *International Social Science Journal* 44 (1992): 217–34. See also Norbert Elias, *The History of Manners*, trans. Edmund Jephcott (New York: Pantheon Books, 1982); idem, *Power and Civility*, trans. Edmund Jephcott (New York: Pantheon Books, 1982).

[84]Richard Quinney, "Suicide, Homicide, and Economic Development," *Social Forces* 43 (1965): 401–6. Citing evidence from a number of countries from the 1970s, Ken Levi, "Homicide and Suicide: Structure and Process," *Deviant Behavior* 3 (1982): 91–115, found only a weak relationship between suicide and homicide rates, on the one hand, and the level of urbanization, on the other. By contrast, he found that suicide varies directly but homicide inversely with industrialization.

[85]Henry Romilly Fedden, *Suicide: A Social and Historical Study* (New York: Benjamin Blom, 1972), 339–41.

[86]Jeffrey S. Adler, "'If We Can't Live in Peace, We Might as Well Die': Homicide-Suicide in Chicago, 1875–1910," *Journal of Urban History* 26 (1999): 3–21.

[87]Halbwachs, *Causes du suicide*, 295–306. Some of the forty-eight countries studied by Quinney, "Suicide, Homicide, and Economic Development," 401–6, had rates that were high or low for both forms of untimely deaths. The United States was rather high for both, ranked sixteenth for suicide (10.3 per 100,000 people) and seventeenth for homicide (4.6 per 100,000); Ireland had very low rates for both, ranked thirty-ninth for suicide (2.6 per 100,000) and forty-eighth for homicide (0.3 per 100,000).

What does the evidence from Geneva reveal? Records indicate that there were 458 homicides in Geneva for the entire early modern period, including infanticides, duels, and killings in self-defense, but excluding casualties of war (see table 18).[88] More murders occurred after 1750 than in the other half centuries, and the noticeable increase in homicides from the first to the second half of the 1700s outpaced population growth. Be that as it may, the per capita murder rate was slightly lower after 1750 than in the first half of the seventeenth century. When one considers that there were important lacunae in the records in the early 1600s, Geneva was less violent in the eighteenth century than in the early seventeenth.[89]

These data on homicides do not include forty-nine deaths (eleven after 1750) that resulted from actions which may be described as involuntary manslaughter or "homicide par imprudence" (see table 19). In these cases, magistrates determined that the person responsible for the death had not intended to harm the victim but was guilty of negligence. Most of these (40 of 49) involved the careless handling of guns that resulted in deaths. A good example of such a death was that of Susanne Cardon, the twenty-four-year-old servant of Bartholomaei Bert, who was unintentionally shot to death by her master's seven-year-old son. The Small Council censured the elder Bert

[88]These homicide figures include thirteen people whom soldiers killed in putting down insurrections in the 1780s and 1790s. In arriving at this total number of homicides, I have not counted criminal proceedings concerning murders committed in foreign lands. Among the *Procès Criminels* in Geneva's archives, there are many investigations of murders committed outside Geneva and its territories. A person may have committed murder in, say, France and hoped to escape prosecution by coming to Geneva and living in anonymity. If informed of the accusations, Genevan authorities arrested the person in question and duly investigated. Moreover, there were dozens of dossiers among the criminal proceedings that were notices from neighboring states—France and Bern, for example—that called for the arrest of individuals wanted on murder charges for crimes committed in those states. Obviously, such foreign murders are not pertinent to the issue of Genevan homicides. I have, however, included a handful of murders of Genevan residents that occurred in places immediately adjacent to Geneva. Three residents of Geneva were murdered in the community of Carouge, for example. Although now part of the canton of Geneva, throughout the early modern period Carouge was under the suzerainty of Sardinia and thus independent of Geneva. Because it was so close, however, Genevan residents commonly passed to and from the two communities on a daily basis. Consequently, a murder committed at Carouge against a resident of Geneva can be viewed as among the quotidian risks that Genevans faced.

[89]The population of Geneva averaged 14,067 for 1600–1650 and 26,877 for 1781–1798. The 103 murders for 1601–50 correspond to an annual homicide rate of 14.6 per 100,000 people. From 1 March 1616, after which the death records are fully extant, through 1650 there were seventy-nine murders, amounting to a homicide rate of 16.1 per 100,000. The sixty-five murders from 1781 through the end of April 1798 represent a rate of 14.0 homicides per 100,000. Population estimates from Perrenoud, *Population de Genève*, 37.

Table 18: Homicides, 1536–1798[a]

Period	Murders	Infanticides	Duels	Self-Defense	Total
1536–1600	55	10	0	2	67
1601–50	76	20	6	1	103
1651–1700	48	25	3	2	78
1701–50	48	28	1	2	79
1751–98	81	42	4	4	131
(1781–98)	(41)	(18)	(2)	(4)	(65)
Total	308	125	14	11	458

a. Source: Etat Civil, Livres des Morts; Procès Criminels; Registres du Conseil.

Table 19: Involuntary Manslaughter, 1542–1798[a]

Period	Total
1542–1600	9
1601–50	6
1651–1700	19
1701–50	4
1751–98	11
Total	49

a. Source: Etat Civil, Livres des Morts; Procès Criminels; Registres du Conseil.

for his negligence in leaving the firearm out in the open, condemning him to court costs and to three days in jail.[90] Predictably, soldiers were often both the victims and the perpetrators of these "homicides par imprudence." On 1 April 1707, the soldiers of the garrison were participating in a military procession. A sergeant ordered the men in his company to put their hair under their caps. Hercule Félix, a soldier from Dauphiné, put his rifle on his shoulder while dutifully tucking his hair under his hat. The rifle, however, slipped and went off, blowing off the head of Pierre de la Rue, a soldier standing immediately behind Félix. For his sloppy handling of his rifle, Félix was con-

[90]AEG, EC, LM 68: 74, 13 August 1793; PC 17035; RC 302: 863.

demned to pay court costs and to do public "réparation," asking forgiveness from God and from de la Rue's widow. Though contrite, Félix was also ordered to leave the city immediately.[91] Since these deaths resembled accidents much more than murders, they have not been included in the homicide totals.[92]

All told, this evidence shows that the increase in the Genevan homicide rate did not come close to matching that for suicide. While homicides easily outnumbered suicides through the mid-eighteenth century (327 to 116), for the period 1751–98 suicides outnumbered homicides by over two to one (288 to 131). The ratio of suicides to murders was even greater in the 1780s and 1790s: 160 to 65. Put another way, while homicides increased by about two-thirds (79 to 131) from the first to the second half of the eighteenth century, suicides were five times more numerous (288 to 54) after 1750 than in the previous fifty years. When one considers that a third of the homicides of the late eighteenth century involved infanticide, Genevan adults of the late 1700s were over three times more likely to commit suicide than to be homicide victims. The frequency of homicide and suicide thus did not vary inversely to each other; rather, they varied independently of each other. Homicides and suicides were both increasing in the late eighteenth century, the former simply at a much slower pace than the latter. In late-eighteenth-century Geneva, anomie contributed to increases in both suicides and homicides.

Though it cannot possibly be confounded with suicide, infanticide warrants a discussion. In addition to the 125 definite cases of infanticide, there were 245 deaths of infants and small children that might have been deliberate. As table 20 reveals, there were far fewer of these questionable infant

[91]AEG, EC, LM 52: 172, 1 April 1707; PC 5780. There were also forty-three accidental deaths by firearms for which no one appeared culpable. Several of these involved people killed by firearms that backfired. While participating in maneuvers in 1682, for example, three soldiers were killed when the cannon they were firing exploded; AEG, EC, LM 45: 2, 9 August 1682.

[92]By its very nature, Geneva's judicial system supported the view that circumstances determined the nature of the crime. Throughout the life of the Republic, Geneva's judicial system was based on the notion of "arbitraire." That is, the judges had enormous latitude in meting out penalties against misdeeds. This stemmed primarily from the fact that the Republic did not have a judicial code that spelled out crimes, misdemeanors, and their respective penalties. Consequently, judicial authorities in Geneva were quite interested in determining whether a violent act, for example, was premeditated. Aggravating circumstances entailed harsher punishments, while mitigating circumstances would likely bring a more lenient sentence; Porret, *Crime et ses circonstances*, 120–21. In dealing with homicides, judges maintained a clear distinction between premeditated murder and "homicide par imprudence," or involuntary manslaughter.

deaths in the eighteenth century than in the seventeenth. They were most numerous at the same time that the murder rate reached its peak: 1601–50. The bulk of these deaths involved babies who were smothered in bed with their mothers or wet nurses.[93] Some of these smotherings were surely intentional, while others were genuine accidents. The precise number of actual cases of infanticide cannot be known.

Table 20:　Questionable Infant Deaths, 1542–1798[a]

Period	Total
1542–1600	46
1601–50	90
1651–1700	63
1701–50	12
1751–98	34
(1781–98)	(15)
Total	245

a. Source: Etat Civil, Livres des Morts; Procès Criminels; Registres du Conseil. In all cases, there is at least a modicum of suspicion of foul play.

I am also convinced that a few of these "suffocations" in bed must have been in reality natural deaths. Among the thousands of infant deaths recorded in early modern Geneva, no mention of course is made of Sudden Infant Death Syndrome (SIDS). I can envision a mother awakening in the morning next to her dead child, the victim of SIDS, and concluding that she must have rolled over and suffocated the baby during the night. It is all too easy to imagine the terrible feelings of guilt that must have plagued such mothers.

As table 21 reveals, these cases of suffocation, whether accidental or intentional, all but disappeared in the eighteenth century. Only five such smotherings occurred in the whole century, only two after 1713. Clearly

---

[93]This decline in the number of deaths of infants by suffocation may have been a trend elsewhere in early modern Europe. Evidence for Stockholm indicates a dramatic decrease in these "roll-over" deaths from the early seventeenth to the late eighteenth centuries; Arne Jansson, *From Swords to Sorrow: Homicide and Suicide in Early Modern Stockholm* (Stockholm: Almqvist and Wiskell, 1998), 22.

Table 21: Infant Roll-Over Deaths, 1542–1798[a]

PERIOD	TOTAL
1541–1600	35
1601–50	84
1651–1700	55
1701–50	4
1751–98	1
Total	179

a. Source: Etat Civil, Livres des Morts; Procès Criminels; Registres du Conseil. These cases involved infants whose mothers or wet nurses allegedly rolled over and smothered them while sleeping in the same bed.

mothers and wet nurses were finally beginning to heed the advice of pastors and physicians that they were not to sleep in the same beds with the infants.[94] When we take into consideration the decline in the questionable infant deaths, the increase in infanticide in the late 1700s may have been illusory. At that time perhaps the number of definite cases of infanticide more accurately reflected the actual number of babies who were killed.[95]

Although mothers of the late eighteenth century were no longer smothering their babies, they were much more likely than ever to abandon them. As table 22 indicates, the half century after 1750, which experienced a rapid increase in illegitimate births, witnessed an explosion in *expositions d'enfants*, accounting for over three-fourths of all abandonments in early modern Geneva.[96] The division between infanticide and abandonment was

[94]In early modern Anjou, synodal statutes forbade the practice of babies' sleeping with adults, but the fact that this interdiction was renewed several times (even as late as 1783) indicates that these accidents still happened; see François Lebrun, *Les hommes et la mort en Anjou aux 17e et 18e siècles* (Paris: Mouton, 1971), 422.

[95]Research on the Parlement of Paris shows that France experienced an "infanticide craze" in the years 1565–1690, while the rate of such deaths declined in the eighteenth century; see Alfred Soman, "Anatomy of an Infanticide Trial: The Case of Marie-Jeanne Bartonnet (1742)," in *Changing Identities in Early Modern France*, ed. Michael Wolfe (Durham: Duke University Press, 1997), 248. See also R. W. Malcolmson, "Infanticide in the Eighteenth Century," in *Crime in England 1550–1800*, ed. J. S. Cockburn (Princeton: Princeton University Press, 1977), 187–209.

[96]See Daniel Aquillon, "'Celui qui se cache bien vit heureux' ou l'exposition d'enfant à Genève entre 1765 et 1785," *Revue de Vieux Genève* 13 (1983): 22–27; see also E. William Monter, "Women in Calvinist Geneva (1550–1800)," *Signs* 6 (1980): 198.

Table 22: Abandonment of Infants, 1540–1798[a]

Period	Total
1540–1600	5
1601–50	10
1651–1700	23
1701–50	141
1751–98	635
Total	814

a. Source: Handwritten inventories in the Archives d'Etat de Genève for the Procès Criminels (1er et 2e Séries).

often blurred. Since the delivery of an unwanted child was performed secretly without the assistance of a midwife, the baby's risk of dying at birth greatly increased. Even if the child did not die immediately, the mortality rate for children taken in by hospitals and orphanages throughout Europe was frighteningly high. In early modern Geneva, 40 exposed babies (36 after 1750, 25 after 1780) had already died when they were found. Although I have included these among the questionable infant deaths, the deaths themselves generally appear to have been unintended. For example, a deceased newborn girl was found wrapped in cloths and placed in a box in the rue des Orfèvres in Geneva. These precautions suggest that the mother, the most likely person to abandon a child, hoped that the baby would be found and saved. The girl was left in a heavily populated area early in the evening and normally would have been found soon.[97] Several other deceased babies were found in front of the entrance to the general hospital, the institution that ordinarily took charge of abandoned children. Although abandoning a child on a doorstep was not tantamount to strangling a newborn and throwing its corpse into the river, a mother must have known that the abandoned child's chances of surviving to adulthood were slim. Magistrates of course would have deemed the mother guilty of abandonment and neglect, although cases of *expositions* were rarely solved. Notwithstanding the peak in definite instances of infanticide, the declining number of questionable infant deaths, combined with the explosion in the number of *expo-*

[97]AEG, EC, LM 67: 36, 8 April 1787; RC 291: 305.

sitions, suggests that, to a degree, abandonment was replacing infanticide in the late eighteenth century.

Contrary to what one may think, infanticide was not directed primarily against female babies.[98] True, girls did outnumber boys somewhat among the definite cases of infanticides: 52 to 41 (for 32 the sex was not revealed). But among the 245 questionable infant deaths, there were 129 boys and 103 girls (and 13 whose sex was unidentified). Of the 40 abandoned newborns who were found dead, there were 26 boys as opposed to only 14 girls. Among babies who were allegedly smothered accidentally by their mothers or wet nurses, boys outnumbered girls by 97 to 77, while the sex of five is unknown. A possible explanation for this last discrepancy is that some of the boys may have died from Sudden Infant Death Syndrome, since male babies are much more likely to die of SIDS than females. A deliberate attempt to eliminate baby boys in particular is most unlikely.

Not surprisingly, males made up the overwhelming majority of the victims of all other forms of homicide. Excluding infanticide, we find that ten times as many men as women (285 to 29) were murdered in early modern Geneva. (Evidence was inadequate to determine the sex of nineteen murder victims, all of whom were killed in the sixteenth and early seventeenth centuries.) Even the victims of involuntary manslaughter were twice as likely to be men as women (32 as opposed to 17). Overall, however, the evidence on the various forms of homicide shows that Genevans of the late eighteenth century were much more prone to killing themselves than others.

There were other ways in which the patterns of Genevan suicides and homicides differed dramatically. The geographical nature of these acts of violence contrasted remarkably: in early modern Geneva suicide was urban while murder was rural, a trend also found in twentieth-century sociological studies. About 90 percent of suicides (356) occurred in the city of Geneva or the immediate surrounding environs, while only forty-four people took their lives in and around the dependent territories (the location of the remaining four suicides being unknown). Since residents of these dependent territories generally numbered no more than a tenth the population of the city, these figures appear roughly in line with the Republic's demographic structure.

[98]Evidence from early modern England and France also indicates that the sex of babies was not a factor in cases of infanticide; see Malcolmson, "Infanticide," in *Crime in England*, ed. Cockburn, 192; Soman, "Anatomy of an Infanticide," in *Changing Identities*, ed. Wolfe, 248–49.

Rural dwellers, however, accounted for a smaller share of suicides than their proportion of the population would have dictated. Some of the suicides committed in the countryside involved urban dwellers who left the city to take their lives. Although suicides most often took place in the privacy of the victims' abodes in town, some sought the quiet of the countryside to end their lives. While suicides were urban, homicides were more characteristic of the sparsely populated countryside: 223 people were killed in the city and suburbs, while 204 met violent deaths in the countryside (the location is unknown for 31 homicides). If we eliminate the data for infanticides (87 out of 125 occurred in or around the city), a clear majority of homicides were rural (168, as opposed to 136 urban homicides).

Do these figures mean that peasants killed each other while the merchants and artisans of the city took their aggression out on themselves? While peasants definitely were less likely to commit suicide than their urban counterparts, the plethora of homicides was tied less to the rural denizens' penchant for violence than to the cover that the isolated countryside offered criminals. While violence might erupt among acquaintances in both town and country, random attacks by hardened criminals were much more likely to happen away from the walls of the city. Roaming bandits and army deserters habitually preyed on people who traveled the roads linking Geneva to neighboring villages. So many murder victims were people who were simply traveling through the countryside rather than permanently living there. A typical murder was that involving Nicolas Bolarue, forty-two, a silk merchant residing in Geneva whose business trip to Burgundy in October 1622 ended tragically when highwaymen ambushed, robbed, and murdered him on an isolated road many miles from the city.[99] The proximity of large numbers of people in town offered protection against such random attacks.

SUICIDES AND SEASONALITY

An issue worth pondering is whether there were seasonal variations with regard to suicide in early modern Geneva. One might expect the number of suicides to rise during the short days and long cold nights of winter. In the *Spirit of the Laws*, Montesquieu in effect blamed the allegedly large number of suicides in England on the bad weather there, and it has long been

[99]AEG, EC, LM 29: 63, 12 October 1622.

assumed that gloomy weather nurtures suicidal despair.[100] A host of studies, however, indicate the opposite is the case. Durkheim found that for almost all countries, the largest number of suicides occur in the summer.[101] More recent sociological research confirms that the peak for self-inflicted deaths tends to be in spring or early summer.[102] In a general way, the evidence from Geneva supports these findings (see table 23). Although it may be rather

Table 23: Suicides and Seasonality, 1542–1798[a]

MONTH	1542–1750	1751–1798	TOTAL
January	11	22	33
February	4	21	25
March	6	13	19
April	10	29	39
May	7	23	30
June	9	38	47
July	9	33	42
August	19	28	47
September	10	22	32
October	11	19	30
November	9	19	28
December	10	21	31
Total	116[b]	288	404

a. Source: Etat Civil, Livres des Morts; Procès Criminels; Registres du Conseil.
b. The date for a late-sixteenth-century suicide cannot be established.

unusual for the nadir of self-inflicted deaths to be in March, the peak unequivocally coincided with the summer months of June, July, and August, followed closely by April. The little evidence that exists for other areas of

[100]Montesquieu, *De l'esprit des lois* (Paris: Garnier Frères, 1927), bk. 14, chap. 12.
[101]Durkheim, *Suicide*, 107.
[102]Dublin, *Suicide*, 56–60; Ronald W. Maris, *Social Forces in Urban Suicide* (Homewood, Ill.: Dorsey Press, 1969), 90.

early modern Europe also shows that self-inflicted deaths were most common in spring and summer.[103]

Why have suicides traditionally been more numerous in the spring and summer than in other times of the year? Although the nineteenth-century Italian social theorist Enrico Morselli believed that climatic factors were key, Durkheim argued that seasonal variations in suicide rates depend entirely on social changes, insisting that suicide rates varied directly with the length of the days. Most suicides occur during the daytime because most human activity, including conflicts and personal reversals, occur during the day.[104] Several studies have pointed out some problems with climatic explanations for seasonal variations, showing that meteorological factors such as the amount of sun or rain or the number of thunderstorms did not influence suicide rates.[105] It is quite possible, however, that psychological problems may be exacerbated by seasonal changes. Perhaps a person's depression is augmented by the rejuvenation of nature around him or her. Suicidal depression has been described as a form of "spiritual winter," and as nature becomes kinder and gentler, the gulf between the warm exterior and the cold, sterile interior becomes wider and less tolerable.[106] Perhaps more important are social factors associated with the changing seasons. Quite likely, during the summer months a person is much more aware of his or her social isolation because the interaction of others is much more visible than in winter.[107]

Interestingly, this seasonal pattern did not exist throughout the early modern period in Geneva. As table 23 further indicates, there were some important differences in the monthly frequency of suicide before and after 1750. The figures for the late eighteenth century reflect quite clearly the predominance of self-inflicted deaths for spring and summer: the months April–August witnessed more suicides than any other month. While the N is admittedly rather small, the data through 1750 paint a noticeably different

---

[103]Michael MacDonald and Terence R. Murphy, *Sleepless Souls: Suicide in Early Modern England* (Oxford: Clarendon Press, 1990), 311–14; Jeffrey Merrick, "Patterns and Prosecution of Suicide in Eighteenth-Century Paris," *Historical Reflections* 16 (1989): 9.

[104]Durkheim, *Suicide*, 104–22; Enrico Morselli, *Il Suicidio: Saggio di statistica morale comparata* (Milan: Dumolard, 1879). See also Fedden, *Suicide*, 334–38.

[105]Lester, *Why People Kill Themselves*, 153–58; Alex D. Pokorny, Fred Davis, and Wayne Harberson, "Suicide, Suicide Attempts and Weather," in *The Sociology of Suicide: A Selection of Readings*, ed. Anthony Giddens (London: Frank Cass, 1971), 298–306.

[106]George Howe Colt, *The Enigma of Suicide* (New York: Summit Books, 1991), 249.

[107]Maris, *Social Forces in Urban Suicide*, 90.

picture. An inordinate number of suicides occurred in August, while voluntary deaths were quite rare in February, March, and May. Otherwise, suicides were fairly evenly distributed among the months of the year. As with the breakdown by gender, the mid-eighteenth century thus marked the beginning of seasonal patterns to Genevan suicides that are typical of modern Western countries. Though to a degree the causes behind these seasonal variations will probably remain a mystery, this evidence, combined with the contemporaneous explosion in suicides, suggests that Genevans were experiencing fundamental changes—be they in mentality or social structure—which anticipated modern experiences with regard to voluntary deaths.

To date, there has been little evidence on the frequency of suicide in premodern Europe. The little work that has been done on suicide in medieval Europe suggests that self-inflicted deaths were very uncommon then, though the extant records are of questionable reliability.[108] There is some evidence to suggest that parts of Europe experienced an increase in suicides in the Reformation era. This probably was in part a reflection of more thorough investigation of questionable deaths and improvements in record-keeping in the sixteenth century.[109] Moreover, even if self-inflicted deaths did become more common in sixteenth-century Europe, evidence thus far indicates that suicide remained quite rare when compared with modern Europeans' penchant to take their own lives.

It is also important to note that the eighteenth-century increase in self-inflicted deaths does not appear to be unique to Geneva. Contemporaries in France and Prussia, for example, experienced similar increases in the number of suicides.[110] In the 1760s Paris witnessed a large number of self-inflicted

---

[108]Barbara Hanawalt, *Crime and Conflict in English Communities 1300–1348* (Cambridge: Harvard University Press, 1979), 101–4; Alexander Murray, *Suicide in the Middle Ages*, vol. 1, *The Violent Against Themselves* (Oxford: Oxford University Press, 1998), 348–78.

[109]H. C. Erik Midelfort, "Religious Melancholy and Suicide: On the Reformation Origins of a Sociological Stereotype," in *Madness, Melancholy, and the Limits of the Self*, ed. Andrew D. Weiner and Leonard V. Kaplan, vol. 3 of *Graven Images: Studies in Culture, Law, and the Sacred* (Madison: University of Wisconsin Law School, 1996), 44; Murray, *Suicide*, vol. 1, *Violent Against Themselves*, 373–78; Michael Zell, "Suicide in Pre-Industrial England," *Social History* 11 (1986): 303–17.

[110]Henri Brunschwig, *Enlightenment and Romanticism in Eighteenth-Century Prussia*, trans. Frank Jellinek (Chicago: University of Chicago Press, 1974), 220–21; Favre, *Mort dans la littérature*, 473; Merrick, "Patterns and Prosecution of Suicide," 1–53.

deaths, reaching a peak in 1769.[111] Claiming in 1782 that suicide was more common in Paris than in any other city in the world, Louis Sébastien Mercier wrote that the French capital experienced 150 suicides a year at that time, amounting to a suicide rate of 18 to 25 per 100,000 people.[112] In the late eighteenth, early nineteenth centuries, the principality of Neuchâtel evidently had an increase in suicides which at least one authority blamed on the antireligious ideas associated with the Enlightenment.[113] In England, a country whose people were believed in the eighteenth century to be especially prone to voluntary death, the suicide rate for greater London in 1700–1706 was twice what it had been three decades before and doubled again in the 1750s, when it reached an unprecedented high, not surpassed until the late 1790s.[114] The important task of identifying the causes of Geneva's explosion in suicide will provide evidence to broader social and cultural changes that may have contributed to the growing numbers of people who took their lives throughout Europe in the late 1700s.

---

[111]John McManners, *Death and the Enlightenment: Changing Attitudes to Death in Eighteenth-Century France* (Oxford: Oxford University Press, 1981), 429–30.

[112]Georges Minois, "L'historien et la question du suicide," *Histoire* 189 (1995): 29.

[113]Philippe Henry, *Crime, justice et société dans la principauté de Neuchâtel au XVIIIe siècle (1707–1806)* (Neuchâtel, Switzerland: Baconnière, 1984), 577–80; Schnegg, "Justice et suicide," 88–89.

[114]Samuel Ernest Sprott, *The English Debate on Suicide from Donne to Hume* (La Salle, Ill.: Open Court, 1961), 71, 97.

2

The Judicial and Intellectual Dimensions of Suicide

IN AN EFFORT TO UNDERSTAND why Geneva experienced an explosion in suicides in the late eighteenth century, we must examine the prevailing attitudes toward and judicial treatment of suicide. Did intellectual and judicial leaders of Geneva and of Europe in general view voluntary death differently in the late 1700s than their predecessors had in the sixteenth century? If so, did changes in ideas about suicide or in the legal treatment of self-inflicted death play a decisive role in the growing numbers of people who took their lives?

CALVIN AND CONTEMPORARIES ON SUICIDE

Appropriately, we must begin with a brief description of the views on suicide of John Calvin, theologian and lawyer, who exerted an enormous influence upon the regulation of Reformed morality in Geneva and elsewhere. Calvin wrote very little on suicide. In fact he treated the issue at length only twice in sermons that dealt with the biblical suicides of Saul and his armor bearer (from 1 Samuel 31, who stabbed themselves rather than be captured by the Philistines), and of Ahithophel (from 2 Samuel 17, who hanged himself after Absalom rejected his plan to assassinate David).[1] In these sermons, the cen-

---

[1] These sermons are found respectively in *CO* 46: 712–22; and *SC* 511–19. The most famous suicide in the Bible is of course that of Judas. In his commentary on Matthew 27:5, however, Calvin showed little interest in self-murder per se. He was much more concerned with Judas's treason than his killing himself; see *CO* 45: 747.

tral argument that Calvin made against suicide is that in taking one's life, one is being disobedient by refusing to submit to the will of God. God has given life to humans; he alone has the right to take it away. In depicting voluntary death as usurping God's powers, Calvin was following closely the logic of Augustine, who in turn drew inspiration from a selective reading of Plato.[2] Their texts emphasized that God has ordered us to be ready for death at every moment, but it is not up to us to determine when we leave this life. Calvin declared:

> Let us wait for the highest commander, who sent us into this world, to call us out of it. Who, pray tell, would praise the soldier who, having been ordered by his commander to be on sentry duty, attacked the enemy in order to gain praise for his bravery? Truly he would be accused of rashness, for which he would be duly punished. Thus God, having sent us in this world, wishes us to stay in it, and he has placed us in a post which we must not abandon until God orders us to do so. Since we have been placed on this duty as in a watchtower, it behooves us to stay watchful and always be prepared to move wherever the commander shall order. This is the virtue of Christians; this is fortitude and constancy.[3]

[2]Augustine *City of God*, trans. George E. McCracken et al. (Cambridge, Mass: Harvard University Press; London: William Heinemann, 1957–72), 1.17–27; cf. Thomas Aquinas, *Summa Theologica*, trans. Fathers of the English Dominican Province (London: R. and T. Washbourne, 1911–24), Secunda Secundae, Quaest. 64, Art. 5. Plato condemned voluntary death as a form of usurping the authority of God. Nonetheless, he asserted that taking one's life was justified if God sends some necessity upon the individual, in effect requiring suicide of him, as in the case of Socrates; see Plato, *Phaedo*, trans. David Gallop (Oxford: Clarendon Press, 1990), 62b–c. In the ninth book of *The Laws*, Plato indicated three situations in which one may be justified to end voluntarily one's life: (1) if the state orders one to do so; (2) if one suffers an "excruciating and unavoidable misfortune"; (3) if one suffers overwhelming shame; see Plato, *The Laws*, translated and with an introduction by Trevor J. Saunders (Middlesex, England: Penguin, 1970), 873c. Plato in short did not issue a blanket condemnation of suicide; rather he disapproved of voluntarily ending one's life without good reason. Augustine may have been influenced more directly by Neoplatonists who tended to take a stronger stand against suicide than Plato. In his *Commentary on the Dream of Scipio*, the Neoplatonist Macrobius, a contemporary of Augustine, wrote that suicides will not have eternal life with God; people must wait for God to free them from the fetters of the body. This, however, still seemed to allow the possibility that one could justifiably kill oneself if so ordered by God; see Albert Bayet, *Le suicide et la morale* (Paris: Felix Alcan, 1922; reprint, New York: Arno Press, 1975), 300, 387–88, 434–46; Arthur J. Droge and James D. Tabor, *A Noble Death: Suicide and Martyrdom Among Christians and Jews of Antiquity* (San Francisco: Harper San Francisco, 1992), 5, 20–22, 41–42.

[3]CO 46: 718–19.

In this passage, Calvin has borrowed the image of the soldier on sentry duty which originated with Pythagoras and served as an important argument for opponents of suicide for over two thousand years.[4]

Describing self-murder as "the worst crime," Calvin suggested that suicides are guilty of hubris. "For the highest and most outstanding virtue, upon which all others are based," Calvin preached, "is faith, to which hope is joined, to which humility next follows, to which virtues human cleverness is most contrary. Whence come the violent deaths that people inflict upon themselves except from impatience and haughtiness?"[5] Saul himself asked his armor bearer to kill him so that the godless Philistines would not gloat over him and kill him. Such words belie, according to Calvin, an impatience, an unwillingness to bear suffering. From such impatience and arrogance, "unbelieving and profane men inflict death upon themselves because they cannot bear disgrace and ignominy." For Calvin, such men are "abominable before God."[6] Calvin declared that Christians must subject themselves to God's will and not "quail from walking through ignominy and infamy, and whatever reproofs and shame may be hurled upon us, let us learn to bear them patiently, as Paul himself teaches us through his example."[7] Calvin acknowledged that the faithful will often pass through difficult times, noting that they may suffer setbacks, tire of living, and long to be free of this world. Nonetheless they must not rebel against God but rather must humbly submit to his will. If God indeed punishes people, it is not to cause them despair but rather to bring them back to the right path. Like Aristotle, Calvin believed that true courage meant to endure hardships.[8]

Echoing Augustine, Calvin observed that "nearly all heathen" heaped

---

[4]Cicero, for example, employed this analogy; see *Tusculan Disputations*, trans. J. A. King (London: William Heinemann; New York: G. P. Putnam's Sons, 1927), 1. 74; Lester G. Crocker, "The Discussion of Suicide in the Eighteenth Century," *Journal of the History of Ideas* 13 (1952): 52.

[5]*CO* 46: 719.

[6]*CO* 46: 719.

[7]*CO* 46: 719; cf. 2 Corinthians 10 and 11.

[8]*SC* 514. Aristotle wrote, "Courage...is confident and endures because it is noble to do so or base not to do so. But to seek death in order to escape from poverty, or the pangs of love, or from pain or sorrow, is not the act of a courageous man, but rather of a coward; for it is weakness to fly from troubles, and the suicide does not endure death because it is noble to do so, but to escape evil." See *The Nicomachean Ethics*, trans. H. Rackham (Cambridge: Harvard University Press; London: William Heinemann, 1982), 3.7.13. As with Plato, Aristotle does not seem to be condemning all suicides but rather those committed for the wrong reasons.

praise on those who, like Saul, took their lives rather than suffer the "ignominy and disgrace" of falling into the hands of their foes.[9] Although he
named no one here, Calvin was surely thinking above all of the Stoics,
aggressive defenders of the right to end one's life voluntarily, provided one
acted rationally. Among the numerous Roman figures who killed themselves rather than submit to their enemies, Cato of Utica (d. 46 B.C.), the
Republican hero who stabbed himself rather than surrender to the forces of
Julius Caesar, served as the model of the "honorable" suicide.[10] Philosophers such as the later Stoic Seneca, who was himself forced to commit suicide by the emperor Nero in 65 A.D., described Cato's demise as a most
noble death and exalted suicide as the ultimate expression of human freedom.[11] Calvin alleged that, according to these "pagan philosophers," Saul
would be considered as having acted bravely and as being "great in soul."[12]

---

[9] *CO* 46: 718; cf. *City of God* 1. 22. Ancient pagan authors were not nearly as unified on the issue of suicide as Calvin and Augustine suggested. Pythagoreans opposed all suicides and, as noted above, Augustine borrowed arguments against suicide from pagan authors, especially from Plato and Neoplatonists.

[10] Yolande Grisé, *Le suicide dans la Rome antique* (Montreal: Bellarmin; Paris: Les Belles Lettres, 1982), 60–63.

[11] Seneca described suicide as a means of liberation in *On Anger*, trans. John W. Basore, 3 vols., *Moral Essays* (London: William Heinemann; New York: G. P. Putnam's Sons, 1928), 3. 15. 3–4. Else-where, Seneca was downright giddy in his praise of Cato: "I do not know…what nobler sight the Lord of heaven could find on earth…than the spectacle of Cato.… Surely the gods looked with pleasure upon their pupil as he made his escape by so glorious and memorable an end!" *On Providence*, trans. John W. Basore, 3 vols., *Moral Essays* (London: William Heinemann; New York: G. P. Putnam's Sons, 1928), 2. 9–12. Even Cicero, who argued that one dare not commit suicide without divine permission, lauded Cato. Cicero believed that both Socrates and Cato had received divine approbation to take their lives; see *Tusculan Disputations*, trans. J. E. King (London: William Heinemann; New York: G. P. Putnam's Sons, 1927), 1. 74; Arthur J. Droge and James D. Tabor, *Noble Death: Suicide and Martyrdom Among Christians and Jews of Antiquity* (San Francisco: Harper San Francisco, 1992), 32–36; Miriam Griffin, "Philosophy, Cato, and Roman Suicide," *Greece and Rome* 33 (1986): 64–77, 192–202. Condemning Cato's suicide, Augustine vowed that a more appropriate role model from pagan Rome for Christians was Regulus, who surrendered to the Carthaginians in the First Punic War and reportedly suffered a most torturous death at their hands; see *City of God* 1. 22–23. It must be noted, however, that no pagan philosopher was promoting suicide. True, Seneca believed that suicide could be a means of liberation and was justified if it spared one from living badly; in certain cases, he deemed it immoral to prevent someone from taking his life. But while he extolled the death of Cato, he found many motives for killing oneself were not justified. He deplored suicides that were acts of passion, the consequences of which had not been thought about, or were motivated simply by weariness of living. Seneca deemed as glorious only those suicides that were based on rational reflection—in short, suicide was an option only for wise people, such as Cato or Socrates, who had valid reasons for ending their lives. One must not take one's life, however, if one could still be useful to others; see Nicole Tadic-Gilloteaux, "Sénèque face au suicide," *L'antiquité classique* 32 (1963): 541–51.

[12] *CO* 46: 718.

Many pagans saw those who took their lives under these circumstances as magnanimous and courageous and mocked the fears of those who hesitated to do so.[13]

Calvin acknowledged nonetheless that not all pagans held this view. Although he did not mention him by name, Calvin was referring to Pythagoras when he extolled the pagan author who originated the analogy, described above, of humans as soldiers on guard duty. According to Calvin, in arguing that humans are thus entrusted with the preservation of their lives, the pagan Pythagoras was divinely inspired. Calvin alleged that God inspired Pythagoras to speak thus in order to remove any excuse for killing oneself.[14] Calvin insisted that since their lives belong to God, not to themselves, Christians, like the faithful soldier, must remain here on earth until God calls them home.

Calvin saw no bounds to the degree of patience required of Christians. Simply put, they were to endure all sorts of torture, misfortune, and disgrace. People who have committed grave sins and are rightly subject to capital punishment, for example, must bear patiently the punishment they deserve. If they confess their sins and ask for forgiveness, theirs shall be an "honorable" death in spite of the apparent dishonor associated with such executions. If they avoid the obstinacy of Saul and Ahithophel in refusing to submit to God's will, "in place of the everlasting confusion and pains which they had deserved, they will find grace with God and his mercy will follow."[15]

In both sermons on suicide, Calvin dealt with the issue of women who, attacked by marauding barbarians, committed suicide to avoid being raped. In this, Calvin addressed an issue that Augustine raised, later commented upon by Aquinas, concerning Roman women who killed themselves rather than be raped by invading Goths in 410. Calvin observed that many praised such women, almost to the point of canonizing them, for having sacrificed themselves in order to remain chaste. For Calvin, however, these women had sinned in taking their lives. Like Augustine and Aquinas,

---

[13]*SC* 513. In *City of God* 1. 21, Augustine wrote that "voluntary death can never be any sign of magnanimity or greatness of spirit."

[14]*SC* 513.

[15]*CO* 46: 722.

Calvin maintained that it is wrong to commit one evil in order to avoid another.[16]

Calvin considered suicide a terribly wicked act not only because it defied the will of God but also because he deemed it unnatural. It was largely because of the unnatural aspect of suicide that in spite of the seemingly dispassionate tone of the Scripture, Calvin described Ahithophel's death as "detestable, even monstrous." Killing oneself is a sin, he preached, because it violates our natural instinct of self-preservation:

> It is against nature that a man kills himself regardless of the method. We have this natural sense to flee from death; we have a certain horror of death, which God has instilled in us. Knowing that death came from God's malediction, we must always be
>
> and proceed in great fear. The pagans knew that death is horrible and that everyone flees it, but they did not know why. [They did not know] that death came into this world because of sin. They thought that people were born mortal and were subject to death from the earliest creation. God engraved in the hearts of all persons this apprehension so that death terrifies and shocks them.[17]

This repugnance causes us to retreat from death whenever possible. Killing oneself, Calvin argued, is behavior that is beneath even that of animals. Even the most savage beasts invariably try to survive and preserve the state in which God placed them. In rejecting suicide as contrary to nature, Calvin was reiterating Aquinas's argument that suicide violated natural law in that

---

[16]*CO* 46: 722; *SC* 515. Augustine argued that since one does not have the right to kill a guilty person, then one certainly must not kill innocent people, such as these women who were about to be raped. He further argued that in killing oneself to avoid another sin, one has committed a sin for which one cannot do penitence. The logical consequence of this endeavor to remain pure and avoid sin, he asserted, is that the Christian ought to commit suicide immediately after baptism. He also criticized Lucretia, the legendary Roman noblewoman whose suicide, following her rape by the king's son, Sextus Tarquinius, led to the overthrow of monarchy and the establishment of the Republic in 509 B.C. Augustine declared that she had punished the innocent victim of rape; *City of God* 1. 16–18, 24, 26. In chapter 25, however, Augustine did acknowledge that it was possible that some of these early Christian female martyrs may have been obeying a divine order to take their lives. Aquinas, like Augustine, said that a woman must never commit the greater sin of voluntary death to avoid the lesser sin of another person. The Bible says, moreover, that one must not do evil so that good may come; Romans 3: 8; Aquinas, *Summa Theologica*, Secunda Secundae, Quaest. 64, Art. 5.

[17]*SC* 512–13.

all things love themselves in the state of nature.[18]

Closely tied to Calvin's view that suicide is unnatural was his belief that self-murder is caused by diabolical possession. Killing oneself, he declared, is a brutish, villainous act; people who commit suicide are "possessed by the devil."[19] Though references associating self-murder with diabolical possession can be found as early as the patristic period, the notion that suicide was diabolical had not always been prominent among Christian thinkers.[20] Neither Augustine nor Aquinas said anything about the devil's causing of suicides. By the late Middle Ages, laypersons and clerics alike commonly attributed suicide to the devil, who was believed to cause despair that led to suicide.[21] In the Reformation era, suicide was associated even more with the work of the devil.[22] For his part, Calvin blamed the devil for suppressing the instinct of self-preservation, which God instills in all creatures. According to Calvin, experience shows that without this diabolical "fury," no one would ever take one's life. A "drop of natural sense" would suffice to prevent some-

---

[18]Aquinas, *Summa Theologica*, Secunda Secundae, Quaest. 64, Art. 5; Bayet, *Suicide et morale*, 426–28.

[19]*SC* 513. Though he viewed the devil as quite powerful, Calvin, unlike Luther, did not in any way construe demonic possession as possibly exculpating those who took their lives. Luther believed that the power of the devil was so great that it simply overwhelmed some people, pushing them to take their lives. Contrary to the views of so many Protestant and Catholic thinkers, Luther denied that suicides were necessarily damned, insisting that they were victims of the devil's powers. Although he was in effect providing a basis for a "demonic insanity defense," Luther nonetheless did not oppose the desecration of corpses, believing that it helped prevent Satan from driving still more people to choose death. Calvin apparently viewed submission to the devil as voluntary and thus blameworthy; see H. C. Erik Midelfort, "Religious Melancholy and Suicide: On the Reformation Origins of a Sociological Stereotype," *Madness, Melancholy, and the Limits of the Self,* ed. Andrew D. Weiner and Leonard V. Kaplan, vol. 3 of *Graven Images: Studies in Culture, Law, and the Sacred* (Madison: University of Wisconsin Law School, 1996): 42, 48. See also Bernard Paulin, *Du couteau à la plume: Le suicide dans la littérature anglaise de la Renaissance (1580–1625)* (Lyon: L'Hermès, 1977), 36–37.

[20]The Church Council that met in Arles in 452 issued a canon that read: "Si quis famulorum cujuslibet condicionis aut generis, quasi ad exacerbandam domini districtionem, se diabolico repletus furore percusserit, ipse tantum sanguinis sui reus erit, neque ad dominum sceleris alieni pertinebit invidia"; cited in Bayet, *Suicide et morale*, 377–78, who convincingly argues that this canon was attacking not suicide in general but only those involving slaves and domestic servants, which were viewed as an attack against their masters.

[21]Jean-Claude Schmitt, "Le suicide au Moyen Age," *Annales: E.S.C.* 31 (1976): 4–5; Michael MacDonald and Terence R. Murphy, *Sleepless Souls: Suicide in Early Modern England* (Oxford: Clarendon Press, 1990), 34–76.

[22]Gabriela Signori, "Rechtskonstruktionen und religiöse Fiktionen: Bemerkungen zur Selbstmordfrage im Mittelalter," in *Trauer, Verzweiflung und Anfechtung: Selbstmord und Selbstmordversuche in mittelalterlichen und frühneuzeitlichen Gesellschaften,* ed. Gabriela Signori (Tübingen: Diskord, 1994), 18.

one from ending his or her life. When God gives life to people, they are clearly to preserve it and to praise God for it. When, however, a person goes so far as to hang himself, stab himself, poison himself, or to jump to his death, he has obliterated this knowledge that God has given him. Such a person has been degraded. Consequently, "we cannot help but conclude that the devil has put such a rage in [that man]; such a man is no longer himself and no longer knows what he is doing and what he is saying."[23]

Calvin almost entirely avoided the problem of the seemingly fine line between martyrdom and suicide among certain early Christians. A number of early martyrs seemed to court death in a manner that bordered on suicide, an issue that Augustine grappled with in arguing that Donatists, whom he considered heretical, were not martyrs but were responsible for their own deaths. Calvin's very brief references to martyrdom in his sermons on Saul and Ahithophel were limited to the apostolic church. On the one hand, Calvin urged his parishioners to follow the examples of the prophets and apostles who patiently suffered the most ignominious treatment: "For some were thrown into irons, others beheaded; some stoned, others cut up; some mocked, others flayed; some... were ill-clad."[24] Their long-suffering for their faith, however, was ultimately quite ennobling.[25]

On the other hand, Calvin treaded rather gingerly in referring briefly to the death of the apostle Peter. The only reference to Peter's death in the Bible is Jesus's somewhat vague prophecy in the Gospel of John. Since the late first century, however, Christian tradition held that Peter was killed in Rome as a martyr for his faith, and the first reference to Peter's being crucified upside down dated from the fourth century. Medieval Catholic tradition held that to be martyrs, Christians had to die of their own free will; if death were inescapable, they had not voluntarily given their lives and thus

---

[23]In spite of his desire to condemn in the strongest manner self-murder, Calvin nonetheless rejected an argument proffered by Aristotle and adopted by Aquinas against suicide. Aristotle declared that suicide offends the state, presumably because it deprives society of one of its members. Calvin found this reasoning cold and vulgar, declaring that it could just as easily be used in favor of voluntarily ending one's life. A terminally ill person might be encouraged to end his or her life in order to avoid being a burden to others. Calvin, however, saw no justification for such a death, even if caused simply by abstaining from eating; *SC* 514–15.

[24]*CO* 46: 721; cf. Hebrews 11: 36–40.

[25]*CO* 46: 722; cf. Hebrews 11: 35–37; 2 Maccabees 6–7.

did not merit martyrdom.[26] Familiar with these traditions of martyrology, Calvin wrote that Peter "definitely died of his own volition, presenting himself as a sacrifice. His death would not have been esteemed as virtuous were it not for the fact that he was impelled to seal the truth of the Gospel."[27] In saying these words, Calvin surely did not mean that Peter actively sought martyrdom. Rather, Peter's death was voluntary in the sense that he could have saved his life by renouncing his Christian faith. Calvin made no mention of the manner in which Peter died, assuming that his audience knew that the apostle's death, though voluntary, was not by his own hand. Calvin avoided entirely the issue of whether God might order someone to commit suicide, an issue that Augustine grappled with, rather unconvincingly, in discussing Samson's death. The reason that Calvin raised the issue of Peter's death was not to dwell on the distinction between martyrdom and suicide but rather to insist that even martyrs, such as Peter, experienced the natural fear of death. Calvin preferred to disregard any gray area between martyrdom and suicide.[28]

All told, Calvin categorically condemned suicide primarily because it was a rebellion against God—a refusal to submit to God's will. It was evil because it was unnatural and resulted from diabolical possession. Calvin's views on suicide are noteworthy not because they were original but because they were representative of his age. He was an articulate spokesman who aptly reflected contemporary attitudes toward suicide shared by Protestants and Catholics. In line with the most important discussions on the topic since Augustine, Calvin's opinions on suicide were neither original nor inordinately harsh, sharing views held by late medieval Catholics.

One can also not help but conclude that in formulating his views on suicide, Calvin uncharacteristically gave less weight to biblical exegesis than to the opinions of past authors such as Aquinas and above all Augustine, the

---

[26]The first mention of Peter's martyrdom was by Clement of Rome in the last decade of the first century (I Clement 5. 1–4, 6.1–2). Clement, however, made no mention of precisely the method by which Peter died. The first mention of his being crucified upside down was made in the fourth-century Latin Acts of Peter, which, like I Clement, has been consigned to the realm of the apocrypha; Angelo Di Berardino, ed., *Encyclopedia of the Early Church* (New York: Oxford University Press, 1992), s.v. "Peter."

[27]*SC* 513.

[28]*SC* 513. Augustine argued that Samson's death, though self-inflicted, was justified because he was fulfilling an order from God; *City of God* 1. 20. In light of the scriptural passage, however, this argument is far from convincing. See also G. W. Bowersock, *Martyrdom and Rome* (Cambridge: Cambridge University Press, 1995), 59–74.

thinker most responsible for Western society's abhorrence for suicide. Neither the Old nor the New Testament clearly condemns voluntary death. The unqualified repugnance that Calvin expressed is not found in the scriptural accounts of the deaths of Saul, Ahithophel, or of any of the other half-dozen biblical self-inflicted deaths. The suicide of Razias is even described as a noble death in 2 Maccabees, which Calvin of course viewed as apocryphal.[29] As Augustine argued, the commandment against killing can be interpreted as forbidding both suicide and murder; Calvin, however, made no mention of self-murder in a sermon and commentary on the sixth commandment, discussing only interpersonal violence.[30] Moreover, in spite of that commandment, there are many examples of divinely sanctioned homicides in the Bible. Could there not also be some exceptional suicides that are divinely approved? In short, Calvin, who rejected virtually all rituals and doctrines that were not solidly based on Scripture, ultimately owed more to authors of pagan antiquity than to the Bible in dealing with the issue of suicide.

Moreover, although his passionate condemnation of suicide was clearly deeply felt, Calvin gave little thought to self-murder. Apart from a couple of tangential references to self-murder, these two sermons were Calvin's only discussions of suicide.[31] Nor did any of his ecclesiastical colleagues in

[29]The Geneva Bible contains the following gloss regarding Razias's suicide: "As this private example oght not to be followed of the godlie, because it is contrary to the worde of God, althogh the autor seme here to approve"; *The Geneva Bible: A Facsimile of the 1560 Edition* (Madison, Wisc.: University of Wisconsin Press, 1969), 2 Maccabees 14: 41. Notwithstanding Scripture, Aquinas condemned Razias's suicide as an act of weakness or cowardice; *Summa Theologica*, Secunda Secundae, Quaest. 64, Art. 5.

[30]*CO* 24: 611–13; 26: 321–34; cf. *City of God* 1. 19.

[31]In a sermon on the passion, based on Matthew 26, Calvin mentioned briefly Judas's suicide. Referring to Judas and other damned souls, Calvin preached about God's anger, "Dieu leur fait sentir leurs pechez, et sont en tel effroy, qu'ils se despitent et crient, helas: mais ce n'est pas pour concevoir quelque esperance, et se presenter à Dieu, c'est plustost une furie qui les pousse.... Aussi l'Evangeliste fait ce recit, à ce que nous contemplions tant mieux l'aveuglement que Satan avoit mis en tous ces reprouvez: et qu'un chacun de nous pense à soy. Et quand Dieu nous propose de tels exemples de son ire et de sa vengence, et qu'il monstre que les hommes sont comme forcenez, qu'ils sont despourvus de sens et de raison, quils sont (brief) abbrutis pour se precipiter avec une furie infernale: c'est afin qu'un chacun de nous baisse la teste, et que nous cognoissions que souvent nous en pourrions là venir, sinon que nous fussions preservez par la bonte et grace de nostre Dieu"; *CO* 46: 882–83. Calvin also wrote a brief preface to a book about Francesco Spiera, who hanged himself in Italy in 1548, allegedly out of despair for having renounced his Protestant beliefs. Calvin's preface, however, is essentially an attack on Italian Catholicism and sheds no additional light on his attitudes toward suicide; *CO* 9: 855–58. See also Michael MacDonald, "'The Fearful Estate of Francis Spiera': Narrative, Identity and Emotion in Early Modern England," *Journal of British Studies* 31 (1990): 32–61; M. A. Overell, "The Exploitation of Francesco Spiera," *Sixteenth Century Journal* 26 (1995): 619–37.

Geneva spend much time worrying about suicide. Not a word about suicide is to be found in the voluminous works of Theodore Beza (1519–1605), the French theologian who served as rector of Geneva's Academy and later succeeded Calvin as head of the Company of Pastors.[32] Indeed, to my knowledge, apart from Calvin's two sermons, the only other Genevan pastor of the Reformation era who left any extant writing about suicide was Lambert Daneau (1530–95). Daneau received a doctorate in law in his native France before coming to Geneva in 1559 where he studied theology briefly at the Academy. After serving as a minister in France, he returned to Geneva in 1572, following the St. Bartholomew's Day Massacre. Here he served as lecturer in theology at the Academy and periodically as pastor, including a stint in the very prestigious position of pastor of the church of Saint Pierre (1574–76) where Calvin himself had preached. He remained in Geneva until 1581 when he left for Leyden.[33]

Among the books Daneau wrote was the *Ethices Christianea,* first published in 1577 in Geneva and reissued six times, the last edition appearing in 1614. Well versed in the classics, Daneau sought to show that Christian ethics could draw support and inspiration from the works of pagan and scholastic authors. Ultimately, however, Daneau argued that Christian ethics had to be based on Scripture and that the "profane" ethics of antiquity did not suffice.[34] In this work Daneau spent less than two pages pondering whether taking one's life can be justified, providing a very brief survey of opinions of great authors. Daneau expressed disapproval of the admiration the ancients had for certain suicides, most notably those of Cato of Utica and Lucretia. Daneau noted, however, that not all pagan authors approved of suicide, observing that Roman jurists such as Papinianus (c. 140–212 A.D.) condemned those who took their lives in order to avoid the punishments of

---

[32]Bernard Paulin, *Du couteau à plume: Le Suicide dans la littérature anglaise de la Rennaissance (1580–1625)* (Lyon: L'Hermès, 1977), 139, avows that Beza once contemplated suicide. In the passage Paulin cites, however, Beza was not suggesting that he had considered killing himself; rather, he simply expressed fear over possibly dying from a serious illness that afflicted him; see Théodore de Bèze, *Correspondance de Théodore de Bèze,* vol. 3, assembled by Hippolyte Aubert, ed. Henri Meylan and Alain Dufour (Geneva: Droz, 1963), 47: "Ecce enim gravissimum morbum mihi infligit, adeo ut pene de vita desperarem." I am most grateful to Max Engammare for assisting me in locating this passage. Having worked on Beza's *Correspondance* for over thirty years, Alain Dufour knows of no reference to suicide in any missive.

[33]Olivier Fatio, *Lambert Daneau et les débuts de la scolastique réformée* (Geneva: Droz, 1976), 1–19.

[34]Fatio, *Lambert Daneau,* 177.

crimes they had committed. (Daneau acknowledged nonetheless that these same jurists believed that people who ended their lives because of "hunger, unbearable pain, or weariness of life" should not be punished nor should their estates be fined.) He further observed that Virgil wrote that those who voluntarily took their lives are condemned, describing the melancholic shadows of suicides in hell.[35] Likewise, the Roman poet Martial (c. 40–c. 104 A.D.) castigated Cato for killing himself rather than face adversity.[36] And he was quick to refer to Pythagoras's metaphor of humans as guards on sentry-duty who cannot leave without the consent of their commander. Daneau wrote approvingly of Augustine's criticism of self-murder, specifically noting the argument that the sixth commandment applies to self-murder, not simply to the killing of one's neighbor.[37] Without describing their arguments, Daneau further listed Plato, Aristotle, Aquinas, and a few others as opponents of suicide. He also insisted, rather unconvincingly, that the apostle Paul explicitly condemned the taking of one's life: "No one ever hates his own body. Instead, he feeds it and takes care of it, just as Christ does the church" (Ephesians 5:29).[38] In short, Daneau was essentially saying that one must not commit suicide because these great thinkers have said that it is unchristian to do so.[39]

Why did Genevan church leaders show such little concern for self-murder? There were two reasons for this paucity of words on suicide. First, suicide did not appear to be much of a problem. As we have seen in chapter 1, suicide was rare in Geneva through the end of the seventeenth century. Second, self-murder was not a source of much debate. Virtually all sixteenth-century thinkers, Protestant or Catholic, agreed that regardless of the circumstances, suicide was clearly wrong.[40]

---

[35]Virgil, *Aeneid* 6.434–39; Augustine cited this passage in disparaging Lucretia, *City of God* 1.19.

[36]"I am not for the hero who buys fame with easy blood, I am for him who can win glory without dying"; "In adversity it is easy to despise life; the truly brave man is he who can endure to be miserable"; Martial, *Epigrams*, 3 vols., trans. D. R. Shackleton Bailey (Cambridge: Harvard University Press, 1993), 1. 8. 5–6, 11. 56. 15–16.

[37]Augustine, *City of God* 1. 20.

[38]Daneau took this passage out of context. Ephesians 5 pertains to husbands and wives, and Paul was instructing men to love their wives just as they love themselves. Interpreting this passage as a ban on suicide requires some imagination.

[39]Lambert Daneau, *Ethices Christianea: Libri tres* (Geneva: Eustathius Vignon, 1579), 197r–v.

[40]The catechism produced by the Council of Trent condemned all suicides, and a series of councils in France—Lyon (1577), Bordeaux (1583), Cambrai (1586), and Chartres (1587)—all forbade the burial

True, Renaissance poets and especially playwrights depicted suicide much more frequently than their medieval counterparts. Among the most memorable scenes in Renaissance literature are the temptation of Marlowe's Faust with the rope and the dagger, and any of a number of suicides from Shakespeare's plays. The increased fascination with suicide is perhaps best exemplified by Hamlet's soliloquy, "To be or not to be." Well before Shakespeare, Thomas More described voluntary euthanasia for the terminally ill in *Utopia*, though elsewhere he condemned suicide in no uncertain terms, associating it with diabolical temptation.[41] Inspired by Stoicism, Montaigne (1533–92) and Pierre Charron (1541–1603) made more serious though still moderate defenses of suicide in the late sixteenth and early seventeenth centuries. In an essay, Montaigne discussed the Greek colony of Ceos (ca. 500 B.C.), in which those who were over sixty or incapacitated by illness were permitted and even encouraged to commit suicide by drinking state-furnished hemlock.[42] John Donne (1572–1631) made a more radical defense of the right to end one's life in *Biathanatos*, written about 1608 but published posthumously in 1647. Donne endeavored to refute Aquinas's arguments that suicide violates the law of nature, the law of the state, and the law of God. He maintained the following: under certain circumstances, some people naturally desire death; voluntary death is not contrary to the law of the state so long as the individual is not motivated by self-interest; and the Bible nowhere condemns suicide per se. Apart from a few isolated voices such as Donne's, however, Renaissance writers and thinkers were still

---

of suicides; see Bayet, *Suicide et morale*, 541–42.

[41]Thomas More, *Utopia*, translated and with an introduction by Paul Turner (London: Penguin, 1965), 102. More wrote that the most horrible fear that one can experience is "where the devill temptith a man to kyll and destroy hym selfe"; More, *The Complete Works*, vol. 12, *A Dialogue of Comfort Against Tribulations*, ed. L. L. Marts and F. Manley (New Haven, Conn.: Yale University Press, 1976), 122, cited in MacDonald and Murphy, *Sleepless Souls*, 90. See also Paul D. Green, "Suicide, Martyrdom, and Thomas More," *Studies in the Renaissance* 19 (1972): 135–55.

[42]Montaigne, "A Usage of the Island of Cea," in *Essays*, translated by George B. Ives with an introduction by André Gide (New York: Heritage Press, 1947), bk. 2, chap. 3. See also Patrick Henry, "The Dialectic of Suicide in Montaigne's 'Coutume de l'Isle de Cea,'" *Modern Language Review* 79 (1984): 278–89. In his discussion of suicide, Pierre Charron, *De la sagesse* (Bordeaux: Simon Millanges, 1601), 2.2, borrowed so heavily from Montaigne that his discussion of suicide borders on plagiarism; see Paulin, *Couteau à plume*, 90–91.

on the whole quite hostile to suicide.[43] They continued to view suicide as morally reprehensible; their considerable interest in the subject stemmed largely from their greater interest in antiquity whose literature and history were replete with self-inflicted deaths.[44] In the seventeenth century, typical were the views of the Lutheran jurist Benedict Carpzov (1595–1666), who viewed suicide as a terrible crime against both God and society that merited punishment, including dishonorable burial and desecration.[45] One would have to wait for the eighteenth-century philosophes for an all-out debate over the legitimacy of suicide. In Europe during the sixteenth and seventeenth centuries, such a debate was no more likely than an argument justifying parricide.[46]

THE JUDICIAL TREATMENT OF SUICIDE, 1542–1650

The intolerance toward suicide of Calvin and other intellectual leaders was reflected in the sentences passed by Genevan magistrates. Judicial authorities of the Reformation period shared Calvin's abhorrence for suicide and his conviction that suicide was caused by diabolical possession. Accordingly, well into the seventeenth century sentences against suicide could be quite harsh. The minimum punishment for suicide was denial of traditional burial rites. Of the 40 suicides that are documented for the period 1542–1650, only one

[43]John Donne, *Biathanatos: A Declaration of that Paradox or Thesis that Self-Homicide Is Not So Naturally a Sin that It May Never Be Otherwise* (London: John Dawson, 1647; reprint, New York: Facsimile Text Society, 1930); Droge and Tabor, *Noble Death*, 7–8; Georges Minois, *Histoire du suicide: La Société occidentale face à la mort volontaire*" (Paris: Fayard, 1995), 109–18. The views on suicide of John Sym, the author of the first English treatise that dealt entirely with suicide, were much more representative of his age than were Donne's. Writing in 1637, the Puritan preacher Sym took a hard line against suicide which he associated with diabolical temptation; see *Life's Preservative Against Self-Killing*, edited and with an introduction by Michael MacDonald (London: Routledge, 1989).

[44]Paulin, *Couteau à plume*, 583–90. Minois, *Histoire du suicide*, 106–40, argues that the writings of playwrights, moralists, and physicians from the period 1580–1620 reflect Europe's first "crise de conscience," an effect of which was the secularization of suicide. In calling this a crisis, Minois exaggerates the influence these writers had on popular opinion and the degree to which Europeans at this time embraced medical as opposed to supernatural explanations for suicide. He himself acknowledges that the belief that suicide was diabolical still prevailed at this time, and that even those who medicalized suicide, such as Robert Burton, had not dissociated it from demon possession.

[45]Craig Koslofsky, "Suicide and the Secularization of the Body in Early Modern Saxony," *Continuity and Change* (forthcoming).

[46]Among certain seventeenth-century thinkers, one can find increased sympathy for those who took their lives. In his *Ethics*, Spinoza (1632–77) argued that there was no such thing as "suicidal agency" or willful self-destruction. Rather, people who take their lives are always victims; see Steven Barbone and Lee Rice, "Spinoza and the Problem of Suicide," *International Philosophical Quarterly* 34 (1994): 241.

person was allowed to be buried with the traditional funerary rites. That case was clearly atypical because it involved a member of a very prominent Genevan family. André Caille, described in chapter 1, was a wealthy merchant who suffered from melancholy for about four months prior to shooting himself with an arquebus in September 1614, the first recorded suicide by firearm in Geneva. Caille's unstable mental state was common knowledge. As a precaution, the physician Isaac Caille, evidently a relative, had been sleeping in the same room with André.[47] Acting on a request from the family who pleaded that this lamentable act was simply the result of his illness, the Small Council decided that Caille's honor was not to be impugned, declaring that "the memory of André Caille must not be sullied or marked with ignominy or suffer any punishment whatsoever, permitting his relatives to bury him."[48] Such words at first glance suggest a secularization of suicide which preceded that described by Michael MacDonald for early modern England. (Beginning in the late seventeenth century, English magistrates became more lenient in dealing with cases of suicide because they saw mental illness rather than diabolism as the root cause of suicide.[49]) But the sentence further noted that Caille's relatives agreed to donate 100 écus from his estate to the city's hospital.[50] It was this substantial donation to the hospital that convinced authorities to be so understanding in dealing with Caille's death. Under the same circumstances, a lesser personage would not have had a chance of being buried with honors. If official attitudes were changing, they were limited to the handling of the suicides of the elite. Typically, those guilty of suicide were at best to be buried after sundown outside the regular cemetery. Most often the corpses of suicides were buried at Champel, where executions took place. At other times, the bodies were interred at the shooting range or in the

[47]AEG, EC, LM 24: 190, 28 September 1614; PC 2e série 2071.
[48]AEG, RC 112: 289.
[49]Michael MacDonald, "The Secularization of Suicide in England 1660–1800," *Past and Present* 111 (1986): 50–100; MacDonald and Murphy, *Sleepless Souls*, 109–216. Even as late as the 1720s, however, one can find authorities who associated suicide with Satan. In 1724 the Puritan Samuel Sewall (1652–1730), Massachusetts's Chief Justice, argued that melancholy did not exculpate those who took their lives, linking that condition to diabolical temptation. Sewall maintained therefore that suicides should be denied Christian burials. This attitude was out of step with prevailing contemporary views; see Howard I. Kushner, *American Suicide: A Psychocultural Exploration* (New Brunswick, N.J.: Rutgers University Press,1991), 14–17.
[50]AEG, RC 112: 289.

cemetery for plague victims. In any event, burial anywhere but the normal cemetery was a sign of ignominy.

Often the judicial authorities deemed that the denial of funerary honors alone was not sufficient punishment. Through 1650, on thirteen occasions they cast further shame on suicide victims by ordering that the corpses be dragged on a hurdle through the streets of Geneva. Dragging the bodies of miscreants or enemies was certainly nothing new—Homer graphically depicted Achilles attaching the body of the vanquished Hector to his chariot and dragging it through the streets. Such an act was intended to dehumanize the victims, to place them on the level of dead beasts.[51] This attitude was surely behind the sentence passed against Bonaventure Gronbon in 1561. A native of Burgundy employed as a soldier in Geneva, Gronbon was wanted in France for the capital crime of counterfeiting. Upon learning of his crimes, Genevan authorities sought to arrest Gronbon. Trying vainly to flee the city, Gronbon was cornered by soldiers on a bridge and deliberately plunged to his death into the ditch below. In condemning this act, magistrates noted that Satan had incited Gronbon to kill himself and ordered that his body be dragged through the streets, then stuffed in a barrel and thrown into the Rhône River, a form of desecration signifying eternal damnation.[52]

More typical were sentences that required that the body be dragged through the streets to Champel where they were buried or, on six occasions through 1650, impaled and left exposed as a deterrent to others. When Jean Jourdain, twenty-six, a farmer living near Geneva, took his life in October 1555, authorities ordered that his body be dragged on a hurdle and then impaled and left exposed outside the city.[53] In February 1564 Julienne Berard was most upset about being convoked by Geneva's Consistory to account for a dispute she had engaged in with her nephew. According to witnesses, Berard was so frightened by the prospect of facing the questions of Calvin and other members of the Consistory that she took her life by throwing herself in the Rhône River. As a result of this evidence, the jurist Ger-

---

[51]Denis Crouzet, *Les guerriers de Dieu*, 2 vols. (Seyssel, France: Champ Vallon, 1990), 1: 84; Alain Joblin, "Suicide à l'époque moderne: Un Exemple dans la France du Nord-Ouest: À Boulogne-sur-Mer," *Revue historique* 589 (1994): 110.

[52]AEG, PC 983. Jean-Claude Schmitt, "Le suicide au Moyen Age," *Annales: E.S.C.* 31 (1976): 12, finds that, according to medieval popular religious culture, the barrel was "a means of transporting the bodies and souls of the damned to the land of the dead."

[53]AEG, PC 552; RC 50: 23v, 25v, 27–28.

main Colladon, a close associate of Calvin, believed that Berard merited having her body dragged through the streets to Champel where it should be hanged. Fearing that her words against the Consistory might cause a scandal, however, Colladon decided that it would be more prudent simply to drag the body to Champel and bury it there.[54] Just two months after the lenient sentence accorded Caille, magistrates in separate cases ordered that the bodies of two rather poor female suicides—one a chambermaid, the other a former servant—be dragged through the streets. The Small Council further ordered in November 1614 that the body of one of these women, the servant Bernarde Cadou, be left exposed and that all her assets be confiscated.[55] Hanging a body to be left for all to view and ridicule was considered the greatest affront possible to the honor of a deceased person.

The punishment of suicide, however, often was not limited to how the corpse was treated. The estate of the deceased could be subject to more mundane penalties. In fact, the first extant Genevan ordinance on suicide, passed in 1568, said nothing about burial or the desecration of the corpse but did call for the confiscation of the goods of those who took their lives, unless they were alienated.[56] In the sixteenth and early seventeenth centuries, judicial authorities did indeed order the confiscation of all the property of five suicides, the corpses of whom were all desecrated in one way or another. Eight other times the Small Council levied fines on the estates of suicides without confiscating all the property, including the de facto fine of Caille's donation. These figures show that the Small Council was not very consistent in passing sentences on suicides.

A look at the political status of the victims reveals a certain bias in sentencing in Reformation Geneva. Of those whose bodies were desecrated by

---

[54]AEG, PC 1179. For the influence of Colladon, see Erich-Hans Kaden, *Le jurisconsulte Germain Colladon, ami de Jean Calvin et de Théodore de Bèze* (Geneva: Georg, 1974).

[55]AEG, EC, LM 24: 194, 26 November 1614; PC 2e série 2076 and 2077; RC 113: 35v, 40, 42v.

[56]The law also ruled that legitimate children should not be deprived of their *légitimes*, that portion of family holdings to which they had hereditary rights. Among the Civil Edicts passed by the General Council in January 1568, Titre 29, Des successions ab intestat, Numéro 16 reads: "Les biens de celuy qui se sera precipité, noyé, pendu ou autrement occis de sa propre main et volenté, non estant aliené de son sens, seront appliquez au fisque, sauf touttefois que s'il a des enfans naturelz et legitimes, leur sera delaissee leur legitime sur cesdictz biens, telle que le droict l'a ordonné"; *Les sources du droit du canton de Genève*, ed. Emile Rivoire and Victor Van Berchem, 4 vols. (Aarau, Switzerland: Sauerländer, 1927–35), 3:228; Laurent Haeberli, "Le suicide à Genève au XVIIIe siècle," in *Pour une Histoire Qualitative: Etudes offertes à Sven Stelling-Michaud* (Geneva: Presses Universitaires Romandes, 1975): 115.

being dragged, impaled, or burned, two were foreign-born permanent residents (Habitants), eight were foreigners, and four were of unknown status. Likewise of the five suicide victims for whom magistrates ordered the confiscation of all assets, the three whose status was identified were all foreigners. Of the ten Citizens who took their lives, extant records reveal only five sentences that went beyond denial of funerary honors: in all five cases, magistrates limited themselves to fines.[57]

Since suicide itself was a crime, attempting to do so was also taken quite seriously, viewed essentially as a form of attempted self-murder. From the mid-sixteenth century through 1650, records survive of twelve cases of people who tried but failed to kill themselves; undoubtedly there were other suicide attempts that went unreported. The jurist Colladon submitted his opinion as to what should be done to Gervais Nadoye, age twenty-eight, a "man of low status." In December 1556 Nadoye tried to hang himself under the Halles du Molard, a busy marketplace, but a man quickly saved him by cutting the rope. Asked why he had tried to kill himself, Nadoye bemoaned the fact that he was a "poor orphan child" and was further upset because a man had accused him of not working hard enough. Considering this case, Colladon recommended capital punishment:

> This act is more heinous and abominable and more of a crime against nature than if he had attempted to kill another person, even one of his parents…. We must go beyond the ancient laws that were made by pagans…who did not consider the seriousness of crimes with respect to the degree to which they were offensive to God or one's conscience. These we must take into consideration given the greater knowledge that God has given us. Moreover, Christian authors have judged such an act to be a capital one that must be punished even if the attempt did not succeed…. All told, he is

---

[57] By comparison, in 1625–29 the male population of the city of Geneva was divided as followed: Citoyens and Bourgeois (while a Citoyen was born a citizen, a Bourgeois was one who acquired citizenship), 38.4 percent; Natifs (permanent residents who were born in Geneva), 13.6 percent; and Habitants and foreigners, 48 percent; see Alfred Perrenoud, *La population de Genève* XVIe–XIXe siècles (Geneva: Société d'histoire et d'archéologie de Genève, 1979), 193. Class biases were also apparent in contemporary England and in late medieval and early modern France, as nobles, clerics, and affluent urban dwellers were generally exempt from punishment, the penalties for suicide being imposed only on humble members of the third estate; see Minois, *Histoire du suicide*, 174; Signori, "Rechtskonstruktionen und religiöse Fiktionen," in *Trauer, Verzweiflung und Anfechtung*, ed. Signori, 40.

worthy of death to set an example. And there is the danger that he will continue his bad ways, considering the insignificant incident that provoked him to try to kill himself.[58]

Acknowledging that he deserved death, the Small Council passed judgment Christmas day, choosing to use "mercy rather than rigor," by sentencing Nadoye to be whipped and banished forever from Geneva under pain of death.[59]

During this period, authorities ordered two other whippings and four other banishments for attempted suicide. In December 1600, the Small Council issued a harsh sentence against Paula Aillod, fifty, who attempted to hang herself after being beaten by her husband. Rumors further indicated that she was physically abused by her adult son. Proclaiming ironically that they were using "mildness rather than rigor," magistrates condemned her to be whipped through the streets of Geneva and banished for life under pain of death, given twenty-four hours to leave town.[60]

As with successful suicides, magistrates seemed to show a certain bias with regard to status in handling attempted suicides. Of the twelve individuals accused of making attempts on their lives through 1650, eight were foreigners, two were Citizens, one was an Habitant, and one was of unknown status. Although the "lowly" Nadoye was a Citizen, the only other Citizen to attempt suicide was a woman who appeared only before the Consistory, which limited itself to admonitions and did not refer her to the Small Council.[61] In cases of suicide and attempted suicide, foreigners and, to a lesser

---

[58]AEG, PC 605. A century later, a French jurist repeated the claim that suicide was a worse crime than murder; see Claude Le Brun de Charette, *Les procez civils et criminels contenans la méthodique liaison du Droict et de la Pratique judiciaire, civile et criminelle* (Rouen, 1661), quoted in Joblin, "Suicide à l'époque moderne," 119.

[59]AEG, RC 52: 167–68.

[60]AEG, PC 1820; RC 95: 213v, 215, 218.

[61]In 1543, Jana, the wife François Bossey, appeared before the Consistory because she allegedly tried to drown herself, having waded into the lake up to her chest while washing clothes. She recognized that what she had done was wrong, explaining that she was upset about finances: she and her husband had debts for their house that they were having difficulty paying; they had two small children to support; and Jana had just spilled some oil and feared her husband would scold her for this waste. She affirmed nonetheless that Bossey had never mistreated her or threatened to beat her. After Jana successfully recited the Lord's Prayer and the confession of faith, Calvin and other members of the Consistory simply admonished her to live honestly. Probably magistrates were gentle with her in part because her suicide attempt appeared halfhearted; *Registres du Consistoire de Genève au temps de Calvin, 1542–1544*, ed. Thomas Lam-

degree, legal residents were apt to be more harshly treated than Citizens.

Does this evidence from judicial records reveal the dawning of an era of severity toward suicide? Since the first extant record of a suicide in Geneva dates from 1542, we cannot know if Reformed Genevans prosecuted suicide more aggressively than their ancestors. There were medieval precedents, however, for every penalty imposed on the bodies and estates of suicides in Reformation Geneva. Ecclesiastical practice denied burial honors to suicides as far back as 563 when the Council of Braga forbade the funerary rites of the Eucharist and the singing of the Psalms to those who killed themselves.[62] In France of the High Middle Ages, church leaders went beyond proscribing prayers and other rituals at interments for suicides: in 1284 the Synod of Nîmes forbade the burial of all suicides in hallowed ground.[63] Burial restrictions in late medieval Germany reflected popular fears that the souls of suicides were likely to haunt those who survived them. To thwart them from finding their way back to survivors, the bodies of suicides were often carried face down or head first to the burial. In Germany of the late Middle Ages, the survivors were even known to change the doors, locks, and windows of the houses in which suicides had lived to prevent them from entering.[64] Medieval French customary law not only denied funerary honors but required the confiscation of the goods of suicides. Legal sources, including compilations of customary laws, further show that in France of the thirteenth, fourteenth, and fifteenth centuries, the bodies of suicides could be

---

bert and Isabella Watt (Geneva: Droz, 1996), 264–65. In 1550 two other women appeared before the Consistory simply because they had talked about suicide. Repentant, both recognized their error before Calvin and other members of the Consistory; AEG, Registres du Consistoire 5:10, 55.

[62]Bayet, *Suicide et morale*, 387–88; Droge and Tabor, *Noble Death*, 5, 22. The *Decretum* mentions the denial of burial rites for suicides, as mandated by the Council of Braga: "Let there be no prayers for those who kill themselves." Likewise, from the Council of Braga, it decreed that for those who voluntarily kill themselves either by the sword, poison, throwing themselves off precipices, hanging themselves, or induce death by any other method, let there be no commemorative prayer, let not their bodies be brought with Psalms to burial; for many usurp these practices for themselves out of ignorance. Similarly, it was also decreed what should be done concerning these [who take their lives], as for those who die for their crimes"; Gratian, *Decretum*, C. 23 q. 5 c. 12, in *Corpus Iuris Canonici*, ed. Emil Friedberg (Leipzig: Bernhard Tauchnitz, 1879), 1: 935.

[63]Bayet, *Suicide et morale*, 434–35.

[64]Jürsten Dieselhorst, "Die Bestrafung der Selbstmörder im Territorium der Reichsstadt Nürnberg," *Mitteilungen des Vereins Geschichte der Stadt Nürnberg* 44 (1953): 63–64.

subject to being hanged, dragged through the streets, or burned.[65] Even the penalty of placing a suicide's corpse in a barrel and tossing it into a river, imposed only once in Geneva, had precedents in medieval France and Germany.[66] Indeed these harsh sentences, which apparently reflected a strong popular abhorrence for suicide, all had their roots in pagan antiquity—the denial of funerary honors, the desecration of the corpses, and even the forfeiture of goods all could be found in pre-Christian Europe. Plato advocated burying suicides "in disgrace," separated from others, on the fringe of the cemetery, in unmarked graves; by contrast, though they attacked suicide more aggressively than Plato, neither Augustine nor Aquinas said anything about burying the bodies of self-murderers.[67]

There are, to be sure, indications that the treatment of the bodies of suicides did become more severe in parts of Europe in the sixteenth and seventeenth centuries. In Reformation England, for example, suicides were

[65]Bayet, *Suicide et morale*, 436–46; Signori, "Rechtskonstruktionen und religiöse Fiktionen," in *Trauer, Verzweiflung und Anfechtung*, ed. Signori, 26–34. Jean Delumeau, *La peur en occident (XIVe–XVIIIe siècles)* (Paris: Fayard, 1978), 84–85, maintains that French burial customs for suicides exemplified the Christianization of pre- or non-Christian rituals. If ecclesiastical and judicial authorities became more severe in handling suicide cases in the thirteenth century, this may have been a reaction to significant numbers of voluntary deaths among the Cathars in southern France. In Cathar theology, once believers repented and joined the ranks of *parfaits*, or perfect ones, they had to lead sinless lives—relapsing into sin meant the eternal damnation of their souls. Consequently, after receiving the *consolamentum*, the equivalent of baptism, Cathars had a strong incentive to hasten death, often abstaining from eating entirely; Joblin, "Suicide à l'époque moderne," 106.

[66]Werner Blesch, "'Sich selbsten leibloß gemacht und aus Verzweiflung erhenkt': Selbsttötungen im 16. Jahrhundert im Raum Mosbach-Eberbach-Sinsheim," *Beiträge zur Volkskunde in Baden-Württemberg* 5 (1993): 323–24; Jürsten Dieselhorst, "Die Bestrafung der Selbstmörder im Territorium der Reichsstadt Nürnberg," *Mitteilungen des Vereins Geschichte der Stadt Nürnberg* 44 (1953): 63; Schmitt, "Suicide au Moyen Age,"12.

[67]Plato, *Laws*, 873c–d. The ancients regularly punished at least some suicides. Thebans and Romans at times left suicides unburied, while Athenians cut off the suicide's hand that was responsible for the death. In ancient Rome, soldiers, among others, who took their lives forfeited their goods because they had neglected their obligations to the state in killing themselves; see MacDonald and Murphy, *Sleepless Souls*, 17. Through the early Empire, there were no laws against suicide. As a result, some prisoners who, if condemned, would have been denied honorable burials and had their assets confiscated, killed themselves to avoid judgment. In so doing, they were buried with honors and their heirs received their patrimony. In the second century, before the influence of Christianity, emperors ceased this practice and confiscated the goods of those who killed themselves because of "criminal remorse"; see Georges Minois, "L' historien et la question du suicide," *Histoire* 189 (1995): 24; Montesquieu, *Esprit des lois* (Paris: Garnier Frères, 1927), bk. 29, chap. 9. Romans found death by hanging particularly repulsive and denied burial to those who took their lives by this method; Grisé, *Suicide dans la Rome antique*, 141–49; Anton J. L. van Hooff, *From Autothanasia to Suicide: Self-Killing in Classical Antiquity* (London: Routledge, 1990), 64–72, 162–66.

regularly buried at crossroads, their hearts often transfixed by a spike. This practice was tied to the widespread popular belief, found elsewhere in Europe, that suicide was the epitome of a "bad death" and that the soul of a suicide was restless, wandering between the world of the dead and the world of the living. Placing the body at the crossroads supposedly hindered the ghost to find its way home, while the spike was intended to pin the dangerous "sleepless soul" in the grave.[68] Significantly, there is no record of the staking of suicides, a practice unique to England, from the medieval period.[69]

The judicial treatment of suicide in Reformation Geneva, though potentially harsh, did not seem unduly severe when compared with legal traditions that predated the sixteenth century. True, the prosecution of attempted suicides in Geneva was unusual.[70] It is also true that judicial authorities in late medieval France were more likely to allow full funerary rites for suicides than their counterparts in Reformation Geneva.[71] Be that as it may, in most cases, the sentences passed against suicide hardly seem extreme. Through the mid-seventeenth century, only a third of suicides were subject to corporal desecration or to fines or confiscation; the sizeable majority of sentences simply forbade funerary honors. Simply put, the penalties imposed on suicide from the conversion to Protestantism through the era of the Thirty Years' War do not appear to deviate dramatically from earlier customs.

In passing judgment on suicides, the Genevan Calvinists also did not appear inordinately harsh vis-à-vis contemporary judicial authorities in both

---

[68]Henry Romilly Fedden, *Suicide: A Social and Historical Study* (New York: Benjamin Blom, 1972), 164; Arnold Van Gennep, *The Rites of Passage*, trans. Monika B. Vizedom and Garielle L. Caffee (Chicago: University of Chicago Press, 1960), 160–61; MacDonald and Murphy, *Sleepless Souls*, 46–47. MacDonald and Murphy describe these English rites of desecration, as "a genuine demotic custom, performed by laymen without clerical participation,…an expression of a deeply held conviction that self-murder was supernaturally evil"; *Sleepless Souls*, 44–45. Similarly, there was strong opposition to burying suicides in community cemeteries in Bavaria in the sixteenth and seventeenth centuries. Popular opinion there, especially among peasants, attributed bad weather, famine, loss of livestock, and pestilence to the interment of corpses in parish cemeteries; see David Lederer, "Aufruhr auf dem Friedhof: Pfarrer, Geimeinde, und Selbstmord im frühneuzeitlichen Bayern," in *Trauer, Verzweiflung und Anfechtung*, ed. Signori, 189–209.

[69]Alexander Murray, *Suicide in the Middle Ages*, vol. 1, *The Violent Against Themselves* (Oxford: Oxford University Press, 1998), 373.

[70]Punishments for attempted suicide were meted out in Puritan Massachusetts. In 1672, a man was sentenced to twenty lashes, a fine, and a brief internment for an unsuccessful suicide attempt; Kushner, *American Suicide*, 22.

[71]Murray, *Suicide*, vol. 1, *Violent Against Themselves*, 207–27; Signori, "Rechtskonstruktionen und religiöse Fiktionen," in *Trauer, Verzweiflung und Anfechtung*, ed. Signori, 9–54.

Protestant and Catholic areas. Denial of "normal" burial and the desecration of suicides' corpses could be found in a variety of forms throughout much of early modern western Europe. In a number of regions of Europe, suicides' cadavers were dragged through the streets and left exposed.[72] Variations on the disposal of the bodies of suicides could be found throughout Europe. In early modern Sweden, for example, the bodies of suicides were to be taken to the woods and burned, unless the victims were deemed mad, in which case the corpses were merely buried outside the cemetery.[73] Likewise, Genevan penalties against the estates of suicides were analogous to sanctions imposed in contemporary Catholic areas such as France.[74]

Certainly Calvin himself cannot be held responsible for the penalties against the bodies and estates of suicides. In fact he showed no interest in withholding burial rites to suicides in order to defame them. He noted that Ahithophel's burial appeared honorable; he was even buried in the sepulcher of his father. According to popular opinion, Ahithophel was thus not subject to disgrace. But, Calvin insisted, this is not to say that he was not punished. God has an infinite number of means of ruining the enemies of the church. For another enemy, God perhaps would not allow the body to be buried; another may be allowed to be buried, but not in the family tomb. We may not always see God's punishments carried out here on earth, but God will surely impose them, if not in this world then in the hereafter.[75]

Preaching about Ahithophel in November 1562, months after the hostilities of the French Religious Wars were unleashed, Calvin referred to the persecution of the French Reformed in dealing with this issue of burial. Aware of the desecration of the corpses of Huguenots, Calvin rejected the importance of burial in the scheme of divine justice and salvation:

> If God wants our enemies to be honored even after their deaths, then let them be buried; or if the poor children of God will be killed and their bodies left exposed, then we must wait patiently. We must

[72]See Joblin, "Suicide à l'époque moderne," 94–95; Alfred Schnegg, "Justice et suicide sous l'Ancien Régime," *Musée Neuchâtelois* (1982): 73–94.

[73]Arne Jansson, *From Swords to Sorrow: Homicide and Suicide in Early Modern Stockholm* (Stockholm: Almqvist and Wiksell, 1998), 12.

[74]As in Geneva, the confiscation of the goods of suicides in contemporary France was imposed inconsistently. The penalty there stemmed from the notion that suicide was a form of lèse-majesté, an offense not against oneself but against the state; Joblin, "Suicide à l'époque moderne," 117.

[75]*SC* 517–19.

hold to this truth today, especially since we see our poor brothers, some of whom are burned and whose ashes are then thrown to the wind; others hanged, others thrown in the water. It would seem as if they were unworthy to be buried in the earth, or rather that the earth is not worthy to have them. This scandal of seeing evil folk thus buried with pomp and glory while the poor children of God are treated with ignominy, could cause us to lose courage unless we have learned this doctrine well.[76]

Quite simply, Calvin clearly viewed the treatment of corpses of good and evil people as ultimately irrelevant.

This should come as no surprise inasmuch as Calvin would have preferred demystifying burials entirely, which he considered heavily laden with pagan superstitions. Ideally, Calvin would have liked to do away with burial rituals altogether. At Calvin's own request, no words or prayers were spoken when he himself was buried in an unmarked grave. Rites for funerals and mourning, however, were an area in which Genevans never entirely embraced the Reformed morality of Calvin. Throughout the early modern period, Genevans remained attached to practices such as the procession to the cemetery, replete with black mourning crêpes. At the cemetery, they offered prayers and sang Psalms. That some suicides were punished by being buried outside the cemetery shows that the notion of hallowed burial ground still resonated among Geneva's rank and file. Calvin and his successors simply had to tolerate certain popular rituals and attitudes.

The same holds true for desecration rites. In a commentary on Deuteronomy, Calvin deplored the practice of leaving criminals' corpses hanging from a gibbet, out of concern not for the deceased but for the general public, fearing they might become insensitive to such "barbaric scenes."[77] Much as he disliked the punishments inflicted on the bodies of miscreants, Calvin at the very least tolerated these practices, in spite of their pagan and medieval Catholic elements. If, as Calvin believed, suicide was tied to diabolical pos-

---

[76]*SC* 519.

[77]In his commentary, Calvin discusses the passage (Deuteronomy 21: 22–23) in which Moses declared that the bodies of executed criminals must not be left hanging from a post but rather ought to be buried on the day of the execution. Calvin maintained that Moses was concerned lest the Israelites become inured to such scenes of barbarism and in turn become more prone to commit homicide themselves; *CO* 24: 629.

session, then he understandably acquiesced in applying these popular punishments which symbolized damnation, the eternal exclusion of the suicide from the Christian community.[78] Quite simply, the often harsh treatment of the corpses of Genevan suicides certainly cannot be attributed to Calvinism but rather to popular practices that predated the Reformation by centuries.

Moreover, during the Reformation period, Genevan authorities began attenuating somewhat this treatment. The desecration of corpses became less common during this century. Through the mid-seventeenth century, the sentence against Bernarde Cadou's body in November 1614 was the last to mandate that a body be left exposed and the next to last to order the corpse be dragged on a hurdle. Thereafter, magistrates evidently viewed denial of customary burials as sufficiently demonstrating the disgrace associated with suicide. Seventeenth-century judicial authorities also became a bit more lenient with respect to the property of suicides. For the era stretching from Calvin's day through 1650, authorities ordered only one confiscation after 1614. Thereafter fines became more common: of the eight fines imposed on the estates of suicides, only one was levied before 1614.

Magistrates also became a bit more moderate in punishing those who attempted unsuccessfully to kill themselves. Authorities imposed the last whipping for an unsuccessful suicide attempt in 1600 and mandated only two banishments after that date. Two people were required simply to do *réparation,* a humiliating formality in which one publicly (usually in church) confessed one's wrongdoing and asked for forgiveness from God, the magistrates, and all those they had offended.[79] The attenuation of the harsh treatment of attempted suicide is aptly seen in the case of Pierre Grisy, a soldier and recent arrival in Geneva. In 1631 Grisy stabbed himself because he was upset for various reasons, especially for having left many personal belongings behind when he came to Geneva to practice the Reformed faith. Concluding that Grisy had stabbed himself as a result of his melancholy, the Small Council ordered that he do *réparation* and be released from prison provided he paid his expenses.[80]

---

[78]MacDonald and Murphy observe with regard to the burial practices surrounding suicides: "Since the Protestant clergy stressed the supernatural causes of self-murder, they had either to replace or to tolerate the popular religious practices that dealt with its supernatural consequences. They chose to tolerate them"; *Sleepless Souls,* 44.

[79]AEG, PC 999, 1137.

[80]AEG, PC 2879; RC 130: 204r–v.

Simply put, Genevan authorities of the sixteenth and early seventeenth centuries certainly viewed voluntary death as a heinous crime and may have been more consistent than some medieval counterparts in "punishing" suicides. Nonetheless, the penalties imposed were by and large commensurate with legal practices found in medieval Europe and in other regions, both Protestant and Catholic, of Reformation Europe. It would be an overstatement, therefore, to suggest that the conversion to Protestantism introduced an era of severity with regard to suicide. Moreover, when the harshest sentences against the bodies and goods of suicides had largely fallen into disuse by the mid-seventeenth century, judicial practice was more in line with the wishes of Calvin.[81]

The Judicial Treatment of Suicide, 1651–1798

The penalties imposed on suicides became even milder after 1650. For all intents and purposes, magistrates stopped desecrating the corpses and confiscating the goods of those who took their lives. Only four times after 1650 did judicial authorities call for the desecration of corpses. Three of these occurred during the years 1669–75, when particular authorities obviously decided to take a hard line against self-murder. Considering the circumstances, the sentence passed against the notary Jean Bardin, who hanged himself in September 1670, may well have been the harshest imposed on a suicide for the entire early modern period. Bardin had suffered some terrible tragedies. He had been emotionally devastated by the deaths, from an explosion, of three of his young children and by the subsequent burglary of his house. In spite of the entreaties of his widow on behalf of their surviving minor children, the Small Council passed an extremely harsh sentence in September 1670, enjoining that Bardin's body be dragged on a hurdle before burial and that his assets be confiscated.[82]

---

[81]Murray, *Suicide*, vol. 1, *Violent Against Themselves*, 373–74, believes that sixteenth-century Europe witnessed both growing severity in the treatment of suicide and an increase in the suicide rate, suggesting that there might be a causal connection between the two. If authorities and communities attacked suicide because of moral indignation, they were apt to pursue suicide more aggressively if they perceived an increase in the number of self-inflicted deaths. While this may be logical, harsher treatment of suicide could serve as an incentive to survivors to cover up suicides. In Geneva the explosion occurred long after the harsh sentences against suicides had fallen into disuse.

[82]AEG, PC 4112; RC 170: 361, 364–65; Manuscrit Historique 133ter. See also Jean-Pierre Ferrier, *Drames et comédies judiciaires de la Genève d'autrefois* (Geneva: Payot, 1930), 51–53.

The body of only one suicide was desecrated after 1675. That isolated case involved Jeanne Berset, forty, who, like her husband, Jean-Pierre Dériaz, was a vineyard worker. Both she and her husband were imprisoned in early 1732 on suspicion of having stolen money from their boarder Georges Boussan, during his absence of a few days. At first Berset blamed burglars for the theft from Boussan's locked trunk, claiming they had also stolen articles of clothing and linens from her while she and her husband were out of the house. A number of inconsistencies were evident in Berset's story. Though she at first denied knowing anything about Boussan's money, Berset later admitted finding a box containing Boussan's money on the ground outside their house, apparently left there inadvertently by the burglars. She reported that she had buried the money near their dwelling and planned on giving the money back to Boussan when he returned. Authorities therefore went with Berset to her home to find the box of money. At first, she said that it was under some rocks; then she claimed that it was in the cellar. Although they looked all over, the box of money was never found. The next day, 27 January, Berset hanged herself in her cell. Authorities decided that they must make an example of Berset, even though they acknowledged that many disapproved of the desecration of corpses of criminals: "Although some scholars criticize the practice of placing on a gibbet the cadavers of criminals who take their lives in order to avoid the shame of punishment, the majority nonetheless holds the opposite view."[83] Accordingly, the body was dragged on a hurdle to Plainpalais where it was hanged on a gallows. Her assets were also confiscated, apart from the legitimate portion that was to go to her surviving son. Boussan was to be reimbursed the amount stolen from Berset's meager assets.[84]

Not only was this the only dragging of a suicide's corpse since 1675; this was the only instance after 1614 that magistrates ordered that the body of a suicide be left exposed as a sign of ignominy. Had Berset's suicide, like Bardin's, resulted from personal tragedies rather than the shame associated with crime, she undoubtedly would not have been judged so harshly. From Berset's death through 1798, eleven other persons hanged themselves while in prison, but no other corpses were desecrated. Berset was also the last suicide

[83]AEG, PC 7890.
[84]AEG, PC 7890.

whose assets were confiscated. Of the 361 suicides that occurred after 1650, Genevan authorities confiscated the estates of only four, including those of Bardin and Berset. In addition, magistrates imposed fines on the estates of four suicides after that date: one in 1669, the other three in the early 1700s.

The case involving Antoine Mallet, who drowned himself in December 1715 at the age of thirty-nine, included an interesting argument against the penalties associated with suicide. An affluent cloth merchant, Mallet had the distinction of being the only person who committed suicide while serving as Auditeur, the officer who investigated suicides and other crimes and misadventures.[85] After another Auditeur had fully investigated Mallet's disappearance and death, Louis Le Fort (1668–1743), who served as Geneva's Procureur Général or prosecutor from 1711 to 1717,[86] reconstructed the last hours of Mallet's life, claiming to show beyond a shadow of a doubt that this was a self-inflicted death. The investigation revealed that about five o'clock of the evening of 13 December 1715, Antoine Mallet took leave of his wife. Le Fort noted that Mallet took nothing of value with him, an indication that he did not want to deprive his heirs of any valuables that might be on his person when he drowned. He left at home his watch, his keys, his overcoat; he changed wigs, taking off his new one and putting on an old worn one. Although his wife twice asked where he was going, Mallet refused to say. His wife and other household members immediately became worried, which, according to Le Fort, suggested that they had reason to suspect that he had bad intentions. Susanne Bonnet, Mallet's wife, sent a female servant out to look for Mallet. When the servant returned, she found that Susanne, her brother, and her father, the former Syndic Jean-Jacques Bonnet, were all extremely worried, indicating, according to Le Fort, that they suspected what Mallet had intended to do.[87]

News soon spread that Mallet's family was worried. The hosier Julian Dombre got wind of this news and went out looking for Mallet sometime between seven and eight o'clock. He found Mallet in the plaza of St. Gervais.

---

[85]There was, however, an ex-Auditeur who took his life. After suffering from illness and "melancholy," Jean-Jacques André Boissier, forty-nine, who had himself investigated a few self-inflicted deaths, drowned himself in October 1766; AEG, EC, LM 63: 319, 17 October 1766; Juridiction Civile F 95; PC 11548; RC 267: 1068.

[86]Michel Porret, *Le crime et ses circonstances: De l'esprit de l'arbitraire au siècle des Lumières selon les réquisitoires des procureurs généraux de Genève* (Geneva: Droz, 1995), xvii.

[87]AEG, PC 6430.

After exchanging pleasantries, Dombre told Mallet that his wife was quite worried about him. Speaking with his ordinary, calm voice, Mallet replied that he must then go and bade Dombre a good evening. They departed in opposite directions, with Mallet heading in the general direction of his residence. After taking about fifteen to twenty steps, however, Dombre looked back and saw that Mallet had turned around and slipped into a narrow alley. Dombre tried to follow him but lost track of him. Not long thereafter, Félise Barthelemy, the widow of Guillaume Dodet, saw Mallet pacing back and forth on a bridge over the Rhône. She noticed that whenever someone approached with a candle, he withdrew and hid in an alley between two buildings on the bridge. When she herself passed by the alley, a candle in hand, she recognized him, but he told her to be on her way. From a short distance, she observed him standing close to the parapet of the bridge, his hat under his arm and his hands folded, as if in prayer. About a half hour later, at approximately nine o'clock, she heard a heavy object fall into the water and then heard thrashing in the water below, sounds which three other people heard about the same time. Though no one saw Mallet jump in the Rhône, he was never seen alive again. Mallet's body was not found until 6 February 1716. The body was lodged against the posts of a mill which was downstream from the bridge where Mallet was last seen alive. The body was quite decomposed and could be identified only by the clothing, which even members of Mallet's family acknowledged were his.[88]

The day after the body was found, the family, led by Jean-Jacques Bonnet, Mallet's father-in-law, and his fellow ex-Syndic Prétet, appeared before the Small Council, requesting permission to bury Mallet with honors, insisting that the death was an accident. However, prosecutor Le Fort countered that the body should be buried in the cemetery but without honors. He also requested that the Auditeur Gédéon Martine be sent to the Mallet household in order to place Mallet's affairs under the control of the state. The Small Council sided with the prosecutor, sending the Auditeur to the Mallet home and ruling, "Without in any way prejudicing the proceeding, ... we permit the burial of Sieur Mallet in the cemetery of

[88]AEG, PC 6430.

Plainpalais in the early evening without any ceremony or procession."[89]

Four days later, the Small Council reconvened. An incensed Syndic Tur-retin revealed that in direct violation of the Council's orders, Mallet had been buried in broad daylight with full honors. Moreover, there was a full procession with sergeants carrying the coffin, accompanied by a considerable number of mourners. Following the burial, the group proceeded to the home of Sieur Cottau, where they prayed and gave thanks and then marched away in pairs. The Auditeur Martine's investigation further revealed that a woman, serving as *prieuse*, passed through the streets of the lower part of town, praying for the funeral cortège. Since he had been at the head of this procession, the former Syndic Bonnet was severely censured for having dis-obeyed the orders of the Small Council. Recognizing his error, Bonnet was fined 50 écus plus court costs.[90]

The question remained as to what was to become of the substantial assets that Mallet left behind. On behalf of Susanne Bonnet, Mallet's widow, and their ten-year-old daughter, the attorney Des Arts made a lengthy appeal to the Small Council for absolution.[91] He argued that the loss of this fine father and husband had already devastated the family. Describing this death as an "unforeseen and most extraordinary accident," Des Arts was most dismayed that some people now wanted to impugn the memory of

---

[89]AEG, PC 6430; RC 215: 79–81. For the identification of the "Auditeur Martine," see Jacques Augustin Galiffe, *Notices généalogiques sur les familles genevoises, depuis les premiers jusqu'à nos jours* (Geneva: Gruaz, 1836), 3: 324–25.

[90]AEG, PC 6430; RC 215: 84–87, 90–92. In the late eighteenth century, a foreign observer viewed a funeral procession in Geneva: "On leaving [Geneva's] city hall, something else caught our attention: it was a funeral procession that was passing in the street. The silence which reigns in these lugubrious cere-monies really struck us. The cortège is always led by a female weeper dressed in black, covered with a mourning crêpe, and accompanied by an usher wearing a cloak and a crêpe which is attached to his hat and hangs down to his belt. Next follows the body in a coffin that is painted black and covered with a large black pall. It is carried by six men dressed like the usher except for the fact that they have sabers hanging at their sides. The procession is completed by a file of relatives and friends, all in black cloaks"; quoted in Charles Du Bois-Melly, *Des usages funèbres et des cimetières à Genève* (Geneva: Jules Carey, 1888), 1. In this scene, the men carrying the bier were corporals or sergeants from the garrison. Du Bois-Melly notes that suicides were supposed to be buried toward the end of the day, as discreetly as possible. The body was to be covered simply by a shroud and carried by prisoners; *Usages funèbres*, 10.

[91]The attorney almost surely was Jean-Philippe Des Arts (1686–1754). After receiving his doctorate in law in 1707, Des Arts served the Republic of Geneva in a number of ways: member of the Council of Two Hundred in 1714, Secretary of Justice in 1718, Auditeur in 1721, Châtelain of Peney in 1726, member of the Small Council in 1728, four times Syndic in 1737–49, and First Syndic in 1753; see Suzanne Stelling-Michaud, ed., *Le livre du recteur de l'Académie de Genève (1559–1878)*, 6 vols. (Geneva: Droz, 1972), 3:88.

Mallet. In response to the prosecutor Le Fort's claim that Mallet committed suicide, Des Arts cited civil law tradition in arguing that one cannot presume suicide "even if a prisoner who was accused of capital crimes were found dead in prison." Insisting that the prosecution lacked proof, Des Arts maintained that the ironclad proof of two eyewitnesses to the suicide was necessary for the confiscation of the assets of the deceased. Even a reduced sentence, such as a fine in lieu of the confiscation of the entire estate, would amount to sullying his memory and finding him guilty without sufficient proof. Des Arts noted all the good qualities Mallet possessed: he had a stable and happy family life; he had very conscientiously fulfilled the duties of Auditeur and had looked after his own business affairs most assiduously; he was a very pious, religious man; he had a sterling reputation; he was very well off financially, having "in his home all the amenities imaginable." In short, Mallet had no reason to commit suicide; the presumptions that would tend to exculpate him were stronger than those that would tend to hold him culpable.[92]

Des Arts further maintained that the Roman Law tradition on the confiscation of goods pertained only to those who were guilty of crimes and killed themselves to avoid punishment. He also asserted that the confiscation of assets was prescribed only for those suicides guilty of lèse-majesté.[93] Des Arts further pointed out that, according to the *Digest of Roman Law,* if people commit suicide because they grow weary of living or because they suffer terribly, their estates are not confiscated but rather are passed on to their heirs.[94]

Having discussed briefly Roman Law traditions, Des Arts then proceeded to mention the customs of neighboring states pertaining to suicide. He observed that Savoy, for example, demonstrated much less severity than Geneva's prosecutor was currently calling for. Des Arts referred to the Savoyard jurist Deville, who avowed that those who were driven to end their

---

[92]AEG, PC 6430. The postmortem inventory of his estate does indeed reveal that Mallet's assets were considerable; Juridiction Civile F 478.

[93]This was not an entirely convincing argument since suicide itself was often construed as a form of lèse-majesté; see Joblin, "Suicide à l'époque moderne," 117.

[94]AEG, PC 6430; "Si quis autem taedio, vel impatientia doloris alieujus vel alio modo vitam finivit, suscessorem habere divus antonius rescripsit"; *Digest*, Book 48, Title 21, in *The Civil Law*, edited and translated by Samuel P. Scott, 17 vols. (Cincinnati: Central Trust, 1932; reprint, New York: AMS Press, 1973), 11:130.

lives by "fury, suffering, or folly must be absolved and deserve pity rather than punishment... because [such a death] is the result of a sudden illness that seizes them and prevents them from being masters of their reason."[95] Des Arts asked rhetorically whether members of the Small Council wanted to be more severe on this issue than the legal traditions of ancient Rome and neighboring states.[96]

Des Arts answered this question by noting quite accurately that recently Genevan magistrates had not themselves punished suicide with anywhere near the severity which they seemed intent on imposing in this instance. Des Arts argued against the confiscation of Mallet's estate by referring to, without naming, a number of recent suicides in Geneva whose estates had been subject to neither confiscation nor fines. While noting that a couple of these involved poor people who in effect possessed almost nothing of value, Des Arts nonetheless insisted that, if confiscation were de rigueur for suicides, then the state should have gone through the formality of declaring their assets forfeited to the state. Otherwise, magistrates would be punishing only the rich, and the law ought to apply to all people equally. Based on recent precedents, Des Arts rightly insisted that Genevan authorities had lately consistently favored clemency over severity in handling cases of suicide. In conclusion, Des Arts besought the Council to allow that the death of Antoine Mallet, which devastated his wife, daughter, and other family members, be the only loss that family must endure.[97] Though insisting that the factual evidence was inconclusive, the attorney Des Arts in effect was further arguing for the decriminalization of suicide, which deserved pity rather than punishment.

In response, Procureur Général Le Fort simply recited the long list of details that showed unequivocally, he believed, that Mallet, in full use of his good senses, had deliberately drowned himself in the Rhône. As a result, Mallet's "body and goods ought to be confiscated to the profit of the seigneurie." The Small Council agreed that Mallet's death was beyond any reasonable doubt self-inflicted. Claiming it was using "mercy rather than rigor," the Council passed judgment 11 March 1716, ordering that Mallet's estate be fined the sum of 2,000 écus, plus court costs. The Council also ordered

[95]AEG, PC 6430.
[96]AEG, PC 6430.
[97]AEG, PC 6430.

that Mallet's estate hand over 3,000 florins, the amount that the family had offered as a donation to the state, no doubt hoping that such a gift would obviate any further fine.[98]

Why did the Small Council impose this substantial fine? In 1716 Genevans clearly had not reached a consensus on how to "punish" suicide. Though long gone was the idea that the devil was behind suicide, some sincerely adhered to the views outlined by the Procureur Général that suicide was a crime that must be punished. The only plausible deterrents to suicide pertained to the body and the estate of those who took their lives. At no time in this case was there any suggestion that Mallet's remains ought to be desecrated—with regard to the body, magistrates were content to limit themselves to burial without honors. The considerable fine was probably the result above all of the Mallet family's defiance. This fine was probably directed more against the contempt shown to the state by burying with honors than against the suicide per se. Nonetheless, the family offered to make a donation to the Republic even before the body was found. This offer was an attempt to curry favor with the magistrates to avoid an actual fine or even confiscation, which seemed like real possibilities, and members of this wealthy family had much to lose. In spite of traditionally showing more restraint in handling cases of suicides of Geneva's elite, in this case magistrates needed to show that no one, including Auditeurs and ex-Syndics, was above the law.

Technically, the last fine imposed on the estate of a suicide was levied in 1733.[99] One unimposed de facto fine was volunteered five years later by the heirs of Jean-Antoine Pelissari, thirty-five, an affluent businessman who owned a small publishing enterprise, Pelissari and Company. Testimony reveals that Pelissari, a bachelor, was rather unstable emotionally and was quite upset over some business conflicts. He left his abode clandestinely in the middle of the night in September 1738, and his body was found in the Rhône about a week later. Although no one saw him jump in the river, his body showed no signs of a struggle, and heavy weights were found in the

---

[98]AEG, PC 6430, RC 215: 133–34.

[99]This involved the fine of 50 écus, plus expenses, imposed on the estate of the watchmaker Pierre Mourgue, who, suffering from "black melancholy," hanged himself in his home because he was upset over the death of his wife several months before; AEG, EC LM 58: 328, 7 May 1733; PC 8043; RC 232: 214–15, 227, 233, 361.

pockets of his coat, indicating that he had placed them there to assure that he would sink and drown.[100]

In considering this case, the deputy prosecutor (Procureur Subrogé) Jacques Martine was the last judicial authority in early modern Geneva to argue that those who took their lives ought to be punished beyond being deprived of burial honors.[101] Martine wrote a lengthy philosophical work dated 26 November 1738, on the legal treatment of suicides. Martine noted that Pelissari left his home clandestinely during the night, leaving behind his watch, his money, his snuffbox, his keys, and everything else of value. There were absolutely no signs of forced entry or of violence to the body, and the weights in his pockets, each weighing thirteen and a half pounds, left no doubt that this was an intentional drowning. In short, to all but those who adhere to the most dangerous form of "Pyrrhonism" in judicial matters, this was clearly a suicide. Then Martine considered what was to be done. Though acknowledging that, particularly since 1734, Pelissari had suffered difficult nights and was tormented by feelings of guilt, Martine maintained that in the days leading up to his suicide, Pelissari had behaved in a normal fashion and that the testimony of those around him did not suggest any alienation in spirit.[102]

Like the attorney Des Arts, Martine acknowledged that Roman Law made a distinction between those who killed themselves because of being tired of living or burdened with sufferings, on the one hand, and those who did so to avoid punishment for crime or infamy, on the other; while the latter were to be subject to the confiscation of body and property, the former were absolved. Nevertheless, Martine argued:

> The wisest of Christian doctors view this distinction as a vestige of pagan ideas concerning self-murder, even attributing to it in certain cases a strength in spirit... [and] heroism. [Cases in point are those of] Cato of Utica who stabbed himself at the news of Scipio's defeat, and Hannibal who poisoned himself out of fear of being handed over to the Romans. The wisest, however, have always recognized

---

[100]AEG, EC, LM 59: 226, 14 September 1738; PC 8581.

[101]Although his first name is not given, this special prosecutor was clearly "Noble" Jacques Martine (1694–1771), an attorney who served the Republic in a number of ways, including as a member of the Council of Two Hundred (1721) and as Auditeur (1734); see Galiffe, *Notices généalogiques*, 3: 324–25.

[102]AEG, PC 8581.

that this supposed magnanimity of a few ancients…did not deserve such an admirable name; in reality, this was merely weakness or desperation. If they had had enough strength in their hearts or the fortitude to endure the ills that afflicted or menaced them, they would have left to posterity more glorious signs of their courage, examples of a more reasonable philosophy.[103]

Martine further cited the most "enlightened" of the pagan authors, who did not share this admiration for suicide. Like Lambert Daneau a century and a half earlier, he quoted the poet Martial who asserted that true bravery meant to face adversity.[104] Martine referred to Cicero, who wrote in his *On Duties*, "We are not born only for ourselves, but our country claims a share of our being, as do our parents and our friends."[105] From Cicero's *The Dream of Scipio*, Martine quoted, "Unless the god, whose temple is everything you see, has freed you from the guardianship of your body, you cannot gain entrance to heaven."[106]

In citing Christian tradition, Martine mentioned in passing the resolute opposition to suicide in Augustine's *City of God* and in Canon Law.[107] He further cited the Parisian poet Madame Deshoulières (1637–98), who held

---

[103]AEG, PC 8581.

[104]AEG, PC 8581; Martial, *Epigrams*, 11. 56 (Martine cited this as Book 11, Epigram 57).

[105]AEG, PC 8581. The text of this treatise in the edition of the Loeb Classical Library does not include the words "partem parentes": only our country and our friends claim a share on our being; Cicero, *De Officiis*, trans. Walter Miller (London: William Heinemann, 1921), 1.22.

[106]AEG, PC 8581; Cicero, *Somnium Scipionis* in *M. Tulli Ciceronis Scripta Quae Manserunt Omnia. De Re Publica*, ed. K. Ziegler (Leipzig: B. G. Teubner, 1958), 6. 15. Martine's very brief remarks about ancient opponents of suicide are at times weak. While Cicero did take a dim view of voluntary death, the key for him was following the divine will. As noted above, Cicero believed that Cato, for example, had received an order from God to take his life. Consequently in certain cases, voluntarily ending one's life is the proper action to take; see *Tusculan Disputations*, 1. 71–75. Martine also quoted a line from an ode of Horace ("And if the broken vault of heaven fall, it will fall on a man undaunted"), which cannot easily be construed as an attack on the legitimacy of taking one's life; Horace *Odes*, bk. 3, ode 3. Although the ode does praise those who face adversity with courage, it does not specifically deal with suicide and indeed is not the best example of antisuicide literature. In this same ode, Horace lauds Hercules, who was responsible for his own death, even if he technically did not die by his own hand. Hercules built his own funeral pyre on Mount Oeta and convinced his friend Philoctetes to light the fire. While his body perished in the flames, Hercules's soul was borne by Jupiter to Olympus where he lived happily ever after. Martine even included Seneca among the opponents of suicide. As we have seen, while Seneca did criticize taking one's life for the wrong reason, his praise of Cato was the most emphatic defense of suicide of ancient times.

[107]AEG, PC 8581. In referring to Canon Law, Martine simply noted that it condemned self-murder, giving the following incorrect citation: "Can. Placuit Caus. 3 quest. 5." As noted above, the passage in question is: Gratian, *Decretum*, C. 23 q. 5 c. 12, in *Corpus Iuris Canonici*, ed. Friedberg, 1.935.

that admiration for ancient suicides was misplaced.[108] In listing opponents of suicide, Martine also referred to recent works by the advocates of Natural Law. He mentioned, for example, the work of the German jurist Samuel Pufendorf (1632–94), a pioneer in the study of Natural Law who insisted that reason was the ultimate ground on which laws were to be based. Contrary to what one may think, the *jusnaturalistes* did not necessarily become defenders of the right to end one's life. As Martine correctly observed, Pufendorf portrayed suicide as a violation of Natural Law, similar to Aquinas's condemnation of suicide as violating the natural instinct of survival. Martine quoted from Pufendorf's *On the Law of Nature and Nations*, "This much is clear, however, that those who interrupt the course of their life, either from mere weariness of the troubles common to life, or from disgust at the evils which would have made them objects of the scorn of society, or from fear of trials which they might have borne with fortitude, and so helped others by their example, can offer no defense so valid that they should not be judged to have sinned against the law of nature."[109]

But, said Martine, it was not necessary to refer to the work of foreign jurists to dispel any controversy that Pelissari's heirs were being mistreated.

---

[108]AEG, PC 8581. Martine cited the following verses:
Quand on éleve au rang des hommes généreux
Ces Grecs et ces Romains dont la mort volontaire
A rendu le nom si fameux.
Qu'ont-ils fait de si grand? Ils sortoient de la vie
Lorsque de disgraces suivie,
Elle n'avoit plus rien d'agréable pour eux.
Par une seule mort ils s'en epargnoient mille.
Qu'elle est douce à des coeurs lassés de soupirer
Il est plus grand, plus difficile
De souffrir le malheur que de s'en délivrer.

See also Antoinette du Ligier de la Garde Deshoulières, "Réflexions diverses," in *Oeuvres*, 2 vols. (Paris, 1770), st. 10, 1:172–73. I am deeply grateful to Alain Dufour for his invaluable assistance in identifying the author and the work, both of which Martine abbreviated almost beyond recognition.

[109]AEG, PC 8581; Samuel Pufendorf, "The Duties of Man Towards Himself," in *De Jure Naturae et Gentium Libri Octo*, trans. C. H. Oldfather and W. A. Oldfather (Oxford: Clarendon Press, 1934), 262, 2: bk. 2, chap. 4. Citing a wide variety of authors, primarily from ancient Rome and Greece, Pufendorf, like Aristotle, believed that taking one's life was a wrong to God and society rather than to oneself. Like Aristotle and Plato, however, Pufendorf did not issue a blanket condemnation of suicide. He condoned the self-inflicted deaths of Cato, Saul, and Samson, and insisted that those "who take their own lives because of some disease which has destroyed the use of their reason" are not guilty of suicide. John Locke too condemned suicide because it violated the natural instinct of self-preservation. See Gary D. Glenn, "Inalienable Rights and Locke's Argument for Limited Government: Political Implications of a Right to Suicide," *Journal of Politics* 46 (1984): 80–105.

On the contrary, this controversy could easily be put to rest on the basis of Geneva's own legal traditions, referring to the ordinance from 1568 which prescribed the confiscation of the goods of those who voluntarily took their lives, unless they were alienated of spirit.[110] Martine acknowledged that he and others were not without compassion and especially commiserated with the innocent people who suffered from this tragedy. Nonetheless, he insisted that magistrates must always do their duty in applying the laws. And in this case, the law unambiguously held that Pelissari's assets should be confiscated. If fear of dishonor alone did not suffice as a deterrent, this further punishment emphasized one's duties toward friends, relatives, and the Republic. As for the exception involving the alienated of spirit, Martine insisted that the law stated that one is presumed of sound mind unless proven otherwise, and nothing suggested that Pelissari was alienated. True, testimony indicated that he suffered some difficult nights. Left to his own reflections, Pelissari was terribly agitated and full of self-reproaches; reason, however, should inevitably emerge victorious when confronted with such thoughts. One witness did reveal that Pelissari wanted to make a general public confession in church, evidence that might imply that he was "on the verge of losing his judgment." But if we assume that Pelissari genuinely wanted to make such a confession, that showed, according to Martine, a soul that was burdened by overwhelming feelings of remorse rather than a demented spirit. Pelissari's public behavior had been quite constant, and he was known to be "eminently gifted in spirit and reason." Furthermore, all those who did business with him and worked with him knew him as a man of good sense.[111]

Martine acknowledged that whenever people take their own lives, there is a certain alienation of spirit. But it was not this type of alienation that legislators had in mind when they made the exception. If such were the case, then no one would be liable to the punishments associated with self-murder. If asked to identify the cause of this suicide—if it were not madness or desperation—Martine would simply reply that he had seen no reason to make it excusable: "Such desperation usually comes either from the fear of punishment or the ignominy that accompanies it, from poverty, from physical sufferings, from ambition or vainglory, or sometimes, although quite rarely,

[110]AEG, PC 8581; as noted above, Titre 29, Des successions ab intestat, Numéro 16, in *Sources du droit de Genève*, ed. Rivoire and Berchem, 3: 228.
[111]AEG, PC 8581.

from love. We find nothing in the life of Sieur Pelissari that suggests that he could have been driven to take his life for any of these reasons."[112] No evidence suggests that he committed any crimes. His fortune was well established, and so poverty surely was not a motive. His health was robust, and there was nothing to suggest that his suicide was driven by ambition or vainglory. "Finally we have learned nothing about his habits with regard to the beautiful sex that would have plunged him into amorous despair."[113] Even if any of these factors had incited Pelissari to take his life, that would not preclude the confiscation of assets. Consequently Martine deemed as futile any further attempt to uncover the real motive of this suicide.[114]

Martine added, "Whoever does not fear to lose his life and to take his own life, is also not at all deterred from taking the lives of others. Such a man is therefore dangerous to society, and society consequently has an interest in ensuring that such men do not become more numerous. They can be restrained only by using very severe punishments."[115] In short, the prosecutor's lengthy argument militated against leniency in handling suicide cases. Apart from the utterly insane, they were responsible for their actions and the state accordingly was to confiscate their assets.

This case of suicide was brought before the Small Council several times during the weeks to follow. In the last appearance, 26 November 1738, Pelissari's siblings, his heirs, announced that they would make a donation of 10,000 florins from their brother's estate to the hospital, asking in return that the case be closed. The Small Council agreed, allowing the siblings to receive Pelissari's inheritance, minus the donation and court costs.[116] This donation—tantamount to a fine for the suicide—was the last time that any amount of money was transferred from the estate of a suicide to the Republic of Geneva. In effect, this marked the last punishment, apart from the denial of funerary honors, imposed on a self-inflicted death. With his well-worn arguments in favor of confiscation, Martine was the last prosecutor who deemed deprivation of funerary honors as insufficient punishment for suicide.

---

[112]AEG, PC 8581; although Martine was correct in saying that romantic love was rarely a motive for ending one's life in his day, later in the eighteenth century a good number of Genevans ended their lives because of romantic misadventure; see chapter 4.

[113]AEG, PC 8581.

[114]AEG, PC 8581.

[115]AEG, PC 8581.

[116]AEG, RC 238: 370–72, 396, 400–1, 405–6, 434, 437–38.

ATTITUDES TOWARD SUICIDE AMONG EIGHTEENTH-CENTURY INTELLECTUALS

Notwithstanding the arguments of Martine in handling cases of suicides, Genevan authorities reflected changing attitudes toward suicide espoused by eighteenth-century intellectuals. That century, particularly the second half, witnessed more debate over the legitimacy of suicide than has ever been seen before or since.[117] The very word "suicide" came into use in French shortly before Martine wrote his opinion concerning Pelissari's property, introduced from English in 1734 by Abbé Nicolas Prévost.[118] Much more important than this linguistic change, however, was the call from many intellectuals for more lenient approaches to suicide. In 1712 Ephraim Gerhardus, a German jurist, authored a treatise that called for the decriminalization of self-murder, though this work found a limited audience outside academic circles.[119] The most famous call for change in the judicial treatment of suicide was that promoted by the Milanese nobleman Cesare Beccaria (1738–94) in the most important eighteenth-century plea for reform of the criminal justice system: *On Crimes and Punishments*, published anonymously in 1764 and quickly translated into French and English. In addition to criticizing capital punishment and the use of torture, Beccaria took issue in this work with the traditional way in which European courts handled cases of suicide. In noting that people love life and are willing to tolerate much evil in exchange for a modicum of contentment, Beccaria seemed to imply, like Pufendorf, that taking one's life is unnatural and a sin against nature. Beccaria insisted, however, that suicide does not lend itself to punishment. Any punishment would be inflicted either on innocent survivors or on a "cold and insensible body." Punishment for suicide is thus unjust and useless:

> Therefore, although it is a fault that God may punish because he alone can punish after death, it is not a crime in man's eyes, for man's punishment, instead of falling on the criminal himself, falls

---

[117]Minois, *Histoire du suicide*, 246–87.

[118]Joblin, "Suicide à l'époque moderne," 86. The word "suicida," referring to the killer of oneself (not the act itself), was used in a treatise written in the late twelfth century by the Augustinian canon Walter of St. Victor. No other reference to that word can be found, however, until Sir Thomas Browne's *Religio Medici*, appearing in 1637; see Murray, *Suicide*, vol. 1, *Violent Against Themselves*, 38–39.

[119]Published in Jena, the treatise was entitled, *Dissertatio juridica de crimine et poenis propricidii, vulgo Vom Selbstmord;* see Paolo Bernardini, "Dal suicidio come crimine al suicidio come malattia: Appunti sulla questione suicidologica nell'etica e nella giurisprudenza europea tra Sei e Settecento," *Materiali per una storia della cultura giuridica* 24 (1994): 88–89.

on his family. To the objection that consideration of such a punishment might, nevertheless, keep a determined man from actually
killing himself, my reply is that anyone who calmly renounces the
advantage of life, who so hates existence here as to prefer an eternity
of unhappiness, is not in the least likely to be moved by the less effi-
cacious and more distant consideration of children and relatives.[120]

As these words indicate, Beccaria viewed suicide as a sin but not a crime.
He in fact recognized three sources for the political and moral principles that
govern humans: divine revelation, natural law, and societal conventions.
Acknowledging the "immutable virtue that emanates from God," Beccaria
deemed suicide to be under the purview of divine judgment alone.[121]

Well before Beccaria, many European intellectuals not only condemned
the traditional treatment of suicide but even expressed admiration for certain
forms of suicide. Throughout the eighteenth century, many prominent intellectuals spoke admiringly of various self-inflicted deaths of antiquity. Many
esteemed Cato's rational choice of death over submission to tyranny, and this
death was the subject of several theatrical works. In England, for example,
Joseph Addison's *Cato*, which justified through Stoic philosophy this self-
inflicted death, enjoyed spectacular success and received rave reviews when
first performed in 1713.[122]

In France the philosophes were unanimous in denouncing traditional
penalties against suicide, and some went beyond the call for decriminalization and defended the right of individuals to choose death under certain circumstances.[123] In his fictitious *Persian Letters*, first published in 1721,
Montesquieu (1689–1755), in a letter from Uzbek to Ibsen, ridiculed Europeans' sentences against the bodies and estates of suicides. Failing to see what

---

[120]Cesare Beccaria, *On Crimes and Punishments*, trans. Henry Paolucci (Indianapolis: Bobbs-Merrill, 1963), 83.

[121]Beccaria, *Crimes and Punishments*, 4, 6.

[122]Michael MacDonald, "The Medicalization of Suicide in England: Laymen, Physicians, and Cul-
tural Change, 1500–1870," in *Framing Disease: Studies in Cultural History*, ed. Charles E. Rosenberg and
Janet Golden (New Brunswick, N.J.: Rutgers University Press, 1992), 94. Less popular was George Lillo's
Fatal Curiosity, which, inspired by Calvinist morality, cast Cato's suicide in a very negative light; see
Stephen L. Trainor, "Suicide and Seneca in Two Eighteenth-Century Tragedies," in *Drama and the Classical Heritage*, ed. Clifford Davidson, Rand Johnson, and John H. Troupe (New York: AMS Press, 1993),
227–40.

[123]Bayet, *Suicide et morale*, 617–86.

crime had been committed, Uzbek asked rhetorically why anyone would want to prevent him from putting an end to his days if he suffered terribly, if his life were sheer misery. If a person no longer received any advantages from society, how could society pretend to have an interest in keeping that person alive? Through Uzbek, Montesquieu ponders the argument claiming that one violates the order of providence in taking one's life: God united the body and soul, and the individual does not have the right to separate them. Insisting ultimately that suicide was a fundamental right of the individual, Montesquieu wrote that human pride was behind this opposition to suicide—people are unable to accept their insignificance in this vast universe: "We imagine that the annihilation of a being as perfect as ourselves would degrade the whole of Nature."[124] In the last letter of the book, Montesquieu even provided an example of a self-inflicted death. Roxanne, whom Uzbek believed the most faithful of his wives, wrote defiantly to him after she had taken poison following her lover's murder, insisting that she had always remained independent in spirit despite her servile status. Asserting that the pact between society and individuals is reciprocal and conditional, Montesquieu's insistence that suicide was not a crime against society if a person received no benefits from society won considerable support among Enlightenment thinkers.[125]

Though expressing concern, as noted in chapter 1, over the high number of suicides in Geneva, Voltaire also defended the right to end one's life, provided one acted rationally. In his correspondence, Voltaire referred to many specific suicides in contemporary Geneva, occasionally expressing approval. In a letter to his niece dated 29 November 1768, Voltaire referred to the death of Marc Pictet who had drowned himself in the Rhône two days before. Pictet, seventy-five, was a former Syndic who had suffered for several months from excruciating abdominal pains, evidently caused by gravel that

[124]Montesquieu, *Lettres persanes*, ed. Antoine Adam (Geneva: Droz, 1965), no. 76, 196–98; see also John McManners, *Death and Enlightenment: Changing Attitudes to Death in Eighteenth-Century France* (Oxford: Oxford University Press, 1981), 412. To mollify critics who were upset with this apology for suicide, Montesquieu added, in the 1754 edition, a very brief and very weak response (letter 77) in which Ibsen suggested that a true Moslem must not kill himself but bear suffering patiently; *Lettres persanes*, 199–200.

[125]Montesquieu, *Lettres persanes*, no. 161, 404–5. Hume and Holbach both reiterated this argument; Bayet, *Suicide et morale*, 652–54; Samuel Ernest Sprott, *The English Debate on Suicide from Donne to Hume* (La Salle, Ill.: Open Court, 1961), 133–36.

brought with it extremely painful urination.[126] Voltaire wrote that the "love-able and pleasant" Pictet "suffered and had no hope of ever seeing an end to his ills.... Only after careful calculation did he take his leave. He is missed and praised in Geneva."[127] Clearly Voltaire believed that this suicide could be justified; this was a rational decision that effectively put Pictet out of his misery.

In his *Philosophical Dictionary*, Voltaire discussed suicide at length in the article, "Cato." Praising Cato for taking his life rather than surrender to the "enemy of Rome," Voltaire claimed that this was not an act of weakness, insisting that courage was needed to overcome the survival instinct. He also noted that to a large degree attitudes toward suicide were culture-bound. Unlike ancient Romans, modern military leaders did not kill themselves after losing battles, and French nobles such as Cinq Mars, convicted of con-spiracy under Louis XIII, preferred execution to suicide. Nonetheless, this did not mean that contemporary French had more or less courage or honor than the Romans; custom simply dictated a different form of behavior. Cul-tural differences also explain why, upon the deaths of their husbands, women of the Malabar coast performed the suttee, a tradition alien to European sen-sibilities. Noting that neither the Old nor the New Testament explicitly con-demned suicide, Voltaire further decried the punishments levied against the bodies and estates of suicides as hurting no one other than the innocent sur-vivors. He suggested that one need not fear that publication of suicide may lead to an epidemic of self-inflicted deaths: nature protects us, offering hope and fear which are very important deterrents.[128] In a letter, he observed that only when one had lost all hope or was afflicted by an intolerable melancholy could one "triumph over this instinct which makes us love the chains of life and draw up the courage to leave this poorly built house."[129]

Like Montesquieu, Voltaire further wrote that the lives of individual human beings are entirely insignificant in the history of the huge universe. The individual is so unimportant that God would surely not notice if a

[126]AEG, EC, LM 64: 51, 27 November 1768; PC 11794; RC 269: 646–47.

[127]Voltaire, *Correspondence and Related Documents,* ed. Theodore Besterman, definitive edition, 51 vols. (Banbury, U.K.: Voltaire Foundation, 1968–77), D 15340. See also Robert Favre, *La mort dans la littérature et la pensée françaises au siècle des Lumières* (Lyon: Presses Universitaires de Lyon, 1978), 478.

[128]Voltaire, "De Caton, du suicide," in *Dictionnaire philosophique*, in *Oeuvres complètes de Voltaire* (Basel: Jean-Jacques Tourneisen, 1786), 38:390–404.

[129]Voltaire, *Correspondence*, D 5708.

person deserted his post here on earth. Nonetheless, Voltaire did not emulate Seneca in holding up suicide as the ultimate expression of individualism and self-determination. The characters in Voltaire's work who long for death are not those bent on determining their own fate but rather people who simply want to be liberated from a miserable existence. In *Candide*, Voltaire described the character of an old woman who, born into wealth, had suffered a series of incredible reversals, including rape, slavery, and mutilation. The elderly woman ruefully said, "a hundred times I wanted to kill myself, but I still loved life. This ridiculous foible is perhaps one of our most disastrous inclinations. For is there anything more stupid than to want to bear continually a burden that we always want to throw to the ground? To regard our being with horror, and to cling to our being? In fine, to caress the serpent that devours us until it has eaten up our heart?"[130] She added that among the "prodigious number of persons" she had known who longed for death, only twelve of them ended their lives, including four Genevans, a further indication that Voltaire perceived a penchant for suicide in Geneva.[131] In *L'ingénu*, the title character, after having been unjustly imprisoned and overwhelmed with grief over the death of his fiancée, inquired of the Jansenist Gordon whether anyone could justifiably prevent him from taking his life. Voltaire wrote:

> Gordon took care not to parade those tedious commonplaces by which people try to prove that it is not permissible to use our liberty in order to cease to be when we are in a horribly bad way, that we must not leave our house when we can no longer remain in it, that man is on earth like a soldier at his post: as if it mattered to the Being of beings whether the collection of a few particles was in one place or another; important reasons to which a firm and considered despair disdains to listen, and to which Cato replied only by a

---

[130]Voltaire, *Candide, Zadig and Selected Stories*, trans. Donald M. Frame (New York: Signet Classic, 1961), 41; Bayet, *Suicide et morale*, 657–59; McManners, *Death and Enlightenment*, 413.

[131]The others were as follows: "three Negroes" (several eighteenth-century accounts referred to slaves committing suicide to escape their miserable existence); four Englishmen, who were believed to be particularly prone to suicide; and "a German professor named Robek"; Voltaire, *Candide*, 41. John Robeck was a Swede who wrote a treatise promoting suicide, *Exercitatio philosophica de morte voluntarii*, which he put into practice by rowing a boat out into the Weser and drowning himself in 1735; see Fedden, *Suicide*, 210–11.

dagger thrust.[132]

Although Gordon remained convinced to the end that suffering is good for the Christian, Voltaire concluded this work by saying that suffering was good for nothing.

When they defended suicide, the philosophes' arguments tended to fall into one of two categories. The first, which would include the reasoning of Voltaire in the above passage, can be described as a "naturalist interpretation." Best exemplified by Holbach, this defense holds that in the grand scheme of this huge universe, the life of a person is really insignificant. Ending one's own life can hardly be said to be a violation of the order of the cosmos. The second form of argument is the "humanist interpretation": emphasizing the importance of human liberty, it suggests that through suicide people can control their own destiny.[133]

The eighteenth century's most emphatic defense of self-inflicted death, David Hume's "On Suicide," stressed this humanist interpretation. The Scottish philosopher Hume (1711–76) wrote this treatise in the 1750s, but it was not published until after his death.[134] While a century and a half earlier, Donne had argued that suicide was not necessarily a sin, Hume insisted that suicide was not a crime. Though not advocating suicide, Hume defended individual liberty, claiming the rational person had the right to end his or her life. The atheist Hume denied that suicide violated the laws of nature. A person suffering from a debilitating illness, for example, may rationally choose death. Such an action no more violates the laws than avoiding a stone that was falling from a cliff onto one's head. In dealing with nature, of which they are a part, humans are free to use their judgment to determine how they react. Hume saw no disjunction between natural phenomena and the voluntary actions of humans. Like Montesquieu, he believed that suicide is not a crime against society if an individual receives no reciprocal benefit from society. Finally, suicide is not necessarily a crime against oneself. If an incurable illness makes life an intolerable burden, death rather than a miser-

---

[132]Voltaire, "Ingenuous," in *Candide and Selected Stories*, 316; McManners, *Death and Enlightenment*, 413–14.

[133]Favre, *Mort dans la littérature*, 473.

[134]"On Suicide" appeared in *Two Essays* (1777) and in *Essays on Suicide and the Immortality of the Soul* (1783); see Sprott, *English Debate on Suicide*, 128.

able existence may be in a person's best interest.[135]

Taking their cue from Montesquieu, many philosophes developed a keen admiration for Roman suicides. In his *Grandeur et décadence des Romains* (1734), Montesquieu wrote admiringly of suicides such as Cato. Montesquieu attributed the Roman penchant to suicide partly to Stoic philosophy "which encouraged it," partly to practical legal concerns (Roman tribunals confiscated the assets of prisoners who were put to death but not those who took their own lives), but above all to a form of heroism. Romans were actors in the play of life and enjoyed the power to determine when their parts were finished, when they exited the stage. The instinct of self-preservation, Montesquieu wrote, can take various forms, and one person may indeed experience the natural desire to end his or her life, overwhelming any instinct toward survival. Reflecting on his own day, Montesquieu lamented, "It is certain that men have become less free, less courageous, less driven to bold enterprises than they were [in Roman times], when, through this power individuals had over themselves, one could, at any instant, escape all other forces."[136]

Enlightenment thinkers were particularly enamored of Cato and Socrates. The author of a tragedy celebrating the death of Cato wrote in 1768, "The situation of a man who, jealous of liberty, prefers a glorious death to a shameful slavery can excite in the soul no other sensations but astonishment and admiration."[137] Philosophes almost universally applauded this ultimate expression of patriotism, in spite of the fact that they themselves lived docilely under absolute monarchy. Diderot, among others, held Socrates in highest esteem, extolling him for selflessly obeying the unfair sentence against him, his crime nothing but telling the truth.[138]

---

[135]Sprott, *English Debate on Suicide*, 128–34.

[136]Montesquieu, *Considérations sur les causes de la grandeur des Romains et de leur décadence*, in *Oeuvres complètes de Montesquieu*, ed. Edouard Laboulaye (Paris: Garnier Frères. 1876), 2: 217–18. In a note in the first edition, which he eliminated from later editions, Montesquieu noted, "If Charles I or James II had followed a religion which allowed them to kill themselves, they would not have had to endure such an [unhappy] death, in the case of the former, or life, in the case of the latter"; *Grandeur des Romains*, 217, n. 3. Montesquieu also discussed Greek and Roman customs on suicide in *Esprit des lois*, bk. 29, chap. 9; see also McManners, *Death and Enlightenment*, 415.

[137] H. Panckoucke, *La mort de Caton: Tragédie* (1768), preface, iii, quoted in McManners, *Death and Enlightenment*, 415.

[138]Voltaire, however, had nothing good to say about Socrates's death. While he sympathized with those who took their lives out of despair, he saw this death as a case of futile martyrdom; see McManners, *Death and Enlightenment*, 416.

It must be noted that the philosophes were not unanimous in praising voluntary death. Eighteenth-century Geneva's most famous son, Jean-Jacques Rousseau (1712–78), for example, was at best ambivalent with regard to suicide. On the one hand, he did write in 1756 that the "wise man" ought to end his life voluntarily if "Nature and Fortune" clearly indicated that was the proper course to take. He admired Cato and conceded that suicide by the terminally ill may be excusable. On the other hand, in *La nouvelle Héloïse* (1761), Rousseau offered, through Milord Edouard, a strong argument denouncing the right to end one's life voluntarily. Arguing with Saint-Preux, who was most distraught over romantic woes, Edouard insisted that one's obligations to others represented the most fundamental reason that suicide was not permissible. Concomitantly, an active life, based on service to others, was the most effective means of dispelling suicidal despair. Milord Edouard did concede that when people suffer utterly incapacitating and incurable physical illnesses, the overwhelming pain can dehumanize them. Under such circumstances, death is a merciful release of the soul, and suicide can indeed be justified. Mental anguish, such as that which plagued Saint-Preux, is a completely different matter. Though suffering from sadness, disappointment, or despair, the soul will heal itself over time.[139] In the early 1760s, Rousseau mentioned three times in correspondence that his own maladies caused him to contemplate putting an end to his days. By 1764, however, Rousseau, though still ill, had forsaken any plans of suicide, resigned to letting nature take its course. Basically he believed that life is worth living and that obligations to others must not be shirked.[140]

In spite of Milord Edouard's argument, Rousseau was at the very least captivated by suicides that were inspired by the motive that had driven Saint-Preux to despair: unhappy love stories. In 1770 a double suicide took place in spectacular fashion in Lyon. A certain Thérèse and her Italian lover, the maître d'armes Faldoni, strongly desired to marry. Faldoni, however, suffered from poor health, and his physicians informed him that he did not have long to live, prompting her father to forbid the marriage. Thwarted in

[139]Jean-Jacques Rousseau, *Julie ou la nouvelle Héloïse*, ed. René Pomeau (Paris: Garnier Frères, 1960), part 3, letters 21–23.
[140]Joseph-Albert Bédé, "Madame de Staël, Rousseau, et le suicide," *Revue d'histoire littéraire de la France* 66 (1966): 55; Fedden, *Suicide*, 206–8; McManners, *Death and Enlightenment*, 419–23; Minois, *Histoire du suicide*, 309–10.

their desire to marry, Thérèse and Faldoni shot themselves in a chapel in Lyon with a pair of pistols that were decorated with pink ribbons. So intrigued was he by this affair that Rousseau wrote an epitaph in honor of the couple: "They lived for each other, and died for each other, the laws condemn them, and unreflective piety notes their transgression, but men of feeling admire them and men of reason remain silent."[141]

Many shared this romantic fascination with suicide, which was also reflected in the sensation caused by the death of Thomas Chatterton in 1770. Subjected to wretched poverty, the brilliant English poet Chatterton poisoned himself at the age of only seventeen, inspiring numerous writers to laud this tragic, misunderstood genius.[142] The same sentiment accounted for the immense popularity of the most famous suicide in eighteenth-century literature: that found in Goethe's *The Sorrows of Young Werther*, published in German in 1774 and available in French translation in 1776. Although Goethe has often been said to have made suicide fashionable, in reality *Werther* was more the culmination of cultural trends that had been developing for years. The debates over the legitimacy of suicide, the letter of Saint-Preux, the fascination with the suicides of the lovers of Lyon and of Chatterton, all had made the reading public receptive to Werther's unhappy love story.[143]

Toward the end of the century, Madame de Staël (1766–1817), the daughter of the Genevan financier Jacques Necker, expressed a strong, almost unrestrained admiration for suicide, especially that motivated by love. Her novellas include many characters who ended their lives voluntarily. Writing on the life and work of Rousseau in 1788, Staël insisted that Saint-Preux's argument, not Milord Edouard's, represented Rousseau's true opinion on suicide. She further suggested that Rousseau took his own life after being betrayed by his lover, Thérèse Levasseur.[144] In her *De l'influence des*

---

[141]Fedden, *Suicide*, 240–41; Minois, *Histoire du suicide*, 308–9. Nonetheless, as McManners, *Death and Enlightenment*, 422–23, rightly observes, Rousseau was surely more concerned with the reunion of lovers in the afterlife than with suicide itself.

[142]MacDonald and Murphy, *Sleepless Souls*, 191–93; Minois, *Histoire du suicide*, 315.

[143]Minois, *Histoire du suicide*, 311.

[144]Gita May, "Staël and the Fascination of Suicide: The Eighteenth-Century Background," in *Germaine de Staël: Crossing the Borders*, ed. Madelyn Gutwirth, Avriel Goldberger, and Karyna Szmurlo (New Brunswick, N.J.: Rutgers University Press, 1991), 172–73. Historical inquiries have not lent support to the view that Rousseau's death was self-inflicted.

passions sur le bonheur des individus et des nations (1796), Staël, who strongly influenced the development of romanticism in France, showed considerable sympathy for those who were driven to take their lives over the death of a loved one. She also believed that suicides resulting from a weariness of life were inspired by "profound reflections, deep introspection." Staël even avowed that suicide for a fault committed revealed a certain "generosity" of spirit. Real criminals hardly ever kill themselves, she wrote, because deprived souls lack the sensitivity and the philosophical prowess needed to kill oneself. She wrote these words amid the passions unleashed by the French Revolution. In 1814, however, she wrote her *Réflexions sur le suicide* in which she regretted her earlier defense of suicide.[145]

A host of eighteenth-century thinkers never shared this enthusiasm for suicide. Echoing Aristotle, several intellectuals viewed suicide as a rejection of one's responsibilities toward society. Though deploring the traditional penalties levied against suicide, Delisle de Sales (1741–1816) asserted that there is a contract between the individual and society; even if a person is rejected by his society, suicide is not defensible. The individual still has the obligation to serve others and can do so by going elsewhere. The philosophes' emphasis on social utility tended to militate against rash defenses of suicide. In spite of his admiration for Socrates, Diderot denied that individuals simply had the right to kill themselves. The likely author of the *Encyclopédie*'s article on suicide which was quite critical of voluntary death, Diderot emphasized the responsibilities people have toward society and maintained that killing oneself is an egocentric act without regard to the harm inflicted on others.[146]

Even Voltaire certainly did not advocate suicide. He lamented the seemingly trivial reasons for which his contemporaries took their lives. Far from the philosophical suicides of antiquity, Voltaire was dismayed that Europeans of his day often took their lives over minor personal reversals, such as loss of wealth, romantic misadventure, or a nonterminal illness, all of which time

---

[145]Bayet, *Suicide et morale*, 700–1, 741–42; Bédé, "Madame de Staël," 52–70; Fedden, *Suicide*, 220–22.

[146]Denis Diderot and Jean Le Rond d'Alembert, eds., *Encyclopédie, ou Dictionnaire raisonné des sciences, des arts et des métiers*, 28 vols. (Paris: Briasson, David, Le Breton, and Durand, 1751–72), s.v. "Suicide"; Favre, *Mort dans la littérature*, 477–78; Fedden, *Suicide*, 224–25; McManners, *Death and Enlightenment*, 424–25; Minois, *Histoire du suicide*, 275.

otherwise would have healed. He maintained that people who, in a fit of melancholy, kill themselves today, would have wished to live had they but waited a week.[147] Even when dealing with royalty, Voltaire dissuaded them from emulating Cato. Faced with losing east Prussia in the Seven Years' War, a desperate Frederick the Great wrote a letter to Voltaire in September 1757, in which he lauded Cato and Otho, the Roman emperor who killed himself after being defeated in battle in 69 A.D., just three months after assuming power. Frederick indicated that he was seriously contemplating following their examples rather than live with defeat.[148] Voltaire responded with a series of letters in which he urged Frederick not even to think of such an action. While ancient societies deemed such figures as heroes, Voltaire warned the Prussian sovereign that he would not be viewed as a martyr for liberty but simply as a man who succumbed to despair. His suicide would mean victory for his enemies and shame for his supporters. Voltaire besought Frederick to think of all those—his subjects, his family, the philosophes— who depended so much on him.[149]

Voltaire asserted that, in contemplating suicide, one must never rush to judgment. He wrote in a letter in 1775 that he did not blame those who wanted desperately to end their lives but urged them to wait at least a week before performing the act. They may change their mind, and things may get better.[150] Voltaire was mortified by the suicide of Jean-Louis Tronchin, twenty-eight, an attorney from a very wealthy and prestigious Genevan family, who shot himself following a brief illness in May 1773.[151] In one letter, Voltaire wrote that he was devastated by the news of Tronchin's death and that he "grieved for the family and for human nature."[152] In another missive, Voltaire bemoaned that he could not understand how this young man, "more handsome and much richer than his uncle [Jacob Tronchin], recently married to a young woman [Anne Caroline Boissier] who was still

---

[147]Voltaire, "Caton," in *Oeuvres complètes*, 38: 390–404. Voltaire was speaking from experience. When he was but nineteen, Voltaire wrote a letter to his lover, Catherine Olympe Du Noyer, in which he threatened to kill himself if she did not leave Holland to come see him; *Correspondence*, D 20.

[148]Voltaire, *Correspondence*, D 7373.

[149]Voltaire, *Correspondence*, D 7400, 7419, 7460.

[150]Voltaire, *Correspondence*, D 19596.

[151]AEG, PC 12450.

[152]Voltaire, *Correspondence*, D 18376. See also Favre, *Mort dans la littérature*, 478.

wealthier and more beautiful than he," could have possibly taken his life.[153] In "Cato" and in letters, Voltaire offered remedies to suicidal proclivities, declaring that idleness was the principal culprit. He claimed, moreover, that urban dwellers kill themselves in greater numbers than rural folk simply because the former have more time on their hands. Accordingly, Voltaire asserted that activity—be it getting exercise, attending the theater, going hunting, enjoying the company of a pleasant woman, or above all, working—was the best means to ward off the desire to leave this world. Voltaire himself suffered from many physical ills and frequent bouts with melancholy, about which he complained constantly in his correspondence.[154] Referring to the former Syndic Pictet's death, Voltaire wrote to a friend, "I will not kill myself as long as I have something to do. But if I had nothing to do, I would be seriously tempted to become another Pictet. Life is good only so long as one puts it to use."[155]

A few Enlightenment thinkers denigrated the suicides of antiquity. A surprising criticism of suicide came from La Mettrie (1709–51), the quintessential materialist and author of *L'homme machine*. In *Anti-Sénèque* (1750) and *Système d'Epicure*, the physician La Mettrie praised Epicureanism, asserting that life should be spent in the pursuit of sensual pleasures, and derided the Stoics, whom he portrayed as proponents of unhappiness. Stressing the duties toward one's family, friends, and country, La Mettrie insisted that, though one must not fear death, at the same time one must not seek it. Preferring the happy fool to the sad philosopher, La Mettrie wrote that people

---

[153]Voltaire, *Correspondence*, D 18389. See also Favre, *Mort dans la littérature*, 478.

[154]In a letter dated 24 January 1754, Voltaire wrote: "I am abandoned to my anxieties and cruel maladies which winter, solitude, and melancholy increase.... As much as I can, I have used work to counteract this gloomy state, but I am quite afraid that this sole consolation will, like everything else, fail in the end and that I will be reduced to face the horror of my situation, in inactivity and pain, until death puts an end to such a cruel life"; *Correspondence* D 5633. Voltaire, who went on to live another twenty-four years, was obviously something of a hypochondriac.

[155]Quotation from Voltaire, *Correspondence*, D 15340; idem, "Caton," in *Oeuvres complètes*, 38: 390–404. See also Favre, *Mort dans la littérature*, 478. In a similar fashion, the Swiss German physician Johann Georg Zimmerman (1728–95) wrote about the connection between solitude and melancholy. Although he viewed a degree of solitude as healthy for stimulating the mind and creativity, he also believed that it could lead to melancholy and even suicide; see Paolo Bernardini, "Solitudine, malinconia e loro esiti 'esiziali' nel Settecento tedesco: Alcune linee di ricerca," *Atti dell'Accademia Ligure di Scienze e Lettere* 51 (1994): 321–41. For eighteenth-century views on the necessary balance between activity and repose to attain happiness, see Antoinette Emch-Dériaz, *Tissot: Physician of the Enlightenment* (New York: Peter Lang, 1992), 90, 133; Robert Mauzi, *L'idée du bonheur dans la littérature et la pensée françaises au XVIIIe siècle* (Paris: Armand Colin, 1969), 125–35.

are to live out their natural life span, attaining as much pleasure as possible.[156] Probably the most important eighteenth-century critic of suicide was the German idealist Immanuel Kant (1724–1804), who condemned suicide under all circumstances, deeming self-inflicted deaths as a violation of nature that was intrinsically immoral to others and especially to oneself.[157]

One point on which all Enlightenment thinkers agreed was that the English had a particular penchant for suicide. In the eighteenth century, suicide was known as the "English malady," a term inspired by a book by the same name by the physician George Cheyne, published in 1733. The British had a reputation of killing themselves over most trivial matters and even for no reason at all when they were demonstratively happy, a reputation perhaps stemming from the English press's paying more attention to suicide than its continental counterparts.[158] As alluded to in chapter 1, Montesquieu blamed this proclivity for suicide on the climate—the English climate impedes the filtration of the "nervous juice," the liquid that supposedly transmitted sensations through the nervous system. When there is a defect in the filtration of this nervous juice, one experiences not pain but rather a certain weariness of life.[159] In 1772 a French author offered an explanation that anticipated the views of Emile Durkheim, asserting that the Protestant Reformation was in large part responsible for the abundance of suicides in England: with the elimination of the confession box, the English had lost an important means of relief from despair. Delisle de Sales, also foreshadowing Durkheim, believed that marriage provided the best salve for anxiety and that the many suicides in England simply reflected the fact that there were too many bachelors there.[160]

---

[156]McManners, *Death and Enlightenment*, 427; Minois, *Histoire du suicide*, 276–77.

[157]Michael J. Seidler, "Kant and the Stoics on Suicide," *Journal of the History of Ideas* 44 (1983): 429–53.

[158]Roland Bartel, "Suicide in Eighteenth-Century England: The Myth of a Reputation," *Huntington Library Quarterly* 23 (1959): 145–58; Minois, "Historien et suicide," 28. Already in the 1760s, Voltaire suggested that the reason that suicide was associated with England was simply because the British gave much fuller press to self-inflicted deaths. Voltaire suggested that in reality there were just as many "mad men" and "heroes" in Paris as in London (intimating that suicide was caused either by insanity or political/philosophical motives). If French journals were less discreet, then the French would rival the English in the area of self-inflicted deaths; see "Caton," in *Oeuvres complètes*, 38:396–97.

[159]Montesquieu, *Esprit des lois*, bk. 14, chap. 12; McManners, *Death and Enlightenment*, 429.

[160]McManners, *Death and Enlightenment*, 429, citing Chomel, *Les nuits parisiennes*, 1.47, and Delisle de Sales, *Essai…sur le corps humain*, 3.322.

The English themselves believed that they were plagued with unusually high numbers of suicides and therefore looked for someone to blame. The Methodists were still convinced that Satan played a decisive role in suicide. They and other religious conservatives blamed the increase in suicide on the free thinking and atheism which they associated with current philosophical trends. By contrast, others blamed the religious zeal of the Methodists and other nonconformists for the increase in self-inflicted deaths. Various Anglicans, such as the physicians Alexander Crichton and William Pargeter, who both wrote in the 1790s, accused the Methodists of contributing to suicide by nurturing the terror of hell, leading people to melancholy and despair. The Anglican clergy viewed a rational religion, free of excesses, promoting social and psychological harmony, as the best safeguard against suicide.[161]

Critics in France bemoaned a dramatic increase in suicide in that country beginning in the 1760s which they blamed on "Anglomania" and on the secular values of the philosophes.[162] A number of French clerics wrote about this "epidemic" of suicides in the late eighteenth century, asserting that unbelief was the root cause. In 1779, Père Laliman, a Dominican, published *Les moyens propres à garantir les hommes du suicide*, in which he criticized medical and climatic explanations for the growing numbers of people who took their lives. Emphasizing moral causes, Laliman believed that the wave of suicide had begun among the English who did not show adequate respect for authority and were receptive to "irreligious speculation." The best way to prevent suicide was to avoid gambling, "possessive love affairs," and immoral literature. Most important, Laliman viewed as paramount the need to discredit the belief that the soul dies with the body. Laliman and other clerical authors observed that the increase in suicide coincided with the growing popularity of works that were antireligious. Laliman even believed that the desecration of corpses was justified as a reminder to others of the eternal punishment that God inflicts for deliber-

---

[161]Minois, *Histoire du suicide*, 255–56.

[162]The printer/bookseller Siméon-Prosper Hardy blamed the growing number of suicides in Paris (1764–89) on the irreligion and immorality of the philosophes; see Jeffrey Merrick, "Patterns and Prosecution of Suicide in Eighteenth-Century Paris," *Historical Reflections* 16 (1989): 2–3. See also Arlette Farge, *Le cours ordinaire des choses dans la cité du XVIIIe siècle* (Paris: Seuil, 1994), 97; Favre, *Mort dans la littérature*, 473; Minois, *Histoire du suicide*, 257.

ately ending one's life.[163]

Similarly, Abbé Nicolas Bergier (1718–90), France's most effective Catholic apologist of the late eighteenth century, authored several antiphilosophe tracts, including an article on suicide. He castigated suicides as lacking the courage to face problems that arise in life. He held the philosophes responsible for the growing frequency of suicide in his day, and favored the most severe penalties against it as a deterrent. Providing the usual Christian arguments against suicide, Bergier insisted that only God, who gives life, may take it away, and that people who commit suicide forsake their responsibility to serve society. Bergier and others also avowed that the philosophes' arguments, with their radical stand on human freedom and their belief in the ultimate insignificance of human life in this vast universe, could be used to condone murder as well as suicide.[164] To some theologians, the issue was quite simple—the growth in unbelief inevitably led to an increase in self-inflicted deaths.

In the late eighteenth century, the philosophes were accordingly on the defensive with regard to suicide. While many philosophes had supported the rational choice of a wise person to end his or her life, they were also sensitive to the criticism claiming that they were responsible for the growing numbers of suicides. Louis Sébastien Mercier derided the notion that the philosophes were to blame for the increase in suicide. Asserting that misery drove people to take their lives, Mercier insisted that the French government was the true culprit because it was responsible for the deplorable social conditions in which so many people lived.[165] In 1770, in his *Système de la Nature*, Holbach endeavored to exculpate the philosophes' defense of suicide. He denied that there is a contract between the individual and society, asserting that the only bond is happiness; once a person has lost happiness, he or she is free to end his or her own life. Holbach insisted, however, that the mere publication

---

[163]McManners, *Death and Enlightenment*, 432–33, citing Laliman, *Moyens propres à garantir les hommes du suicide* (1779), 14, 16–37, 55, 115. In the eighteenth century, the English debated at length the issue of suicide. Theologians issued the same religious arguments against suicide that were later proffered by Laliman. For example, in *A Defense Against the Temptation to Self-Murther* (London, 1726), Isaac Watts blamed the growing number of suicides on "the Sceptical Humour and growing Atheism of the Age with the Disbelief of a future State and of all the Terrors of another World," quoted in Sprott, *English Debate on Suicide*, 117.

[164]Lester G. Crocker, *An Age of Crisis: Man and World in Eighteenth-Century French Thought* (Baltimore: Johns Hopkins Press, 1959), 14; Minois, *Histoire du suicide*, 251–52.

[165]Farge, *Cours ordinaire*, 98.

of this truth was not itself responsible for suicides. While there might be a few modern Catos who were motivated by the desire to escape tyranny, Holbach claimed the huge majority of suicides were caused by physical and mental maladies, many of which were hereditary. Suicide resulted not from philosophical reflection but rather from defects of nature and physical malfunctions, such as a bilious and melancholic constitution.[166] Similarly, Voltaire stressed the connection between suicide and insanity, claiming: "Suicide is not always due to madness. It is said that at times a wise man may take this path. But in general, people do not kill themselves in a fit of reason."[167]

All told, where did Enlightenment thinkers stand with regard to suicide? As a rule, the philosophes enjoyed undercutting the religious arguments against suicide. But while they were in many ways the champions of the rights of the individual, they nonetheless stressed the duties of individuals to society. And while they defended the right to end one's life in the abstract, the philosophes were too much enamored with this world to promote suicide actively in practice. Moreover, like the ancient philosopher Seneca, the philosophes approved of suicides that were motivated by rational consideration. But only a tiny number of the wave of self-inflicted deaths in the late 1700s resembled the heroic, politically motivated suicides of Cato or Socrates;[168] the large majority appeared the result of mental derangement or simple weariness of life, motives with which the philosophes were none too comfortable. The assertions of Holbach, Voltaire, and others on the insignificance of the individual in this vast universe—and concomitantly, the ultimate meaninglessness of the individual's life—certainly did not deter suicidal proclivities. Be that as it may, as John McManners aptly observes, "Even as it faded into the irrationalities of romantic despair, the Enlightenment was less than half sincere in its defense of suicide."[169]

The most important aspect of the Enlightenment's impact on suicide is

---

[166]Paul Henri Thiery d'Holbach, *The System of Nature*, trans. Samuel Wilkinson (London: Thomas Davison, 1820; reprint, New York: Garland, 1984), 1: 341–48; McManners, *Death and Enlightenment*, 433–34; Minois, *Histoire du suicide*, 257.

[167]Voltaire, *Correspondence*, D 13995.

[168]Patrice Higonnet, "Du suicide sentimental au suicide politique," in *La Révolution et la mort*, ed. Elisabeth Liris and Jean-Maurice Bizière (Toulouse: Presses Universitaires du Mirail, 1991), 137–50, maintains that the French Revolution marked a turning point in regard to the way suicide was treated in literature. While suicides depicted in French Enlightenment literature were generally motivated by love, with the Revolution the patriotic, political suicide predominated.

[169]McManners, *Death and Enlightenment*, 437.

the mere fact that the debate on its legitimacy was even taking place. Even if the philosophes' defense of suicide was half hearted, the eighteenth century marked the first time since antiquity that a significant number of Western thinkers did not deny categorically the right to end one's life voluntarily. Even if the philosophes did not advocate voluntary death, eighteenth-century thinkers certainly changed permanently the discourse on suicide. Almost absent from the debate on suicide, even among clerics such as Père Laliman and Abbé Bergier, was any reference to diabolical possession as the cause of suicide. By the late 1700s, Laliman and others who still defended the desecration of the corpses of suicides were definitely going against the tide of opinion concerning the judicial treatment of suicide.

As in Geneva, magistrates throughout Europe stopped confiscating the estates and dragging the bodies of those who took their lives. The Dutch were in the vanguard in this regard. In Amsterdam the last trial conducted against the body of a suicide was in 1658.[170] Authorities abolished the confiscation of the goods of suicides in the American colonies of Pennsylvania and Delaware in 1701, while in 1751 Frederick the Great rescinded penalties against suicide in Prussia.[171] In France the criminal ordinance of 1670, which called for the desecration of suicides' corpses, was not rescinded until the Revolution, but its application became less and less common during the course of the century.[172] While the French royal government favored traditional penalties against the bodies and estates of suicides in the first half of the eighteenth century, thereafter it limited itself to forbidding the publication of accounts of suicide and favored discreet burials over the desecration of corpses. By 1780 French jurists were virtually unanimous in condemning the traditional punishment of suicide, though by that date the penalties were basically dead letters.[173] In Neuchâtel as well, apart from the suicides of prisoners, eighteenth-century judicial authorities became lenient in handling

---

[170]Pieter Spierenburg, *The Broken Spell: A Cultural and Anthropological History of Preindustrial Europe* (New Brunswick, N.J.: Rutgers University Press, 1991), 176–77.

[171]Minois, *Histoire du suicide*, 343.

[172]Fedden, *Suicide*, 229; Joblin, "Suicide à l'époque moderne," 107; Minois, "Historien et suicide," 27.

[173]Minois, *Histoire du suicide*, 338–42. Merrick, "Patterns and Prosecution of Suicide," 30, found that of the 218 suicides recorded in Paris for the years 1764–89, authorities ordered the desecration of only three corpses, the last one in 1772. In late-eighteenth-century Brittany, harsh sentences were still imposed occasionally for suicide. In adjudicating the case of a peasant who had killed himself two years earlier, a tribunal ordered that his assets be confiscated and his body be dragged on a hurdle, hanged by

cases of suicide, in effect decriminalizing it, viewing it as the result of mental illness.[174] In Nürnberg, suicide ceased to be punished in 1778; thereafter the corpses were subject to "quiet" but holy burials.[175] In rural Swabia, while suicides had been cremated in the sixteenth century, they were simply buried without honors in the eighteenth.[176] Though England did not officially decriminalize suicide until 1961, the last country to do so, Parliament abolished the profane burial of suicides in 1823 and the forfeiture of the property of suicides in 1870. The repeal of these laws, however, merely reflected that they had rarely been applied since the late eighteenth century.[177] In short, eighteenth-century Europe witnessed a general de facto if not de jure decriminalization of suicide.

We cannot attribute this attenuation in Geneva and elsewhere specifically to the thought of Beccaria, Montesquieu, or the philosophes in general. At no time in the second half of the eighteenth century do Genevan criminal proceedings or the registers of the Small Council cite any of these thinkers on the issue of suicide. Moreover, while the most important writings in this regard date from the second half of the eighteenth century, with a handful of exceptions, as noted above, the penalties stopped in Geneva in the mid-seventeenth century. The evidence from Geneva suggests that the views on

---

the feet for three hours, and then thrown on the refuse dump; see Minois, *Histoire du suicide*, 325–26. The fact that authorities took so long to arrive at this decision mirrors the fact that by the 1770s such severity was out of step with contemporary mores. McManners, *Death and Enlightenment*, 411, aptly observes, "In a century of progressive refinement in the arts of civilization, the abandonment of the ceremony of dragging on the hurdle, which, on any showing, was of little use, does not require an explanation from the history of ideas."

[174]Philippe Henry, *Crime, justice et société dans la principauté de Neuchâtel au XVIIIe siècle (1707–1806)* (Neuchâtel, Switzerland: Baconnière, 1984), 577–80. Alarmed at what they believed were unprecedented numbers of suicides, Neuchâtel's magistrates in the early nineteenth century did, however, reassert traditional restrictions regarding funerary rites, denying burials with honors to those who took their lives. This practice ended, however, in 1831; see Schnegg, "Justice et suicide," 86–91.

[175]Dieselhorst, "Bestrafung der Selbstmörder," 65, 168.

[176]Karl Wegert, *Popular Culture, Crime, and Social Control in Eighteenth-Century Württemberg* (Stuttgart: Franz Steiner, 1994), 69–70. Wegert further notes the popular opposition among eighteenth-century peasants to the burial of suicides, even without honors, in village cemeteries. For similar popular resistance, see Michael Frank, "Die fehlende Geduld Hiobs: Suizid und Gesellschaft in der Grafschaft Lippe (1600–1800)," in *Trauer, Verzweiflung und Anfechtung*, ed. Signori, 152–87. No trace of such opposition can be found in contemporary Geneva's urban setting.

[177]Patricia Jalland, *Death in the Victorian Family* (Oxford: Oxford University Press, 1996), 70; Minois, *Histoire du suicide*, 344.

penal reform of Beccaria and other Enlightened thinkers were more the effect of changing mentalities already under way than the agents of change themselves.[178] Years before the publication of *Crimes and Punishments*, Geneva witnessed the de facto decriminalization of suicide, even though authorities still viewed it with abhorrence. Many magistrates no doubt shared Pufendorf's view that suicide was wrong because it violated Natural Law. But eighteenth-century authorities understandably did not punish those who sinned against Natural Law with the same rigor that their sixteenth-century counterparts demonstrated toward the "diabolically possessed." While Pufendorf held that suicide violated Natural Law and some philosophes believed it breached the pact between society and the individual, these were not wrongs that lent themselves to punishment. Though they condemned most suicides, neither Pufendorf nor Diderot said anything about punishing suicide as a crime.[179]

As elsewhere in Europe, the last vestige of penalties against suicides was the denial of funerary rites, which ultimately was more symbolic of divine opprobrium than a form of punishment itself. Of the 404 definite suicides that occurred during the course of the early modern period, the Small Council specifically denied traditional funerary rites to 180 suicides. While some of these sentences amounted to a simple statement of "to be buried without

[178]Merrick, "Patterns and Prosecution of Suicide," 40, claims that, in handling suicide cases, French magistrates of the late eighteenth century ceased enforcing "standards of Christian conduct," not because they were rejecting their faith in favor of the Enlightenment but simply because with the expansion of civil jurisdiction, religious imperatives were subordinated to public order. This explanation cannot apply to contemporary Geneva. The city council's jurisdiction was never seriously questioned since the Reformation, and as we shall see in chapter 5, the attitudes of the clergy itself changed dramatically during the course of the eighteenth century. Recent research further suggests that the abolition of judicial torture in many European states in the late eighteenth century owed less to the writings of Beccaria, Voltaire, and other advocates of judicial reform than to changes regarding what could be considered as judicial evidence. John H. Langbein, *Torture and the Law of Proof: Europe and England in the Ancien Régime* (Chicago: University of Chicago Press, 1977), has argued persuasively that the disappearance of torture resulted above all from legal changes whereby judges no longer felt bound to attain absolute certainty of guilt, a requirement that had necessitated judicial torture in order to elicit confessions. Judicial authorities were given more freedom in evaluating evidence and were less compelled to impose capital punishment for serious crimes. In Geneva the abolition of judicial torture (1738) preceded by decades Beccaria's famous treatise; see Porret, *Crime et ses circonstances*, 57–58.

[179]Pufendorf, *De Jure Naturae*, 2: 259–63. MacDonald, "Medicalization of Suicide," 97, asserts that "enlightened" thinkers had only a limited impact on the ruling elite of England on the treatment of suicide; the latter ignored the philosophes' call to repeal laws against suicide, though the penalties were rarely imposed in the late eighteenth century.

honors," others prescribed conditions for the burial which precluded burial with honors. As noted above, being buried outside the normal cemetery was a sign of ignominy. Other interments were ordered to be performed without prayers, without a procession, or without any of the trappings associated with honorable burials. While sixteenth- and seventeenth-century magistrates regularly forbade even the closest survivors to attend the burials of suicides, their eighteenth-century counterparts were generally much more lenient, often allowing a limited number of mourners. In April 1736, for example, Ezechiel Revilliod, sixty-eight, a former military officer and a member of a prestigious family, hanged himself after suffering from an illness, which, on the basis of his physician's testimony, resembled manic depression. Jean Du Pan (1682–1757), Procureur Général for the years 1735–41,[180] declined to prosecute a case against either the body or the estate of Revilliod. The Small Council ruled that Revilliod could be buried in the ordinary cemetery, but that the body could be accompanied by only "five rows of relatives" and that there were to be no prayers said at the interment.[181]

In over 150 cases, the Small Council registers mention a death, often even indicating that it was self-inflicted, without passing any sentence whatsoever. This is particularly true in the late eighteenth century during the explosion of suicides. After 1750, the Small Council specifically allowed full funerary rites for thirteen suicides, denied them for 116 others, but made no statement concerning the interment of the remaining 159. By the end of the eighteenth century, magistrates were above all interested in determining how a person died—they investigated suicides primarily to make sure they were not murders. Although magistrates still denied funerary rites to a little over a fourth of the suicides after 1780, they were decidedly less interested in "punishing" the suicides than their predecessors had been.[182]

By the very end of the period, even the denial of funerary rites fell by the wayside. The last sentence that denied full burial rites for a suicide was that

---

[180]Porret, *Crime et ses circonstances*, xvii.

[181]AEG, EC, LM 59: 84, 29 April 1736; PC 8373; RC 236: 263, 265, 267, 272, 297.

[182]After 1780 the Small Council passed no sentence regarding burial for fully two-thirds of the suicides. Of the 160 suicides, 5 were specifically allowed funerary honors, 45 were denied them, while no mention of burial is made for the 110 others. The demise of 88 of these 110 people was at least mentioned in the Council's registers.

involving the artist-painter Gabriel George, who shot himself in August 1791 after suffering from melancholy and delirium.[183] With the establishment of the new regime in 1792, the de facto decriminalization became de jure, and magistrates even stopped denying funerary rites to suicides. This action paralleled judicial changes in France. Killing oneself was officially decriminalized in the Revolutionary period, when the new penal code of 1791 did not mention suicide at all.[184]

All told, the evidence from Geneva reveals dramatic changes in the judicial treatment of suicide during the course of the early modern period. The evidence from the Reformation era shows that the attitudes and judicial treatment of suicide, though uncompromising and harsh, were in line with intellectual and legal traditions that predated Protestantism by centuries, making it difficult to argue that the conversion to the Reformed faith introduced an age of severity toward suicide. Authorities' suspension of the penalties inflicted on the corpses and estates of suicides mirrored and at times even anticipated the views of European intellectual leaders. Although they did not articulate why they stopped taking actions against the bodies and goods of suicides, Genevan magistrates apparently believed, as Beccaria later declared, that such actions were useless and harmed no one but innocent survivors. The fact that authorities still occasionally denied funerary rites after 1750 to those who took their lives shows that they still abhorred suicide. But even if some Genevan magistrates continued to view suicide as a sin, by the late 1700s they had long stopped ascribing it to demon possession and in effect ceased treating it as a crime. With regard to the judicial treatment of suicide, Geneva definitely experienced a secularization of suicide, similar to that experienced in England beginning in the late seventeenth century.[185] By the very end of the eighteenth century, people who took their lives had been fully transformed from criminals to victims.[186]

---

[183]AEG, EC LM 67: 264, 2 August 1791; PC 16495; RC 298: 1123.

[184]Fedden, *Suicide*, 223.

[185]MacDonald, "Secularization of Suicide"; MacDonald and Murphy, *Sleepless Souls*, 109–216.

[186]See Minois, *Histoire du suicide*, 348.

3

The Social, Economic, and Political Dimensions of Suicide

HAVING EXAMINED the frequency of suicide in early modern Geneva and changing views on and penalties against suicide, we must now look more closely at the suicides themselves. Who committed suicide and why? Did the propensity for suicide vary directly or indirectly with wealth? Some sociologists have found that the very poor and the very rich are both overrepresented among suicides. While wretched poverty may drive some to take their lives, a decline in status or reputation may devastate a wealthy person, perhaps leading to suicide.[1] Can the composite picture of those who took their lives help explain why there was such a dramatic upswing in the number of suicides in Geneva in the late eighteenth century? Were these growing numbers of suicides reflecting dramatic societal changes, akin to Durkheim's anomic suicides? Did self-inflicted deaths mirror the economic vicissitudes of early modern Geneva? Or were cultural changes more important in the growing frequency of voluntary deaths? This and the following two chapters will endeavor to answer these vitally important questions.

MOTIVES FOR SUICIDE

As for motives, the investigations of suicides reveal much about what pushed people to take their lives. From the first extant records until the French Rev-

---

[1]Louis I. Dublin, *Suicide: A Sociological and Statistical Study* (New York: Ronald Press, 1963), 65.

olution, Genevan authorities sought to determine not only whether a death was self-inflicted but also what causes lay behind such voluntary deaths.[2] Indeed identifying motives for suicide was an important part of the process in determining whether a particular death was suicide. Witnesses gave testimony concerning the suicides' character and state of mind, their physical and mental health. Investigations often revealed whether these people had recently suffered personal reversals of a wide variety of forms. In the late eighteenth century, a number of people left suicide notes, many of which tried to explain or justify their actions.

Not all scholars believe that one should even try to determine what pushed individuals to take their lives. Durkheim viewed suicide as a social phenomenon, the explanations for which lie outside individuals, and asserted that the supposed motives for suicide are only the apparent causes. The actual causes are the great collective forces that exist in a given society. He further insisted that statistics concerning motives are nothing more than the opinions of officials who investigate the death: upon discovering a suicide, they simply examine the background of the person to find a likely motive. Durkheim, though he trusted officials' judgment in identifying self-inflicted deaths, viewed their data on motives as unscientific.[3] Other scholars have insisted that the social causes of suicide are not limited to society's great collective forces. The everyday life experiences that push some individuals to kill themselves are every bit as important in determining which people take their lives. Individual motives are ultimately tied to the mores that permeate society: family sentiment, religious beliefs, and attitudes toward wealth are all part of a given culture that will influence the numbers of suicides.[4] Apart from rare cases of mass suicides—or the altruistic suicides, such as the suttee,

---

[2]The criminal proceedings from 1794 on are very sketchy, however. Magistrates for these years were content to establish that a death was suicide and not murder. As a result, I have been unable to identify any motive for sixteen of the last twenty-eight suicides occurring from July 1794 through April 1798.

[3]Emile Durkheim, *Suicide: A Study in Sociology,* trans. John A. Spaulding and George Simpson, edited and with an introduction by George Simpson (New York: Free Press, 1951): 148–49, 297–325.

[4]Maurice Halbwachs, *Les causes du suicide,* foreword by Marcel Mauss (Paris: Félix Alcan, 1930): 512–13. Steve Taylor, *Durkheim and the Study of Suicide* (New York: St. Martin's Press, 1982), 164, has the following defense of studying individual cases of suicide: "The rules or laws of social life...operate only through the conscious, intentional and reflective activity of individuals. It seems reasonable to suppose, therefore, that any student of human behavior should, as far as possible, examine both the intentions of social actors and the details of the social contexts in which they act, for it is precisely these that we seek to explain."

which Durkheim associated with primitive societies—suicide appears to be the ultimate expression of individualism. Accordingly, we ought to investigate why some individuals in a given society choose death.

True, we need to use caution in evaluating the evidence from witnesses and suicide notes. If we were to believe all the testimony of witnesses, then we would have to conclude that many suicides in Reformation Geneva were the direct result of demon possession. The evidence, however, is usually extensive enough, if combined with a little common sense, to give a good idea of what was behind a certain suicide. For example, the criminal proceeding concerning the suicide of Elizabeth Paschal, who jumped to her death in November 1625, makes several references to the devil and demons who tormented her during the months before her death. The evidence of her incoherent speech and outbursts of temper, however, denotes a form of mental illness that was exacerbated by some bitter disputes with her husband.[5] Likewise I have paid little heed to the testimony of a mistress who maintained that her chambermaid who drowned herself in November 1614 had often spoken of the devil and criticized the Reformed faith. I have given more weight to the testimony of other witnesses who avowed that the mistress had made the young woman's life miserable by frequent vicious verbal attacks.[6]

Nonetheless, one may still wonder to what degree we can trust the criminal proceedings with regard to the motives for suicide. Witnesses were perhaps relying excessively on the insight of hindsight in offering explanations as to what drove others to take their lives. Perhaps they gave too much importance to one factor and not enough to another. While the evidence from the criminal proceedings should be used with a degree of caution, it certainly can show some important changes in mentality. Testimony from one era may equate suicide with demon possession, while that from another may see mental illness as the root cause of most self-inflicted deaths. That does not mean of course that demons torment people in one century and disappear in the next, nor that mental illness was suddenly born at a particular time. Such evidence would indicate, however, a very significant change in mentality, denoting the secularization and medicalization of suicide. Like-

[5] AEG, PC 2681bis.
[6] AEG, PC 2e série 2077.

wise, what does it mean if we find many suicides from one period, but none from another, that were allegedly motivated by romantic despair? Even if we cannot be absolutely certain that the witnesses correctly identified the motive behind the suicide, such a change reveals much about popular mentality. If unhappy love stories suddenly began appearing as alleged motives for suicide, this surely means that popular culture in general was placing more importance on romantic love.[7]

On the basis of criminal proceedings and the registers of the Small Council, I have identified plausible motives for 358 of the 404 suicides (see table 24).[8] Although, as we have seen, many eighteenth-century intellectuals

Table 24: Motives for Suicide, 1542–1798[a]

MOTIVES	TOTAL
Physical Illness	96
Problems Related to the Family	89
Alienation	79
Melancholy	71
Poverty	29
Financial Concerns or Reversals	29
Prison/Avoiding Arrest	23
Alcohol	16
Politics	8
Disputes with Masters	8
Miscellaneous Motives	4
Motive Unknown	46
Total Suicides	404

a. Source: Procès Criminels; Registres du Conseil. It was not uncommon for more than one motive to be cited for a suicide.

[7]The most common motive for suicide cited among the ancient Greeks and Romans was shame, an apt reflection of the great importance that Greco-Roman culture placed on honor; see Anton J. L. van Hooff, *From Autothanasia to Suicide: Self-Killing in Classical Antiquity* (London: Routledge, 1990), 107–20.

[8]The 46 for which no motive can be deduced occurred as follows: 2 in 1542–1650, 3 in 1651–1700, 8 in 1701–50, and 33 in 1751–98 (28 after 1780).

admired Seneca and Cato, Genevans were not killing themselves for philosophical reasons but rather for various forms of suffering. Not surprising is the considerable number of suicides in which physical illness, melancholy, or alienation was cited as a factor. Also predictable was the fair number of people who took their lives in prison, some of whom were subjected to torture, or committed suicide to avoid arrest and punishment. Perhaps less predictable is the large number of suicides motivated by concerns pertaining to the family, including the death of a loved one, romantic misadventure, generational conflict, pregnancies outside of marriage, and illegitimate births.[9]

But what is most surprising is the fact that poverty and financial concerns were alleged as motives so infrequently. Destitution and fiscal concerns appear to have been a direct factor in only about a sixth of the suicides with identifiable motives (58 of 358). Not all of those for whom financial concerns were a motive were themselves poor. A few simply were not satisfied with their material wealth, even though they had assets that would have been the envy of most Genevans. Some others killed themselves after a financial reversal which, though lowering their standard of living, did not reduce them to poverty. Does this mean that the poor and downtrodden were not, as one may expect, those most likely to end their lives? People down on their luck, the chronically unemployed, the homeless, skid-row alcoholics, people who feel they have nothing to live for, may seem most prone to end their lives. On the other hand, throughout history many wealthy, powerful, and famous people have taken their lives, causing bewilderment among others envious of their station in life. Did material well-being fail to offer any immunity to suicide in early modern Geneva?

A thorough examination of the social-economic status of those who took their lives in early modern Geneva is necessary to answer these questions. It is essential of course to know how people who committed suicide made a living. Were they in rich and prestigious walks of life, or were they confined to the most humble occupations? Occupational information and other evidence allow us to evaluate the financial status of suicides—were the poor, affluent, or those in between most prone to take their own lives?

[9]The most common motives cited for suicides in Paris of the late 1700s were debts, finances, family problems, and unhappy love stories. Interestingly, only 7 percent of suicides, both attempted and completed, were motivated by illness; Jeffrey Merrick, "Patterns and Prosecution of Suicide in Eighteenth-Century Paris," *Historical Reflections* 16 (1989): 13–19.

Finally, to what degree were suicides integrated politically in the society in which they lived? The rights enjoyed by the residents of early modern municipalities varied immensely depending on political status, and the question arises whether the frequency of suicide varied according to political status. Finally, were there differences between male and female suicides with regard to class and status?

POLITICAL STATUS AND ECONOMIC STRUCTURE IN EARLY MODERN GENEVA

As noted above, the polity established in Geneva in 1536 was no democracy. From its creation through 1792, Citizens generally comprised only a small minority of people living in Geneva. Only those who had citizenship had the right to participate in the General Council, and only a minority of Citizens (in general, wealthy merchants and attorneys) could sit upon the smaller councils. From its inception, the Republic of Geneva was governed by and for the interests of an upper-middle-class elite. While in the early Reformation period pastors provided a certain moral check on the ruling patricians, by the seventeenth century the pastorate was entirely assimilated within the narrow oligarchy, whose power was essentially unfettered by any popular controls. The oligarchic government was paternalistic, as the hardworking patricians recognized they had an obligation to the city's poor. They were consistently obstinate, however, in dealing with the political aspirations of those below them.[10]

Residents of Geneva were divided into six different groups of political status. At all levels, a man's status determined that of his wife and children. At the top of the ladder was Geneva's so-called Bourgeoisie, referring to all those who held citizenship in the Republic: that is, the Citizens and Bourgeois. While one was born a Citizen, a Bourgeois acquired citizenship through naturalization; the Republic recognized as Citizens all those who were born in Geneva to fathers who were Citizens or Bourgeois.[11] Male Citizens had complete political and economic rights; they alone had the right to

---

[10]Patrick O'Mara, "Geneva in the Eighteenth Century: A Socio-Economic Study of the Bourgeois City-State During Its Golden Age" (Ph.D. diss., University of California, Berkeley, 1954), 10, 155–57.

[11]A child of a Genevan Citizen who was born outside the city, even in territory under the jurisdiction of the Republic, ordinarily did not receive citizenship, unless the father had been required to be absent from the city in order to fulfill services to the Republic; see Alfred Perrenoud, *La population de Genève XVIe–XIXe siècles* (Geneva: Société d'histoire et d'archéologie de Genève, 1979), 182, n. 1.

sit on the Small Council. The Small Council determined who would be admitted to the Bourgeoisie, and one had to purchase a "lettre de Bourgeoisie" to become a Bourgeois. Like the Citizen, the Bourgeois had the right to take part in any industrial or commercial activity. Only Citizens and Bourgeois had the right to practice certain professions—they alone could be attorneys, bankers, and, with few exceptions, merchants. The Bourgeois, as members of the General Council, had the right to vote but were excluded from the smaller councils and the principal magisterial positions, such as the office of Syndic. Together, Citizens and Bourgeois were the political community of Geneva. Neither could be expelled from the city of Geneva, unless so sentenced by judicial decree.[12]

All others were essentially considered foreigners, and being born in Geneva did not itself convey any rights of citizenship. Nonetheless those without citizenship were divided into a number of different political categories with varying levels of liberties and privileges. At the bottom were those residing in the city who were, strictly speaking, foreigners. Some of these foreigners sojourned only very briefly in Geneva, while others lived and worked there for years without obtaining the right to residency. The children born of foreigners in Geneva were themselves considered foreigners, unless they petitioned for legal residency. Similar to the status of foreigner was that of Sujet or subject. A large number of rural communities and districts surrounding Geneva—such as Petit-Saconnex, Vandoeuvres, Jussy, Peney, Dardagny, Russin, Avusy—had been fiefs held by Geneva's prince-bishop. With the overthrow of the bishop, these lands passed into the hands of the Republic, and people living in these villages were subjects to the Republic of Geneva. The status of Sujet conveyed no rights of citizenship or even of residency in the city of Geneva, and most Sujets remained in their villages where they did have the right to reside. Some Sujets came to the city to live and work, but unless they petitioned for permanent residency, they had the same rights (or lack thereof) as foreigners.

Habitants and Natifs were, politically speaking, between the Bourgeoisie and foreigners. The status of Habitant was a product of the First Refuge, when Protestants, especially from France, flocked to Geneva in the sixteenth century. Initially magistrates awarded this status, which accorded the right to

[12]Perrenoud, *Population de Genève*, 182–83.

reside in the city, to almost all new arrivals, provided they accepted the Reformed faith. Already in the sixteenth century, however, Genevan magistrates introduced restrictions on immigration. In 1572 the Small Council began demanding that all new arrivals receive its approval in order to stay. In effect, magistrates stopped admitting those who were without any financial resources, particularly those who had entire families to support. Only one form of residency permit existed until 1626, when an important distinction was made between those who petitioned to stay only a few days in Geneva and those who sought to reside there more or less permanently. Henceforth the status of Habitant was clearly defined. An Habitant was a foreigner who received permission to live, work, and marry in the city, provided he leave a deposit with the hospital, which was responsible for poor relief. Magistrates reviewed the residency permits every one to three years, reserving the right to revoke them.[13]

Initially indistinguishable from the Habitants were the Natifs, so called because they were born in Geneva to parents who were either Habitants or themselves Natifs. Magistrates began distinguishing the Natifs from the foreign-born Habitants in the mid-seventeenth century. Natifs enjoyed certain advantages, the most important being the right to purchase, beginning in 1677, a lettre de Bourgeoisie at a reduced rate.[14] Although permitted to reside in Geneva, Natifs and Habitants had no political voice. To obtain the right to vote, a person had to petition to join the ranks of the Bourgeoisie.

During the course of the early modern period, however, the cost of

---

[13]At times Habitants were also required to pay an annual fee for the "right to protection." Such fees were imposed, for example, in the 1650s and 1660s; see Perrenoud, *Population de Genève*, 183–84. A variation of the Habitant was introduced in the second half of the eighteenth century as a result of the increase in immigration. The Domicilié received permission to stay in Geneva on an annual or four-month basis. I have included the Domicilié suicides, of which there were very few, among those of the Habitants. In the late eighteenth century, the difference between the ease of receiving temporary residency and the difficulty of attaining permanent residency was remarkable. In 1789 Genevan authorities admitted 43 people to permanent residency: 14 were Sujets, 17 Swiss, 7 French, and 5 Germans or Vaudois. In the same year, magistrates issued 2,263 *cartes de séjour* (1,356 to Protestants and 907 to Catholics), and renewed residency permits for 744 others (467 for Protestants and 277 for Catholics). These permits, which cost a florin each, were required both of men and women, as evidenced by the Small Council's noting that the *cartes de séjour* (temporary residence cards) were provided free of charge to the wives of soldiers in the garrison; AEG, RC 294: 788–89. It seems highly unlikely that authorities would have admitted 2,263 new residents into the city in a single year. This figure almost certainly includes some people who were already residing in Geneva; see Perrenoud, *Population de Genève*, 328.

[14]Perrenoud, *Population de Genève*, 183.

admission to the Bourgeoisie became increasingly expensive. In the second half of the sixteenth century, the cost of a lettre de Bourgeoisie ranged from 50 to 100 florins, rising to an average of 745 florins in the 1650s, 2,900 florins in the 1680s, 4,800 florins in the 1720s, and 8,400 florins in the 1740s. The exorbitant nature of these prices is evidenced by the fact that in the eighteenth century, a journeyman mason or carpenter typically earned two florins a day. In the 1740s, a lettre de Bourgeoisie would thus be equivalent to ten years of wages for such a worker, if he worked six days a week.[15]

As a result of the rising costs of attaining citizenship, admissions to the Bourgeoisie never again reached the all-time high established at the time of the First Refuge. During the period 1551–75, Geneva received 1,019 people into the Bourgeoisie, including Geneva's most famous refugee, John Calvin. In the following quarter century, admissions fell to 514 and continued to fall thereafter, reaching the nadir in 1676–1700, when only 133 people were admitted. In the first three-quarters of the eighteenth century, magistrates admitted to the Bourgeoisie 298, 164, and 251 people, respectively. In response to political turmoil, 569 new Bourgeois were admitted during the years 1775–92.[16]

Variations in the price of admission to the Bourgeoisie understandably effected significant changes in the breakdown of Geneva's various juridicpolitical groups. Together Citizens and Bourgeois comprised 38.4 percent of Geneva's male population in 1625–29, reaching a peak of 51 percent in 1650–54. Thereafter the percentage of the male population that enjoyed the franchise decreased steadily, dropping to 37 percent in the 1690s and ranging between 28 percent and 30 percent for the first half of the eighteenth century. By the 1770s, less than a fifth (18.8 percent) of men living in Geneva had the right to vote. As one may imagine, with entry into the Bourgeoisie becoming increasingly difficult, the ranks of the Natifs swelled. While they represented only 13.6 percent of the male population in the 1620s, Natifs surged to 26.7 percent in the 1660s, reaching 30.8 percent in the 1740s when they outnumbered Citizens and Bourgeois for the first time. If we look at Habitants, foreigners, and Sujets together—as sources do not always adequately distinguish among these various immigrants—we find

[15]Perrenoud, *Population de Genève*, 185–86.
[16]Perrenoud, *Population de Genève*, 186–87.

that their proportion of the male population declined from 48 percent in the 1620s to 25 percent in the 1660s. Thereafter they increased, fluctuating from the 1690s through the 1780s between about 40 and just over 50 percent of Geneva's male population.[17]

An individual's position in Genevan society was determined not only by political status but also by the profession he or she exercised. A foreigner who worked as a menial laborer would have been worlds apart from a foreign merchant or military officer. To study the occupations of suicides, it is essential first to describe the various professions exercised by Genevans. Genevan professions for men and women (as we will see below, identifying occupations for women is much more challenging) can be divided into two broad categories: those involved in production and those involved in services. Of course the two are not always clear-cut. A goldsmith, for example, often not only produced jewelry but also sold it. Nonetheless insofar as most artisans, such as goldsmiths, spent much more time producing than selling, the division is usually not difficult to discern. Genevan men were indeed a very productive lot. Alfred Perrenoud found that from 1625 to the 1770s, men involved in production averaged from two-thirds to three-fourths of the active male population.[18] Under the rubric of those in production, I have divided occupations into three subcategories, the first of which is comprised of those working in agricultural production: farmers and day laborers, gardeners, vine growers, and so on. Given the urban setting, this was understandably a rather small group, representing 8.7 percent of the active male population in 1625–50 and 3 to 4 percent throughout most of the eigh-

---

[17]In the 1780s these figures for the male population were broken down as follows: Habitants and foreigners respectively comprised 23 percent and 15.4 percent in 1781, and 28.9 percent and 19.9 percent in 1788. I have included the figures for the Domiciliés under the rubric of Habitants. For 1788 Sujets made up 2.6 percent of the male population of the city; see Perrenoud, *Population de Genève*, 192–95. For a brief description of the fluctuating rights of different political rubrics throughout the Old Regime, see Liliane Mottu-Weber, "Le statut des étrangers et de leurs descendants à Genève (XVIe–XVIIIe siècles)," in *Les immigrants et la ville: Insertion, intégration, discrimination (XIIe–XXe siècles)*, ed. Denis Menjot and Jean-Luc Pinol (Paris: L'Hartmattan, 1996), 27–42.

[18]Perrenoud, *Population de Genève*, 156. In his samples, Perrenoud found that those involved in production ranged from 70.1 percent in 1700–1704 to 76.2 percent in 1745–49. Among those he included in production, however, were people employed in *alimentation*. I believe that such occupations—grocers, wine vendors, cheese sellers, and so on—more properly belong in the service sector. Thus, if we exclude those in *alimentation*, we find that Genevans employed in production ranged from 64.8 percent in 1700–1704 to 74.1 percent in 1745–49.

teenth century.[19] The other two groups under the rubric of production are those involved in the creation of nonperishables primarily for local use and those producing largely for export. The former includes those employed in the construction industry, such as carpenters, masons, painters, and woodworkers. Artisans who worked with nonprecious metals—such as blacksmiths, tinsmiths, ironmongers, and locksmiths—made tools, utensils, and arms to serve the needs of Geneva and the surrounding countryside. Those making clothing (other than hosiery) and leather goods—shoemakers, tanners, tailors, and hatters—were also producing almost exclusively for the local market. A handful of other artisans, such as wigmakers and perfumers, also produced for local consumption.[20]

More important in terms of numbers were those involved in production for export. After French refugees established a number of print shops in the Reformation period, publishing became Geneva's first export industry.[21] Soon Geneva became an important publishing center, as printers produced significant amounts of Reformed literature, much of which was destined for France. The paper and printing industry, however, was not very labor-intensive, never employing more than 2.5 percent of the male workforce in early modern Geneva.[22] Other sectors involving the manufacture and export of certain luxury goods employed far more people. As Geneva was poor in natural resources, its residents were understandably attracted to labor-intensive activities. Following the first wave of religious refugees in the mid-sixteenth century, Geneva became an important center for the production of various textiles. Woollen draperies, silk hose and lace, and colorful cotton fabrics known as *indiennes* were all produced in Geneva at various times during the early modern period. Although the volume and value of its exports were rather modest, the wool industry enjoyed the greatest longevity of Geneva's textile industries.[23] Exporting serges, entrepreneurs in the wool industry employed a wide range of workers including carders, spinners, weavers,

---

[19]Perrenoud, *Population de Genève*, 156.

[20]Liliane Mottu-Weber, "Les activités manufacturières," in *L'économie genevoise de la Réforme à la fin de l'Ancien Régime XVIe–XVIIIe siècles*, ed. Anne-Marie Piuz and Liliane Mottu-Weber (Geneva: Société d'histoire et d'archéologie de Genève, 1990), 411–23.

[21]E. William Monter, *Calvin's Geneva* (New York: Robert E. Krieger, 1975), 21.

[22]Perrenoud, *Population de Genève*, 154–56.

[23]Mottu-Weber, "Activités manufacturières," in *Economie genevoise*, ed. Piuz and Mottu-Weber, 423.

dyers, fullers, and shearers. More numerous were those who earned their living working with silk. As a result of the influx of the First Refuge, the silk industry established itself in Geneva in the 1540s. Sundry artisans threw and dyed silk thread, oversaw the mechanical knitting of silk hose, and manufactured velvet and taffeta. The most important part of Geneva's silk industry was the manufacture of passementerie—products such as ribbons, braids, cords, edging, fringes, and other works that were intended as ornamentations for clothing or furniture. Those who produced passementerie and other silk products made up about three-fourths of all textile workers throughout much of the seventeenth century, but their numbers began to decline in the early eighteenth century.[24]

The production of *indiennes* or printed cotton cloth first appeared in Geneva in the late seventeenth century, and reached its peak in the second half of the eighteenth century. Beginning in 1785, however, the printed-cloth industry suffered as a result of French protectionism and disappeared completely in the early nineteenth century. In a certain sense, the printed-cloth industry was quite different from other manufacturing endeavors in early modern Geneva. The manufacture of *indiennes* was the only activity in early modern Geneva that can be described as factory production. While other sectors often utilized various forms of the putting-out system, the printed-cloth industry brought together large numbers of workers in one shop. A few of the largest producers of *indiennes* oversaw all stages of production, receiving raw cotton which was spun and woven into sheets which were then bleached and finally printed in colorful patterns. More common were workshops that received unbleached sheets of cotton, while the smallest shops limited themselves to printing the prepared fabrics. The total process involved washing and bleaching the pieces of fabric which were then stretched out on long tables, and later printed with designs by being pressed with engraved wooden boards or copper plates dipped in dyes. More detailed designs were added by paintbrush, and background colors were added by immersing the fabrics in tubs of dyes. Some of these tasks were performed by skilled artisans—most notably, the contributions of the engravers who made the wooden or copper molds that produced the designs. For the most part,

---

[24]Mottu-Weber, "Activités manufacturières," in *Economie genevoise*, ed. Piuz and Mottu-Weber, 437–55; Perrenoud, *Population de Genève*, 158.

however, the printed-cloth industry involved relatively unskilled laborers who performed a variety of tasks. Unlike other sectors of the textile industries, the manufacture of *indiennes* in Geneva and elsewhere was not at all governed by guilds or any corporate body whatsoever. Most *indienneurs* were members of a semiskilled "proletariat" who generally did not own the means of production and earned modest wages. Moreover, a large portion of the workforce in printed cloth was temporary and seasonal, as most shops shut down entirely in winter.[25] Taken together, the wool, silk, and cotton industries steadily declined in favor of other forms of employment during the course of the early modern period.[26]

While textiles were the most important Genevan export in the sixteenth and seventeenth centuries, they were overtaken by the various products of La Fabrique in the eighteenth century. La Fabrique refers to the manufacture of a variety of goods made with jewelry or precious metals, the most important areas being gilding in the seventeenth century and watchmaking in the eighteenth century. It is rather ironic that Geneva became an important producer of jewelry in the later sixteenth century. The Reformed morality of John Calvin and Theodore Beza forbade personal ostentation and eliminated from the churches the ornate jeweled crosses, chandeliers, statues, and chalices made of silver or gold. Forced to produce for export, religious refugees from France, Italy, and Flanders established themselves in Geneva as goldsmiths, lapidaries, and engravers, effecting dramatic growth in the jewelry trade in the later 1500s. Gilding united the production of silk with metalwork (producing gold and silver thread to decorate braids, lace, and brocades) and employed large numbers of men and women by the late seventeenth century. Although initially less numerous, watchmakers also introduced their trade at the time of the First Refuge. These professions quickly took hold and thrived, and artisans did not wait long to form corporations: the goldsmiths' guild was formed in 1566, and the watchmakers' in 1601.[27] Together those

---

[25]Mottu-Weber, "Activités manufacturières," in *Economie genevoise*, ed. Piuz and Mottu-Weber, 458–66.

[26]Perrenoud, *Population de Genève*, 156, 170.

[27]Mottu-Weber, "Activités manufacturières," in *Economie genevoise*, ed. Piuz and Mottu-Weber, 487; idem, "Women's Place of Work in Geneva under the Old Regime (sixteenth to eighteenth centuries)," in *Forgotten Women of Geneva*, ed. Anne-Marie Käppeli, trans. Rebecca Zorac (Geneva: Metropolis, 1993), 104–7; Anne-Marie Piuz, *Affaires et politique: Recherches sur le commerce de Genève au XVIIe siècle* (Geneva: Jullien, 1964), 14–18, 399–401.

engaged in La Fabrique became ever more important to Geneva's economy during the course of the early modern period. Although La Fabrique employed only 5 percent of the active male population for the period 1625–50, it employed 20 percent in 1725 and about 40 percent by 1788. According to some estimates, by 1788 out of a total population of more than 27,000, 3,000 men and women were employed in watchmaking alone, and 5,000 in all facets of La Fabrique. Estimates have further suggested that by the 1780s, Geneva produced as much as a sixth of the world's watches.[28]

The experiences of those in La Fabrique show that some of these occupations changed considerably during the course of the early modern centuries. When watchmaking originally took hold in Geneva, for example, it resembled a traditional artisanal industry. In a typical shop, a master watchmaker and his journeymen performed all phases of production from beginning to end. In the eighteenth century, by contrast, watchmaking had developed a sophisticated division of labor, built upon a hierarchy of the various phases of production. By the latter part of the eighteenth century, a master watchmaker contracted out the less prestigious tasks in the process of making watches, such as polishing, affixing crystals, making chains, and the like. Moreover, while the watchmaking industry was at first rather open to newcomers, guild rules made admission to the ranks of masters increasingly difficult in the eighteenth century.[29] In spite of these important changes, the similarities between watchmakers of the seventeenth and eighteenth centuries far outweigh the differences. Although less open than before and built upon a greater division of labor, the watchmaking industry of the eighteenth century was still based upon the labors of master artisans and their journeymen and apprentices whose production was regulated by a guild.

La Fabrique definitely provided the most prestigious and most lucrative work for artisans in early modern Geneva. By the eighteenth century, many watchmakers were making a very good living. Many owned their own apartments or even entire buildings, renting out rooms to others. Some watch-

---

[28]Mottu-Weber, "Activités manufacturières," in *Economie genevoise*, ed. Piuz and Mottu-Weber, 487–88; Perrenoud, *Population de Genève*, 156, 170, 176, 178, 544–55; Anne-Marie Piuz, "Négoce et négociants: Les espaces commerciaux," in *Economie genevoise*, ed. Piuz and Mottu-Weber, 556. See also David S. Landes, *Revolution in Time: Clocks and the Making of the Modern World* (Cambridge: Harvard University Press, 1983), 237–56.

[29]Perrenoud, *Population de Genève*, 147.

makers were wealthy enough to acquire plots of land in the surrounding countryside where they built small cottages. It was not uncommon for watchmakers to employ servants, acquire libraries, and invest capital in bonds and annuities.[30] Throughout the early modern period, artisans of all types were for the most part content with their lot, as they rarely agitated for change. On the few occasions that artisans did rise up in protest during the Old Regime, their goals were generally quite modest—rarely did they call for anything more than an increase in pay.[31]

About a fourth to a third of early modern Geneva's active male population was engaged in various areas of services. This group included all those engaged in provisioning or hostelry such as grocers, vendors of wine or cheese, and those who ran taverns, cafés, or inns. Those employed in provisioning consistently represented less than 5 percent of the active male population, and those involved in hostelry represented less than 1 percent.[32] Although not nearly as numerous as those engaged in textiles or La Fabrique, those in provisioning provided sustenance that was essential to the survival of any city. Some of these professions involved formal apprenticeships, and one needed to receive municipal permission to exercise most of them.

The elite in the service sector and in Geneva in general was comprised of merchants and the so-called liberal professions. Merchants, along with bankers and attorneys, were the wealthiest inhabitants of Geneva and had a monopoly on the most powerful positions in the Republic. Some merchants were involved in the commerce of textiles, jewelry, or watches. Others were entrepreneurs in the printing and publishing trade or in the clothing business. Still others were involved in long-distance trade of commodities that passed through Geneva to other locations. Even those who were involved in strictly local commerce could become quite well-to-do through trade in and around Geneva. Those involved in commerce usually comprised about 10 percent of Geneva's population. The liberal professions provided various legal, cultural, and scientific services, and included attorneys and clergymen

---

[30]O'Mara, "Geneva in the Eighteenth Century," 34–37.

[31]Liliane Mottu-Weber, "'Tumultes,' 'complots' et 'monopoles': De quelques mouvements de protestation ou de revendication chez les artisans genevois d'Ancien Régime," *Des archives à la mémoire: Mélanges d'histoire politique, religieuse et sociale offerts à Louis Binz*, ed. Barbara Roth-Lochner, Marc Neuenschwander, and François Walter (Geneva: Société d'histoire et d'archéologie de Genève, 1995), 235–56.

[32]Perrenoud, *Population de Genève*, 156, 170.

who all came from rather prestigious families. Educators and those engaged in the fine arts and health-related fields—physicians, barber-surgeons, and apothecaries—also fall under this rubric, as do clerical workers and administrative assistants. The so-called liberal professions usually represented a little over 5 percent of the active male population.[33]

At the lowest end of the social scale under service are the categories of soldiers (officers, however, were always from well-to-do families) and unskilled workers such as street sweepers, woodcutters, coalmen, laborers, and domestic servants. Workers in these areas did not go through apprenticeships and required no licensing to perform such poorly paid tasks.

There are certain ambiguities inherent in these classifications. A woodworker could be involved in construction, the manufacture of furniture, or both. When the records refer to a painter, we cannot be sure if he was an artist or a painter of buildings. Although records generally indicate those painters employed in La Fabrique as *peintre en émail* or *peintre en vernis*, it is possible that some identified simply as *peintres* were engaged in such production. Barring evidence to the contrary, I have assumed that those men identified simply as painters were employed in painting buildings, as they were undoubtedly more numerous than professional artists. Despite minor shortcomings, these various categories successfully reflect the male workforce in early modern Geneva.

Individuals' political status to a considerable extent determined which occupations were open to them. The economic rights of non-Citizens went through three great phases. Until 1670 Habitants and Natifs could practice virtually the same professions as members of the Bourgeoisie; although they were excluded from the liberal professions, Habitants and Natifs could work as merchants. This was followed by a period of suppression of the economic rights of non-Citizens, lasting roughly from 1670 to 1720. Beginning in 1696 non-Citizens were excluded from commerce, unless they received special permission from Genevan magistrates. They were also denied the possibility of being masters in the principal artisanal professions. Non-Citizens, including Natifs, were denied entry to the apprenticeships of the most lucra-

---

[33]Those men engaged in commerce ranged from a high of 12.4 percent (1625–50 and 1700–1704) of the active population to a low of 6.8 percent in 1725–27. In 1788 merchants made up 8.1 percent of the active male population. The liberal professions, of which attorneys were a part, ranged from 8.2 percent (1725–27) to only 1.2 percent in 1788; Perrenoud, *Population de Genève*, 151, 156, 170.

tive artisanal occupations: *tireurs d'or* (1682),[34] watchmakers (1690), goldsmiths (1701), and engravers (1716). Unless they received special dispensations, the Natifs and Habitants were thus relegated to the more humble professions. For the remainder of the eighteenth century, however, the non-Citizens gradually won back these lost rights. From 1738 to 1753, the Natifs regained the right to work in the various branches of La Fabrique. Under pressure from below, magistrates passed an edict in 1768 allowing Natifs the right to work in commerce and certain liberal professions. In 1782 Natifs were recognized as having the same economic rights as Citizens and Bourgeois, while Habitants were permitted to work in commerce, provided they received permission from the Small Council. With the end of the Old Regime in December 1792 all such class barriers came to an end.[35]

In spite of protectionism, the elite professions were never as closed as the Bourgeoisie's edicts would suggest. Indeed, protectionism was itself a response to important changes in the makeup of those working in commerce and the liberal professions. In the 1620s to 1640s, 90 percent of those in the elite professions were Citizens or Bourgeois. During 1675–94, the Bourgeoisie comprised less than three-fourths of these professions, the remainder held by Habitants and foreigners. As a result of the influx of many affluent Huguenots with the Second Refuge, which followed the Revocation of the Edict of Nantes in 1685, Citizens and Bourgeois made up just over half of those in commerce and the liberal professions in the early 1700s. Habitants and foreigners made up a third of this elite workforce during this time. By the 1720s, the Bourgeoisie again comprised three-fourths of those working in these sectors, although this figure fell to 61 percent in the early 1770s. What these figures show is that notwithstanding the Bourgeoisie's protective measures, a significant number of non-Citizens did indeed receive permission to work in these most lucrative sectors. Citizens and Bourgeois were, quite simply, not numerous enough to fulfill all the commercial needs of Geneva.[36]

---

[34]A *tireur d'or* was an artisan who pushed gold through polished, narrowing holes in order to make fine gold thread; Denis Diderot and Jean Rond d'Alembert, eds., *Encyclopédie, ou Dictionnaire raisonné des sciences, des arts et des métiers*, 28 vols. (Paris: Briasson, David, Le Breton, and Durand, 1751–72), s.v. "Tireur d'or et d'argent."

[35]Perrenoud, *Population de Genève*, 184–85.

[36]Perrenoud, *Population de Genève*, 198–200.

Contrary to what one may think, Habitants were much more likely than Natifs to be allowed to enter these privileged sectors. Although theoretically enjoying fewer privileges than the Natifs, the Habitants outnumbered Natifs among the wealthy of Geneva. By definition foreign-born, some Habitants came to Geneva already quite wealthy. About a fifth of the Huguenots who were admitted as Habitants in the 1690s were merchants, for example. A good number of these new arrivals had the financial means and the business savvy to receive permission to work in commerce or various liberal professions. Even long after the Second Refuge, a third of men employed in commerce and the liberal professions in Geneva were Habitants or foreigners, and up to one in ten members of these political categories worked in these elite occupations.[37]

The Natifs were a more homogeneous group than either the Habitants or the Bourgeoisie. For the seventeenth century as a whole, the Bourgeoisie, who formed 43 percent of the population, had a virtual monopoly on commerce and the liberal professions (84 percent of those fields) and comprised 69 percent of the workforce in La Fabrique. Citizens and Bourgeois, however, represented only 29 percent of those employed in less prestigious artisanal activities (such as those who produced textiles, clothing, leather commodities, and goods made of nonprecious metals) and 9 percent of those in construction and agriculture, areas that were still less remunerative. The Natifs, 21 percent of the population, were not involved at all in commerce but comprised 14 percent of the workforce in La Fabrique, 32 percent of other artisans, and 21 percent of those in construction and agriculture. For Habitants and foreigners, 36 percent of the population, the figures were: 15.4 percent in commerce, 16.5 percent in La Fabrique, 39.3 percent among other artisans, and 70 percent in construction and agriculture. In the eighteenth century, the Bourgeoisie, down to 28 percent of the population, still dominated commerce and the liberal professions, though to a lesser extent (68.4 percent). They no longer were in the majority in La Fabrique (45 per-

---

[37]At no time did the number of Natifs equal that of Habitants in commerce and the liberal professions. Natifs comprised 11.1 percent of those working in these sectors in 1700–1704, at a time when Habitants and foreigners were 33.3 percent of this workforce. In 1770–72, Natifs, on the one hand, and Habitants and foreigners, on the other, respectively made up 6.8 percent and 32.2 percent of men who worked in commerce and the liberal professions. In 1700–1704, 13.3 percent of all Habitants and foreigners were engaged in commerce or the liberal professions; Perrenoud, *Population de Genève*, 198–205.

cent) and almost disappeared among lesser artisans (8 percent) and construction and agriculture (2 percent). Natifs, now 28 percent of the residents of Geneva, made up 7 percent of the elite professions, 41 percent of La Fabrique, 33 percent of other artisans, and 22 percent of construction and agriculture workers. Now comprising 45 percent of the population, Habitants and foreigners increased considerably their share of those in commerce and the liberal professions (25 percent). At the same time, they saw their share of the workforce in La Fabrique decline slightly to 14.5 percent, but now made up half of all lesser artisans and dominated still further the occupations in agriculture and construction (76.5 percent).[38]

These statistics show that to a degree, Geneva's juridic-political categories reflected real class differences. During the course of the seventeenth and eighteenth centuries, the Bourgeoisie increasingly abandoned artisanal production outside La Fabrique. By the 1770s, Citizens and Bourgeois essentially worked either as watchmakers or goldsmiths, on the one hand, or as merchants or practitioners of liberal professions, on the other.[39] Although it was possible to find individual Citizens who were poor, members of the Bourgeoisie tended to range from comfortable to wealthy.

Moreover, the new admissions to the Bourgeoisie changed considerably during the course of the early modern period. In the sixteenth century, artisans made up a majority of the new Bourgeois. With the inflation of the costs of procuring the lettres de Bourgeoisie, however, artisans gave way to members of the liberal professions, who comprised 42.4 percent of all Bourgeois for the seventeenth century. Thereafter, merchants came to predominate among the new admissions to the Bourgeoisie, representing only 5.9 percent of those admitted for 1651–90 but 42.1 percent for 1690–1725, the period of the Second Refuge.[40]

By contrast, the Natifs were the artisanal class par excellence. Throughout the seventeenth and eighteenth centuries, fully 90 percent of Natifs were engaged in production. Natifs far outnumbered Habitants in watchmaking and related industries throughout the eighteenth century, comprising the majority of such workers by the 1770s. Indeed, at that time, half of all Natifs

---

[38]Perrenoud, *Population de Genève*, 203–4.

[39]In 1770–72, 41.4 percent of the Bourgeoisie was employed in commerce or liberal professions, and 46 percent worked in La Fabrique; Perrenoud, *Population de Genève*, 205.

[40]Perrenoud, *Population de Genève*, 187–90.

were employed in La Fabrique. Virtually excluded from the most lucrative professions in commerce and the liberal professions, the Natifs as a group did not enjoy the wealth of the Citizens and Bourgeois. Individual Habitants, on the other hand, tended to be either richer or poorer than the mass of Natifs. While they were amply represented among the elite occupations, the Habitants along with foreigners dominated the most humble professions. Throughout the seventeenth and eighteenth centuries, a fifth to a third of all Habitants and foreigners worked in construction and agriculture, and an eighth to a fourth produced clothing or leather goods, all occupations that were not very remunerative.[41]

Through an examination of marriage contracts from the beginning of the eighteenth century and from the 1770s, Alfred Perrenoud found evidence that confirms the economic differences among the Bourgeoisie, Natifs, and Habitants. Convincingly showing that the large majority of couples signed contracts before marrying, Perrenoud found a strong concentration of wealth in the Bourgeoisie. At the beginning of the century, the Bourgeoisie accounted for about a third of the contracts but three-fourths of the wealth that couples brought into marriage. By the 1770s Citizens and Bourgeois formed only a fourth of the contracts but still represented three-fourths of the wealth. At the other extreme were the Natifs who in 1700–1704 formed a fifth of the marriages but had less than 5 percent of the wealth in all marriage contracts; in the 1770s, Natifs signed a third of the contracts but brought just a twelfth of the total wealth into marriage. Put another way, the typical marriage contract for Citizens and Bourgeois involved wealth that exceeded that for Natifs by tenfold in the early eighteenth century and almost twelvefold in the 1770s. Between these two groups were the Habitants and foreigners, who formed 40 percent to 45 percent of the contracts. The assets that they brought into marriage on the average exceeded those of Natifs by 50 percent to 75 percent.[42]

These data from the marriage contracts demonstrate that the dramatic economic boom Geneva experienced from 1730 to 1785 did not benefit everyone equally. If the assets described in marriage contracts are a reliable barometer, Citizens and Bourgeois on the whole enjoyed a substantial

[41]Perrenoud, *Population de Genève*, 200, 205.
[42]Perrenoud, *Population de Genève*, 209–14; idem, "La population," in *Economie genevoise*, ed. Piuz and Mottu-Weber, 74–77.

increase in their standard of living. Although this increase held true virtually across the board for the Bourgeoisie, it was most pronounced for those in the most lucrative professions—commerce and the liberal professions—for whom the average assets at the formation of marriage increased by over half.[43] The economic boom of eighteenth-century Geneva widened the gap between the elite and everyone else.

Natifs and Habitants were both less homogeneous in the later eighteenth century than at the beginning of the century. The Habitants and foreigners, whose richest, poorest, and intermediate segments were all better off than their Natif counterparts in 1700, had a larger proportion of poor people than the Natifs in the 1770s. Wealthy Habitants, however, continued to outnumber affluent Natifs. Among the Natifs, the poorest and the richest were more numerous in the 1770s than in 1700.[44]

These developments in the relative wealth of the political categories were related to changes in the wealth associated with various professions. The humblest occupations—those employed in agriculture, provisioning, woodworking, construction, and the military (excluding officers)—experienced a decrease in the standard of living. The next step up the ladder, involving artisans in textiles, clothing, and metallurgy, experienced substantial gains (more than 30 percent) in their standard of living, as witnessed by their marriage contracts. Above them were artisans associated with La Fabrique. Watchmakers and goldsmiths signed contracts involving assets worth more than twice those of other artisans in the early 1700s, but their standard of living tended to stagnate during the course of the century. The assets brought into their marriages, though still noticeably higher than other artisans', had increased only modestly by the 1770s. Nonetheless, while the primary beneficiaries of the growth in wealth were the Bourgeoisie, the Natifs also improved their condition considerably, as the proportion of the Natif workforce engaged in La Fabrique tripled. Contemporaneously, their share of those working in agriculture, construction, woodworking, and the military

---

[43]Perrenoud, *Population de Genève*, 221.

[44]The increasing number of poor among the Habitants, however, was something of a fluke. The large number of wealthy merchants and artisans who came to Geneva during the Second Refuge produced a very atypical group of Habitants. Thereafter, immigrants, and consequently Habitants, took on a more traditional complexion, with large numbers of unskilled workers; see Perrenoud, *Population de Genève*, 212–17.

diminished by one-half. While a minority of Habitants and foreigners became wealthier, most were becoming more concentrated in humbler professions which were losing ground financially.[45] Thus while the rich were getting richer in the eighteenth century, those in the humblest professions became poorer. While the largest sector of Geneva's economy, La Fabrique, continued to offer the most lucrative artisanal occupations in the later eighteenth century, its workers were not benefitting to the same degree as merchants and bankers. As we shall see, watchmakers experienced a major decline in their standard of living as their industry entered into a serious crisis beginning in the 1780s, coinciding with the explosion in suicides.

POLITICAL AND ECONOMIC STATUS OF SUICIDE

This background to early modern Genevan society allows a better appreciation of the breakdown by occupation and political and financial status of the suicides of early modern Geneva. Information about the status of those who took their lives is of course fundamentally important to understanding suicide as a social phenomenon. Durkheim himself associated high social status and low external restraint with high suicide rates, and some more recent sociological studies indicate that suicide tends to be less common among those engaged in crafts and manual labor than those employed in more remunerative professions, such as business management.[46] In their work on modern suicide and homicide, Andrew Henry and James Short argued that aggression is often the result of frustration, which can be triggered by economic crises that produce changes in the hierarchical ranking of people and thwart the realization of individuals' goals. As noted in chapter 1, they avowed that people subject to strong external restraint were more likely to commit homicide, while those subject to strong internal restraint were more susceptible to suicide. They believed that people occupying the highest rungs of the social ladder were those most susceptible to suicide; those at the bottom were the least likely to take their lives.[47] Several studies suggest,

---

[45]Perrenoud, *Population de Genève*, 218–21, 226.

[46]Henry Romilly Fedden, *Suicide: A Social and Historical Study* (New York: Benjamin Blom, 1972), 333–34.

[47]Andrew F. Henry and James F. Short, *Suicide and Homicide: Some Economic, Sociological, and Psychological Aspects of Aggression* (Glencoe, Ill.: Free Press, 1954); Ronald W. Maris, "Sociology," in *A Handbook for the Study of Suicide*, ed. Seymour Perlin (New York: Oxford University Press, 1975), 102–5. Martin Gold, "Suicide, Homicide, and the Socialization of Aggression," *American Journal of Sociology* 53

however, an inverse rather than direct relationship between status and suicide. This may mean that strong external restraint may cause frustration which in turn nurtures aggression not only against others but also against oneself. People of the lowest status may be most prone to kill themselves simply because they are the least likely to realize common social goals. Indeed one may argue that the "anomie" which Durkheim described was essentially frustration, not having the means to satisfy one's needs.[48] Moreover, the few extant records of suicide from the medieval period suggest that peasants and artisans, not the affluent, were those most likely to take their lives.[49]

What does the evidence from Geneva reveal? Table 25 shows the civil status of suicides for the entire early modern period. At first glance, the extremes of political status appear quite prominent. Leaving aside the sixteen suicides whose status was unknown, we see that a third of the suicides were Citizens or Bourgeois and a fourth were foreigners. The figure for Citizens, however, is a bit misleading. The Revolution of December 1792 conveyed citizenship to all those who had previously been Habitants or Natifs. True, from then until Geneva's absorption into France in 1798, all Citizens—including the former Habitants and Natifs—enjoyed the same rights and privileges. Yet one may wonder if the economic advantages that Citizens had enjoyed before the Revolution might have given them a degree of wealth which survived the Revolution. It is more appropriate to take into account the pre-Revolutionary status for all those who took their lives during the years 1793–98. Using these criteria, we see in table 26 that Citizens and Bourgeois, Natifs, and foreigners each made up around a fourth of the suicides in early modern Geneva. Close to 15 percent of the suicides were Habi-

---

(1958): 651–61, has rightly questioned whether those of higher social status are less restrained externally. He suggests, for example, that the behavior of army officers may indeed be more limited by "external" restraints—the recognized norms of behavior—than that of enlisted men.

[48]Ronald W. Maris, *Social Forces in Urban Suicide* (Homewood, Ill.: Dorsey Press, 1969), 117–31. See also Warren Breed, "Occupational Mobility and Suicide Among White Males," *American Sociological Review* 28 (1963): 179–88. Elwin Powell, "Occupations, Status, and Suicide," *American Sociological Review* 23 (1958): 137–39, found that suicide rates were highest at opposite ends of the social scale among white males—those in professional-managerial positions and in unskilled labor.

[49]Georges Minois, *Histoire du suicide: La société occidentale face à la mort volontaire* (Paris: Fayard, 1995), 54.

Table 25: Civil Status of Suicides, 1542–1798, Version 1[a]

| STATUS | TOTAL NUMBER AND PERCENTAGE OF POPULATION | | | | | |
| | Males | | Females | | Total | |
	n	%	n	%	n	%
Citizen	94	34.8	29	24.4	123	31.6
Bourgeois	10	3.7	5	4.2	15	3.9
Natif	48	17.8	24	20.2	72	18.5
Habitant	32	11.8	16	13.4	48	12.3
Sujet	22	8.2	14	11.8	36	9.3
Foreigner	64	23.7	31	26.0	95	24.4
Unknown	5	n/a	10	n/a	15	n/a
Total	275		129		404	

a. Source: Etat Civil, Livres des Morts; Procès Criminels; Registres du Conseil. The fifteen people whose civil status cannot be determined are not included in the percentages.

tants, and a little under 10 percent were Sujets.

This breakdown by political status for the entire early modern period differed only slightly among male and female suicides. The most noticeable difference is that the percentage of male suicides who came from the ranks of the Citizens and Bourgeois was somewhat higher than that of female suicides. By the same token, the proportion of female suicides who were foreigners was slightly higher than that for men. As we shall see, this reflects the fact that wealthy suicides were proportionally less common and poor ones more frequent among women than among men.[50]

Taken together, foreigners, Habitants, and Sujets appear to be represented more or less proportionally for much of the early modern period, particularly for male suicides. As they represented between 40 and 50 percent of

[50]Women of course did not have citizenship. They could neither vote nor hold office. Nonetheless the wives, daughters, and mothers of Citizens enjoyed the right to reside permanently in the city and to receive support from the Republic, should they fall into indigence. More important, since their husbands and fathers enjoyed greater economic opportunities than other juridic groups, the wives and daughters of Citizens were likely to enjoy greater financial comfort than women among the ranks of other juridic groups.

Geneva's male population in the early seventeenth century and from the 1690s on, it does not seem out of line that they comprised a little less than half of all early modern suicides, male and female. Among these three groups, however, foreigners predominated. As we have seen, the percentages of people in these various political categories varied throughout the life of the Republic, although foreigners who had not received residency never

Table 26: Civil Status of Suicides, 1542–1798, Version 2[a]

STATUS	TOTAL NUMBER AND PERCENTAGE OF POPULATION					
	Males		Females		Total	
	n	%	*n*	%	*n*	%
Citizen	64	23.8	23	19.5	87	22.5
Bourgeois	12	4.5	5	4.2	17	4.4
Natif	67	24.9	27	22.9	94	24.3
Habitant	38	14.1	18	15.2	56	14.5
Sujet	24	8.9	14	11.9	38	9.8
Foreigner	64	23.8	31	26.3	95	24.5
Unknown	6	n/a	11	n/a	17	n/a
Total	275		129		404	

a. Source: Etat Civil, Livres des Morts; Procès Criminels; Registres du Conseil. The pre-Revolutionary status is used for those Citizens who took their lives after December 1792. The seventeen people whose civil status cannot be determined are not included in the percentages.

made up a fourth of Geneva's population. Foreigners understandably were less integrated in Genevan society than any other group. They were the ones most likely to be lacking a support network of family, friends, and neighbors. Although they might have found some institutional assistance—most notably, French people might be eligible for assistance from Geneva's bourse française—foreigners ran the highest risk of being required to leave the city in case of indigence or even rather minor indiscretions.[51] Still, considering

[51]See Jeannine E. Olson, *Calvin and Social Welfare: Deacons and the Bourse Française* (Selinsgrove, Penn.: Susquehanna University Press and London: Associated University Press, 1989).

that they made up 15 to 20 percent of Geneva's male population in the 1780s, the prevalence of foreigners among suicides does not appear to have been exaggerated.

As for Sujets, their position among suicides is paradoxical. At no time during the early modern period did Sujets comprise a tenth of the population living in the city of Geneva; in 1788 only 2.6 percent of the city's males were Sujets. On the other hand, they made up more than a tenth of the population if we include the territories dependent on Geneva, which were home to the Sujets.[52] Of the 38 early modern suicides involving Sujets, 21 took place in the dependent territories and only 15 in the city itself (evidence is insufficient to pinpoint the location of the other two suicides). When we take the population of the dependent countryside into account, Sujets were thus slightly underrepresented among suicides, a finding that is not very surprising insofar as suicide tended to be less common in rural than in urban settings. The Habitants also appear to be rather underrepresented among suicides. Although we cannot trace with precision the Habitants' proportion of the population over the early modern period, they definitely made up more than 15 percent from the 1690s on.

As the proportion of the population in various political categories fluctuated widely over the early modern period, it is difficult to analyze the suicides of these groups for the entire two and a half centuries. For example, the Bourgeoisie, comprising a little over a fourth of all suicides, appear underrepresented vis-à-vis the population at large for the Reformation era but overrepresented for the late eighteenth century. In any event, information pertaining to political statuses provides only a partial portrait of a suicide's position in Genevan society.

Other information must complement the data on political categories to shed light on the relative wealth enjoyed by individual suicides. The criminal proceedings themselves often provide considerable insight to the financial status of suicides. Occupations and municipal functions alone often sufficed to indicate the class to which a suicide belonged. From the Reformation to

---

[52]For example, in 1789 the population of the city of Geneva was 26,140. Its suburbs had a population of 4,104, which included villages such as Cologny and Petit-Saconnex whose residents were Sujets. In addition, the population of the dependent territories was 4,475. If we include only the population of these dependent territories, then Sujets comprised 12.5 percent of the population of Geneva and the surrounding land under its jurisdiction; AEG, RC 294: 788–89.

the French Revolution, all servant-girls and all soldiers other than officers were of very humble means. By contrast, all members of the Council of Two Hundred and the Small Council were affluent. The testimony of suicides' landlords, servants, co-workers, relatives, and neighbors can also shed important light on their economic status.

Beyond the criminal proceedings, postmortem inventories shed valuable light on the financial status of individuals. Such inventories were routinely made for those who died intestate or left minor children; authorities wanted to ensure that other interested parties did not disregard the rights of minors. Inventories were also made on request when there was a dispute over a person's inheritance. For the entire early modern period, postmortem inventories were conducted for 100 of the 404 definite suicides. Extant inventories are quite rare for those who took their lives prior to the mid-eighteenth century. Only two such inventories (the first in 1679) were made for suicides that occurred before 1700, and only six for people who took their lives for the period 1701–50. They became much more common, however, in the second half of the eighteenth century. Postmortem inventories were conducted for about a third (92 of 288) of the suicides in this half century.[53]

Who was most likely to be the subject of a postmortem inventory? The inheritance of a person who possessed virtually nothing would not likely have been a point of contention. The poor, however, could of course leave minor children, and there were indeed several cases of people who, though very poor, were nonetheless subjects of postmortem inventories. Fanchette Dupont, for example, was a humble servant-girl from the Pays de Vaud who drowned herself in January 1779, apparently because she was pregnant for the second time and suffered from a venereal disease. At the request of her brother, an inventory was made, revealing assets of only a few personal

---

[53]An important shortcoming of these sources is that they were inventories of assets only; they made no mention of the debts of the deceased; see Alfredo Mallet, "Structure et évolution des fortunes à Genève au XVIIIe siècle (d'après les inventaires après décès)" (Mémoire de licence, Université de Genève, 1981), 20. For a good introduction to the nature of these inventories, see Liliane Mottu-Weber, "Inventaires de biens et histoire des activités manufacturières à Genève (XVIe–XVIIIe siècle): Un premier bilan," in *Inventaires après décès et vente de meubles: Apports à une histoire de la vie économique et quotidienne (XIVe–XIXe siècle)*, ed. Micheline Baulant, Anton Schuurman, and Paul Servais (Louvain-La-Neuve: Academia, 1987), 233–42; Barbara Roth-Lochner, *De la banche à l'étude: Une histoire institutionnelle, professionnelle et sociale du notariat genevois sous l'Ancien Régime* (Geneva: Société d'histoire et d'archéologie de Genève, 1997), 378, n. 30.

effects, worth 214 florins.[54] At the other extreme was Jean-Louis Tronchin, alluded to in chapter 2, an attorney who shot himself at the age of twenty-eight following a brief illness in May 1773. The son of Jean-Robert, the former Procureur Général who was best known for his conflict with Rousseau, Tronchin came from a very wealthy and influential Genevan family. The inventory revealed that Jean-Louis, the father of an infant daughter, had brought with him into marriage 72,000 livres.[55] Although the legacies of the wealthy understandably generated more interest than those less affluent, the wealthy were also the least likely to die intestate and the most likely to detail how their estates were to be distributed. Consequently postmortem inquests were made on the estates of less than half of the suicides who were wealthy or comfortable.

Together the various sources provide ample information about the financial status of almost all suicides. Of the 404 definite suicides, I was able to find adequate information on the financial status of all but 44. Excluding these, we find that 47 (13.1 percent) were clearly affluent, 150 (41.7 percent) were poor, and 163 (45.4 percent) were of modest to comfortable means. As noted above, examining these suicides by sex, we find that female suicides tended to be poorer than males. Leaving aside the 34 of unknown financial status, we find that 35 male suicides (14.5 percent) were affluent, almost half (115 of 242) were modest to comfortable, and 93 (38.4 percent) were poor. By contrast, of the female suicides, only 12 (10.2 percent) were wealthy, 48 (40.7 percent) were neither rich nor poor, while half (58 of 118) lived in poverty. (Eleven female suicides were of unknown financial status.)

There were also some variations with regard to the financial status of suicides throughout these two hundred fifty years. When compared to the figures for the entire two and a half centuries, the statistics for the period 1542–1650 were tilted slightly more toward the lower end of the social scale (8.6 percent were well-to-do and 45.7 percent for both those of poor and medium means). For the following century, 1651–1750, however, the wealthy were definitely overrepresented. For that century, over a fourth (17 of 67) of the suicides whose financial status was known were affluent, while 30 (44.8 percent) were poor, and 20 (29.9 percent) were between the two

[54]AEG, EC, LM 65: 249, 13 January 1779; Juridiction Civile F 724; PC 13265.
[55]AEG, Juridiction Civile F 747.

extremes. After 1750 the breakdown by wealth of suicides (10.5 percent wealthy, 40.3 percent poor, and 49.2 percent medium) resembled much more that for the Reformation period than for the century that immediately preceded the explosion.

These data show that in both the Reformation period and in the late eighteenth century, the affluent comprised a little less than one in ten suicides, a figure that is probably roughly in line with their share of the population at large. In the late seventeenth and early eighteenth century, the wealthy were far more prominent among suicides than they were among the general population. Since the early eighteenth century also witnessed the growing gap between the rich and the poor, does this mean that, far from offering a degree of immunity to suicide, wealth helped stimulate suicide? Perhaps, but the fact is that suicide was quite rare through the end of the seventeenth century. Although the suicide rate increased perceptibly after 1700, suicide remained quite uncommon, as Geneva experienced only one suicide per year for the first half of the eighteenth century.

The data on the political statuses of suicides up to 1750 also differ in important ways from the pattern for the entire period (see table 27). For-

Table 27: Civil Status of Suicides, 1542–1750[a]

	TOTAL NUMBER AND PERCENTAGE OF POPULATION					
	Males		Females		Total	
STATUS	n	%	n	%	n	%
Citizen	15	24.6	9	20.9	24	23.1
Bourgeois	7	11.5	2	4.7	9	8.7
Natif	2	3.3	2	4.7	4	3.8
Habitant	11	18.0	7	16.3	18	17.3
Sujet	11	18.0	6	13.9	17	16.3
Foreigner	15	24.6	17	39.5	32	30.8
Unknown	4	n/a	8	n/a	12	n/a
Total	65		51		116	

a. Source: Etat Civil, Livres des Morts; Procès Criminels; Registres du Conseil. The twelve people whose civil status cannot be determined are not included in the percentages.

eigners were more prominent among suicides in the two hundred years before 1750 than in the half century thereafter. Excluding the suicides of unknown status, Habitants, Sujets, and foreigners combined to represent almost two-thirds of all pre-1750 suicides, even though these groups never made up more than about half the population. Thus, foreign-born people who were politically marginal in Geneva really predominated among suicides, killing themselves much more frequently than other groups. For women, this tendency was even more pronounced. This can be attributed to the fact that a good number of female suicides were domestic servants, almost all of whom were foreign born.

Rather surprising was the large number (close to a third of the total) of Citizens and Bourgeois who took their lives during these two centuries. Although this is less than the Bourgeoisie's percentage of the population through the late seventeenth century, Citizens and Bourgeois were proportionally committing more suicides than other groups, save foreigners, in the early eighteenth century.[56] Most surprising of all, however, was the almost total absence of Natifs (only 4 out of 117 suicides), even though ever since the mid-seventeenth century at least one in four inhabitants of Geneva was a Natif. For the first two hundred years of this study, suicide in Geneva, although relatively rare even in the early eighteenth century, involved mainly those who were most and least integrated politically in the Genevan Republic. Citizens and Bourgeois, on the one hand, and foreigners, on the other, had a stronger penchant for suicide than members of other juridic categories.

Concomitantly, for the first two hundred years of this study, there was a real dichotomy with regard to the financial status of suicides. Among Citizens and Bourgeois, over half of those whose financial status was known were obviously wealthy.[57] Among the Habitants, Sujets, and especially the foreigners, however, the poor predominated. Although two of them came from affluent families, twenty-six of the thirty-two foreign-born suicides who took their lives through 1750 were poor.

---

[56]For the period 1701–50, of the fifty-two suicides whose political status was known, nineteen (36.5 percent) were Citizens or Bourgeois. At no time during this half century did the Bourgeoisie represent more than 30 percent of the male population.

[57]Of the thirty-three Citizens and Bourgeois, sixteen were clearly affluent and ten seemed at least comfortable. Although there were two of modest means and five of unknown status, not one Citizen or Bourgeois was poor.

Table 28: Employment Sectors for Male Suicides, 1542–1798[a]

	1542–1750	1751–98	(1781–98)	TOTAL
1. Production for Local Consumption				
Agriculture	9	14	(12)	23
Clothing	1	4	(2)	5
Construction	2	7	(2)	9
Leather	2	10	(2)	12
Nonprecious Metals	1	5	(3)	6
Woodworking/Furniture	0	3	(3)	3
Miscellaneous	0	7	(5)	7
2. Artisanal Production for Export				
La Fabrique (except watches)	0	17	(6)	17
Indiennerie	1	2	(1)	3
Printing	0	1	(0)	1
Silk	0	4	(2)	4
Watchmaking	4	58	(39)	62
Wool	2	1	(0)	3
3. Services				
Clergy	1	1	(0)	2
Clerical/Admin. Assistance	1	3	(2)	4
Commerce/Finance	10	11	(8)	21
Education and Art	1	4	(3)	5
Health	0	2	(1)	2
Hostelry	1	3	(2)	4
Law/Magistracy	2	7	(1)	9
Military	5	12	(4)	17
Provisioning	6	5	(5)	11
Unskilled Labor	2	16	(11)	18
4. Other				
Students	0	6	(4)	6
No Profession	2	5	(2)	7
Profession Unknown	12	2	(2)	14
Total	65	210	(122)	275

a. Source: Etat Civil, Livres des Morts; Procès Criminels; Registres du Conseil.

A full understanding of a person's status obviously depends to a large degree on his or her occupation. Records provide ample evidence for the professions of the vast majority of male suicides (see table 28). Both the death records and the criminal proceedings regularly identified the occupations of adult males. Information about women's work unfortunately is much more difficult to obtain (see table 29). Of the 129 female suicides, I can identify occupations for 43, exactly one-third.[58]

Table 29: Employment Sectors for Female Suicides, 1542–1798[a]

Sector	Total
1. Production for Local Consumption	
Agriculture	3
Clothing	7
2. Artisanal Production for Export	
Indiennerie	1
La Fabrique	1
Silk	2
Watchmaking	2
3. Services	
Domestic Service	24
Education and Art	1
Provisioning	1
Retail Sales	2
Washing	1
Wet-Nursing	1
4. Other	
Profession Unknown	86
Total	129

a. Source: Etat Civil, Livres des Morts; Procès Criminels; Registres du Conseil.

[58]I have listed as *ouvrières de terre* the wives of three rural laborers even though no occupation was listed for the women themselves. In these cases, I have assumed that they performed work typical of women associated with peasant households. I included only those whose husbands' occupations were specifically mentioned and have not assumed that every married woman who lived in the Genevan countryside was involved in agriculture. See also Liliane Mottu-Weber, "Les femmes dans la vie économique de Genève, XVIe–XVIIe siècles," *Bulletin de la Société d'histoire et d'archéologie de Genève* 16 (1979): 388.

That is not to say that the remaining women did not work. On the contrary, they certainly made very important contributions to the household economy. The wives of many artisans, for example, assisted their husbands in their shops, and the contributions of peasant women were invaluable to their households' economies. Many young women spent a few years working in domestic service. Throughout the early modern period, women played important roles in textile industries, reeling silk and spinning wool, tasks most often performed at home. Women from the surrounding countryside often came to Geneva to sell milk, eggs, fruits, and vegetables. Female urban dwellers often worked as retailers; most notably, they commonly operated secondhand shops, ran taverns, and worked in other forms of provisioning.[59]

As in other areas of Europe, however, the economic opportunities available for women declined toward the end of the sixteenth century.[60] A fairly significant number of Genevan women went through apprenticeships in the late sixteenth century, including some who successfully became velvet makers, haberdashers, and even goldsmiths. By the early 1600s, however, such opportunities became much rarer as women were pushed more and more into work that was considered unskilled. In effect, master craftsmen were tightening the controls over their professions. As guilds were formed and became better organized, women were gradually excluded from all the upper levels of trades governed by master craftsmen. In 1566 goldsmiths were the first to exclude women officially from the ranks of masters, and masters for all other trades followed suit. Even when allowed to go through apprenticeships, women could not establish their own shops. Thus by the early seventeenth century, women could work as pinmakers but only as an employee of a male master, and a seamstress generally could work only for her husband, provided that he was a master tailor. Some guilds began accepting female apprentices only if they were the daughters of masters and then eliminated even this privilege during the course of the seventeenth century.[61]

---

[59]Mottu-Weber, "Women's Place of Work," in *Forgotten Women*, ed. Käppeli, 100–3.

[60]See, for example, Natalie Zemon Davis, "Women in the Crafts in Sixteenth-Century Lyon," in *Women and Work in Preindustrial Europe*, ed. Barbara A. Hanawalt (Bloomington, Ind.: University Press, 1986), 167–97.

[61]Mottu-Weber, "Femmes dans la vie économique," 387–400. As in other early modern cities, widows enjoyed the greatest liberties in the area of work. Interestingly, Geneva's largest gilding enterprise

Even when a woman worked outside the home, the judicial documents and death records ordinarily identified her simply as the wife or daughter of a certain man, whose profession was mentioned. At times, the criminal proceedings nonetheless provide valuable evidence of the work that women performed. For example, Gabrielle Gallet, who took her life in June 1762, was described as the daughter of the late Jean Gallet, a master goldsmith. The twenty-four-year-old Gabrielle lived with her mother and brother, a master watchmaker. Having suffered from alienation for several weeks, she had made earlier attempts on her life, causing family and friends to look after her closely. A neighbor woman, Louise Charlotte Bousquet, sixty-two, "out of pity and friendship" had spent the past two weeks living with Gallet, trying to look after her. The afternoon of 11 June, Gallet encouraged Bousquet to get some rest and lie down beside her on the bed. Bousquet agreed. Pretending to sleep for a few minutes, Gallet soon got up. When Bousquet asked where she was going, she replied that she was going to her workbench to do some silk work. Finding the window next to the bench open, however, Gallet jumped out, falling four stories to the street below, dying several hours later.[62] It is only thanks to this remark that we know Gallet worked as a lacemaker. Of the forty-three women whose employment is mentioned, only four were married at the moment of their deaths. Five others were widows and two were separated from their husbands. The remaining thirty-two were single. Women who were most likely to have an occupation listed were those who were unmarried and did not live with their parents.

One reason for the limited evidence on females' work is that, unlike men, the women of early modern cities generally did not identify themselves

---

of the later seventeenth century was headed by a widow, Elisabeth Baulacre, who demonstrated considerable business savvy and has been described as one of the great merchant capitalists of early modern Geneva. When she died in 1693, she had the second largest fortune in the city; see Anne-Marie Piuz, "La fabrique de dorures d'Elisabeth Baulacre," in *A Genève et autour de Genève aux XVIIe et XVIIIe siècles: Etudes d'histoire économiques* (Lausanne, Switzerland: Payot, 1985), 166–83.

[62]The medical treatment that Gallet received could not have helped. The physician Baumgartner had examined her a number of times because of her alienation. He had bled her twice, the second time on 8 June. On 11 June, he prescribed that she be given a mild "purgation" the following day (i.e. the day she jumped). Baumgartner also came to examine her, as she lay dying after jumping. The surgeon Cabanis had administered first aid to her, having stitched up a wound on her head. Baumgartner found that she was still alive, though was rather weak. He immediately ordered that she be bled again! AEG, PC 11018.

with a particular occupation. Female work identity tended to be quite weak in large part because they generally received little formal training for the work they performed. Unlike male artisans, Genevan women—particularly, as we have seen, by the early seventeenth century—usually did not learn their skills through formal apprenticeships and were not members of guilds.[63] Moreover, wages women earned often served to supplement the family income. As Natalie Davis has noted, women therefore had to be very flexible with regard to work. They needed to adapt their work habits to the different stages in their lives, to the needs of their families, and to changes in market conditions and in employment areas that were open to females. Required to do whatever work was available to them at a particular time, urban women had to change the work they performed far more frequently than men. Consequently, women identified themselves much less with their work and much more with their families or neighborhoods.[64]

The one form of female employment that the records consistently identified was that of domestic service, a traditional female domain. Throughout this 250-year period, twenty-four female servants took their lives. A part of a household economy by definition, domestic service was throughout the early modern period the form of work which women could find most readily. The master had responsibilities toward the servant that were similar to those of a father, and women in domestic service were identified not as the wife or daughter but rather as the servant belonging to a particular man or woman.

Extant records reveal that twelve female servants committed suicide during the two hundred years prior to the mid-eighteenth century, and another twelve did so after 1750. While this suggests an increase in the frequency with which servants took their lives in the late eighteenth century, more striking is the decline in the proportion of servants' suicides vis-à-vis those of other women. Up to 1650 servants made up a third of all female suicides (six of eighteen). From the beginning of extant records through 1750, servants comprised over a fourth of all female suicides (twelve of forty-five).

---

[63]Even in the eighteenth century, however, there are a few cases of women going through apprenticeships. For example, Judith Aubert, who drowned herself at the age of seventeen in 1778, had completed an apprenticeship with the seamstress Jeanne Helene Landri from Nyon. During the three years of this apprenticeship, Aubert lived with Landri, just as many male apprentices lived with their masters. Thereafter Landri employed Aubert as an *ouvrière tailleuse* (journeywoman seamstress); AEG, PC 13236. See also E. William Monter, "Women in Calvinist Geneva (1550–1800)," *Signs* 6 (1980): 200.

[64]Davis, "Women in Crafts," in *Women and Work*, ed. Hanawalt, 167–97.

In the second half of the eighteenth century, however, servants made up less than a sixth of all women who took their lives (twelve of seventy-eight). Thus more striking than the increase in the number of suicides among servants was the growing number of suicides among women who were not engaged in domestic service. Moreover, the data suggest that while servants were overrepresented among suicides through the seventeenth century, they killed themselves with a frequency that was not too out of line with their total numbers. At the very end of the period under study, half (49.3 percent) of Geneva's active female population was engaged in various forms of service. The so-called active female population, however, represented only 31.5 percent of all females in Geneva at that time. Consequently, approximately 15.5 percent of all Genevan females were employed in domestic service in 1798, a percentage almost identical to servants' share of late-eighteenth-century suicides.[65] To be sure, servants were still overrepresented among female suicides, as the total population would have included large numbers of children who would have been unlikely candidates for suicide.[66] Still, these data provide palpable evidence that suicide involved less exclusively the economically marginal in the second half of the eighteenth century. The increase in suicides in the late 1700s affected the women and men of Geneva in general, not simply poor servant-girls and soldiers.

If we look at the occupations of male suicides, the figures for the first two hundred years of this study show that suicide was spread out among a wide variety of professions and, consequently, of classes. Of the sixty-six men who took their lives prior to 1750, we know the occupations of fifty-four of them. It is dangerous to make conclusions on the basis of such limited numbers of suicides whose professions can be identified. With this caveat in mind, we nonetheless see some surprising statistics. Although those engaged in production consistently outnumbered those in services by at least two to one in the population at large, suicides were more common among the services: thirty to twenty-two. The most dynamic sectors of Geneva's economy

---

[65]At the end of the eighteenth century, 92.4 percent of those employed in domestic service were women; Perrenoud, *Population de Genève*, 176.

[66]Servants were disproportionately common among female suicides under the age of twenty-five in Victorian Hull, a trend that can be attributed to their vulnerability and their isolation from their families; Victor Bailey, *"This Rash Act": Suicide Across the Life Cycle in the Victorian City* (Stanford: Stanford University Press, 1998), 184–85.

were textiles in the seventeenth century and La Fabrique in the eighteenth. Nonetheless, only seven men working in these sectors took their lives from the mid-sixteenth century through 1750. Records reveal that only three men in textiles killed themselves during these two centuries—two weavers committed suicide in 1591 and 1704, and an *indienneur* took his life in 1735. In La Fabrique, four watchmakers committed suicide, all in the 1730s and 1740s. From the early seventeenth century to 1750, textiles and La Fabrique employed from a fourth to almost 40 percent of Geneva's male labor force. Nonetheless, to the mid-eighteenth century, these two sectors comprised only about an eighth of the male suicides whose professions were known. Equally rare were suicides among artisans producing for local consumption: only six suicides involved men engaged in construction, clothing, leather, and nonprecious metals, even though a fifth to a fourth of Genevans were engaged in these industries.[67]

At first glance, agricultural workers appear overrepresented. Nine peasants, vine workers, and gardeners (16.7 percent of the suicides whose occupations were known) took their lives during the first two centuries of this study. Ever since the early seventeenth century, however, agricultural workers never amounted to more than 8.7 percent of the workforce of the city of Geneva. This discrepancy can be explained, however, by the fact that six of these nine men were Sujets who lived in the neighboring countryside. Consequently, the three agricultural workers in the city of Geneva who took their lives were not out of line with regard to the overall workforce.[68]

Although the military has often been associated with a high incidence of suicide, only five soldiers, including one officer, took their lives during these two centuries. They thus represented 9.3 percent of the male suicides whose occupations were known. It is impossible to know precisely the military's percentage of Geneva's active male population throughout the first two centuries of this study. Death records from the 1730s, a time of peace, suggest that the army comprised 12.6 percent of Geneva's active male population, while the figure for 1798 was only 2.1 percent.[69] The percentage of the population that was engaged in military service undoubtedly varied considerably over the course of these two centuries. It stands to reason that as the threat of

---

[67]Perrenoud, *Population de Genève*, 156.
[68]Perrenoud, *Population de Genève*, 156.
[69]Perrenoud, *Population de Genève*, 154, 170.

invasion declined, the number of soldiers needed in the garrison also diminished. Though three of these suicides took place after 1700—a time when Geneva was not threatened by neighboring states—the military was not a hotbed of suicidal proclivities.

Another sector that is worthy of note among the services is that of provisioning. Six men—a grocer, three confectioners, a vinegar seller, and a baker—committed suicide during the first two hundred years. They thus represented 16.7 percent of the pre-1751 male suicides whose professions were known, more than twice their share of the Genevan workforce.[70] Interestingly, four of these suicides occurred during the years 1639–69. Although this preponderance of those in provisioning among suicides was also found in the late eighteenth century, it appears that this was entirely by chance both in the seventeenth and eighteenth centuries. An ill baker was in a frenzy when he jumped to his death from an upper-story window in August 1639.[71] A pastry cook shot himself in February 1644, suffering from depression three weeks after his wife had died during childbirth.[72] A vinegar maker was violently insane, suffering from paranoia and hallucinations, when he jumped in the Rhône in June 1645.[73] A seventeen-year-old apprentice confectioner, described as melancholic, hanged himself in November 1669.[74] In short, there does not seem to be any socioeconomic basis for the significant number of those involved in provisioning—unless the insane and melancholic were especially attracted to provisioning, or the provisioning trades tended to lead to mental disorders.

Most striking about the professions of suicides before 1750 is the large number of merchants, members of Geneva's elite who enjoyed wealth, political clout, and prestige. Ten merchants—two Habitants and eight Citizens or Bourgeois—committed suicide, thus amounting to almost a fifth of the pre-1751 suicides whose professions are known, outnumbering all other sectors. Eight of these ten merchants took their lives in the first half of the eighteenth century. In Geneva for the years 1701–50, a total of twenty-eight men took their lives, three of whom had no profession listed. Consequently, for that

---

[70]Perrenoud, *Population de Genève*, 156.
[71]AEG, LM 33: 45, 25 August 1639; RC 138: 576–78, 585.
[72]AEG, EC, LM 34: 39v, 14 February 1644; PC 2e série 2476; RC 143: 23v–24, 28.
[73]AEG, EC, LM 34: 72v, 26 June 1645; PC 2e série 2485; RC 144: 66v, 122v.
[74]AEG, Manuscrit Historique 133ter.; PC 4066; RC 169: 404.

half century, merchants comprised about a third of the male suicides whose professions are known, while they made up around 10 percent of the active male population.[75] It was these merchants who were responsible for the affluent being overrepresented among suicides in the late seventeenth and early eighteenth centuries.

The large number of self-inflicted deaths among these affluent, powerful men might appear to suggest that high status came at the price of vulnerability to suicide. Neither the economic history of Geneva nor the criminal proceedings provide evidence that they suffered major reversals, however. Of the eight merchants who took their lives in the early eighteenth century, at least six were clearly quite affluent. Although Jean-Antoine Pelissari, who owned and ran a printing company, had complained about some conflicts with another businessman, his affluence was enviable. Clearly his suicide was more the result of his unstable personality than of any business failure.[76] In only one of the eight suicides were financial concerns referred to as a possible motive for suicide, and that case involved disappointment over an inheritance rather than business reversals.[77] Three of the remaining six suicides had suffered from physical illnesses, another had suffered from melancholy and alcohol abuse, and no motive was cited in the other two cases. Commerce in general thrived in early-eighteenth-century Geneva. Simply put, socioeconomic motives do not appear to have been behind the considerable number of suicides among merchants in the first half of the eighteenth century. As we shall see in the following chapter, cultural explanations are more plausible for this preponderance of wealthy merchants in the early 1700s.

The evidence on both the financial and political status of suicides thus shows that, particularly in the early eighteenth century, wealth and citizenship offered only limited immunity to suicide. This is not to say of course that the handful of affluent Citizens who committed suicide did so because of their wealth and power. Almost all the Citizens and Bourgeois who took

---

[75]Perrenoud, *Population de Genève*, 156.

[76]AEG, PC 8581.

[77]David Gérard was a rather wealthy seventy-year-old clothing merchant who was devastated following his wife's death. According to all reports, however, he was upset not because he had lost his beloved companion, but because his wife had not, as promised, left him half of her estate. The postmortem inventory suggested, however, that his assets were substantial even without his wife's inheritance. His clothing merchandise and real estate holdings (four substantial buildings) were worth tens of thousands of florins; AEG, EC, LM 61: 87, 19 January 1749; Juridiction Civile F 359; PC 9545; RC 249: 28, 31.

their lives through 1750 suffered from physical or mental illnesses.[78] Although affluent Citizens of course did not have a monopoly on mental and physical maladies, foreigners and poor people had so many additional motives to end their lives. Accordingly, up to 1750, physical illnesses, melancholy, and other mental maladies apparently played a role in just under half of the foreign suicides.[79]

The rarity of suicides among the Natif artisans through 1750, however, is quite striking. Politically speaking, the Natifs had reason to be dissatisfied with the status quo and were in the best position to protest Geneva's polity. Born in Geneva, the Natifs knew no home other than the city on the lake. Even if their families had been in the city for generations, Natifs had no political voice, were generally excluded from the most lucrative professions, and were subject to higher taxes than Citizens. They clearly resented their inferior moral status which was implied, for example, by the mandatory deposit upon marriage required of Natifs (but not of Citizens) as a safeguard against their falling into poverty and having children who became wards of the state.[80] As entry into the Bourgeoisie had become prohibitively expensive, few Natifs could expect ever to have the right to vote, which might have enabled them to alter the status quo. The Natifs also continually lost leaders who might have carried the banner for reform; those rich enough to purchase membership into the Bourgeoisie invariably shifted their loyalties and became defenders of the privileged Citizens and Bourgeois. Although Geneva's oligarchy made concessions on a number of occasions, the Natifs remained second-class residents throughout these two centuries. Nonetheless, despite occasional political agitation, the Natifs for the most part accepted their lot. Heavily concentrated in the artisanal professions, Natifs were industrious and were generally assured of making an adequate living in Geneva where they in effect had the right to spend their entire lives. In spite of the Bourgeoisie's protectionist measures, the Natifs became quite promi-

---

[78]Apart from the four suicides for whom no motive can be discerned, mental or physical illness was a factor in all but six of the thirty-three suicides involving Citizens and Bourgeois.

[79]Mental or physical illness was alleged in fifteen of the thirty-two foreign suicides that occurred through 1750.

[80]Natifs and Habitants received tax equality with Citizens in 1782. Previously, they had paid double the rate of Citizens in customs and a third more on real estate transfers. In all fairness, however, the patricians did pay a considerable share of taxes. In cases of financial emergencies, they generally shouldered the burden; O'Mara, "Geneva in the Eighteenth Century," 131, 231–49.

nent in La Fabrique in the early eighteenth century, thus filling the most remunerative artisanal positions. By and large, the Natifs willingly remained in a Republic where they enjoyed a level of financial security unattainable elsewhere. Occasional political frustration was not sufficient to drive Natifs to kill themselves.[81]

But why were Natifs less prone to suicide than the Citizens and Bourgeois? Did the Citizens feel overwhelmed with the burden of governing? That seems implausible inasmuch as Antoine Mallet was the only suicide during these two centuries who was a significant player in Genevan politics, and as an Auditeur, he was not yet a part of the upper echelons of Genevan leaders. A more likely explanation can be found in the lifestyle of Natifs. Throughout these two centuries, the Natifs were consistently able to support themselves and their families by working hard. Unlike foreigners, Natifs rarely were driven to crime or sent to prison, and their daughters generally did not have to work as domestic servants. Although less numerous among the elite professions, Natifs were well established as artisans and, at least after 1700, were less likely to suffer from poverty than foreigners or Sujets. Barring criminal activity, a Natif's risk of being expelled from the city was virtually nonexistent. Unlike some of the wealthiest Citizens, they also did not have the leisure to allow themselves the luxury of getting depressed.[82] In short, up to the mid-eighteenth century, Natifs were likely to be spared the severe hardships and despair that some foreigners suffered in Geneva. But they were also too busy working to make ends meet to succumb to the physical and mental ills that drove a number of wealthy Citizens to take their lives.

More broadly, through 1750 economic trends had virtually no impact on the frequency of suicide. In Reformation Geneva suicides were prominent among the marginal, people who for various reasons were cut off from the community, suicides who apparently conform roughly to Durkheim's

[81]Only eight times during the entire early modern period did people commit suicide apparently because they were upset with political events. All eight—involving four Citizens, three foreigners, and an Habitant—occurred during the chaotic 1780s and 1790s. See below.

[82]A number of eighteenth-century intellectuals and physicians blamed various "maladies of the soul" on idleness, which they associated with the rich, particularly with women of means; Antoinette Emch-Dériaz, *Tissot: Physician of the Enlightenment* (New York: Peter Lang, 1992), 5, 90, 133; Robert Mauzi, *L'idée du bonheur dans la littérature et la pensée françaises au XVIIe siècle* (Paris: Armand Colin, 1969), 160–65.

egoistic suicides, or who suffered from the social isolation which Halbwachs viewed as the quintessential cause of suicide. Prisoners, including four suspected witches, who were by definition pariahs, were prominent among suicides. Nine of the forty-one recorded suicides through 1650 involved people who were either in prison or about to be arrested. To be sure, suicides that took place in prison were invariably discovered, and one might think that this could skew their importance among the total number of self-inflicted deaths. Other evidence confirms, however, that suicide in Reformation Geneva involved above all people who were not well integrated into Genevan society. The prevalence of servants is indicative, as servants not only were poor but were outsiders who often lacked moral support because they were separated from their families. In Reformation Geneva, poorer sorts—the economically marginal—were vastly overrepresented among those who committed self-murder. Through 1650, sixteen of the suicides whose material status could be determined were clearly poor, while only three were rather well-to-do. For the most part, however, the poor, though overrepresented among suicides, were not killing themselves directly because of their poverty or financial reversals. The poverty of the prisoners, suspected witches, and domestic servants who took their lives in Reformation Geneva was only indirectly related to their suicides. Poor people were those most likely to commit theft and to be accused of witchcraft. The miserable conditions in jail and the torture that prisoners endured could cause a reasonable person to look for an escape through death. Mauris de Marset, forty-five, had been in prison for months, suspected of having stolen a large quantity of linen. He was subjected to various forms of torture in order to get a confession and to elicit information on assets he may have hidden. On the morning of 17 July 1613, the day after a torture session, Marset was found hanging by a string from a peg on the wall.[83] Among the half dozen female servants who took their lives during the Reformation period, none did so directly because of their poverty. For example, two twenty-year-old servants drowned themselves in 1612 and 1619 after their masters accused them, respectively, of being pregnant and stealing.[84] In other cases, people were driven to suicide

[83]AEG, EC, LM 24: 155v, 17 July 1613; PC 2151; RC 111: 24, 64, 77, 97, 114, 120r–v, 163, 193r–v.

[84]AEG, EC, LM 24: 129v, 5 August 1612; PC 2e série 2051 and 2130; RC 109: 212r–v.

not by poverty per se but by a particular misfortune or turn of events. In 1629, for example, Maurice Giron, a peasant living near Geneva, hanged himself after suffering from paranoia and alienation after losing a pair of oxen. By all reports, Giron had been an honest, stable, and industrious day laborer until his oxen wandered off into the forest, never to be found again.[85] Although Giron had always been rather poor, it was the loss of the oxen that fatally disrupted his mental equilibrium.

If poverty itself were largely responsible for suicide, one would expect the frequency of suicide to follow directly the ups and downs of the local economy. Historians have suggested that suicide in seventeenth-century France increased in years of bad harvests, high prices of foodstuffs, and outbreaks of the plague. Subsistence crises, aggravated by the devastating wars of the late seventeenth and early eighteenth centuries, certainly did produce growing numbers of poor people in France, for example.[86]

Through the end of the seventeenth century, however, there was no correlation between economic fluctuations and the frequency of suicide in Geneva. In fact, Geneva did not witness a heavy concentration of suicides at any time during the first one hundred fifty years of this study. Famines occurred without provoking a flurry of suicides. A subsistence crisis occurred in 1586–87, but there are no records of any suicides between 1569 and 1591. To be sure, surviving documents are rather spotty for those years. By the end of the seventeenth century, however, death records are entirely intact, and criminal proceedings have been well preserved. The area around Geneva and western Europe in general suffered a number of serious famines in the 1690s (1692, 1693–94, 1698, 1699).[87] In Geneva, the cost of wheat skyrocketed, increasing by about 150 percent in a matter of months in 1693. Aggravating the situation was the presence of large numbers of refugees from France (ever since the 1680s). In 1693 there were 3,300 refugees out of a population of 16,111. To make matters worse, the most dynamic part of Geneva's economy in the latter seventeenth century—the manufacture of

---

[85]AEG, PC 2e série 2293; RC 128: 136.

[86]Minois, *Histoire du suicide*, 181, 219.

[87]In Anjou the price of wheat nearly tripled from November 1691 to September 1693. The famines of 1693–94 caused a large increase in mortality and a significant decline in conceptions in that region of France; François Lebrun, *Les hommes et la mort en Anjou aux 17e et 18e siècles* (Paris: Mouton, 1971), 136, 338–47; Pierre Goubert, *Louis XIV and Twenty Million Frenchmen*, trans. Anne Carter (New York: Vintage Books, 1970), 215–19.

gilded braids and trimmings—went through a very difficult period beginning in 1690. From that date the huge German market was effectively closed to Genevan gilded articles, a reprisal for Geneva's allegedly favoring Louis XIV in his war against the Holy Roman Empire. True, for the previous four decades Geneva's economy had been growing. Genevans averted disaster by encouraging many poor refugees to leave and by the effective administration of "La Chambre des Blés," which oversaw the purchasing, stocking, and distribution of grain.[88] Nonetheless, one would think that the crisis of the 1690s could have spawned a large number of suicides. In fact, only one person committed suicide during the years 1692–99. A single woman of thirty-two, who came from an affluent family, drowned herself in a state of delirium in January 1699. Significantly, her suicide was not the result of food shortages.[89]

We do begin to see a noticeable increase in suicides in the years 1701–30, a period of recession in Geneva. But far from declining, the suicide rate increased considerably during the economic expansion of 1740–85. Although, as noted above, not all Genevans enjoyed a higher living standard during this expansion, fluctuations in cereal prices during these decades had no effect on suicides. In spite of high grain prices, there were only four suicides in 1748 and 1749. Cereal prices were again dangerously high in 1770–71,[90] but there were just six suicides during these two years, as opposed to seven in 1769 alone.

By and large, the evidence from Geneva through 1750 shows that poorer sorts were overrepresented among suicides, although they generally were not killing themselves directly because of their poverty. The most important point of all, however, is that during these two hundred years, suicide was rare for all residents of Geneva, regardless of social class or political rubric. The perceptible upturn in the number of people who took their lives after 1700 was in large part fueled by a burst of suicidal tendencies among affluent merchants. This upswing, however, was independent of social and economic develop-

---

[88] Anne-Marie Piuz, "Chertés et disettes," in *Economie genevoise*, ed. Piuz and Mottu-Weber, 372–78.

[89] Marguerite Revilliod was the daughter of Pierre Revilliod, a member of the Council of Two Hundred; AEG, EC, LM 51: 64v, 19 January 1699.

[90] Anne-Marie Piuz, "Genève des Lumières," in *Histoire de Genève*, ed. Paul Guichonnet (Toulouse: Edouard Privat, 1974), 228–29.

ments. Regardless of whether this resulted from inward aggression associated with high status or, more likely, from cultural changes that simply hit the better-educated people first, even with this increase, Geneva still witnessed on the average just one suicide per year in the first half of the eighteenth century.

THE SOCIAL STATUS OF SUICIDES, 1751–98

What groups of people were most responsible for Geneva's explosion in the late eighteenth century? As for financial status, while the poor were overrepresented among Genevan suicides throughout the early modern period, they comprised a somewhat smaller proportion of suicides in the late eighteenth century (40.3 percent) than that for the previous two centuries (45.1 percent). At the same time, those of modest to comfortable means reached their peak, making up half of the post-1750 suicides, as opposed to 35.3 percent for 1542–1750. If we think in terms of absolute numbers rather than percentages, we see that the most dramatic growth in suicides in the late eighteenth century occurred among those in the middle group. The number of wealthy suicides more than doubled and poor suicides quadrupled from the first to the second half of the eighteenth century. Contemporaneously, however, the number of suicides who were between these two financial extremes increased tenfold, largely because of the growing numbers of suicides among Natif artisans.

Since the proportion of suicides who were poor was lower after 1750 than before, one might assume that poverty and financial concerns must have declined as factors in suicide in the late eighteenth century. That, however, was not the case. As we have seen, the poor who killed themselves in the Reformation era were generally not killing themselves because of their poverty. Moreover, poverty at times could be as much an effect as a cause. A mental illness may be the cause of a person's poverty and may ultimately lead to suicide. In such a scenario, poverty would be at most tangentially related to the suicide. In April 1789, for example, Abraham Saussine, fifty-eight, a poor Natif and former setter of watchcasings, hanged himself in the hospital, where he had been incarcerated for alienation for six months. A hospital worker described him as an "imbecile" who had never done anything wrong to anyone.[91] His insanity was the root cause of his poverty and his suicide.

---

[91]AEG, PC 15680.

Interestingly, of the 58 suicides for whom poverty or financial reversals appeared as motives, 49 of them occurred after 1750. Prior to 1750, poverty and financial affairs were not largely responsible for suicides. Poverty itself appeared as a motive for suicide only twice before 1750, as opposed to 27 times thereafter (23 times after 1780). Other financial concerns were factors in suicides only 7 times before 1750 but 22 times thereafter (12 times after 1780). In short, poverty and financial anxiety were more often motives for suicide after 1750, even though suicide cut across class lines more than ever before.

This may appear to suggest that poverty was more a problem in the late eighteenth century than before. We have seen that the poor got poorer in the eighteenth century and that the 1780s and 1790s were quite turbulent. Many experienced a drop in their standard of living, and there surely were proportionally more poor people in Geneva in the 1790s than a half century before. Moreover, contemporaries, such as Madame de Staël, certainly felt that poverty and financial ruin were fundamentally important in the increase in suicides in France toward the end of the century.[92]

Be that as it may, the appearance of significant numbers of suicides for financial reasons after 1750 had more to do with personal values or cultural changes than with the fluctuations of the economy. Poverty is likely to be a motive for suicide only in highly developed capitalistic societies. In an underdeveloped society where poverty is ubiquitous, few would likely be pushed to end their lives by their material status. In a capitalistic society, however, the loss of money can bring with it a loss of political power, prestige, and self-esteem.[93] In February 1771 the watch merchant Pierre Delor, forty-seven, shot himself the very day that he was making arrangements with creditors for his impending bankruptcy. A widower and father of five, Delor had been most despondent, undoubtedly because of being financially embarrassed. Records reveal that he left assets of 76,000 livres, though his debts were still greater. The bankruptcy agreement that was eventually reached provided for a plan for the payment of creditors while leaving the Delor family with ample resources to continue to lead a rather comfortable exis-

[92]Fedden, *Suicide*, 237.
[93]Fedden, *Suicide*, 54.

tence. In short, Delor's suicide was not motivated because he feared that his children were going to be hungry and dressed in rags. Rather, the shame at having failed in his business pursuits weighed far more heavily on Delor than any form of economic duress that his family suffered.[94]

Durkheim found that anomie was endemic in the society he lived in, and he placed considerable blame for it on moral deregulation vis-à-vis economic pursuits. Traditionally, social equilibrium had been maintained by a moral regimen, accepted by all social classes, which prescribed the relative wealth to which each class could aspire. Durkheim asserted:

> Under this pressure, each in his sphere vaguely realizes the extreme limit set to his ambitions and aspires to nothing beyond.... Truly, there is nothing rigid or absolute about such determination. The economic ideal assigned each class of citizens is itself confined to certain limits, within which the desires have free range.... This relative limitation and the moderation it involves, make men contented with their lot while stimulating them moderately to improve it; and this average contentment causes the feeling of calm, active happiness, the pleasure in existing and living which characterizes health for societies as well as for individuals.[95]

Durkheim claimed, however, that for over a century this moral regulation had been shattered, destroying the social equilibrium. The growth of unbridled capitalism had reduced society to a constant state of anomie as all social classes gave free rein to material desires which could never be satisfied, thus causing frustration and despair. Durkheim viewed the high suicide rates of his day as evidence of the moral ill health of his society, related in large part to capitalistic greed.[96]

The historian Georges Minois believes that capitalism was a key factor in the increase in French and English suicides in the eighteenth century, citing as possible causes the speculative ventures of England's South Sea Bubble and France's "Mississippi Bubble" (associated with John Law's Company), both of which ruined so many investors in 1720. Based on rugged individualism, competition, and risks, capitalism was a source of instability.

---

[94]AEG, Juridiction Civile Fc 12 and Ga 1: 219–58; PC 12133.
[95]Durkheim, *Suicide*, 250.
[96]Durkheim, *Suicide*, 246–57.

As the solidarity of guilds and corporations weakened, the individual became more isolated and more vulnerable to financial ruin. Government protection was quite weak as economic controls were rudimentary at best. In France from 1715 on, banking and finance offered both the greatest possibilities of striking it rich and the greatest dangers of fiscal disaster.[97]

Surely Genevans and western Europeans in general were becoming increasingly materialistic in the eighteenth century. Well before Adam Smith, European thinkers were divorcing economics from morality and appealing to humans' desire for wealth. Already in 1681 John Locke had defended the unequal distribution of goods, even justifying the unlimited accumulation of riches.[98] Anne Robert Jacques Turgot (1727–81), a physiocrat who served as controller-general under Louis XVI, wrote *Réflexions sur la formation et la distribution des richesses* (1766), in which he lauded people who strove to get rich as useful to the state and described as reasonable those who wanted to enjoy their riches. Totally absent from this discussion of economics were issues of morality and legitimacy.[99] Himself a financier, Voltaire acquired considerable wealth through commercial speculation, unabashedly pursuing gain through investments in the African grain trade, Parisian lotteries, and very unpredictable life annuities. While a few philosophes, such as Rousseau, condemned luxury as the greatest source of vice, Voltaire and many other intellectuals, far from being embarrassed by their riches, viewed the accumulation of wealth as the means of becoming independent men of letters.[100]

While sixteenth-century Geneva represented a religious ideal, in the eighteenth century it was the "Bourgeois Republic," serving to protect and

---

[97]Minois, *Histoire du suicide*, 218.

[98]John Locke, *Second Treatise of Civil Government*, in *Political Writings of John Locke*, edited and with an introduction by David Wootton (New York: Mentor, 1993), 273–86.

[99]By contrast, Jacques-André Naigeon (1738–1810) was out of step with contemporary morality when he wrote under "Richesse" in the *Encyclopédie* that wealth led to the corruption of morals; see Yves Citton, "La richesse est un crime: (Im)Moralité de l'accumulation de John Locke à Isabelle de Charrière," in *Etre riche au siècle de Voltaire*, ed. Jacques Berchtold and Michel Porret (Geneva: Droz, 1996), 47–65. In that same volume, see also Marco Geuna, "Richesse, commerce et corruption dans la pensée d'Adam Ferguson," 81–95.

[100]Jacques Berchtold and Michel Porret, introduction to *Etre riche*, ed. Berchtold and Porret, 8–11. In the same volume, see Bronislaw Baczko, "Les richesses de l'Eldorado," 195–203; and Gabriella Silvestrini, "Luxe et richesse dans la pensée de Rousseau," 117–34. Cf. Simon Schama, *The Embarrassment of Riches: An Interpretation of Dutch Culture in the Golden Age* (Berkeley: University of California Press, 1988).

promote the interests of middle-class wealth and status. According to one scholar, for Geneva's middle classes, the eighteenth century was truly the golden age, both literally in the amount of wealth they accumulated and figuratively in the contributions that certain Genevans made to European culture.[101] One issue that is beyond doubt is that eighteenth-century Geneva attained a much higher level of commercial development and greater overall wealth than ever before. Goods from all over the world passed through Geneva, which served as a center of distribution for, among others, the French *Compagnie du Levant*. As noted above, the watchmaking industry flourished until 1785, employing thousands in a sophisticated division of labor. Geneva had also become one of the most important centers for the production of printed cloth.

Geneva was also home to some of the most successful bankers of Europe and, as a financial center, may have been surpassed only by Paris, London, and Amsterdam.[102] The Wars of the League of Augsburg (1688–97) and of the Spanish Succession (1701–14), though devastating to much of Europe, proved most lucrative to bankers in the neutral Republic of Geneva. Since the French banking system was still underdeveloped, Louis XIV had to look elsewhere for loans at high interest in order to pay for mercenaries. In the early decades of the 1700s, Genevans were the trendsetters in European investment banking; though Genevan bankers turned their attention above all toward Paris, where many of them opened offices, they also invested heavily in the East India Company and the Bank of England. Genevan investors escaped largely unscathed by the liquidation of John Law's Company, having had the foresight to withdraw before the disaster of 1720. Toward the end of the century, Genevans possessed about a fifth of the capital in the French Company of the Indies.[103]

---

[101]O'Mara, "Geneva in the Eighteenth Century," 4–5.

[102]O'Mara, "Geneva in the Eighteenth Century," 5–6. For the fullest discussion of Genevan banking and investment in the eighteenth century, see Herbert Lüthy's *La banque protestante en France de la Révocation de l'Edit de Nantes à la Révolution*, 2 vols. (Paris: Service d'Edition et de Vente des Publications d'Education Nationale, 1959–1961).

[103]Dominique Zumkeller, "La banque, genevoise et internationale," in *Genève et la Suisse: Un mariage d'amour et de raison*, ed. Marian Stepczynski (Geneva: Bourse de Genève, 1992), 43–45. One Genevan who did go bankrupt from the Law debacle was the banker Jean-Robert Tronchin (1670–1761). Though a member of a very powerful Genevan family, this Tronchin was not a direct ascendant of his namesake whose son committed suicide in 1773: the former was the first cousin of the latter's father; Lüthy, *Banque protestante*, vol. 2, *De la banque aux finances (1730–1794)*, 177–78.

To be sure, Genevan pastors called for frugality and warned that luxury led to vanity, covetousness, laziness, and moral decadence in general, themes that were echoed by Rousseau who criticized his native city. Be that as it may, men and women of eighteenth-century Geneva could not be deterred from pursuing riches.[104] As the century progressed, residents of Geneva were increasingly drawn to pursue wealth in highly speculative ventures that differed little from gambling. Genevans even of rather modest means shared this lust for gain, as demonstrated in their heavy investment in foreign (especially French) lotteries.

In the second half of the eighteenth century, many Genevans—magistrates, pastors, artisans, bankers, and financiers—engaged in very risky speculative ventures. The most popular form of investment was an unusual form of annuity, devised by Genevan bankers. Jacques Necker (1732–1804), the Genevan who served as controller-general under Louis XVI, aggressively promoted this form of annuity to provide the French monarchy with cash to cope with its ever increasing debts. Through bankers, people could make unusual actuarial investments that in effect amounted to gambling on whether certain other individuals would live. Girls from well-to-do families, usually aged four to seven, were most often the objects of these investments. Probably the most famous of these schemes involved the thirty immortelles de Genève, so called because almost all thirty girls were Genevans. A person would invest an agreed upon sum on the "head" of a girl, receiving annually a fixed sum in return as long as the girl lived. Upon her death, the principal was forfeited and payments stopped. In order to reduce risks, speculators typically invested on the lives of several girls. Interestingly, unless they invested themselves in these annuities, neither the girls nor their families benefitted directly from these bets made on their lives. These investments could not be made, however, without the consent of the girls' parents, many of whom did indeed invest heavily in these life annuities. For the French crown, the advantage of such annuities was that there was no need ever to pay back the principal. The disadvantage for the throne (and the appeal for investors) was that they yielded a higher return: typically 9–10 percent on

---

[104]In the first two decades of the eighteenth century about a third of the Genevans who invested in British securities were women, almost all of whom were widows or had never married; Monter, "Women in Calvinist Geneva," 202.

the principal annually as opposed to about 5 percent for more traditional loans.[105]

To a considerable extent, investments such as these were responsible for Geneva's prosperity, which reached its early modern peak for the city as a whole during the years 1750–85. During those years, Geneva was transformed into a city of investors, where even artisans and retailers often received more money from their investments with the French royal treasury than from practicing their professions. While in 1763 Genevans were reaping approximately 3 million livres a year from such investments, in 1785 they were bringing in four times as much.[106]

Genevans had long been known for their industriousness, making their living through hard work as artisans and merchants while maintaining a modest lifestyle. Calvin had set the tone by abolishing all holidays, meaning that Sundays were the only days off work for Genevans. While Genevan Protestants were not unique in establishing sumptuary laws, into the seventeenth century they were unusually strict in enforcing them.[107] In the eighteenth century, however, Genevans were not averse to flaunting their wealth. Referring to Geneva, Voltaire avowed that there was no city in Europe whose

---

[105]Lüthy, *Banque protestante*, vol. 2, *Banque aux finances*, 464–591; Zumkeller, "Banque genevoise," in *Genève et la Suisse*, ed. Stepczynski, 49–51.

[106]Piuz, "Genève des Lumières," in *Histoire de Genève*, ed. Guichonnet, 233–34. In a sampling of postmortem inventories from the 1770s, Mallet, "Structure et évolution des fortunes," 26–34, found that those in the top quartile had almost three-fourths of their wealth in annuities and stocks. Not surprisingly, postmortem inventories for people from the countryside in the late 1700s reveal the majority of wealth was in land; see Laurence Wiedmer, "Le cadre de vie matériel dans la campagne genevoise au XVIIIe siècle," *Revue du Vieux Genève* 12 (1982): 50–58.

[107]David Hiler and Laurence Wiedmer, "Notes sur le prix du pain et les budgets populaires à Genève dans la première moitié du XVIIIe siècle," *Bulletin du Département d'histoire économique: Université de Genève* 15 (1984–1985): 37; E. William Monter, *Studies in Genevan Government (1563–1605)* (Geneva: Droz, 1964), 67–68; Corinne Walker, "Images du luxe à Genève: Douze années de répression par la Chambre de la Réformation (1646–1658)," *Revue du Vieux Genève* 17 (1987): 21–26. For example, the Small and General Councils passed sumptuary ordinances in October 1626, forbidding, among many other things, gold or silver book clasps and all combinations of gold or silver with silk (e.g. in embroidery, belts, tassels, etc). Weddings and funerals were to be kept simple. For people of low condition, all rings worth more than three écus were prohibited, while the limit was 25 écus for those of average wealth; see *Ordonnances somptuaires* (Geneva: Pierre Aubert, 1631). Into the early seventeenth century, Genevan sumptuary laws were closely tied to religious values, while eighteenth-century laws were based more on socioeconomic than on moral or religious arguments. In the sumptuary law that was passed in 1772, criticism of luxury was quite attenuated compared to earlier laws; Corinne Walker, "Les lois somptuaires ou le rêve d'un ordre social: Evolution et enjeux de la politique somptuaire à Genève (XVIe–XVIIIe siècles)," *Equinoxe: Revue Romande de Sciences Humaines* 11 (1994): 111–27.

residents had more spacious dwellings in proportion to the available territory. Notwithstanding the sumptuary laws, he observed most luxurious furnishings and carriages, which he deemed at least equal to those found at Lyon.[108] In the later eighteenth century, splendid, ostentatious town houses were built for members of Geneva's elite, such as Jean-Robert Tronchin, whose son, Jean-Louis, committed suicide.[109] Evidence from postmortem inventories reveal that the city of Geneva witnessed the birth of a consumer society in the second half of the eighteenth century. Genevans from a wide range of social strata slept in canopied beds, adorned their walls with draperies and tapestries, and sat in easy chairs while they smoked their pipes.[110] Even in death, Genevans became more ostentatious: while Calvin had hoped to see an end to all burial rituals, eighteenth-century Genevan authorities felt compelled to pass ordinances that prescribed which relatives could wear mourning attire, prohibited as ostentatious certain forms of mourning clothes, and forbade the family of the deceased to offer any gifts other than gloves to those in attendance.[111]

It is important to remember, however, that not everyone benefitted from this prosperity. While bankers, financiers, merchants, and many artisans enjoyed increasing levels of wealth into the 1780s, many people below these ranks saw their real wages declining. As we have seen, the eighteenth century witnessed a growing gap between the rich and the middle classes, on the one hand, and the poor, on the other. The economic expansion of the eighteenth century had witnessed the concentration of great sums of wealth in the hands of certain Genevans, enabling them to indulge in conspicuous con-

---

[108]O'Mara, "Geneva in the Eighteenth Century," 89.

[109]Linda Kirk, "'Going Soft': Genevan Decadence in the Eighteenth Century," in *The Identity of Geneva: The Christian Commonwealth, 1564–1864*, ed. John B. Roney and Martin I. Klauber (Westport, Conn.: Greenwood, 1998), 145. Geneva's elite began building large, beautiful town houses in the early 1700s, a trend that accelerated later in the century.

[110]David Hiler and Laurence Wiedmer, "Le rat de la ville et le rat des champs: Une approche comparative des intérieurs ruraux et urbains à Genève dans la seconde partie du XVIIIe siècle," in *Inventaires après décès*, ed. Baulant, Schuurman, and Servais, 131–51. In a sampling of postmortem inventories, Mallet, "Structure et évolution des fortunes," 26–34, found that valuables such as jewelry, silverware, and art objects increased from 6 percent of the value of inventories of the 1730s to 20 percent in the 1770s. In the latter period, even the lowest quartile was putting more wealth into such items than had been the case four decades before.

[111]Charles Du Bois-Melly, *Des usages funèbres et des cimetières à Genève* (Geneva: Jules Carey, 1888), 12–13; Walker, "Images du luxe," 25.

sumption that would have violated sumptuary laws of earlier periods.[112] As the gap between the rich and the poor increased and as Genevan society became more materialistic, individuals were less willing to tolerate the status quo. Even though most levels of Genevan society were better off than ever before for most of the eighteenth century, higher material expectations were more difficult to fulfill, and the increasing difficulty in realizing aspirations provoked dissatisfaction and helped fuel suicidal tendencies. The greater emphasis on materialism clearly was a factor behind the explosion in suicide in late-eighteenth-century Geneva, and probably a significant factor in contemporary increases in self-inflicted deaths elsewhere in Europe.[113]

The French monarchy, however, simply was not going to be able to continue to pay the interest on its colossal debt. When the Revolution arrived in France, its consequences were soon felt in Geneva. Exacerbating a crisis that already existed in La Fabrique and the printed-cloth industry, the fall of the French monarchy brought with it the collapse of several Genevan banks in the early 1790s, leaving many individuals with nothing to show for their investments. Not surprisingly, bankruptcies among Genevans, which had increased dramatically since 1770, reached their peak in the years 1792–96. The collapse of banks certainly had an immediate impact on many Genevans.[114]

---

[112]David Hiler, "Fiscalité, conjoncture et consommation à Genève au XVIIIe siècle," *Bulletin du Département d'histoire économique: Université de Genève* 13 (1982–1983): 40–45; idem, "Permanences et innovations alimentaires: L'évolution de la consommation des Genevois pendant le XVIIIe siècle," *Bulletin de la Société d'histoire et d'archéologie de Genève* 18 (1984): 23–48; Corinne Walker, "Les pratiques de la richesse: Riches Genevois au XVIIIe siècle," in *Etre riche*, ed. Berchtold and Porret, 135–60.

[113]Observing an increase in suicides in Prussia in the 1780s, contemporaries cited debts as the most common motive, which in turn stemmed from the spread of luxury; see Henri Brunschwig, *Enlightenment and Romanticism in Eighteenth-Century Prussia*, trans. Frank Jellinek (Chicago: University of Chicago Press, 1974), 220. Fedden, *Suicide*, 200–3, suggests that a moral factor may have contributed to poverty as a motive for suicide. He correctly observes that Puritans (and, one may add, early modern Calvinists in general) increasingly viewed the poor as morally responsible for their plight. Moreover, some Calvinists viewed prosperity as a sign of election and, concomitantly, poverty as a mark of being damned. As this view became assimilated, the poor of eighteenth-century England were both social and moral outcasts and suffered more than ever before.

[114]Jean-David Dallinge, "Dépôts de bilans et papiers de faillites à Genève durant la seconde moitié du XVIIIe siècle" (Mémoire de licence, Université de Genève, 1992). Following the overthrow of the Old Regime, however, the financial situation soon improved, resulting in the establishment of several new banks beginning in the mid-1790s. These new banks effectively helped restore stability to Geneva, investing in commercial activities associated with silk, precious metals, insurance, and transportation; see Zumkeller, "Banque genevoise," in *Genève et la Suisse*, ed. Stepczynski, 53–54.

What impact did the economic crisis have on suicide? Durkheim asserted that dramatic economic change—be it increasing prosperity or a depression—contributed to growing numbers of suicides, arguing that changes in either direction contributed to anomie or moral deregulation.[115] Most sociological studies of suicide indicate, however, that suicide rates generally increase with economic depressions but decline in times of prosperity and full employment—studies in fact have shown that the suicide rate for unemployed American workers is thirty times the national average.[116] We can say without hesitation that Geneva's economic tribulations of the 1780s and 1790s contributed to the explosion in suicides of those two decades.

The statistics concerning the professions of male suicides for the years 1781–1798 yield some interesting results (see table 28). If we compare the proportions of men employed in the three major categories—production for local markets, production for export, and services—the percentages conform roughly to those of the active male population in each. Excluding students and those of unknown employment status, we find that those working in the service sectors comprised 32.5 percent of the suicides, just a little over their share for the male population as a whole. Those producing for export were overrepresented among suicides by about 2 to 3 percentage points, and those producing for local markets were underrepresented by about 5 percentage points.

It is worth looking at a few occupations that stand out among suicides. At first glance, agricultural workers appear to have killed themselves in disproportionately large numbers, a finding that seems to contradict the traditional belief that suicide is more an urban than a rural phenomenon. However, since five of these twelve men were Sujets living in dependent territories (and therefore not counted in the city's population) and two were foreigners who committed suicide in prison, agricultural workers did not have an undue penchant for suicide. Artisans producing for local markets— be they in construction or the manufacture of wooden products, clothing

---

[115]Durkheim, *Suicide*, 241–47.

[116]Steven Stack and Ain Haas, "The Effect of Unemployment Duration on National Suicide Rates: A Time Series Analysis, 1948–1982," *Sociological Focus* 17 (1984): 20. See also Dublin, *Suicide*, 17, 65; Halbwachs, *Causes du suicide*, 362–74; Andrew F. Henry and James Short, "Suicide and External Restraint," in *The Sociology of Suicide: A Selection of Readings*, ed. Anthony Giddens (London: Frank Cass, 1971), 63.

and leather goods, or products of nonprecious metals—tended to be under-represented among suicides after 1780. Relatively few carpenters, coopers, tailors, and blacksmiths took their lives, even though their jobs were considerably less remunerative than those in La Fabrique (and their standard of living declined vis-à-vis those in more prestigious occupations in the eighteenth century). Among those producing for local markets, only wigmakers were overrepresented among suicides after 1780. Significantly, all four of these wigmakers took their lives in the 1790s. It stands to reason that during periods of economic distress, wigmakers may have had trouble finding work. Wigs and other luxury goods would logically have been among the first products that people would have renounced, and quite simply wigs, particularly for men, were declining in popularity. Moreover, during the Revolutionary period—three of the suicides occurred after the Revolution of 1792—the powdered wigs of men could be viewed as symbolic of Old Regime aristocratic decadence. Indeed, one master wigmaker, Marc Galland, who shot himself to death in August 1793, had complained to his brother that he had little work since the Revolution.[117] In short, wigmakers should have felt acutely the economic woes of the late eighteenth century. With the exception of wigmakers, however, those who produced for local consumption tended to be underrepresented or proportionally present among late-eighteenth-century suicides, a trend that also held true for most occupations involved in production for export.

Watchmakers, by contrast, comprised the largest occupational group among suicides and were strikingly overrepresented among them. Fifty-eight male watchmakers took their lives between 1751 and 1798, thirty-nine of them after 1780. The dominant sector in La Fabrique, watchmaking employed 28.4 percent of Geneva's male workforce in both 1788 and 1798. After 1780, however, those employed in the various stages of watchmaking comprised 34.2 percent of the male suicides whose occupation is known. In other words, suicides among watchmakers were 20.4 percent more common than their importance in the workforce would have dictated.

This propensity for suicide leads one to ponder whether watchmakers were subject to occupational hazards, such as industrial contamination that might lead to mental problems and, subsequently, to suicide. Although gild-

[117]AEG, Juridiction Civile F 831; PC 17025.

ers did run the risk of mercury poisoning which could cause physical and mental illnesses, including depression, this does not appear to have been a factor behind the plethora of suicides in watchmaking. To begin with, the criminal proceedings provide no evidence that these men had suffered from the various physical ailments, such as tremors, resulting from mercury poisoning. More important, women, as the majority of those who performed the lowly task of gilding,[118] were at considerable risk of mercury poisoning, yet the watchmakers who took their lives in the last two decades of the eighteenth century were all males.

Social and economic causes therefore appear to have been the culprit. For most of the eighteenth century, La Fabrique flourished in Geneva, although there were some brief periods of troubles. In 1766, for example, France forbade the importation of watches and related products, a blockade that lasted several months. In 1770 Genevan authorities made certain concessions to disgruntled Natifs who sought enhanced rights to work in La Fabrique. At the same time, however, Genevan magistrates decided to take legal action against the ringleaders of these Natifs. By so doing, they caused the emigration of a considerable number of artisans employed in La Fabrique, who, encouraged by Voltaire, established themselves in France at Versoix and Port-Choiseul, in direct competition with Genevan watchmakers. Apart from these ephemeral vicissitudes, La Fabrique flourished until the crisis that began in 1785, and lasted for decades.[119] Significantly, of the sixty-four people (sixty-two men and two women) involved in watchmaking who committed suicide during the life of the Genevan Republic, thirty of them (all men) did so from 1785 on. Quite simply, a growing number of watchmakers found themselves in difficult situations beginning in 1785.

For some in the watchmaking industry, a difficult situation was made worse by technological change. Changes in watchmaking techniques rendered obsolete the skills of some artisans. In December 1785, the Natif Abraham Delaine, twenty-three, a setter of watchcasings, killed himself by taking arsenic. According to his employer, Jean Pierre Rivoire, Delaine had showed considerable talent and had made a decent living when he worked in the manufacture of "the old style" of watches. With the introduction of new

---

[118]Mottu-Weber, "Women's Place of Work," in *Forgotten Women*, ed. Käppeli, 102–5.
[119]Mottu-Weber, "Activités manufacturières," in *Economie genevoise*, ed. Piuz and Mottu-Weber, 495.

styles and techniques, however, Delaine found himself compelled to come work for Rivoire to learn the new methods. This was almost as if he were beginning a second apprenticeship, and Rivoire attested that Delaine was upset about the considerable loss in income that he suffered as a result of technological change.[120] Another good example of the trials and tribulations of Genevan watchmakers was the suicide of Pierre Dombre, who shot himself in June 1787 at the age of forty-seven. A Natif and amateur poet, Dombre left a number of letters explaining and justifying his decision to take his life. Among various personal reversals, Dombre complained that the switches he made for watches had largely become obsolete, replaced by "rollers" which Dombre did not know how to make. Without work, Dombre explained that he had neither the courage nor the will to learn a new trade and was thus condemned to a life of poverty.[121]

Of course, suicidal proclivities and work failure might both stem from other problems, such as depression or alcoholism.[122] Nevertheless, when a jump in the number of suicides coincides with economic crisis (with particularly large numbers of self-inflicted deaths in those sectors that are especially hard hit), we cannot help but conclude that economic reversals nurture suicidal tendencies. In both eighteenth-century Geneva and contemporary Western societies, job loss may cause a loss of self-confidence and self-esteem, stress resulting from economic hardship, depression, avoidance of friends, and general social isolation, all of which make one more susceptible to suicide.[123]

Although the economic downturn played a vitally important role in the large number of suicides involving people in the watchmaking industry, it is interesting to note that these generally did not involve the most modest of these professions. By the eighteenth century, the watchmaking industry's sophisticated division of labor involved about forty different categories of work. Unable to become master watchmakers, women comprised the majority of some watchmaking occupations. These included polishers, gilders, emptiers, case coverers, and makers of hairsprings, bows, hinges, small

---

[120]AEG, PC 14795.
[121]AEG, PC 15188.
[122]See Maris, "Sociology," in *Handbook for Study of Suicide*, ed. Perlin, 108.
[123]See Steven Stack, "Divorce and Suicide: A Time Series Analysis, 1933–1970," *Journal of Family Issues* 2 (1981): 79; Stack and Haas, "Effect of Unemployment Duration," 19.

chains, and watch hands, all of which involved tasks that were poorly paid and at times posed health dangers, such as mercury poisoning.[124] While some of the sixty-two male watchmakers who committed suicide were identified with a specialized function—such as setter of watchcasings or polisher—forty-three were simply identified as *horlogers*, or watchmakers. Only one of the sixty-two was specifically identified as an apprentice, although undoubtedly there were others (such as the eighteen-year-old André de la Rue who poisoned himself in October of 1793).[125] More of them were journeymen watchmakers who worked for masters. Most likely, some of the men described as *horlogers* did work that was limited to some of the less well paid tasks in watchmaking. But a few clearly were master craftsmen themselves. Ferdinand Kannenworf, who shot himself in June 1793, was specifically listed as a master.[126] Even if most who committed suicide did not have their own shops, these watchmakers were generally not from the lower echelons of the industry. The watchmakers who took their lives had acquired knowledge and skills through years of work. They enjoyed good prospects for making a decent living up until 1785. Suffering from frustrated expectations, so many watchmakers, like Pierre Dombre, were unwilling or unable to find employment in other areas.[127]

Quite different, however, were the experiences of those engaged in the other sectors of La Fabrique. Jewelers, goldsmiths, and other similar occupations made up about 10 percent of the workforce, but only six men in these professions took their lives after 1780. At first glance this striking discrepancy is most surprising since it is difficult to separate entirely these *industries d'art* from watchmaking. In Geneva much of the work of goldsmiths and jewelers was in service to the watchmaking industry. Nevertheless, even though the same merchants tended to sell both watches and jewelry, they found less opposition to jewelry than to watches in France. To protect the

---

[124]Mottu-Weber, "Activités manufacturières," in *Economie genevoise*, ed. Piuz and Mottu-Weber, 491.

[125]AEG, EC, LM 68: 82, 16 October 1793; PC 17092.

[126]Be that as it may, financial concerns clearly were a motive for this suicide. Friends reported that Kannenworf had complained about not having enough work; AEG, PC 16952.

[127]In the city of Hull in the Victorian era, Victor Bailey, *"This Rash Act,"* 161, found that an inordinate number of male suicides and a significant, though smaller, percentage of female suicides were unemployed. Overrepresented among men and women who took their lives were skilled and semiskilled workers.

Parisian watch industry, the French passed a number of edicts intended to ruin the Genevan and Swiss watchmaking industries. In 1796, for example, the French forbade the passage of Genevan watches through France to Spain, alleging that they were of inferior quality and contained parts made of English steel.[128] Those involved in the jewelry industry did not face the same hostility; Genevan jewelers and goldsmiths were accordingly not in as difficult a situation as watchmakers.

The experiences of textile workers with regard to suicide could not have been more different from those of watchmakers. Although by the 1780s La Fabrique had long surpassed textiles as the dominant sector in Geneva's economy, the years 1765–85 marked the zenith for the manufacture of *indiennes* with fully eleven factories in operation. The precise number of people involved in the production of *indiennes* cannot be known. Although census data indicate fewer than three hundred people employed in *indiennerie* in the 1780s and 1790s, reliable contemporary accounts indicate that in 1784 there were 1,900 employees in one factory alone, the Fazy Fabrique des Bergues, and about three thousand altogether engaged in *indiennerie* in Geneva and its environs. Part of the discrepancy in the sources concerning the numbers employed can be attributed to the use of child labor: the occupations of children were not listed on census roles, and elsewhere children made up about a third of the labor force involved in printed cloth. Moreover, many of those employed in Geneva's factories came not from the city but from the suburbs—Plainpalais, Eaux-Vives, Petit-Saconnex, Cologny, Chêne, and so on—or the surrounding countryside. These suburbanites would not have appeared on the census data for the city itself. Thus while textile workers in general may have comprised a very small percentage of the workforce for the city of Geneva (about 3 percent of the active male population in both 1788 and 1798), in the early 1780s there were probably about two thousand adults employed in the manufacture of *indiennes* at a time when the city and its suburbs had a population of about 29,500 (children included).[129] When we

[128]Anne-Marie Piuz, "Négoce et négociants," in *Economie genevoise*, ed. Piuz and Mottu-Weber, 558.

[129]Mottu-Weber, "Activités manufacturières," in *Economie genevoise*, ed. Piuz and Mottu-Weber, 463–65; Perrenoud, *Population de Genève*, 160–61. On 31 December 1788, the Syndic Rilliet reported that based on surveys made in the *dizaines* the previous spring and summer, there were 25,525 people living in the city of Geneva and an additional 4,038 in the suburbs of Plainpalais, Pré-l'Evêque, Eaux-

include workers from the suburbs and countryside, the printed-cloth industry surely employed more than 10 percent of the workforce.

An issue that is beyond dispute is that Geneva's printed-cloth industry declined after 1785, when Louis XVI's controller-general, Charles-Alexandre de Calonne, issued a decree forbidding the importation into France of various fabrics. Faced with difficult times, *indiennerie* nonetheless persevered in Geneva. In 1787 five of the eleven factories were still in operation, though all with a reduced workforce.[130] Since those living in the suburbs and countryside were under the city's jurisdiction, any unnatural deaths among them would have been investigated by Auditeurs or Châtelains. Since the printed-cloth industry reduced its workforce by several hundred in the 1780s, one might think unemployed *indienneurs* would have swelled the ranks of the disaffected and contributed to the growing numbers of suicides. Nothing could be farther from the truth. The crisis in printed cloth, unlike that in watchmaking, did not fan suicidal flames. During the 1780s and 1790s only three men in textiles took their lives. Only one of these was an *indienneur*, and he killed himself in 1781, well before the crisis in the printed-cloth industry.[131] There was also a young woman who worked in the printed-cloth industry who killed herself in 1791 because she was upset about the death of a family member.[132] Together these four represent less than 3 percent of the total suicides after 1780.

Why were textile workers, particularly *indienneurs*, underrepresented among suicides? One explanation is that unlike virtually all others engaged in production for export, most *indienneurs* were unskilled. They had not spent years as apprentices learning a trade. They had in effect invested little financially or intellectually in that industry. As noted above, work in the printed-cloth industry also tended to be seasonal, as most shops shut down

---

Vives, Cologny, Chêne, Pâquis, Châtelaine, and Petit-Saconnex, for a total of 29,563; AEG, RC 292: 1096–97.

[130]Mottu-Weber, "Activités manufacturières," in *Economie genevoise*, ed. Piuz and Mottu-Weber, 461–66.

[131]AEG, PC 13746; the other two men were in silk—one was a deranged hosier who took his life in 1790, the other was a poor man involved in passementerie (braids and trimmings), killing himself in September 1793; PC 16022 and 17057.

[132]AEG, EC, LM 67: 270, 22 September 1791; PC 16543; RC 298: 1338.

for winter. *Indienneurs* therefore identified themselves less with a profession than did watchmakers and were not reluctant to seek other forms of unskilled labor when opportunities in printed cloth diminished. In fact, it is quite likely that some of the suicides among unskilled workers or "laborers" involved people who at one time had worked in *indiennerie*.

The virtual absence of *indienneurs* among suicides sheds some important light on the issue of industrialization and suicide. Some believe that industrialization has played a very strong role in determining the suicide rate of a given society, asserting that suicide rates are higher in industrialized societies because of increased social mobility. In contrast to a peasant society, people associated with industry no longer inherit their work and farm or means of production from their parents. Rather, they reach a certain economic status through education and hard work. Sociologists have maintained that if people in an industrialized society have invested much of themselves in a certain vocation but then see their efforts come to naught, failure may push them to suicide.[133] While this trend may indeed hold true for the industrial and postindustrial societies of the late twentieth century, it does not apply to the very early phases of industrialization, as seen in the experiences of printed-cloth workers. After receiving only minimal training and earning relatively poor wages, they identified themselves much less with a profession than did skilled artisans and showed very weak suicidal proclivities. Simply put, the experiences of *indienneurs* suggest that industrialization did not cause an increase in the suicide rate.[134]

[133]See interesting comments in Steven Stack, "Suicide and Religion: A Comparative Analysis," *Sociological Focus* 14 (1981): 207–20. Among the many works dealing with the issue of industrialization and suicide, see Ken Levi, "Homicide and Suicide: Structure and Process," *Deviant Behavior* 3 (1982): 91–115; Richard Quinney, "Suicide, Homicide, and Economic Development," *Social Forces* 43 (1965): 401–6.

[134]The findings on *indienneurs* support Olive Anderson's thesis that the appearance of industrialization did not cause a general increase in suicide; see "Did Suicide Increase with Industrialization in Victorian England?" *Past and Present* 86 (1980): 149–73; see also her *Suicide in Victorian and Edwardian England* (Oxford: Clarendon Press, 1987). By contrast, Roger Lane, *Violent Death in the City: Suicide, Accident, and Murder in Nineteenth-Century Philadelphia* (Cambridge: Harvard University Press, 1979), sees industrialization as the key to the sharp rise in suicides and the contemporary, though less dramatic, decrease in homicides in late-nineteenth-century Philadelphia. According to Lane, with the advent of industrialization and mandatory public education, people became accustomed to harsh discipline and supervision, running their lives according to strict time schedules. As people internalized this work and educational discipline, they achieved much greater self-control and were more likely to vent aggression against themselves than against others. Philadelphia's suicide rates of the late 1800s, however, were much lower than Geneva's for 1781–1798, even though the latter must be considered a preindustrial city.

If we turn our attention to the service sector, we see considerable variations in the frequency of suicide after 1780 among the different occupational subcategories. Although the N is not very large—37 suicides for all services—we see that most occupational groups are either underrepresented among suicides or killed themselves in numbers commensurate to their percentages of the workforce. As we have seen, when the suicide rate began to increase perceptibly if not dramatically in the first half of the eighteenth century, those most responsible for the increase were merchants. Although they may have been influenced by cultural trends, their propensity for suicide was not a result of economic fluctuations. In the late eighteenth century, merchants were less prominent among suicides, primarily because other sectors of the population were simply catching up with them. In absolute terms, suicide among merchants did not decline during the course of the eighteenth century. There were more suicides among such businessmen in the second half of the eighteenth century than in the first half (eleven to eight). If we group attorneys, magistrates, and merchants together, there were eighteen suicides among members of these elite professions after 1750, more than twice the number of the first half of the century. Be that as it may, members of Geneva's elite were underrepresented among suicides after 1780. During these two decades no attorneys committed suicide and no banker took his life during the entire early modern period.[135] After 1780 only five merchants, one broker, and two who simply lived off their investments (one of whom was a former merchant) killed themselves, thus comprising 7 percent of the suicides among those engaged in production and services. Those directly engaged in commerce, however, made up from 8.3 percent to 13.5 percent of the male workforce. One may think that merchants would have been adversely affected by the same dynamics that caused crises in the manufacture of watches and *indiennes* beginning in the mid-1780s. Contrary to what one may suspect, however, Genevan merchants as a group did not suffer unduly from French protectionism.

---

[135]As for pastors, only one Protestant clergyman committed suicide in early modern Geneva. In October 1758 Jean Pierre Chapponnier, pastor and regent at Le Collège, drowned himself after a long illness; AEG, PC 10602. A former Catholic priest committed suicide in 1545; AEG, RC 39: 111–12; RC 50: 27. See also Gabriella Cahier-Buccelli, "Dans l'ombre de la Réforme: Les membres de l'ancien clergé demeurés à Genève (1536–1558)," *Bulletin de la Société d'histoire et d'archéologie de Genève* 18 (1987): 386.

The main reason their experiences differed so from those of watchmakers is that merchants traded in a wide range of products coming from all over the world. Those merchants involved in the export of watches and jewelry were a small minority of the people involved in commerce in Geneva.[136] Farmers in the territory of Geneva produced a wide variety of crops but were never able to produce enough cereals to provide enough bread for Geneva's population. Throughout the life of the Republic, Genevans needed to import grains; and by the late eighteenth century, grain and flour came from as far away as Russia and the Black Sea region, Sicily and Sardinia, northern Africa, Spain, England, and even the United States.[137]

More important, as alluded to above, Geneva served as a place of exchange for products from all over the world. Geneva was strategically located at the source of the Rhône and at the crossroads of very important trade routes linking Milan to Paris and Marseille to southern Germany. The city furthermore had important cultural ties both to northern and southern Europe. Religiously and politically, Geneva had strong affinities to northern Teutonic culture. Demographically and linguistically, Geneva shared a common culture with France and Savoy, whose political rivalry assured the independence of the small neutral Republic. These factors explain why Geneva served as a vitally important commercial link between the north and the south. The city was especially important as an intersection for goods in transit from Marseille to the Swiss cantons and other places to the north. Sugar and tobacco from the Americas, coffee from the Antilles, olive oil from the Mediterranean, cheeses from Switzerland, and textiles from England, Holland, and Picardy all passed through Geneva.[138] Although the French impeded the export of Genevan watches, they of course wanted to pass on various products to the north through Geneva. Since locally manufactured products comprised a small proportion of the goods traded in Geneva, the

---

[136]Rarely did the criminal proceedings, the death records, or the registers of the Small Council specify in what areas of commerce merchants worked. We know the specialties of only two of these merchants who committed suicide after 1780. Jacques Mirabeau, discussed below, was a spice merchant. Alexandre Gaud, who took his life in June 1793, was a tobacco merchant; AEG, EC, LM 68: 68, 26 June 1793; Juridiction Civile F 831; PC 16965; RC 302, 677.

[137]Anne-Marie Piuz, "Les subsistances et le ravitaillement," in *Economie genevoise*, ed. Piuz and Mottu-Weber, 256–60. See also Dominique Zumkeller, *Le paysan et la terre: Agriculture et structure agraire à Genève au XVIIIe siècle* (Geneva: Editions Passé Présent, 1992), 107.

[138]O'Mara, "Geneva in the Eighteenth Century," 45–48; Piuz, "Négoce et négociants," in *Economie genevoise*, ed. Piuz and Mottu-Weber, 501–59.

merchants did not feel the brunt of the crisis in *indiennes* and La Fabrique. The fact that there were few suicides among merchants in the late eighteenth century, almost none motivated by financial reversals, is therefore understandable.

If we proceed a bit further down the social scale, we notice that those engaged in a variety of services were proportionally represented. As for the first two centuries of this study, those engaged in provisioning and hostelry were slightly overrepresented. Men employed in these areas comprised 4.9 percent of the workforce in 1788, 3.9 percent in 1798, and 6.1 percent of the male suicides after 1780 whose professions are known. Even though three sellers of wine or spirits took their lives, there is no evidence that in the turbulent 1780s and 1790s Genevans reduced their prodigious consumption of a half-liter of wine per person per day, an average maintained from the sixteenth through the eighteenth centuries.[139] In short, the frequency with which those in provisioning and hostelry killed themselves was apparently an aberration.

Most striking is the fact that the explosion in suicides after 1750 cut across class and occupational lines.[140] Only one sector, watchmaking, both deviated significantly from the norm and was large enough to make a significant difference in the suicide rate for the city as a whole. Watchmaking was the sector that employed the largest number of people and suffered the most in the late eighteenth century. The crisis in watchmaking, affecting hundreds of skilled craftsmen, the vast majority of whom were Natifs or Citizens, made a very important contribution to the growth in Genevan suicides, palpably showing the growing gap between material aspirations and financial realities. Be that as it may, all branches of La Fabrique represented about 38 percent of the male workforce and accounted for only 37.7 percent of all male suicides, 40.4 percent of those whose occupations are known. The crisis in watchmaking alone therefore cannot account for the very high suicide rates of the last two decades of this study. What is most noteworthy about suicides and professions is that so many sectors were roughly in line with the figures concerning the total workforce. While the

[139]Anne-Marie Piuz, "Le vin," in *Economie genevoise*, ed. Piuz and Mottu-Weber, 307–8.

[140]Similarly, in late-eighteenth-century Paris, evidence suggests that lower-class individuals—domestics, unskilled workers, apprentices, and journeymen—were most prone to commit suicide, but one could also find some suicides among master artisans, clergymen, lawyers, and magistrates; see Merrick, "Patterns and Prosecution of Suicide," 8–9.

economic crisis of the late eighteenth century was an important contributing factor to the increasing frequency of suicides, it does not suffice to
explain the growing numbers of people who took their lives. The virtual
absence of suicides among *indienneurs* after 1785 militates against a monocausal explanation based on economics.

Moreover, as previously noted, poverty and financial concerns were not
among the most prominent motives for taking one's life in early modern
Geneva. Poverty and financial concerns appeared to be factors in only a sixth
of all suicides for which motives could be established (58 of 359). One may
try to argue, however, that we cannot trust the criminal proceedings with
regard to the motives for suicide. Witnesses were perhaps relying excessively
on the insight of hindsight in offering explanations as to what drove people to
take their lives, thus erring in identifying the real motives. Perhaps they gave
too much importance to one factor and not enough to another. While these
are possibilities, there is no getting around the fact that financial misery could
not possibly have been a factor for most suicides. The majority of suicides
throughout the early modern period were not poor. Even if we made the dangerous assumption that all poor suicides took their lives because of their poverty, that would still leave us looking for explanations for the remaining 60
percent of self-inflicted deaths. Poverty definitely did have an aggravating
effect—causing various problems in one's life that could in turn lead to suicide—and could be a major factor in leading to marital breakdown. Poverty
could exacerbate certain "melancholic" tendencies that preceded many suicides, and could prevent some from getting sufficient repose to recover from a
variety of illnesses that were so commonly cited as motives for suicide. But it
is important to emphasize that poor suicides declined vis-à-vis others from
the first to the second halves of the eighteenth century.

It is also important to note that Geneva's economy did not undergo a
fundamental structural change from the seventeenth to the late eighteenth
century. Though watchmaking had become more stratified, Geneva's was still
essentially a guild economy. Indeed, the guilds even survived the overthrow of
the Old Regime and the establishment of democracy in late 1792.[141] Family

---

[141]Far from dismantling the guilds, the Revolution reinforced them. During the years 1792–98, artisans who had never before organized petitioned to have the right to form guilds; Liliane Mottu-Weber,
"Economie et société à Genève à l'époque de la Révolution," in *Regards sur la Révolution genevoise 1792–
1798*, ed. Louis Binz and others (Geneva: Société d'histoire et d'archéologie de Genève, 1992), 73.

connections generally were quite important throughout the early modern period to attain higher status work. Like their eighteenth-century descendants, artisans of the seventeenth century had invested much of themselves in pursuing their professions. Some, such as those trained in passementerie, saw employment opportunities decline considerably, and all Genevans experienced a serious crisis in the late 1600s that rivaled that of a century later. The fact that seventeenth-century Genevans, even when faced with hard times, did not take their lives indicates that factors other than economics played important roles in the explosion in suicides of the late 1700s.

SUICIDE AND POLITICAL CRISIS

As eighteenth-century Geneva witnessed political as well as economic crises, perhaps many suicides were politically motivated. Throughout the eighteenth century, the governing oligarchy of Geneva feared and hated democracy more than anything else. First it was the lesser Bourgeoisie who agitated for change. Geneva experienced political turmoil in 1707, 1718, and 1734 as the petty and middle Bourgeoisie—master craftsmen and other Citizens below the ranks of the patricians—called for change, advocating that political supremacy reside with the General Council rather than the small councils. So great was their fear of democracy that three times (1738, 1766, and 1782) members of Geneva's ruling elite called upon France, Bern, and Zurich to intervene militarily on their behalf to put down democratic uprisings. The upper and lower Bourgeoisies appeared to be reconciled in 1738 when they agreed that the General Council had the right to approve all tax measures and all new laws in general. The calm was disrupted, however, in June 1762 when the Small Council condemned as subversive *Emile* and *The Social Contract*, among the best-known works of Jean-Jacques Rousseau, himself a product of Geneva's lower Bourgeoisie. Rousseau's claim that all people in a society, regardless of their birth, must freely come together and form a social contract from which government is created, found a receptive audience among Geneva's lower Bourgeoisie and Natifs. In response to the ban, a group of Citizens put forward a "représentation," or protest, which the Small Council, invoking its "droit négatif," or right of refusal, did not deign to accept. This affair spawned two competing political parties in the second half of the eighteenth century: the "Négatifs," who supported the ruling oligarchy; and the "Représentants," who sought a more democratic government, arguing that the General Council rather than the Small Council should be the supreme governing body. The ideas of each group were expressed in two different works: Jean-Robert Tronchin (1710–93), Procureur Général from 1760 to 1767, published his *Lettres écrites de la campagne* in 1763 to justify the Small Council's actions; in response, Rousseau wrote the much more famous *Lettres écrites de la montagne.*[142]

The disputes of the 1760s helped stimulate political activism among the Natifs. An edict in 1738 had allowed Natifs to serve as master craftsmen and another in 1768 provided other professional advantages, including the right to serve as Master Jurymen—the heads of different crafts. The more economic privileges they enjoyed, however, the less the Natifs could tolerate being utterly bereft of political rights. Eventually the Natifs and lower Bourgeoisie allied to call for a democratic government. Upset that the Small Council had rejected their petition for political equality, the Représentants, comprising a large group of lesser Citizens, rose up in arms with the support of the Natifs and effectively took control of the city on 7 April 1782. The insurgents declared there was political equality among all the former Citizens, Natifs, and Habitants. Many of the leaders of the Négatifs were arrested and remained in prison throughout this crisis. This first experience with democracy was short-lived, as patrician leaders fought back by calling for help from their stronger neighbors. Surrounded by 11,000 troops from France, Bern, and Sardinia, the Genevans, through a representative assembly, voted by a narrow margin to surrender, allowing the troops to enter the gates 2 July 1782. Geneva's oligarchy was quickly restored, many of the leaders of the insurrection were banished, and the division between the upper and lower Bourgeoisie had never been wider and more bitter.[143]

In 1791 Genevans accepted a new constitution whereby the General Council was recognized as sovereign. Though Natifs and Habitants were to enjoy "civil equality" with Citizens, they still did not have the franchise, an omission that proved fatal. Inspired by the democratic rhetoric from Revolutionary France, members of the lower Bourgeoisie, Natifs, and Habitants

[142]Lucien Fulpius, "Les institutions politiques de Genève dès origines à la fin de l'ancienne république," in *Actes de l'Institut National Genevois*, nouvelle série 3 (1965): 22–23; O'Mara, "Geneva in the Eighteenth Century," 251–91; Porret, *Crime et ses circonstances*, 92–96.

[143]Édouard Chapuisat, *La prise d'armes de 1782 à Genève* (Geneva: Jullien, 1932); O'Mara, "Geneva in the Eighteenth Century," 297–318.

together formed radical political clubs, such as the *Cercle de la Grille* and the *Cercle du Tiers-Etat*, which called for the overthrow of the Old Regime. Members of these various clubs were behind the armed insurrection which began the night of 4–5 December 1792. In response to this agitation, the General Council decreed 12 December that citizenship was to be granted to Natifs and Habitants, effectively bringing to an end the oligarchic regime. Two weeks later the Small Council was forced to dissolve, replaced by a provisional government which was formed by the political clubs. This group embraced a new slogan for the new regime: "Liberty, Equality, Independence." The Revolution in Geneva took a decisive turn to the left in July 1794 when, in response to food shortages and economic crisis, radicals assumed power and aggressively pursued the redistribution of wealth, the leveling of social classes, and the "purification" of Genevan society by eliminating the rich. Harking back to the words of their hero Rousseau, many viewed riches and virtue as incompatible. Such excesses were over, however, by September of the following year when authorities invited members of the former patriciate who had fled the country to return to Geneva. Subject to an economic blockade, the General Council voted 15 April 1798 to be incorporated into Napoleonic France, thus ending 262 years of independence.[144]

What impact did these events have on suicide? After 1750 suicide affected all levels of political status, as members of all political rubrics killed themselves in numbers roughly commensurate to their share of the Genevan population (see table 30). Citizens made up well over a third of the suicides during these decades, but this figure is skewed by the large number of Habitants and Natifs who acquired citizenship through the Revolution. If we consider the pre-Revolutionary status of all those who took their lives during the years 1793–98, then Citizens and Bourgeois comprised a fourth of all suicides for this half century (see table 31). The Bourgeoisie's share of suicides was thus roughly in line with their numbers in the overall population; at most, Citizens and Bourgeois were slightly overrepresented among those who killed themselves.[145] The immunity to suicide that Natifs had enjoyed

---

[144]O'Mara, "Geneva in the Eighteenth Century," 395–456.

[145]The Bourgeoisie comprised 18.8 percent of Geneva's population in the early 1770s, but 26.5 percent in 1781. Since many Citizens emigrated during the turbulent 1780s, the Bourgeoisie declined to 23.7 percent of the population in 1788. If we look only at Geneva's adult population for that year, Citizens and Bourgeois made up only 20.9 percent; Perrenoud, *Population de Genève*, 193–95.

during the previous two hundred years disappeared during this half century—for every Natif who had committed suicide through 1750, over

Table 30: Civil Status of Suicides, 1751–1798[a]

Status	Totals	
	n	%
Citizen	99	34.7
Bourgeois	6	2.1
Natif	68	23.9
Habitant	30	10.5
Sujet	19	6.7
Foreigner	63	22.1
Unknown	3	n/a
Total	288	

a. Source: Etat Civil, Livres des Morts; Procès Criminels; Registres du Conseil. The three people whose civil status cannot be determined are not included in the percentages.

Table 31: Civil Status of Suicides, 1751–1798[a]

STATUS	TOTAL NUMBER AND PERCENTAGE OF POPULATION					
	Males		Females		Total	
	n	%	*n*	%	*n*	%
Citizen	49	23.6	14	18.7	63	22.3
Bourgeois	5	2.4	3	4.0	8	2.8
Natif	65	31.3	25	33.3	90	31.8
Habitant	27	13.0	11	14.7	38	13.4
Sujet	13	6.3	8	10.7	21	7.4
Foreigner	49	23.3	14	18.7	63	22.3
Unknown	2	n/a	3	n/a	5	n/a
Total	210		78		288	

a. Source: Etat Civil, Livres des Morts; Procès Criminels; Registres du Conseil. The pre-Revolutionary status is used for those Citizens who took their lives after December 1792. The five people whose current or pre-Revolutionary civil status cannot be determined are not included in the percentages.

twenty took their lives in the last half century of the Republic's existence. Nonetheless, Natifs' suicides were not out of proportion to their share of Geneva's population.[146] Even foreigners were not unduly present among suicides in the late eighteenth century. Twice as many foreigners killed themselves after 1750 as in the previous two centuries, but their importance fell vis-à-vis other political categories. As they committed a little over a fifth of post-1750 suicides, foreigners were at most just slightly overrepresented among those who killed themselves.[147] Only for Habitants did the share of suicides differ noticeably from their percentage of the population. Habitants, who generally made up about a fourth of the population but committed only 13.4 percent of the suicides, clearly killed themselves less frequently than other juridic groups. As for the previous two hundred years, Sujets living in the city killed themselves more often than others, while suicide was less common among those who remained in their rural villages than among urban dwellers of all juridic categories.[148]

In short, after 1750 no juridic-political group was immune to suicide. Even though they were less prone to suicide than others, twice as many Habitants killed themselves after 1750 as in the previous two hundred years. Apart from the Habitants, the two groups that appeared to deviate even slightly from their proportional norms were at opposite ends of the spectrum of political privilege: foreigners and the Bourgeoisie. Suicide made for

[146]Natifs comprised 33.7 percent of Geneva's population in 1770–72 and 34.1 percent in 1781. By 1788, however, the proportion fell to 24.8 percent. Fearing the agitation from below, Citizens had allowed a number of Natifs to join the ranks of the Bourgeoisie; Perrenoud, *Population de Genève*, 193–95.

[147]In 1781, 15.4 percent of Geneva's population was foreign, increasing to 19.9 percent in 1788. Looking only at the adult population, we find that 30.1 percent of the population was foreign in 1788. If this figure were true for the entire second half of the eighteenth century, we would have to say that foreigners were underrepresented among suicides. The higher percentage of foreigners among adults resulted from so many foreigners' being poor and single; Perrenoud, *Population de Genève*, 195. The proportion of the population that was foreign declined with the Revolution, however. In 1793 the provisional government expelled foreigners who did not have a profession that was "useful to the Nation," such as male domestic servants; see David Hiler, "La pomme de terre révolutionnaire," in *Regards sur la Révolution*, ed. Binz and others, 98–99.

[148]In 1781 Habitants and Domiciliés comprised 12.1 percent and 11.9 percent, respectively. Seven years later these figures were 17.2 percent and 11.7 percent. In 1788, 2.6 percent of the males living in the city of Geneva were Sujets, while the eleven Sujets who killed themselves while residing in the city of Geneva amounted to 4.3 percent of suicides after 1750. Nine other Sujets committed suicide in their villages, while for one suicide, it is not clear if he was living in Geneva or in the dependent countryside; population figures from Perrenoud, *Population de Genève*, 195.

strange bedfellows in Geneva during the late 1700s.

As table 31 indicates, the breakdown into juridic categories was quite similar for male and female suicides. The most obvious difference between female and male suicides is that the percentage of Sujets was higher among women while that of foreigners was higher among men. All this shows is that among those who came to Geneva, men tended to come from farther away than women. When combined, the percentages of these two groups (whose juridic status was identical within the city of Geneva) were virtually the same for male and female suicides. The overall trend, including the dramatic increase in the Natifs' share of suicides, holds true for male and female suicides. Throughout the early modern period, the sex of suicides was thus not an important variable in influencing the proportions of suicides from members of the various political rubrics.

Did the political turmoil of the 1780s and 1790s have an impact on the contemporary explosion in suicides in Geneva? France, for example, witnessed a large number of suicides among political leaders in the Revolutionary period. During the time of the Terror, Girondins such as Condorcet and Etienne Clavière (the latter a Genevan and former Représentant who had been exiled in 1782[149]) committed suicide in prison; Pétion, Buzot, Ledon, Roland, and Valazé also took their lives. With the Thermidor reaction, it was the Jacobins' turn to commit suicide rather than submit. When troops approached to arrest them, Lebas successfully took his life by shooting himself in the head, while Robespierre merely wounded himself with a pistol shot to the jaw. The so-called martyrs of Prairial, Montagnards, convoked by the Military Tribunal, collectively decided to kill themselves rather than be executed. Five of them succeeded while the other two were carried wounded to the guillotine.[150] In France, revolutionaries who took their lives during the Terror or Thermidor tended to identify with Brutus or Cato, while counterrevolutionaries saw themselves as a modern version of early Christian martyrs.[151] Were Genevans also committing suicide because they were disillusioned with the course their revolution was taking?

---

[149]See André Gür, "Quête de la richesse et critique des riches chez Etienne Clavière," in *Etre riche*, ed. Berchtold and Porret, 97–115.

[150]Patrice Higonnet, "Du suicide sentimental au suicide politique," 137–50; McManners, *Death and Enlightenment*, 417.

[151]Though suicide was decriminalized during the Revolution, French authorities continued to view it with opprobrium: those who took their lives were forswearing their services to the state; Minois, *His-*

The evidence on the political status of suicides for those years appears to be roughly proportional to the breakdown of the population as a whole (see table 32). If we look at their pre-Revolutionary status for 1793–98, the number of suicides among Citizens and Bourgeois almost perfectly reflected their numbers in the population at large. While Habitants killed themselves less often than other groups, proportionally more Natifs took their lives than members of any other rubric. Foreigners may have represented a larger proportion than their share of the population would have dictated, but not by much.[152]

Table 32: Civil Status of Suicides, 1781–1798[a]

Status	Total	
	n	%
Citizen	32	20.5
Bourgeois	4	2.6
Natif	51	32.7
Habitant	23	14.7
Sujet	12	7.7
Foreigner	34	21.8
Unknown	4	n/a
Total	160	

a. Source: Etat Civil, Livres des Morts; Procès Criminels; Registres du Conseil. The pre-Revolutionary status is used for those Citizens who took their lives after December 1792. The four people whose current or pre-Revolutionary civil status cannot be determined are not included in the percentages.

Nonetheless, how can we explain that the suicidal urge seemed to hit the Bourgeoisie and foreigners a trifle harder than others, and the Habitants a bit less? An explanation that immediately comes to mind centers on the political changes of the 1780s and 1790s. As for foreigners, they were without a polit-

---

toire du suicide, 349–55. See also Dorinda Outram, *The Body and the French Revolution: Sex, Class and Political Culture* (New Haven, Conn.: Yale University Press, 1989), 90–105.

[152]Perrenoud, *Population de Genève*, 195.

ical voice in the Republic both before and after the Revolution. As the group that was most marginalized politically, economically, and socially, foreigners might be expected to kill themselves in greater numbers than others. The Habitants, by contrast, gained the most from the Revolution. Until December 1792, they were third-class residents of Geneva, having no political rights and economic rights that were, at least theoretically, below those of the Natifs. With the Revolution of 1792 the Habitants attained citizenship, achieving political parity with the former Citizens, Bourgeois, and Natifs. One would think therefore that the relative paucity of Habitant suicides reflected their general satisfaction as they approached the end of the 1700s.

Members of the upper Bourgeoisie, by contrast, lost more than anyone else with the fall of the Old Regime. Many members of Geneva's traditional elite were so distraught with the change of events that they emigrated. The former members of the upper Bourgeoisie who remained lost their privileged status, as the oligarchy that had defended the rights of the Bourgeoisie for over two and a half centuries came to an end. What the Bourgeoisie had hated and feared most—democracy—had become a reality, as all nonforeign men living in Geneva attained citizenship. The peak year for suicide in early modern Geneva was 1793, immediately after the fall of the Old Regime. This fact conjures up visions of former Citizens taking their lives out of despair over the course of events.

Certain problems arise with these explanations, however, if we look at the pre-Revolutionary political status of those who committed suicide between December 1792 and the end of the Republic in 1798 (see table 33). The former Citizens and Bourgeois, who had just witnessed the elimination of their privileged status, made up just over a fifth of the suicides, almost exactly equal to their share of the pre-Revolutionary population. Had they been so devastated to see the Old Regime fall, one would think the former Citizens and Bourgeois would have killed themselves in greater numbers than others. Although ex-Habitants were underrepresented among suicides after 1792, the former Natifs, having comprised about a fourth of the population, made up almost half the suicides during these years. Together with lesser Citizens, the Natifs had been largely responsible for establishing this democratic republic. They, along with the Habitants, were the primary beneficiaries of the New Regime, achieving equality with members of the former Bourgeoisie. The years of the democratic Republic also marked the only period in early modern Geneva when foreigners were underrepresented among suicides. In short, the data for suicides after 1792 militate against a simple political explanation for suicides in the waning years of the Genevan Republic.

Table 33: Pre-Revolutionary Civil Status of Suicides, 1793–1798[a]

Status	Total	
	n	%
Citizen	8	16.3
Bourgeois	2	4.1
Natif	22	44.9
Habitant	9	18.4
Sujet	2	4.1
Foreigner	6	12.2
Unknown	2	n/a
Total	51	

a. Source: Etat Civil, Livres des Morts; Procès Criminels; Registres du Conseil. The two people whose civil status cannot be determined are not included in the percentages.

Why then were more suicides committed in 1793 (the first twelve months that followed the end of the Old Regime) than in any other year in early modern Geneva?[153] Suicide by imitation is unlikely in that, as noted in chapter 1, these were all separate cases of suicides involving people who apparently were not associated with one another. Interestingly, the seventeen people who took their lives in Geneva that year were all men who killed themselves in the city itself, a fact that at first glance lends credence to the view that they could have been politically motivated since at no time were the rights of women even raised in the political turmoil of the 1780s and 1790s. Nonetheless for the most part, this surge in suicide was not a reflection of the despair of the former Bourgeoisie. Of the seventeen suicides, only

[153]This finding does not support the contention that like war, political crises generally cause a drop in the number of suicides, as people are too consumed with political enthusiasm to turn their aggression inwardly. See Durkheim, *Suicide*, 208; Halbwachs, *Causes du suicide*, 328–32.

six had enjoyed citizenship before the Revolution. As they made up about a fifth of the population but a third of the suicides for this year, the former Bourgeois and Citizens evidently were somewhat more prone to suicide during those twelve months than members of other former political rubrics. But the majority of the suicides for that year were precisely those who in theory benefitted most from the Revolution: Natifs and Habitants. Eight former Natifs and one former Habitant took their lives during the first twelve months that they enjoyed citizenship in the New Regime of the Republic of Geneva.

If we trust the descriptions of motives in the criminal investigations, only three of the seventeen suicides appeared to be even partially motivated by politics.[154] Only one of these three had been a member of the Bourgeoisie. On 4 July 1793, Jacques Mirabeau, forty-five, a wealthy spice merchant, took his life by firing two pistols simultaneously, one into each ear. Mirabeau, married and the father of four minor children, had reportedly been sick and depressed for a long time. Nevertheless, his business partner, Jacques Guigonat, asserted that he knew of no motive for this suicide other than the fact that Mirabeau had been preoccupied for some time with "affairs in France." Exactly what these affairs were is not clear. Perhaps he was upset about the Revolution in France, or he may simply have found his business hindered by the Revolution. In any event, this suicide appears to have been at most tangentially related to the end of the Old Regime in Geneva.[155]

The suicide of 1793 that was most clearly politically inspired involved a Frenchman who was upset about events back home. Charles Dalloz, thirty-five, was an aide-de-camp from the French town of St. Claude, not far from Geneva, who shot himself in October 1793. Fearing a misfire, Dalloz, like Mirabeau, simultaneously fired pistols into both ears. In a suicide note to his

[154]Among other motives cited were romantic misadventures (3), poverty or financial concerns (7), and physical illnesses (3). Interestingly, melancholy or alienation was cited as a motive only twice.

[155]The postmortem inventory revealed that Mirabeau had affluent holdings in real estate. He also had a substantial library, comprising thirty-six titles, many of which were in several volumes. Included among his books were the *Oeuvres* of Rousseau (25 volumes), Voltaire (57 volumes), and Fielding (15 volumes). He also owned some religious works, including collections of sermons, a New Testament, and Calvin's *Institutes*. Out of the one hundred postmortem inventories I consulted, this was the only one that listed the *Institutes* among the library holdings. Mirabeau also owned books of local interest such as the two-volume *Histoire de Genève* and another two-volume work, *Révolutions de Genève;* AEG, EC, LM 68: 69, 4 July 1793; Juridiction Civile F 831; PC 16974; RC 302: 714.

friend, "the Citizen Christin of St. Claude," Dalloz wrote:

> I had only three paths to take, my dear Christin: return to live under
> tyranny, emigrate, or die. The first would have been a despicable act.
> The second runs contrary to my principles and would endanger my
> friends and relatives and mean victory for my enemies. I have
> chosen the third and am going to join Cato. I have seen the disgrace
> of France being tyrannized by the most vile scoundrels. At least I
> won't have to see the last convulsions of its ignominious agony. I
> leave my mother for you to console. If my brother is still alive, I
> hope he will not despise my memory. I would prefer leaving [the
> money] in my desk to my sister for her husband's voyage, should he
> be obliged to leave France, rather than consuming it myself by
> hanging on for a few more days to this gloomy existence.... I die
> calm and content that I have not knowingly offended anyone.... I
> have never hated anyone except the brigands who are tearing France
> apart.... I hope that those who call themselves patriots will stop per-
> secuting my mother, who sacrificed everything for the most disas-
> trous of all revolutions.[156]

An excellent example of a political suicide, Dalloz had been a revolutionary
who became disillusioned with the Jacobin Dictatorship and the Reign of
Terror. His suicide, which took place just a day after he arrived in Geneva,
was clearly independent of Genevan political events.[157]

More typical was the suicide of Noé Pelin, a setter of watchcasings and
former Natif, who shot himself in the heart in his home 30 May 1793.
According to witnesses, Pelin was upset about not having work, as his
employer closed his shop just the day before Pelin took his life. Interestingly,
magistrates found on Pelin's body a medallion of the *Club Fraternel des*

---

[156]AEG, PC 17079.

[157]The only other suicide of 1793 that, according to the criminal proceedings, was motivated at
least in part by political events was that of Germain Jeanrenaud, a former Natif. Jeanrenaud was a twenty-
nine-year-old setter of watchcasings who shot himself in April of that year. According to two witnesses,
Jeanrenaud, married and the father of two minor children, was rather melancholic. Moreover, a neighbor
believed that perhaps the recent political developments, in which Jeanrenaud had been very actively
involved, may have driven him to this act. His employer of the past four years also affirmed that Jeanrenaud was quite involved in politics, which took considerable time from his work; AEG, EC, LM 68: 60,
11 April 1793; Juridiction Civile F 830; PC 16884; RC 301: 429.

Révolutionnaires Genevois. In other words, this Revolutionary took his life out of economic despair just five months after seeing his desire for citizenship fulfilled. As this case demonstrates, financial concerns drove more people to suicide than purely political motives.[158]

In fact, if the criminal proceedings are accurate in identifying the motives of suicides, then there were only eight suicides in the entire early modern period in which political events were motives. All eight, involving seven men and one woman, occurred from July 1782 to November 1793. In addition to Mirabeau, only two others were members of the traditional Bourgeoisie, both of whom committed suicide during the last years of the Old Regime. The connection between political events and suicide was quite clear in the death of the Citizen George Charles Boin, a setter of watchcasings, who shot himself in the head 3 October 1792. Married and the father of two minors, Boin, forty-four, left a suicide note in which he declared that he could no longer tolerate the diffusion of "modern philosophy." Writing just two months before the fall of the Old Regime, Boin complained:

> Having been heartbroken several times upon learning of the cruel atrocities committed since the reign of modern philosophy and seeing this terrible spectacle drawing near to our dear country, I had neither the strength nor the courage to tolerate being a passive eyewitness to such cruelties. Having invoked providence concerning the fate of my children and my worthy and virtuous wife, and commending them to honest, charitable people, I for my part see that I can no longer be useful to them since I am absolutely convinced that I would succumb. I pray to God to forgive me for this last act of my life, having done nothing else to merit reproach. I beg my brother-in-law, the minister, to have the charity to take in my wife, my daughter, and my son, if possible.[159]

Abhorring the events of the French Revolution and foreseeing the arrival of democracy in Geneva, Boin was the only member of the Bourgeoisie—and he was not a member of the patriciate—to commit suicide unequivocally because he was upset about political developments in Geneva.

---

[158]AEG, EC, LM 68: 66, 30 May 1793; PC 16945; RC 301: 596.
[159]AEG, PC 16769.

In the peak year of 1793, the typical profile of a suicide was a male watchmaker and former Natif who was anxious about his financial situation. In his late thirties, he was married and the father of minor children. In this year, neither marriage nor parenthood offered much immunity to suicide. Many of those most prone to suicide throughout the early modern era—prisoners, soldiers, servants, foreigners, menial laborers—were nearly or totally absent in 1793. Suicide in 1793 involved almost everyone but the marginal.[160]

SUICIDE, GENDER, AND SOCIOPOLITICAL STRUCTURE

As noted above, studies have consistently shown that men kill themselves much more frequently than women in modern Western societies. As we have seen in chapter 1, this also held true for Geneva during the late eighteenth century, whereas there was a much smaller discrepancy between the numbers of men and women who killed themselves prior to 1750. This discrepancy was most pronounced after 1780. These last seventeen years and four months witnessed 39.5 percent of the recorded suicides during these two and a half centuries. Although more women killed themselves than ever before, the extraordinary suicidal impulse unleashed at this time particularly affected Genevan men. Up until 1750, men had outnumbered women among suicides by a modest margin. By contrast, men outnumbered women by over three to one from 1781 on (122 to 38).[161] Put another way, these seventeen and a third years witnessed 44.2 percent of male suicides, as compared to 29.5 percent of the female suicides, for the entire early modern period.

Sociological studies have offered a host of explanations for the gender gap, some of which are quite unsatisfactory. Durkheim claimed to reject all nonsocial factors—such as those pertaining to race, climate, and biology—in determining variations in suicide rates. In explaining differences between rates among men and women, however, Durkheim apparently embraced

---

[160]Of the seventeen men who took their lives in 1793, nine were married, seven were watchmakers, and the average age of these suicides was 39.9 years.

[161]For the first two hundred years of this study, 59 men (56.7 percent) and 45 women (43.3 percent) took their lives. Even for the years 1751–80 the proportion of suicides who were male was not as high as in the last two decades of this study. During these thirty years, 82 men (70.7 percent) and 34 women (29.3 percent) committed suicide.

biological determinism: "Women's sexual needs have less of a mental character because, generally speaking, her mental life is less developed. These needs are more closely related to the needs of the organism, following rather than leading them, and consequently find in them an efficient restraint. Being a more instinctive creature than man, woman has only to follow her instincts to find calmness and peace."[162] Today, no scholar seriously believes that women are less prone to kill themselves because they are more dominated by biological instincts than are men.

Suicidologists have suggested that ideas about masculinity and femininity help explain why men kill themselves in greater numbers than women. According to Jean Baechler, "The social image of man is characterized by an exaggeration of strength and a denial of dependence. The former places emphasis on ambition and success, and increases the chances of failure. The second denies some forms of behavior to men."[163] Accordingly, men may not feel free to seek consolation from others if they are depressed or unhappy with their lot. Men may deem it unmanly to show their emotions, and have no safety valve for their frustrations, ultimately finding solace only through death. Moreover, Baechler argues that aggressiveness—be it against oneself or others—is the province of males, based on education, social custom, and physiology.[164]

These explanations may indeed have some validity both for contemporary Europe and North America and for Geneva of the late 1700s. Though

---

[162]Durkheim, *Suicide*, 272. See also Philippe Besnard, "Durkheim et les femmes ou le *Suicide* inachevé," *Revue française de sociologie* 14 (1973): 27–61.

[163]Jean Baechler, *Suicides*, trans. Barry Cooper (New York: Basic Books, 1979), 290.

[164]Baechler, *Suicides*, 290, further argues that if a couple had a serious conflict, the woman might make a half-hearted suicide attempt in order to put pressure on her male lover to modify his behavior. Such unsuccessful suicide attempts are much rarer for men. In dealing with conflicts with their spouses or lovers, men are much more apt to commit murder, completed (as opposed to attempted) suicide, or murder-suicide. Attempted suicide is of course much more difficult to study than completed suicides. Although in early modern Geneva attempted suicide was subject to criminal investigation—and in the Reformation period, to criminal penalties—authorities investigated only thirty-five unsuccessful suicide attempts, involving twenty-five men and ten women, during the 250 years of this study. Seventeen of these attempts occurred after 1750, eighteen before. These findings do not support the contention that women attempt suicide more often than men, but we have good reason to suspect that many suicide attempts went unreported. While authorities diligently investigated and recorded every death in Geneva, they did not inquire into every injury. By comparison, statisticians for Metropolitan Life Insurance Company of New York estimate there are six or seven attempts for every successful suicide, an estimate that may be rather conservative; see James M. A. Weiss, "The Gamble with Death in Attempted Suicide," in *Sociology of Suicide*, ed. Giddens, 387.

very detailed, the postmortem investigations do not provide enough information to generalize whether men were more prone than women to suppress
their fears and frustrations until they reached the breaking point. But if this
were indeed a principal cause of the difference in suicide rates, one still must
explain why Genevan males and females killed themselves in equal numbers
in the first half of the eighteenth century. No evidence suggests that social
mores governing gender roles changed noticeably during the course of the
1700s. Similarly, if physiology was a key determining factor behind male
aggression, how can one explain the parity between male and female suicides
before 1750? Surely Genevan men of the late eighteenth century did not
have higher levels of testosterone, which is associated with aggressiveness,
than their forefathers.

Another explanation that suicidologists offer for the discrepancy
between the numbers of men and women who kill themselves is that males
are much more prone to toxicomania, especially alcoholism, which greatly
increases the risk of self-inflicted death.[165] The criminal investigations of
questionable deaths always include a surgeon's report that gives a description
of the corpse and cites the probable cause of death, but they generally do not
provide a detailed medical history of the deceased. The reports of witnesses,
however, do often mention whether people had a drinking problem before
their untimely deaths. Based on this testimony, only sixteen suicides apparently suffered from alcoholism, a figure that surely underreports the actual
number of suicides with problems with alcohol. Of these, all but one were
men, and only one killed himself before 1750. This evidence suggests that
alcohol may have contributed in a very minor way to the discrepancy
between male and female suicides in the late eighteenth century. One cannot
help but wonder, however, why alcohol abuse was behind only one suicide in
the previous two hundred years.[166]

Although the increase in self-inflicted deaths in the late 1700s affected
all classes of people, socioeconomic and political factors help explain why

[165]Baechler, *Suicides*, 290. Some recent studies suggest that alcoholics comprise 5 percent of the
general population but 30 percent of the suicides in the United States in the late twentieth century; see
George Howe Colt, *The Enigma of Suicide* (New York: Summit Books, 1991), 266–67.

[166]True, in eighteenth-century France, the elites complained more than ever before about the
drunkenness of members of the lower classes. Other evidence suggests, however, that these moralists were
exaggerating the problems associated with drink and the taverns; Thomas Brennan, *Public Drinking and
Popular Culture in Eighteenth-Century Paris* (Princeton: Princeton University Press, 1988), 187–227.

suicide became increasingly a male phenomenon at this time. True, one can find examples of women who were pushed to take their lives at least in part by financial reasons. A good example was Antoinette Martin, thirty-two, the wife of the master surgeon Sieur Antoine Laurent, a man thirty years her senior. Martin, who took her life by taking arsenic in October 1759, was clearly dissatisfied with the amount of wealth she had. Her husband revealed that she had been plagued with melancholy off and on for years, suffering continuously since August. Martin's emotional instability was blatant, as "a hundred times" she had gone to the top floor of the house to jump out a window, but someone had always managed to stop her. Both Laurent and a physician had prescribed some remedies, all to no avail. Martin was quite high-strung, having argued with and even slapped her married stepdaughter. Though affluent by the standards of the vast majority of Genevans, Martin, a member of a French noble family, had nonetheless married beneath her station. Witnesses indicated that she complained to friends about her material status and, without her husband's knowledge, even borrowed money from some of them. Although her unstable character was clearly the main factor in this suicide, dissatisfaction with her financial status definitely contributed to her emotional malaise.[167]

Martin's case, however, was atypical. Most who took their lives in part because of financial concerns or reversals were not well-to-do, and almost all who did so were men rather than women. Although there were proportionally more poor among female suicides than among males, poverty and financial concerns in general were very rarely cited as motives for suicide among women. Throughout the early modern period, fifty-eight female suicides, compared to seventy males, were clearly poor. Nonetheless poverty appeared as a motive in the suicides of only four women, as opposed to twenty-five men. In addition, other financial concerns, but not poverty per se, were

---

[167]AEG, EC, LM 62: 321, 20 October 1759; PC 10707. This case drew international attention. Upon learning of this death, Antoinette Martin's sister in France, the countess d'Allegrin, wrote for information about the death from Sieur Jean-François Sellon, a banker who served as the de facto ambassador for the Genevan Republic in Paris; RC 259: 460–61, 481, 489; Lüthy, *Banque protestante*, vol. 2, *Banque aux finances*, 292. Though there was no postmortem inventory after Martin's death, an inventory was made after the demise of her husband, who succumbed to natural causes sixteen months later. The inventory revealed that Antoine Laurent enjoyed a very comfortable life. He possessed bonds and stocks worth 43,399 livres, and his four-story home with a courtyard on La Grande-Rue was estimated at 70,000 florins; Juridiction Civile F 710.

behind the suicides of six other women, only one of whom can be characterized as poor, as compared to twenty-three males.

The most plausible explanation of why Genevan men were more likely
than women to be pushed to kill themselves by financial concerns resided in
their different attitudes toward work. As previously noted, women's work
was generally considered supplementary. Whether they were married or single, their labor, paid or unpaid, most often was needed to bolster the family
economy. Even though some women performed certain tasks in various
branches of La Fabrique that required considerable training and skill,
women in general did not identify themselves with particular professions. As
noted above, women never enjoyed the prospects of being master artisans or
performing the most highly paid jobs. Since they were used to changing the
work they performed, women were also much more willing than men to
modify work patterns as dictated by market conditions. Few women in early
modern Geneva would have felt as did Pierre Dombre, the unemployed
watchmaker who committed suicide in part because the skills he had learned
had become obsolete as the result of technological change. Although
Dombre could not bear the thought of learning a new trade, many women
performed the same job as he and faced the same dilemma. Though women
comprised up to 30 percent of those employed in watchmaking, none of the
twenty-one women who took their lives from 1785 on worked in the watchmaking industry, while thirty male watchmakers took their lives during
those same years.[168] Even when they possessed the same skills as men,
women simply identified themselves much less with a particular profession
and were more willing to change their line of work in response to changing
market conditions.

The fact that women had lower expectations for earnings is another
reason that poverty and financial concerns were less likely to be motives for
suicide among women. Even when performing the same work, early
modern women invariably were paid less than men, rarely earning more

---

[168]In 1788, women comprised 16 percent of the people involved in watchmaking and 30 percent
in 1798, a time when 20 percent of all active women were engaged in some way or another in the watchmaking industry; Mottu-Weber, "Activités manufacturières," in *Economie genevoise*, 488; Perrenoud,
Population de Genève, 170, 176, 178.

than half the wages of their male counterparts.[169] Among married couples, the husband was invariably expected to provide the principal source of income. Consequently, men were more likely than women to feel they had failed as providers for their families. True, various studies have shown that women, as those who put food on the table, often initiated grain riots.[170] From the seventeenth century on, however, Genevans did not run the risk of starvation. Since the Republic of Geneva did not have nearly enough land to provide an adequate food supply for its population, its leaders established in 1628 La Chambre des Blés, mentioned above, which effectively stockpiled grains and intervened in times of crisis to assure that Geneva's population could be fed. In spite of its very limited agricultural resources, Geneva's grain reserves were generally sufficient to feed the entire population of Geneva for two years. Indeed, throughout the eighteenth century, Genevans were generally able to satisfy their preference for wheat bread, as opposed to the less expensive types such as rye.[171] True, on several occasions in the eighteenth century, Geneva endured popular unrest because of high bread prices. Nonetheless, from the early seventeenth century, no Genevans died directly from hunger.[172] Simply putting bread on the table was thus not a problem for the women of seventeenth- and eighteenth-century Geneva. In fact, Genevans were remarkably well fed. During the course of the eighteenth century, the consumption of bread

---

[169]Even when they performed such delicate tasks as fine-tuning the watches, which was a rarity by 1780, women were poorly paid; Mottu-Weber, "Women's Place of Work," in *Forgotten Women of Geneva*, ed. Käppeli, 100–5. For further information on women and work in early modern Geneva, see Liliane Mottu-Weber, "L'évolution des activités professionnelles des femmes à Genève du XVIe au XVIIIe siècle," in *La Donna nell'economia, secc. XVIII–XVIII*, ed. Simonetta Cavaciocchi (Florence: Le Monnier, 1990), 345–57; idem, "Femmes dans la vie économique," 381–401.

[170]Suzanne Desan, *Reclaiming the Sacred: Lay Religion and Popular Politics in Revolutionary France* (Ithaca, N.Y.: Cornell University Press, 1992), 199–200, 205–7; Olwen Hufton, "Women in Revolution, 1789–1796," *Past and Present*, 53 (1971): 104–8.

[171]See Hermann Blanc, *La Chambre des Blés de Genève 1628–1798* (Geneva: Georg, 1941); Hiler, "Fiscalité, conjoncture et consommation," 28–30; Laurence Wiedmer, *Pain quotidien et pain de disette: Meuniers, boulangers et Etat nourricier à Genève (XVIIe–XVIIIe siècles)* (Geneva: Editions Passé Présent, 1993), 32–39. Even well before 1628, Geneva's authorities had intervened to ensure that its population could be fed. See, for example, Liliane Mottu-Weber, "A propos de la crise de 1586–1587 à Genève: Du devoir des magistrats de nourrir le peuple et du droit des pasteurs de leur résister," in *Quand la Montagne aussi a une Histoire: Mélanges offerts à Jean-François Bergier*, ed. Martin Körner and François Walter (Bern: Paul Haupt, 1996), 151–65.

[172]Wiedmer, *Pain quotidien*, 11, 359–420; see also Perrenoud, *Population de Genève*, 444–46.

steadily declined in the Genevan diet while the consumption of meat—especially veal—increased.[173] Of course a family could be adequately fed yet still suffer from abject poverty. In such cases it was the father above all who suffered feelings of guilt for failing as a provider. Men who were married and the fathers of dependent children were especially prone to take their lives directly because of poverty. Significantly, though, as we will see in chapter 4, the majority of all suicides were unmarried—only a third of the men who took their lives out of poverty were bachelors.

In short, men enjoyed far more opportunities for economic success than women, but they accordingly had many more reasons to feel like failures. These findings bring to mind a number of sociological studies on twentieth-century suicide, which show an important connection between work failure and high suicide rates among males. In twentieth-century America, as in eighteenth-century Geneva, a male's status, his general relationship to society, is determined above all by his occupation. Evidence from the mid-twentieth century showed that suicide rates were much higher for retired men than for men of the same age who were still working. American evidence indicated that the greatest strain for males was to be out of work, as prevailing values implied that for a man to be without work was to live without purpose. As in early modern Europe, women in twentieth-century Western societies have often been restricted to lower-status, lower-wage jobs, which do not foster strong job identification. As a result, work failure and job loss generally have not produced the same feelings of failure as they do for men.

---

[173]For the years 1718–22, Genevans annually consumed 63–66 kilograms of meat per person, increasing to 83–88 kilos per person in 1780. At 85 kilos per person, even the Genevan hospital's annual meat rations were unusually generous for the years 1796–99. Even more impressive is the quality of the meat Genevans were consuming. In 1780 two-thirds of the meat they ate was beef and, amazingly, 35 percent of the total meat consumed was veal. By comparison, residents in the French Department of Le Léman consumed on the average only 6.5 kilograms of meat annually in 1813; David Hiler, "Permanences et innovations alimentaires: L'évolution de la consommation des Genevois pendant le XVIIe siècle," *Bulletin de la Société d'histoire et d'archéologie de Genève* 18 (1984): 26–31; Piuz, "Genève des Lumières," in *Histoire de Genève*, ed. Guichonnet, 228–29. According to official statistics, the average American consumed 80.7 kilograms of meat in 1995; 36.5 percent of this total was beef, but only 0.4 percent was veal; U.S. Bureau of the Census, *Statistical Abstract of the United States: 1997*, 149. The abundance of meat can be explained by the fact that the mountainous area around Geneva is better suited for pasture than for agriculture; Anne-Marie Piuz, "Note sur les rapports entre le prix du pain et le prix de la viande à Genève au XVIIIe siècle," *Bulletin du Département d'histoire économique: Université de Genève* 15 (1984–85): 47–51. Indeed, in the late eighteenth century, fully 26.5 percent of Genevan territory was in the form of meadows for grazing, primarily for cattle; Zumkeller, *Paysan et terre*, 177, 184.

Likewise, changes in the labor market have had a direct bearing on the suicide rates for males but far less impact on the frequency with which women kill themselves.[174] Since women's expectations were low, they were less likely to be disappointed.

What was true for the successes and failures associated with economic opportunities applied equally to political rights and privileges. The events preceding and immediately following the Revolution of December 1792 caused great disruption in Geneva. Even if for the most part people were not killing themselves specifically because of the fall of the Old Regime, the Revolution, combined with an economic crisis that continued unabated, nurtured a certain angst that cut across political and class lines. People were disturbed by the tumultuous times in which they lived and concerned about their finances and the futures of their children. Men alone were political actors in the Republic of Geneva, and in this period of political and economic instability, the well-being of most women depended in large part on the fortunes or misfortunes of their husbands and fathers. Regardless of the status of their husbands and fathers, women themselves had no political voice either before or after 1792.

While female activists promoted their rights in Revolutionary France, the political rights of women were never an issue in the Genevan conflicts of the 1790s. Geneva produced no Mary Wollstonecraft, and its female inhabitants never threatened or even seriously questioned the male bastions of political and economic privileges. As was so often the case in early modern Europe, even when women were actively involved in popular protests—as they certainly were in the Genevan unrest—they generally were not agitating for the rights of women.[175] The absence of feminist revolutionary activists

---

[174]Dennis A. Ahlburg and Morton Owen Schapiro, "Socioeconomic Ramifications of Changing Cohort Size: An Analysis of U.S. Postwar Suicide Rates by Age and Sex," *Demography* 21 (1984): 97–108; Maris, *Social Forces*, 95; Powell, "Occupations, Status, and Suicide," 131–39. Warren Breed's explanation about the connection between work failure and suicide among males could easily be applied to eighteenth-century Geneva: "Measuring up to the standard gives the individual a feeling of achievement and self-satisfaction; falling below it produces a painful sense of failure, or self-devaluation, of shame. Using this criterion, many of our suicides were shown to lack competence on the job. And because in American society the work role is central for man, work failure is not inadequacy in just one role among many, but spreads through other roles and the self-image to threaten a general collapse of life organization." See his "Occupational Mobility and Suicide," 188. See also Dublin, *Suicide*, 66.

[175]Judith M. Bennett's *Ale, Beer, and Brewsters in England: Women's Work in a Changing World, 1300–1600* (New York: Oxford University Press, 1996), 152, found no records of female brewers protest-

surely explains why Genevan male insurgents saw little need to embrace the aggressive antifeminism in contemporary France, where Jacobins shut down women's clubs and silenced female revolutionaries in October 1793.[176] Simply put, no evidence indicates that women rebelled against the political and economic limitations placed on their sex in Geneva. As a result, while they undoubtedly shared the hopes and fears of male family members, political setbacks weighed less upon Genevan women than on their husbands and fathers. In this age of patriarchy, men had more to win and more to lose politically and economically. In both politics and economics, men had far more opportunities than women to feel like successes or failures.[177]

These social mores governing gender roles, however, were nothing new in the late eighteenth century. Long before the founding of the Republic, political power in Geneva had rested solely in male hands. Men had a much stronger work identity than women in the sixteenth and seventeenth centuries. Though employment opportunities for women were probably more circumscribed in the eighteenth century than in Calvin's day, men had always been expected to be the principal breadwinners and invariably earned better wages even when performing similar work. Quite simply, patriarchy was not born in the eighteenth century. Thus, though the Genevans' growing materialism and the political and especially economic crises of the late 1700s con-

---

ing the obstacles that they faced as women. Similarly, Ralph A. Houlbrooke, "Women's Social Life and Common Action in England from the Fifteenth Century to the Eve of the Civil War," *Continuity and Change* 1 (1986): 171–89, finds that in early modern England there was rarely anything even vaguely feminist about the protests in which women participated.

[176]On the role of women and attitudes toward women in the French Revolution, see Jane Abray, "Feminism in the French Revolution," *American Historical Review* 80 (1975): 43–62; Darline Levy, Harriet Applewhite, and Mary Johnson, eds. and trans., *Women in Revolutionary Paris* (Urbana: University of Illinois Press, 1979); Linda Kelly, *Women of the French Revolution* (London: Hamish Hamilton, 1987); Annette Rosa, *Citoyennes: Les femmes et la Révolution française* (Paris: Messidor, 1988). In Revolutionary Geneva, only a couple of incidents bear even the slightest trace of feminism. In 1794 a Genevan Jacobin complained about the presence of women at the Great Fraternal Club, provoking the wrath of a host of female members who came close to beating him up. In 1797 a group of women proposed a new liturgy for marriage which "would better respect the rights of *homesses* [sic]"; see Monter, "Women in Calvinist Geneva," 207, n. 76.

[177]Referring to twentieth-century Western society, Baechler, *Suicides*, 290, notes that men generally experience a wider range of life's possibilities in professional, political, private life. Consequently, men also face a greater variety of problems than women, and a higher proportion of men are likely to fail in realizing their aspirations. This certainly was the case in early modern Geneva.

tributed to the suicide explosion and the widening gender gap among suicides, they do not suffice as explanations. Why had economic downturns and political unrest not been accompanied by rising numbers of suicides prior to the eighteenth century? What changes in mentality had occurred that made men and women, when faced with adversity, more willing to choose death?

4

The Cultural Dimensions of Suicide: Part 1

MARRIAGE, LOVE, AND THE FAMILY

While economic and political crises made a significant contribution to the growth in suicides in the late eighteenth century, cultural changes surely played an important role. Although a consensus has not been reached, a growing body of literature testifies to the increasing importance of romantic love in the formation of marriage and to closer emotional ties within the family in the eighteenth century.[1] This chapter will examine whether changes in attitudes toward marriage, romantic love, and the family contributed in any way to the suicidal explosion. Marriage and the family are arguably our most fundamental and influential institutions. Durkheim and other

---

[1] See, for example: Philippe Ariès, *Centuries of Childhood: A Social History of Family Life*, trans. Robert Baldick (London: Jonathan Cape, 1962); Rudolf Braun, *Industrialisation and Everyday Life*, trans. Sarah Hanbury Tenison (Cambridge: Cambridge University Press; Paris: Editions de la Maison des Sciences de L'Homme, 1990); Jean-Louis Flandrin, *Families in Former Times: Kinship, Household and Sexuality*, trans. Richard Southern (Cambridge: Cambridge University Press, 1979); Michael Mitterauer and Reinhard Sieder, *The European Family: Patriarchy to Partnership from the Middle Ages to the Present*, trans. Karla Oosterveen and Manfred Hörzinger, foreword by Peter Laslett (Chicago: University of Chicago Press, 1982); Edward Shorter, *The Making of the Modern Family* (New York: Basic Books, 1975); Lawrence Stone, *The Family, Sex and Marriage in England 1500–1800* (London: Weidenfeld and Nicolson, 1977); Randolph Trumbach, *The Rise of the Egalitarian Family: Aristocratic Kinship and Domestic Relations in Eighteenth-Century England* (New York: Academic Press, 1978); Jeffrey R. Watt, *The Making of Modern Marriage: Matrimonial Control and the Rise of Sentiment in Neuchâtel, 1550–1800* (Ithaca, N.Y.: Cornell University Press, 1992).

social scientists have long recognized that strong emotional support from one's family is one of the most effective safeguards against suicide: the stronger the family ties are, the greater immunity a person has against suicide.[2]

Accordingly, we must analyze the marital status and family situations of the suicides themselves. The criminal proceedings and death records almost always suffice to determine the marital status of women. The records identified women as being the wives or widows of their current or late husbands. If unmarried, a woman was identified as being the daughter of such and such a man or as the servant of her master. Consequently, we know the marital status of all but four of the 129 female suicides. For men, identifying the marital status is not so easy. The death records never mentioned if a man was married, although they at times indicated if he left minor children. In describing the events surrounding suicides, the criminal proceedings at times give enough evidence to indicate if a man was married; Auditeurs often but not always interrogated the widows of suicides. At times, we must look to other sources to ascertain if male suicides were married. Apart from some foreigners, most men, if they married, would have done so in Geneva or the surrounding countryside. Consequently, I have consulted marriage records to determine if male suicides were ever married and the death records to determine if their wives were still living at the time of the suicide. (I also consulted the baptism and death records to see if male and female suicides had any children who survived them.) Notwithstanding all these efforts, there were still twenty-five male suicides whose marital status I was unable to determine.[3]

The evidence from Geneva shows that suicide tended to be much more common among those who were single than among those who were married: single people were overrepresented and married people underrepresented among suicides. For the entire early modern period, only about a third of both male and female suicides were married at the time of their deaths (see tables 34–36). These findings support the view of Durkheim and subsequent schol-

---

[2]Emile Durkheim, *Suicide: A Study in Sociology*, trans. John A. Spaulding and George Simpson, edited and with an introduction by George Simpson (New York: Free Press, 1951): 171–89, 202. See also Nick Danigelis and Whitney Pope, "Durkheim's Theory of Suicide as Applied to the Family: An Empirical Test," *Social Forces* 57 (1979): 1081–1106; Henry Romilly Fedden, *Suicide: A Social and Historical Study* (New York: Benjamin Blom, 1972), 326; Ronald W. Maris, *Social Forces in Urban Suicide* (Homewood, Ill.: Dorsey Press, 1969), 108–10.

[3]The baptism, marriage, and death records for both the city and the countryside are most accessible thanks to superb indices.

ars who have found that suicide was much more common among single than married people. Durkheim and others have argued that marriage generally offers considerable immunity against suicide. Marriage serves as a means of

Table 34: Marital Status, Male and Female Suicides, 1542–1798[a]

Marital Status	Total	%
Single	172	45.9
Married	134	35.7
Widowed	52	13.9
Separated	15	4.0
Divorced	2	0.5
Unknown	29	n/a
Total	404	100.0

a. Source: Etat Civil: Livres des Baptêmes, Mariages et Morts; Procès Criminels; Registres du Conseil. The twenty-nine suicides whose marital status cannot be determined are not included in the percentages.

integration and thus protection from social isolation, and as a source of regulation, requiring that one take into account the interests of another person (before contemplating suicide, a married person must consider the impact on the spouse). Among those whose marital status was known, the percentage of suicides who were married was very slightly higher among men than among women. But perhaps a more telling figure is that the division by sex of the suicides who were married was essentially identical to that of suicides in general. Women comprised 31.3 percent of the married suicides and 31.9 percent of all suicides. This, combined with the fact that the largest category of suicides were those who had never married, indicates that marriage offered equal immunity to suicide to both men and women. This finding runs contrary to Durkheim's assertion that men benefitted more from marriage than women, and thus accordingly received more immunity to suicide. That is, the difference between the suicide rates for the married and unmarried was more pronounced for men than for women.[4] Simply put, marriage did not influence

[4]Durkheim, *Suicide*, 183–85. For Victorian England, Victor Bailey, *"This Rash Act": Suicide Across the Life Cycle in the Victorian City* (Stanford: Stanford University Press, 1998), 187, also found that the suicide rates of men and women were much higher among the single and widowed than among the married.

the gap between the numbers of men and women who took their lives.

Table 35: Marital Status, Female Suicides, 1542–1798[a]

DATES	SINGLE		MARRIED		WIDOWED		SEPARATED		DIVORCED		UNKNOWN		TOTAL
	n	%	n	%	n	%	n	%	n	%	n	%	n
1542–1600	0	–	2	66.7	1	33.3	0	–	0	–	1	–	4
1601–50	6	42.9	6	42.9	0	–	2	14.3	0	–	0	–	14
1651–1700	3	50.0	2	33.3	1	16.7	0	–	0	–	1	–	7
1701–50	12	48.0	7	28.0	5	20.0	1	4.0	0	–	1	–	26
1751–98	33	42.9	25	32.5	17	22.1	1	1.3	1	1.3	1	–	78
Total/Avg.	54	43.2	42	33.6	24	19.2	4	3.2	1	0.8	4	n/a	129

a. Source: Etat Civil: Livres des Baptêmes, Mariages et Morts; Procès Criminels; Registres du Conseil. The four women whose marital status cannot be determined are not included in the percentages.

We do see differences by sex, however, among the widowed suicides. The percentage of suicides who were widowed was noticeably higher among women than among men. This comes as no surprise insofar as widows traditionally were much more numerous than widowers in early modern cities, in part because women tended to be younger than their husbands. In eighteenth-century Geneva, widows in fact outnumbered widowers three to one. Both widows and widowers were clearly overrepresented among Genevan suicides throughout the early modern period. In Geneva's population at large, the widowed never made up more than about 8 percent of adults. Widowhood apparently reached a peak at the very end of this period, when 9.5 percent of adult females and 3.6 percent of adult males were widowed.[5] The widowed understandably were older than most suicides. While the average age of all suicides was 42.2 years (42.9 for males and 40.6 for females), the average age of widowed suicides was 57.5 years: 60.2 for widowers and 54.1 for widows. The widowed tended to be about ten years older than married suicides and about twenty-five years older than single suicides. (The average ages for single and married suicides were, respectively, 33 and 48.6 for men and 31.1 and 42.9 for women.) As they grew older, the widowed were more subject to the physical ailments that were common motives for

[5]Alfred Perrenoud, La population de Genève XVIe–XIX3 siècles (Geneva: Société d'histoire et d'archéologie de Genève, 1979), 81–82.

suicide. More often than not, the widowed lived in isolation; any children they may have had usually no longer lived with them. Living alone, they ran greater risks than others of suffering from depression and of falling into indigence, should they no longer be able to work. This latter eventuality was particularly dangerous for women, whose employment opportunities were

Table 36: Marital Status, Male Suicides, 1542–1798[a]

DATES	SINGLE		MARRIED		WIDOWED		SEPARATED		DIVORCED		UNKNOWN		TOTAL
	n	%	*n*	%	*n*	%	*n*	%	*n*	%	*n*	%	*n*
1542–1600	1	25.0	3	75.0	0	–	0	–	0	–	6	–	10
1601–50	3	27.3	7	63.6	1	9.1	0	–	0	–	1	–	12
1651–1700	7	50.0	7	50.0	0	–	0	–	0	–	1	–	15
1701–50	14	53.9	9	34.6	3	11.5	0	–	0	–	2	–	28
1751–98	93	47.7	66	33.9	24	12.3	11	5.6	1	0.5	15	–	210
Total/Avg.	118	47.2	92	36.8	28	11.2	11	4.4	1	0.4	25	n/a	275

a. Source: Etat Civil: Livres des Baptêmes, Mariages et Morts; Procès Criminels; Registres du Conseil. The twenty-five men whose marital status cannot be determined are not included in the percentages.

much more limited. Often faced with illness, isolation, and poverty, the widowed understandably committed suicide in disproportionate numbers.

Was widowhood equally difficult for men and women? In early modern Geneva, men made up a slight majority of widowed suicides (28 of 52), but because they constituted only about a fourth of the widowed population, their propensity to commit suicide was more than three times greater than that of widows. Among married suicides, in contrast, men outnumbered women by about two to one (92 to 41). Put another way, the proportion of male suicides in equal populations of men and women was 68.7 percent among the married but 77.8 percent among the widowed. For the half century after 1750, men were even more conspicuous among widowed suicides, accounting for 80.9 percent in equal populations of males and females. This evidence seems to lend credence to Durkheim's contention that men lost more than women in passing from marriage to widowhood.[6] Men may indeed have had a harder time dealing with widowhood because they lacked

[6]Durkheim, *Suicide*, 192. See also Bailey, *"This Rash Act,"* 213.

the domestic skills needed to live independently. This discrepancy, however, can also be explained in part by age. Genevan widowers in general, including those who committed suicide, were older than their female counterparts and thus more prone to suffer the illnesses that pushed several to take their lives.

During the course of the early modern period, the breakdown of suicides by marital status changed somewhat. As tables 35 and 36 indicate, the unmarried predominated among suicides in both the first and the second halves of the eighteenth century. If we look at the first 150 years of this study, however, we see that there were proportionally more people who were married and fewer who were single or widowed among suicides. For the years 1542–1700, among those whose marital status is known, a majority of male (17 of 29) and a large proportion (43.5 percent) of female suicides were married. Caution of course must be used in dealing with such small numbers. With this caveat in mind, we can nonetheless ask why the numbers of suicides of both sexes who were single or widowed grew vis-à-vis those who were married. Could it be that the proportion of Geneva's population that was married was declining in the eighteenth century? Evidence does indicate that the Genevans' average age at first marriage increased over time, but only very modestly: from 27.9 for husbands and 25.6 for wives in the seventeenth century, to 29.2 and 27.9, respectively, in the eighteenth.[7] An increase in the age at first marriage of a little more than one year for men and two years for women could not possibly have caused the proportion of the married population to drop to such an extent.

Other demographic evidence utterly contradicts the theory that the percentage of Genevans who married declined from the seventeenth to the eighteenth century. The proportion of Geneva's population, children included, that was married increased from 31.9 percent in 1720 to 36.2 percent in 1798, apparently resulting in part from a decrease in the number of people who never married. The declining numbers of the permanently single were the indirect result of Geneva's falling birthrate. From the late seventeenth

---

[7]The earliest age at marriage was 24.6 for women in 1625–44 and 27.3 for men in 1650–84. The latest average age at first marriage was 29.2 for men and 28 for women in 1725–27. No significant variations occurred for the rest of the eighteenth century. These figures refer to all marriages celebrated in Geneva, even those of foreigners; Alfred Perrenoud, "Les comportements démographiques," in *L'économie genevoise de la Réforme à la fin de l'Ancien Régime XVIe–XVIIIe siècles*, ed. Anne-Marie Piuz and Liliane Mottu-Weber (Geneva: Société d'histoire et d'archéologie de Genève, 1990), 86–88.

century, members of all social classes in Geneva intentionally limited family size—apparently through coitus interruptus—resulting in the steady reduction in the number of children per family.[8] With fewer children, parents were more likely to have the means to establish sons in apprenticeships and to provide dowries for daughters, thus facilitating marriages for both and accordingly decreasing the numbers of the permanently single. Simply put, the declining proportion of married men and women among suicides in the eighteenth century ran contrary to demographic trends in Geneva. Thus while it appears likely that for the first century and a half of this study, married men—and perhaps also married women—were overrepresented among suicides, there is no doubt that for the eighteenth century single people were overrepresented and married people underrepresented among suicides. Consequently, while the suicide rates increased for all categories of marital status in the late eighteenth century, they were clearly growing at very different rates.[9] Concentrating on the eighteenth century, we must ask why married people were less likely to take their lives than the unmarried.

One possible reason for the discrepancy between married and single suicides is a form of matrimonial selection. Not everyone who wants to marry is able to do so. The sick, the destitute, the insane, among others, are all at a disadvantage in finding mates. Such people may stand out from the population at large by a higher mortality rate, greater criminality, and even stronger suicidal tendencies. If such is the case, then marriage and the family in and of themselves may not offer protection from suicide. Rather, only the more stable would be admitted to the ranks of the married, and the unmarried would include the less stable and the more suicide-prone.

The evidence from Geneva suggests that matrimonial selection played a certain role. The suicide of Jean Dittmar is a case in point. Dittmar, twenty-nine, a Natif in the watchmaking industry, shot himself to death in August 1772, eleven years after castrating himself as protection against "the temptations of the flesh and the desire to marry."[10] An industrious but solitary

---

[8]The average number of children per family for all classes fell from 5.7 in 1650–74, to 3.7 in 1745–49 and 1770–72, reaching a nadir of 2.5 in 1800–1810; Perrenoud, "Comportements démographiques," in *Economie genevoise*, ed. Piuz and Mottu-Weber, 105.

[9]By contrast, evidence from nineteenth-century France shows that suicide rates increased at roughly the same pace for both married and unmarried people; Maurice Halbwachs, *Les causes du suicide* (Paris: Félix Alcan, 1930), 490–91.

[10]AEG, PC 10868.

young man, Dittmar wrote a suicide note, declaring that his wound alone, which was becoming ever deeper and more painful, had pushed him to this extreme act. Clearly Dittmar suffered from mental instability that had driven him first to mutilate and then to kill himself. In light of the castration, it is not surprising that Dittmar never married.[11]

Although Dittmar's case was clearly exceptional, many other suicides involved mentally unstable people, for whom marriage was unlikely. The Citizen Jean-Philippe Roux, thirty-three, was incarcerated for dementia when he hanged himself at the hospital in April 1769. According to members of the hospital staff, Roux had tried unsuccessfully to hang himself before and had often asked members of the hospital staff for a knife or a rifle, though they understandably did not honor that request. The Auditeur affirmed that Roux had been incarcerated and labeled "crazy" by order of the Small Council a full year before his suicide.[12] Marie-Anne Moulinier, twenty-six, who drowned herself in "a fit of craziness" in May 1790, apparently suffered from congenital mental illness. The criminal proceeding indicates that Moulinier's mother, already "crazy" at the time of Marie-Anne's birth, spent the last several years of her life in Geneva's hospital, confined and labeled insane. Raised by the hospital, Moulinier never proved herself capable of living independently. As a young woman, she developed an "insane passion" for a man with whom she had never exchanged a word. This disruptive passion led eventually to her being incarcerated in 1787 in the same institution where her mother had been kept. Later, she again demonstrated erratic behavior, saying she wanted to marry or become a nun, an odd request for a Protestant.[13] In light of their mental state, Moulinier and Roux were unlikely to find spouses. Though not necessarily insane, Jean-Robert Badollet, twenty-seven, a Citizen in the watchmaking industry who shot himself to death in July 1789, was described as "feebleminded." He was

[11]AEG, EC, LM 64: 245, 21 August 1772; PC 12363; RC 273: 482.

[12]AEG, EC, LM 64: 77, 22 April 1769; Juridiction Civile F 597; PC 11865; RC 270: 237. A small but not insignificant statistic is that of the nine suicides (five women and four men) involving people who were incarcerated for alienation, only one, a woman, was married at the time. Four were single (one woman and three men), three women were widows, and one man was of unknown marital status.

[13]AEG, EC, LM 67: 209, 14 May 1790; PC 16053. Moulinier obviously was Protestant insofar as her minister, a certain pastor Fontanes, had counseled her at length. Moulinier was ordered to be buried without honors, the last time that authorities denied customary funerary honors to a suicide; RC 295: 558–59.

entirely without education and unable to read or write—most unusual for a Citizen artisan at this time. He was also physically handicapped and walked with a limp, which he believed prevented him from finding a wife. Chances are, however, his intellectual limitations proved a greater hindrance in finding a wife than his physical imperfections.[14]

All these examples reveal unmarried suicides who were relegated to the fringe of society. In these specific cases, however, it appears that they were single because they were marginal and not marginal because they were single. Because of their mental instability, intellectual limitations, or physical unattractiveness, they and some others had not been able to attract mates. Although Dittmar expressed a fear of marriage, Moulinier and Badollet clearly wanted to marry. It appears therefore that matrimonial selection did play a certain role in accounting for the disproportionate number of suicides who had never married. In particular, those lacking mental stability were both more likely to commit suicide and less likely to attract spouses.[15]

Be that as it may, matrimonial selection can account for only a small part of the discrepancy between the suicide rates of the married and unmarried. To begin with, single people definitely did not have a monopoly on insanity and bizarre behavior. Pierre Puech, seventy-nine, was an eccentric, marginal character who drowned himself in the Arve River in April 1763. Having been widowed two years before his death, Puech, according to his nephew by marriage, had been a hosier but had renounced his trade twenty-five years ago in order to dedicate himself simply to gathering roots, frogs, and snails. The nephew believed that Puech, though poor, did not kill himself out of poverty; rather he did so simply because he was deranged and led an animal-like existence without cares and without any regard to cleanliness.[16] If he had always acted in this fashion, one cannot help but be amazed that he ever married at all. Of course, mental illness could develop just as easily after marriage as before. Jean Bovard, the vinegar maker referred to briefly in chapter 2, was married well before he started suffering from violent delusions. Just before jumping in the Rhône, Bovard was hallucinating, stabbing with a knife an imaginary man in his bed, and running wildly about as if chased by someone. Until less than a year before his death, however,

[14]AEG, PC 15762.
[15]Cf. Durkheim, *Suicide*, 180–85.
[16]AEG, EC, LM 63: 107, 28 April 1763; PC 11131; RC 263: 151.

Bovard had reportedly led a normal existence.[17] Examples such as these are intended to show that the lower suicide rates for married people were not simply a case of matrimonial selection. Mental and physical infirmities, along with poverty, did make the formation of marriage difficult for some. These same plights, however, could also occur after marriage and could, as we have seen, help lead to suicide. The lower incidence of suicide among married people must mean that marriage itself offered a certain immunity to suicide.

But what was it about marriage that provided a degree of safety against suicide? The most plausible explanation is in the area of sentiment. The reason that the percentage of married people declined among suicides from the sixteenth and seventeenth centuries to the eighteenth was because people were investing more of themselves emotionally in marriage and the nuclear family. Significantly, between 1751 and 1798, over a fourth of the suicides (75 of 288) were motivated at least in part by family concerns, such as grief over the loss of a loved one, domestic disputes, romantic misadventures, or generational conflicts. By comparison, such motives figured in only fourteen suicides during the previous two hundred years, eight of which took place in the first half of the eighteenth century. If the companionate marriage was gaining popularity in the eighteenth century, then the more intense emotional support offered by matrimony should have offered more protection than ever against suicide. By the same token, the higher percentage of married people among pre-1700 suicides may simply reflect that marriage was less emotionally based and consequently offered less immunity to suicide. Moreover, if in the eighteenth century more emphasis was placed on romance which was expected to lead to marriage, then more single people would likely feel emotionally unfulfilled. In such circumstances, it should come as no surprise to find some suicides among emotionally frustrated single people.

Conversely, if a society puts little emphasis on romantic love, then one would surely think that failure in love would rarely incite people to take their lives. The rarity of references to suicide for love among the Greeks and Romans has quite plausibly been attributed to the ancients' giving little

[17]AEG, EC, LM 34: 72v, 26 June 1645; PC 2e série 2485; RC 144: 66v–67, 122v.

importance to romantic love.[18] Similarly, in sixteenth- and seventeenth-century Geneva, not one suicide can realistically be attributed to a romantic misadventure.[19] Even in the first half of the eighteenth century, only one such suicide occurred. This first case, from 1734, shows that in the choice of marriage partners, interest and emotion at times conflicted, causing unrest in some Genevan families. Samuel Pellet, thirty, was a haberdasher who courted Catherine Pansie for three years with the hope of marrying her. At first his parents opposed this match because they considered her too poor. They eventually agreed and Pellet's mother even gave Pansie a ring in an informal ceremony, "showing all the signs of affection that one expects on such occasions."[20] The couple also made the announcements for their marriage in November 1733. Pellet's parents' reservations did not disappear, however. François Verceil, a friend and neighbor, reported that Samuel spoke to him about his parents' opposition. Samuel even told him that he was considering breaking his marriage with Catherine because of his parents' pressure. Verceil told him he thought such a move would be unwise and even impossible, and Samuel acknowledged that he shared a great intimacy with Catherine and that, all things considered, he really wanted to marry her. On Tuesday, 27 January 1734, unbeknownst to Pellet's parents, Samuel and Catherine were married at the morning church service. Samuel then went alone to his parents' house to tell them about the marriage and to get some rings and a belt buckle that he wanted to give his bride. When he told his mother the news, she became absolutely furious and began slapping her son, causing Samuel's brother-in-law to intervene and subdue her. When Samuel returned to his own abode, he recounted this incident to Catherine and to Verceil and his

---

[18]Fedden, *Suicide*, 51–53.

[19]Jürsten Dieselhorst, "Die Bestrafung der Selbstmörder im Territorium der Reichsstadt Nürnberg," *Mitteilungen des Vereins Geschichte der Stadt Nürnberg* 44 (1953): 130–33, did find a few suicides motivated by unhappy love stories or by marital breakdown in sixteenth- and seventeenth-century Nürnberg. In studying insanity in seventeenth-century England, Michael MacDonald found that woes associated with courtship and marriage were the source of mental anguish for 40 percent of those who sought professional psychological help; see *Mystical Bedlam: Madness, Anxiety, and Healing in Seventeenth-Century England* (Cambridge: Cambridge University Press, 1981), 88–94. Religious literature from the later Middle Ages includes several examples of suicidal inclinations that were motivated by *chagrin d'amour*. Moreover, a number of completed medieval suicides were attributed to issues pertaining to love and marriage; Terence R. Murray, *Suicide in the Middle Ages*, vol. 1, *The Violent Against Themselves* (Oxford: Oxford University Press, 1998), 251–94, 400.

[20]AEG, PC 8123.

wife who were present. Devastated by this reaction, Catherine threw herself in the Rhône the next morning. Their marriage had thus lasted one day.[21]

While this was the only such suicide before 1750, in the latter half of the eighteenth century seventeen people—twelve men and five women—were driven to take their lives because of unrequited love or because a romance had not led to marriage as hoped. Jeanne Renée Dunant, forty-nine, a member of an affluent family, drowned herself in June 1757, after suffering from "alienation of spirit" for a number of years. According to witnesses, her mental instability resulted from a love affair that went awry with a certain Sieur Frelitte—a man with whom she had a four-year liaison. Frelitte reportedly had led her on with promises of marriage but married another woman in 1751. Upon learning of that marriage, Dunant had tried to commit suicide by jumping into a well, though she was immediately fished out without serious injuries. Although thereafter Dunant was often lucid, she invariably became most upset whenever she saw a bride passing through the streets.[22] Similarly, the watchmaker Louis Marcinhes, thirty-six, shot himself to death in September 1779 because of his failure in love. According to friends and to a series of letters he wrote immediately before shooting himself, Marcinhes had been badly hurt by two successive romantic misadventures. His more recent passion appeared particularly hopeless—he was infatuated with a woman in a Roman Catholic nunnery.[23] In July 1785 Christine Scherff, twenty-four, was seen jumping in the Rhône just shortly after her fiancé had reproached her, saying he would not marry her unless she changed her behavior.[24]

One couple committed double suicide when their happy affair was threatened. Pierre Adam Rey, a carpenter from the Pays de Vaud, and Jeanne Bovay, a servant, appeared to be an ordinary, happily married couple. In reality, their union was bigamous. After they drowned themselves in January 1780, a number of documents and letters found in their apartment allowed authorities to piece together this sad story. Rey had been married in the Pays de Vaud twenty-two years before to another woman. The registers of the city council of Lausanne revealed that this was an unhappy marriage. Rey's wife

---

[21]AEG, PC 8123. Of course this particular case itself does not help explain the large number of single suicides since Pansie was technically married at the time of her death.

[22]AEG, EC, LM 62: 182, 19 June 1757; PC 10454; RC 257: 354–55.

[23]AEG, PC 13389.

[24]AEG, EC, LM 66: 343, 28 July 1785; PC 14677; RC 289: 803.

was so violent that the council ordered the couple to leave Lausanne, though it did write an attestation to Rey's good behavior. When he left Lausanne in 1776, Rey separated from his wife, but the two were never formally divorced. The two most recent documents found in Rey's apartment were extremely angry letters, both dated 6 January 1780, from Rey's brother and son. Both were furious that Rey had married Bovay and threatened to expose their bigamy. Neighbors had seen Rey and Bovay most upset on 7–8 January. They were last seen 9 January, jumping in the Rhône—the bodies were never found.[25]

Jeanne Pernette Diauville and Abraham De Fernex, both twenty-three, were lovers who committed suicide a few hours apart in June 1782 in a manner reminiscent of Romeo and Juliet. Witnesses testified to the love they had for one another, a love, however, that "was so violent that at times they quarreled over very insignificant things, always convinced that their passion was at stake in even the slightest things."[26] According to witnesses, the couple strongly wanted to marry but had encountered a certain amount of resistance from both fathers. Just before their suicides, De Fernex had spoken to Diauville's father and became most upset when the latter intimated that, though he did not object, Jeanne herself was less than enthusiastic about the match. In a note to her, the hurt De Fernex complained about her wavering, declaring that he loved her more than ever. He further asked rhetorically what good it did to get her family's consent to the match if he could not obtain hers, adding that the family's approval was merely to complement her decision. After crying much of the following day, Diauville took a large dose of opium before going to bed, and she died about noon the next day. Unaware of her death, De Fernex arrived at the Diauville home about an hour later. Upon hearing the sad news, the hysterical, weeping De Fernex threw himself on his fiancée's corpse, which he hugged and kissed repeatedly. Only with difficulty could he be torn from the body. About 5:00 P.M. that same day, De Fernex took his life by shooting himself in the chest, leaving a short suicide note that read: "Father, this is the last sorrow I will cause you."[27] This lovers' dispute proved fatal to them both.

[25]AEG, PC 13447; RC 281: 56, 114.
[26]AEG, PC 13889.
[27]AEG, EC, LM 66: 132, 2 June 1782; PC 13889; RC 283 bis: 336, 340. Quotation from PC 13890.

In considering the companionate marriage against the marriage of convenience, we must keep in mind that this is a question of degrees. It is wrong to suggest that prior to the Enlightenment, all marriages were formed solely on the basis of wealth and status and were arranged by parents with no regard to the inclinations of their sons and daughters.[28] It is equally incorrect to suggest that beginning in the latter part of the eighteenth century, young people enjoyed unbridled freedom in forming marriages that were based exclusively on love. Dowries and other material concerns were still factors in the formation of marriages. As the case of Diauville and De Fernex suggests, parental consent to a union, which was required until the age of twenty-five, was still considered an important part of the process of forming a marriage. Thus, in 1793 Matthieu Jourdan, a twenty-four-year-old soldier, shot himself in front of his parents' house, reportedly upset about his mother's opposition to his proposed marriage.[29]

Another love story with an unhappy ending involved Pierre François Varlet, forty, an actor from Paris who drowned himself in November 1790 because he feared his upcoming marriage plans would be thwarted. Jean Samuel Muller, an Habitant and dance instructor, testified that his daughter and Varlet had engaged in a love affair for the past five years. Muller had long refused to grant Varlet's request for his daughter's hand in marriage because he did not want his daughter following the migrations of a theater troupe. After Varlet promised to give up acting, Muller agreed to the match and the

---

[28]As early as 1619 we have clear evidence of a Genevan couple marrying for love. The Consistory referred a couple to the Small Council, disapproving of the match because the woman was thirteen years older than her fiancé: "Sur le renvoy dudit Consistoire portant que Pierre Mauris et Sarra Deroches vefve de Jacques Levet se sont promis en mariage de paroles tant seulement, et que ladite Sarra a advoué d'estre aagée de quarante cinq ans, et ledit Mauris a fait foy d'un extrait du livre des Baptesmes par lequel il se trouve n'estre aagé que de trente deux ans; Les parties ayant esté ouys et protesté de ne se vouloir ni pouvoir separer à cause de la grande amitié et affection qu'ils se portent reciproquement, A esté arresté qu'on leur permet de se marier"; AEG, RC 118: 129v. As this couple was older and the woman a widow, it is unlikely that parents, even if alive, would have played any role whatsoever in the formation of this marriage.

[29]AEG, EC, LM 68: 73, 1 August 1793; PC 17012; RC 302: 809. In 1545 Calvin composed laws governing marriage, which served as the basis of the actual marriage laws that were adopted in Geneva in 1561. Calvin proposed requiring parental permission to marry until the age of twenty-four for men and twenty for women, but magistrates changed these ages to twenty and eighteen, respectively, in the ordinances; *CO* 10/a, 33–34, 105; Jeffrey R. Watt, "The Marriage Laws Calvin Drafted for Geneva," in *Calvinus Sacrae Scripturae Professor*, ed. W. H. Neuser (Grand Rapids, Mich.: Eerdman's, 1994), 247. The *Edits civils* of 1713 raised the age at which one could marry without permission to twenty-five for both men and women; E. William Monter, "Women in Calvinist Geneva (1550–1800)," *Signs* 6 (1980): 194.

couple planned to marry around Easter 1791. Muller spoke quite highly of Varlet and his pleasing disposition, and various witnesses testified to the strong affection the couple had for each other. Varlet spent considerable time in the evenings at the Muller household and often accompanied his daughter to the various places where she evidently gave private music lessons of some sort. At first, no one had a clue as to what pushed Varlet to commit suicide, the news of which absolutely devastated his fiancée. Muller produced a letter Varlet had written him while the acting troupe was performing in France. There is a hint that Varlet regretted having to give up the theater, but the joy of marrying the woman he loved apparently far outweighed this professional sacrifice. The Auditeur found among Varlet's personal effects a letter from his father in Paris, dated 28 April 1790, in which he gave his consent to any marriage the younger Varlet might contract, provided he marry a Catholic woman. There is no evidence to indicate that Muller was Catholic, but it is unlikely that the forty-year-old Varlet was doing anything more than going through a formality in asking for a generic paternal permission to marry. A more likely motive for suicide involved a love triangle. Shortly after Varlet's death, a fellow actor received a letter from a colleague who worked with the theater in Lyon. The letter revealed that when Varlet's troupe had been in Lyon for an extensive period, Varlet had developed a liaison with a woman there. The two of them lived together, and the woman claimed to have a written marriage promise which Varlet had signed. This affair, which produced a child who was baptized with Varlet's name, took place after Varlet had proposed to Muller but before he had received her father's consent. The letter inquired as to how the woman could make a claim on Varlet's estate.[30] Evidence thus indicates that Varlet feared that this affair and marriage contract would be exposed and would prevent him from marrying Muller whom he loved. Varlet and others clearly shared the view of Madame de Staël, who wrote in 1796 that love was among the most sublime justifications for suicide.[31]

In addition to these unhappy love affairs, instances of vicarious passions led to suicides in the late eighteenth century. Three young bachelors were inspired to take their lives after reading Johann Wolfgang von Goethe's *The*

[30]AEG, PC 16236.
[31]Lester G. Crocker, "The Discussion of Suicide in the Eighteenth Century," *Journal of the History of Ideas* 13 (1952): 55.

Sorrows of Young Werther. The first of these involved Ami Pattey, a nineteen-year-old Citizen and apprentice watchmaker who lived with his parents and grandfather. About noon on Sunday, 27 June 1779, the young Pattey briefly paid a visit to Jaqueline Brodon, a widow who lived in the same building. He sat down in her apartment and showed her a book, saying, "I have a nice book here." After reading silently for a few minutes, Pattey asked Brodon if she had a pistol. When she said she did not, he got up and left. About two that afternoon, a loud bang was heard coming from the shop on the fourth floor where Pattey and other watchmakers worked. Pattey had shot himself in the head with a rifle. Beside the body was a French translation of Goethe's *Werther*, the same book that Brodon had seen him reading shortly before. No other plausible motive for suicide was found.[32]

Before committing suicide in September 1783, the nineteen-year-old Etienne Pestre had worked as an apprentice grocer. His employer was generally satisfied with Pestre's job performance, though he had reproached him several times for reading novels on the job. According to his cousin, Jacques Girod, just before his death, Pestre had spoken admiringly about a man who had drowned himself just three weeks earlier, insisting that a virtuous man can indeed take his life. He also spoke highly of the novel *Werther*, of which he owned a French translation. About 9:45 on the evening of 23 September, Pestre passed by Girod's abode for a brief chat. When he took leave of Girod, Pestre said that he was going to spend the night with the book he held under his arm, the title of which he did not want to reveal. When his brother and another man forced open Pestre's locked door the next morning, they found his body seated in a chair with a gunshot wound to the head. By his side were a discharged pistol and a blood-splattered copy of *Werther*, apparently the same book Girod had seen the previous evening.[33]

The third youthful suicide to draw inspiration from *Werther*, André De La Rue, eighteen, an apprentice watchmaker, was the only one who appar-

---

[32]AEG, EC, LM 65: 277, 27 June 1779; PC 13346; RC 280: 334.

[33]The Auditeur found three letters that Pestre had written just before shooting himself, including one to his mother and another to his sister. In these letters, he begged for forgiveness for causing them pain. Referring to her as "the best of all mothers," Pestre wrote to his mother that it was his melancholy, his "black humor that was driving him to the tomb." To both of them he complained that nature had made him too sensitive: "What character, what soul has nature given me? Should I call it sensitive or criminal?" He also regretted having lost his father too young and was looking forward to seeing him again "up above." Asking his sister to console their mother, Etienne told her that he wished with all his heart

ently had an unhappy love affair. After he died by poisoning himself in October 1793, a witness spoke of an unhappy liaison. Several testified that De La Rue had a rather melancholic personality and had read Goethe's *Werther* and other similar novels.[34] Clearly the maudlin misadventures of Werther hit a responsive chord among Geneva's artisanal youth.

A greater emphasis on sentiment in marriage and the family could lead to more suicides among married in addition to single people. Marriage based more on sentiment than on material concerns is an example of the growing individualism which, according to Durkheim and others, is responsible for increasing numbers of suicides. One may argue that the emphasis on the importance of romance in marriage has reduced considerably the significance of other duties that spouses have traditionally owed one another.[35] In eighteenth-century Geneva, as romantic love grew in importance, loveless marriages were becoming less tolerable. After 1750 thirteen Genevans, ten men and three women, were driven to commit suicide at least in part because of unfulfilling marriages or marital breakdown (only three suicides, all involving females, were so motivated prior to 1750).[36] One such suicide involved Pierre Dombre, referred to in chapter 3, who shot himself in June 1787. Not only did he lament his poverty, the result of technological change; the unemployed watchmaker also suffered from marital breakdown and

---

that he could spare his mother this pain. He claimed, however, that he just could not go on. "Each day,…each minute" was a death for him, he wrote. "I was dying a thousand times, simply for not dying once." Ending the letter to his sister, Etienne wrote, "Farewell, the most excellent of sisters. Live happily—that's the wish of your brother who has only a few minutes left to live"; AEG, PC 14170.

[34]Before taking poison, De La Rue wrote a letter to his parents in which he insisted that he was leaving this world not because he did not love them. On the contrary, it grieved him greatly to leave such good parents who did not deserve to have such an unworthy son. He also begged forgiveness of them and of his sisters, to whom he wished all the happiness possible, and bade farewell to his friends, hoping that they would not regret having befriended him; AEG, EC, LM 68: 82, 16 October 1793; PC 17092; RC 302: 1052.

[35]Anthony Giddens, "A Typology of Suicide," in *The Sociology of Suicide: A Selection of Readings*, ed. Anthony Giddens (London: Frank Cass, 1971), 99.

[36]One of these early suicides, that of Sarah Garnier in December 1722, was motivated more by public humiliation than by conflicts with her husband. The wife of Jean Pautet of the village of Choully, Garnier reportedly had been rather unstable emotionally ever since giving birth to their son about twenty months before. Though her husband tried to be accommodating, they had a bitter quarrel a week before her death in which Garnier became violent and broke a jar over Pautet's head, badly injuring him. Though Garnier begged her husband for forgiveness, news of this violent attack spread, and other villagers, particularly the youth, decided that Garnier needed to be taught a lesson and so organized a charivari.

unrequited love. Dombre was a very cultivated man and an amateur poet who left behind many writings. In one letter he bitterly complained about his wife, from whom he was now separated, intimating that she had gone to Lyon, taking their son with her, in order to abort a fetus she had conceived in an adulterous affair. Abandoned by his wife, Dombre was now hopelessly in love with an unidentified married woman. In a letter to her, Dombre wrote that he had passed three days without eating or drinking anything, but not from want of money. Now at his last gasp, he begged her to come to his room with a cup of hemlock so that he could die at her feet. He professed his love for her and proclaimed that her husband was not worthy of her. After she refused to come, returning his letter, Dombre wrote that beautiful women were both the cure and the cause of his ills.[37]

Jean Bertrand, a wine seller from Bourdigny in France, shot himself in August 1792 because he was most upset that his wife had left him two weeks before.[38] After drinking a bottle of wine, Jean Alexandre Fontaine, thirty-five, shot himself in the head in July 1777. According to witnesses, Fontaine, employed in watchmaking, had become quite alienated and degenerate since his recent divorce. Having attempted suicide once already by stabbing himself, Fontaine was the only person in early modern Geneva to take his life directly because of a divorce.[39]

Antoinette Jaquet, thirty-three, a seamstress who was married to the enameler Thomas Nogué, jumped to her death in March 1778. According to some neighbors, Jaquet, the mother of two young daughters, had been quite melancholic recently, which they attributed to domestic discord. She reportedly had been upset by the recent birth of an illegitimate child that her husband had fathered. Nonetheless, according to one witness, Jaquet told her husband that it did not matter and she would not love him any less.

Congregating in front of the Pautet home, they forced Garnier to come outside and be ridden on a donkey. Following the charivari, the humiliated Garnier drowned herself in a stream; AEG, PC 7028. The charivari, found in rural societies throughout western Europe, was a means of maintaining social mores in communities. When one violated the accepted code of behavior, one ran the risk of the humiliation associated with a charivari. See Natalie Zemon Davis, "The Reasons of Misrule," in *Society and Culture in Early Modern France* (Stanford: Stanford University Press, 1975), 97–123.

[37] AEG, PC 15188.
[38] AEG, EC, LM 68: 29, 11 August 1792; PC 16742; RC 300: 967.
[39] AEG, EC, LM 65: 150, 2 July 1777; PC 12990; RC 278: 303.

Far from accepting graciously this forgiveness, Nogué continued to treat her unkindly and suggested that they separate.[40] Jaquet shortly thereafter committed suicide.

For Dame Antoinette Martin, referred to in chapter 3, her marriage was also a factor in her suicide, but for very different reasons. In addition to regretting having married beneath her station, this French noblewoman took her life in October 1759 in part because she had a husband she considered kind and thoughtful but a bit boring. At sixty-two, her husband for the past twelve years, the surgeon Antoine Laurent, was thirty years her senior. On the morning of her death, Martin, unbeknownst to anyone else, swallowed a considerable quantity of arsenic. As she lay ill in bed, she bade her ten-year-old daughter to draw near. Taking the girl's hand which she squeezed tightly, Martin told her "to be good to her dear father and to follow all his orders."[41] A female friend reported that Martin nonetheless had complained that her husband was too old for her and regularly bemoaned her lot in life. Several witnesses revealed that Martin had developed a strong romantic interest in a young man before she married Laurent and that this inclination continued after her marriage. Her friend, Marie Pepin, reported seeing her sitting close to this gentleman, engrossed in a conversation. Pepin rebuked Martin, telling her that the wife of a jealous man should be more prudent in the way she acted. Although no evidence suggests that Martin was having an affair, several witnesses testified that Laurent was quite jealous—apparently insecure of his wife's affection for him. Although her unstable character, replete with volatile temper and frequent depressions, was ultimately responsible for this suicide, Martin's dissatisfaction with her marriage clearly contributed to her emotional malaise.[42] Martin respected her husband as a decent man who genuinely cared for her and their daughter. She felt, however, emotionally unfulfilled and regretted having agreed to this marriage of convenience. In the second half of the eighteenth century, the suicides of eight other people, all men, were apparently motivated at least in part by marital breakdown, be it an unhappy union or the wife's departure. Simply put, the growing importance of the love match made loveless marriages less tolerable, inciting several unhappily married Genevans to take their lives.

[40]AEG, EC, LM 65, 202, 11 March 1778; PC 13098; RC 279: 126.
[41]AEG, PC 10707.
[42]AEG, PC 10707. See also EC, LM 62: 321, 20 October 1759; RC 259: 460–61, 481, 489.

A growing emphasis on the companionate marriage could thus cut both ways with regard to marital status. Some single people who failed at love took their lives, while some married people committed suicide because their marriages failed or proved unsatisfying. The emphasis on romance, however, ultimately weighed more on unsuccessful single people than on those who were unhappily married. For those in miserable marriages, divorce might have been an option, providing relief from an unhappy union and the possibility of a future remarriage. Although the acceptable grounds for divorce had not changed—they were still basically limited to adultery and desertion—Geneva witnessed a dramatic increase in divorces in the second half of the eighteenth century which paralleled the increase in suicides.[43] Even when a person did not have valid grounds for divorce, there were ways of getting out of unhappy unions, much to the dismay of contemporary moralists. In the late eighteenth century, the number of illicit separations increased and for the first time, a large number of men received divorces on the basis of desertion, a ground previously alleged almost exclusively by abandoned wives. According to contemporary accounts, numerous women left their husbands and Geneva. Once their husbands divorced them, many returned and remarried.[44] In an ironic manner, increasing numbers of divorces and separations denoted the growing importance of sentiment in marriage, reflecting the desire to escape unhappy marriages and perhaps form new, happier unions. In short, although some people committed suicide because of marital breakdown, far more preferred separation or divorce.

Durkheim maintained that the suicide rate is higher for divorcees than for all other marital statuses; as divorce represents conjugal anomie, Durkheim asserted that divorce and suicide increase contemporaneously,

---

[43]While there were only 67 divorces in the first half of the eighteenth century, Genevan magistrates accorded 282 divorces after 1750, 169 of which were granted in the years 1781–1798. See Laurent Haeberli, "Le suicide à Genève au XVIIIe siècle," *Pour une Histoire Qualitative: Etudes offertes à Sven Stelling-Michaud* (Geneva: Presses Universitaires Romandes, 1975), 123, n. 2; Bernard Sonnaillon, "Etude des divorces à Genève dans la seconde moitié du XVIIIe siècle" (Mémoire de licence, Université de Genève, 1975), 50.

[44]Monter, "Women in Calvinist Geneva," 195–96; Liliane Mottu-Weber, "Des ordonnances ecclésiastiques au Code civil (1804): Jalons pour une étude du divorce à Genève de la Réformation à la Restauration," in *Dossier Helvetik–Dossier Helvétique*, ed. Christian Simon, vol. 2, *Structures sociales et économiques: Histoire des femmes* (Basel: Helbing; Frankfurt am Mein: Lichtenhahn, 1997), 167–85; Thérèse Pittard, *Femmes de Genève aux jours d'autrefois* (Geneva: Labor et Fides, 1946), 31–34.

showing a causal connection between the two.[45] The number of suicides who were divorced or separated is not large enough to lend itself to statistical analysis. During the entire early modern period, there were only two divorced suicides, involving a man in 1777 and a woman in 1778. There were also fifteen suicides who were officially or unofficially separated, twelve of whom (eleven men and one woman) took their lives after 1750. Divorce and separations therefore played at most a very minor role in directly influencing the suicide explosion of the late eighteenth century. Divorce and suicide appear rather to have been alternative options to marital unhappiness. Along with the love match, suicide and divorce represented an important change in mentality: increased individualism.[46] Marriage for love and separation or divorce for its absence reflected a growing desire for personal fulfillment in matrimony. Terminating one's life, like ending a marriage, generally involved putting one's own concerns above those of others. This enhanced emphasis on individualism shows that the Republic of Geneva was a much less tightly integrated society in the late 1700s than before.

Increased individualism was also the source of friction within families, as different generations had conflicting views on their rights and responsibilities. Generational conflicts were behind fifteen suicides after 1750 (as opposed to only three before), involving twelve males and three females. Five individuals, all men, were driven to commit suicide at least in part because of conflicts with their grown sons or daughters.[47] For example, Isaac Jarre, who was married, shot himself in September 1629 after having been quite sad for about a year, especially about the marriage engagement of his eighteen-year-old daughter.[48] The other four cases, involving three widowers and a man

---

[45]Durkheim, *Suicide*, 259–62. American sociological studies that show very high suicide rates among divorcees include the following: K. D. Breault, "Suicide in America: A Test of Durkheim's Theory of Religious and Family Integration, 1933–1980," *American Journal of Sociology* 92 (1986): 628–56; Jack P. Gibbs, "Marital Status and Suicide in the United States: A Special Test of the Status Integration Theory," *American Journal of Sociology* 74 (1969): 521–33; Steven Stack, "Divorce and Suicide: A Time Series Analysis, 1933–1970," *Journal of Family Issues* 2 (1982): 77–90; idem, "The Effects of Marital Dissolution on Suicide," *Journal of Marriage and the Family* 42 (1980): 83–92. In another work, Stack asserts that suicide is more common among American Protestants than Catholics simply because divorce is more common among the former; "Religion and Suicide: A Reanalysis," *Social Psychiatry* 15 (1980): 65–70.

[46]See Haeberli, "Suicide à Genève," 123.

[47]A sixth man killed himself because he was angry with his nephew who reneged on his promise to take care of him in his old age; AEG, PC 12679.

[48]AEG, PC 2e série, 2292.

who was separated from his wife, all occurred in the second half of the eighteenth century. These generally involved poorer men who were upset that they were not getting adequate assistance from their sons and daughters. The widower Isaac De Curnex, eighty-six, drowned himself in February 1778, after spending the last year of his life as a boarder at the hospital. Some fellow inmates suggested that he was upset that his son and daughter-in-law did not want to take him in.[49] In March 1786 a sixty-year-old widower killed himself after some bitter disputes with his daughter. The conflict came to a head when the daughter married and kicked the father out of the house.[50] René Aval, sixty, whose wife was in prison, suffered from an illness before drowning himself in May 1792. In the weeks prior to his death, his landlady tried to persuade him to go to the hospital to live, as she could no longer cope with him in his state—he was full of vermin and often incontinent. Aval was upset by this proposition and hinted that he would commit suicide. Concerned, the landlady went to talk to Aval's eldest son, who curtly replied that he did not care what happened to his father. The elder Aval took his life three days later, and witnesses indicated that all his children had neglected him.[51]

This is not to say that the sons and daughters of these men were necessarily guilty in dealing with their fathers. The Small Council censured Aval's son for neglecting him and for saying he did not care what happened to his father. For his part, the younger Aval denied saying those words and claimed that he had often helped his father. Although this contention does not square with the testimony of other witnesses, his bitter complaints about his parents were probably well founded. Claiming that he had been left to fend for himself since the age of ten, the young Aval avowed that it was through his efforts alone that he was able to find "an honest means of making a living" to support his wife and children, a veiled reference to the fact that both the elder Aval and his wife had twice been convicted of running a house of prostitution in their own home. The elder Avals surely had not been the ideal parents and had alienated their children.[52] In another case, Jeanne

---

[49]AEG, EC, LM 65: 198, 25 February 1778; PC 13090; RC 279: 104.
[50]AEG, EC, LM 66: 370, 1 March 1786; PC 14826; RC 290: 200.
[51]AEG, EC, LM 68: 19, 20 May 1792; PC 16693; RC 299: 602–3.
[52]AEG, RC 299: 629. On the first conviction in 1776, Aval was condemned to the time he had spent in prison awaiting the trial, plus one additional month, including eight days on bread and water.

Martin, a young seamstress and the daughter of Isaac Martin, probably would not have been able to offer much financial assistance to her bitter father, who drowned himself in July 1786.[53]

For most of these cases of generational tensions, we see the conflicting desires of helping elderly parents and enjoying the privacy of the nuclear family. In all eighteenth-century cases, except that of Martin, the sons or daughters in question were married, and obviously preferred not taking their fathers into their homes. This may have reflected an increased desire on the part of young couples in the late 1700s to enjoy more independence and privacy from kin. Apart from Aval's case, magistrates themselves did not express any opprobrium toward the sons and daughters of the older men. In the case of De Curnex, the Auditeur revealed that the son, Jean-Pierre De Curnex, forty-two, had placed his father at the hospital, paid for his keep there, and provided him with spending money every week. The elder De Curnex came to visit Jean-Pierre and his family every week, bringing his laundry which they washed for him.[54] The Auditeur and members of the Small Council gave not the slightest hint of disapproving of this arrangement. Magistrates evidently understood the younger couple's desire for privacy; the financial and moral support that the couple provided the elder De Curnex was considered sufficient.

It was no coincidence that these suicides of older parents not taken in by children were all men. Fathers had ruled in their households, wielding considerable authority over their sons and daughters. Young couples understandably feared that, once they moved in with them, the fathers would be unwilling to take orders from their former protégés. A mother would have

His wife, Marion Bourget, was to stay an additional four months in prison, including one month on bread and water, beyond the time she had already spent incarcerated; PC 2e série 4369. On the second occasion, in 1790, both the husband and wife were censured and were required to do *réparation*. While Aval was sentenced to just three days in prison, beyond the time already spent there, Bourget was to spend five years in prison. Obviously, she was considered the ringleader; PC 15909.

[53]AEG, EC, LM 67: 2, 21 July 1786; PC 14927; RC 290: 655.

[54]AEG, PC 13090. Throughout the early modern period, three-generation families were quite rare. One does see a noticeable increase in the percentage of the elderly who died at the hospital, increasing from 4.7 percent in 1592 to 17 percent in 1780. The infirm were much more likely to spend their last days in the hospital in the late 1700s; Liliane Mottu-Weber, "Etre vieux à Genève sous l'Ancien Régime," in *Le poids des ans: Une histoire de la vieillesse en Suisse Romande*, ed. Geneviève Heller (Lausanne, Switzerland: Editions d'en Bas et Société d'histoire de la Suisse Romande, 1994), 51–52.

proved less a threat in this regard, and couples were more likely to allow a mother into their household.[55] After all, it was her son or son-in-law who was the principal breadwinner and who determined the legal status of the entire family. Nonetheless, the impression from the court records is that married couples who had a parent living with them were clearly exceptional for the entire early modern period. The reason we find these cases of suicides involving parents who felt abandoned by their adult children only in the late eighteenth century surely reflected a greater desire for privacy at that time. Although Genevans were living a bit longer in the late 1700s than ever before, the increase in life expectancy was not sufficient to make a significant difference in the number of single elderly people living in Geneva.

Generational conflict, however, was more often a motive for suicide among Geneva's youth. Twelve young people, nine males and three females, took their lives following disputes with their parents.[56] Nine of these, involving six men and three women ranging in age from fourteen to twenty-six, took their lives after 1750, complaining of parents who were overbearing or negligent. Interestingly, the conflicts were primarily with the mother in eight cases (including those of the three female suicides), and with the father in only four. Philippe Brun, at age fourteen one of the youngest suicides in early modern Geneva, took his life following serious conflicts with his father. On the evening of 9 July 1753, Brun's mother accompanied him to prison, where he was incarcerated at the request of his father, the weaver Etienne Brun, who was upset with his son's libertinage. According to prison employees, the young Brun spent much of the following day crying in his cell, begging to see his mother—a request that was denied. At four that afternoon they discovered that he had hanged himself by a string in his cell. Imprisoned by means of the Genevan equivalent of the French lettre de cachet, the young Brun apparently took his life in order to punish his parents for the way they handled their differences.[57] In a similar fashion, in September 1793, the watchmaker Etienne Haim, twenty-two, shot himself in his room after writing a letter to his father. As in the case of Matthieu Jourdan, described previously, Haim was upset because of opposition to "a marriage

---

[55]See also Bailey, *"This Rash Act,"* 98.

[56]Cf. Olive Anderson, *Suicide in Victorian and Edwardian England* (Oxford: Clarendon Press, 1987), 179–82.

[57]AEG, EC, LM 61: 389, 10 July 1753; PC 9989; RC 253: 315.

on which he had staked his happiness."[58]

These suicides reflect a certain tension between the increasing independence that young people asserted, on the one hand, and the persistent efforts of parents to influence the major decisions in their children's lives, on the other. The growing importance of romantic love as a legitimate motive for marrying—one of the most important expressions of eighteenth-century individualism—at times conflicted with parents' interest in seeing their sons and daughters form advantageous matches. These suicides can also be explained in part by the growing importance of sentiment in the nuclear family. With the strengthening of the emotional bonds of the nuclear family, family dysfunction, like marital dysfunction, became less tolerable.

Similarly, with emotions more centered on the nuclear family, the death of one of its members weighed more heavily on the survivors. Throughout early modern Geneva, twenty-three people—fifteen males and eight females—took their lives out of grief over the loss of a family member. Eighteen of these suicides—eleven males and seven females—occurred in the second half of the eighteenth century. These included Louis-Etienne Du Trembley, a watchmaker's son, who jumped to his death from his family's fifth-floor abode in October 1780. At eleven years of age, Du Trembley was the youngest suicide in early modern Geneva. According to his parents, the boy had always been rather sickly and sad, but his melancholy had redoubled since the death of his sister the previous February.[59] Du Trembley's death, however, was exceptional both because of his youth—only twelve people under the age of eighteen committed suicide in 250 years—and of the person whose death pushed him to suicide.[60]

More common as motives for suicide were the deaths of parents (five

---

[58]AEG, EC, LM 68: 77, 5 September 1793; PC 17054; quotation from RC 302: 935.

[59]AEG, EC, LM 66: 10, 46, 13 October 1780; PC 13572. The parents, Jean-Pierre Du Trembley and Rose De La Planche, lost two other children in 1780 in addition to Louis-Etienne: Catherine, aged four and a half (EC, LM 66: 10, 12 February), and Jean-Pierre, aged fifteen months (EC, LM 66: 38, 8 September), both of whom died of natural causes.

[60]By contrast, Terence Murphy found that people under twenty-one accounted for over a third of the early modern British suicides whose ages are known. The corresponding figure for Geneva is 7.2 percent. Murphy's figures are not trustworthy, however, as the ages of over 90 percent of those suicides cannot be determined; "'Woful Childe of Parents Rage': Suicide of Children and Adolescents in Early Modern England, 1507–1710," *Sixteenth Century Journal* 17 (1986): 260–61. Cf. Michael Zell, "Suicide in Pre-Industrial England," *Social History* 11 (1986): 303–17. For Geneva, the ages are unknown for only forty-five suicides (only eight after 1750).

such suicides, all after 1750). The twenty-one-year-old François Des Arts took his life because he mourned the death of his father, who died of natural causes four days before François shot himself in the head in May 1754. The Des Arts family not only enjoyed considerable wealth but was also one of the most prestigious and politically powerful of eighteenth-century Geneva: François's father, Philippe, was a member of the Small Council and had served as First Syndic. According to his physician, the young Des Arts had suffered from melancholy and hypochondria and had led a reclusive and sedentary life for several years. Other witnesses further testified to his mental instability and often bizarre behavior, noting, for example, that for the past three years François had habitually drunk his own urine. Three of the family's servants noted that while François had long been melancholic, his sadness greatly intensified in the days following his father's demise. During those four days, François paced through the house, eating little, and reading the Bible constantly, which he had not been wont to do. Although François Des Arts by nature was a rather eccentric lad, his suicide certainly was triggered by his father's death.[61]

Another case featured Jean-Jacques Danel, fifteen, an apprentice in the watchmaking industry, who drowned himself in September 1777, less than three months after his father died. Danel's mother was already deceased and he had no siblings. Described as rather serious and sad, Danel clearly felt quite alone and, as a result, decided to take his life.[62]

Still more common were suicides following the death of a spouse or fiancé. Prior to 1750 there is only one case in which the death of a spouse appeared as a motive for suicide. In the latter half of the eighteenth century, however, eight people were so motivated to end their lives. Daniel Dupras, forty-four, a blacksmith and toolmaker, drowned himself in April 1779. Witnesses reported that he had not recovered from his wife's death five weeks before.[63] The carpenter Jean Louis Definot, seventy-five, committed suicide only hours after the death of his wife, Pernette Moré, who died of natural causes in July 1755. Neighbors reported that Definot was devastated by her unexpected demise and could not forgive himself for not being with her during her last moments. Various friends and neighbors tried to console

[61]AEG, EC, LM 62: 24, 25 May 1754; PC 10087.
[62]AEG, EC, LM 65: 162, 8 September 1777; PC 13018; RC 278: 384.
[63]AEG, EC, LM 65: 264, 5 April 1779; PC 13311; RC 280: 187.

him, preparing meals for him and checking in on him. Despite their entreaties, Definot insisted on being alone to stay awake with the body. A little after nine that evening, Definot jumped to his death from his window into the courtyard below.[64]

A similar case occurred in November 1781 when Guillaume-Louis Reinhart, an apothecary from Alsace, drank heavily immediately before shooting himself in the head with a pistol. His suicide, however, was not the result of a drunken whim. Earlier in the day, a sober Reinhart had written a number of letters, to be sent after his death to several people, in which he explained the action he was about to take. From all reports, Reinhart had been a stable person until the recent death of his fiancée. According to witnesses, Reinhart grieved terribly over her death for which he felt responsible—she was pregnant with his child, and the pregnancy evidently caused her death.[65] Pernette Reffet of the village of Crête, near Geneva, hanged herself in June 1772 because she was devastated that her husband, the watchmaker Jean Chambaud, was apparently terminally ill and had only weeks to live. The previous year she had been overwhelmed with grief over the death of a child and had to be restrained from drowning herself at that time. (Witnesses also reported that when Chambaud found his wife's hanging body, he became hysterical and wanted to kill himself; several people were required to prevent him from doing so.) Apparently, the prospect of losing her husband after losing the child the previous year was more than Reffet could bear.[66]

Interestingly, this was one of only a handful of suicides for which the death of a son or daughter was cited as a probable motive. In August 1724, Louise Guy, thirty-eight, the wife of the cloth merchant Antoine Aubert, jumped to her death from their third-floor apartment after suffering from melancholy since the death of a child two months before.[67] The watchmaker Jean-Louis Lyanna, seventy-four and a widower, committed suicide in December 1747 in part because of the grief over the loss of his son, who had taken his own life five months earlier. This was the only example of a father and a son both committing suicide in early modern Geneva. The son, thirty-five and a watchmaker, was described as a voracious reader and a loner who

---

[64]AEG, EC, LM 62: 87, 13 July 1755; PC 10241.
[65]AEG, EC, LM 66: 103, 28 November 1781; PC 13803; RC 282: 634.
[66]AEG, PC 12329.
[67]AEG, EC, LM 57: 24, 13 August 1724; PC 7211; RC 223: 344.

rarely spoke even when spoken to, having suffered from melancholy for two years before shooting himself in July 1747.[68] Witnesses, including his surgeon, reported that the elder Lyanna had been ill in body and spirit ever since his son's death. Devastated by the loss of his son, Lyanna was also upset about the impending marriage of his daughter, who lived with him. Although his fears appeared groundless, Lyanna apparently believed that, left without children, he would fall into poverty. To assuage his fears, his daughter and her fiancé stipulated in their marriage contract that they would take care of Lyanna for fifteen months in return for seven cuts of wheat. About 9:30 A.M., Sunday, 10 December, Lyanna's daughter left to go to church to get married. Too sick and upset to attend the ceremony, Lyanna stayed at home with their two servant-girls. About ten o'clock, one of the servants discovered that he had hanged himself in a closet. The fact that he chose the very moment of his daughter's wedding to commit suicide is indicative. Already distraught by his son's suicide, he could not bear the prospect of the complete disintegration of the family.[69]

All told, however, the loss of a child was not a common motive for suicide in early modern Geneva.[70] Only six times in two and a half centuries (three times after 1750) did the death of a son or daughter lead to suicide, and there were usually further aggravating circumstances. In these cases, Reffet's husband's illness, and Lyanna's illness and his daughter's marriage all exacerbated the situation. By and large, Genevan parents evidently were able to deal with the grief associated with the loss of a child, be it a newborn or a fully grown son or daughter.[71]

One might think that being a parent could be an important deterrent to suicide. Durkheim and other sociologists have argued that parenthood doubles the immunity to suicide offered by marriage, especially for women: concerns for one's children reportedly deter mothers more than fathers from

---

[68]AEG, EC, LM 60: 388, 10 July 1747; PC 9393; RC 247: 255.

[69]AEG, EC, LM 61: 16, 10 December 1747; PC 9425; RC 247: 359.

[70]Medieval miracle literature reveals a number of cases of suicidal despair provoked by the loss of a child; Murray, *Suicide*, vol. 1, *Violent Against Themselves*, 251–94.

[71]Concern for living offspring was the major factor behind a couple of suicides. In separate incidents from the 1770s, two older men committed suicide because they were upset about their sons' departures. In both cases the sons left town after getting into trouble with the law, and their fathers feared they would never see them again; AEG, PC 12808, 13002.

taking their lives.[72] To what extent does the evidence from Geneva support this contention? The baptism records are very effective in determining if a person had children born in Geneva and its territories. In this time of high infant and child mortality, it is important to know not only how many suicides produced children but also how many had children who survived. Presumably, the immunity to suicide provided by parenthood disappears upon the death of the children. Indeed, one would expect those who lost their children to be at a greater risk of suicide than those who never had children. As a result, it is also important to consult the death records to determine if the suicides had children who survived.[73] As the death records themselves indicate the age of the deceased and often the name of the father, I have been able to determine if a certain person was the child of the suicide in question or, instead, was only a homonym.

There are some obstacles to determining the parental status of every suicide, however. There are some lacunae in the registers of the baptism, marriage, and death records for the sixteenth and seventeenth centuries, particularly for the Genevan countryside. More important, these sources provide information only for those who were born, married, or died in Geneva and its territories. It is particularly difficult to determine the parental status of foreigners, who made up over a fifth of the total suicides. In spite of the best efforts, for fifty-seven suicides (14.1 percent of the total), it was impossible to determine whether they had produced and left any children.

Among those whose parental status is known, fathers and mothers were clearly in the minority among suicides throughout the early modern period (see tables 37 and 38). Most striking is the fact that the percentages are quite uniform among both male and female suicides: for both sexes, if we exclude those whose parental status remains unknown, only about 40 percent of suicides had children who survived them.[74] It would be most useful of course to compare these figures with the proportions of men and women who were parents in Geneva's population at large. Unfortunately, such detailed infor-

---

[72]Danigelis and Pope, "Durkheim's Theory of Suicide," 1081–106; Durkheim, *Suicide*, 185–89; Fedden, *Suicide*, 326; Halbwachs, *Causes du suicide*, 221; Maris, *Social Forces*, 108–10.

[73]There were indeed six suicides, five men and one woman, who had produced offspring but had no children who survived them. Luc Bosson, for example, who shot himself in March 1798 at the age of fifty-eight, had fathered three children, all of whom died as small children; AEG, PC 19649.

[74]The proportion of suicides who left children was lower for the previous two centuries, but the high number of suicides whose parental status was unknown is problematic.

mation does not exist. We do know, however, that the number of married couples in Geneva who bore no children ranged from 12.5 percent to 16.9 percent from the late seventeenth to the late eighteenth century.[75] These figures refer only to those couples who produced no births; they do not include couples whose children did not survive. Among those suicides who were married, very few left no children. Of the ninety-two married male suicides, only sixteen were not survived by children. Excluding the eight for whom it

Table 37: Female Suicides Survived by Offspring[a]

DATES	LEGITIMATE		ILLEGITIMATE		NONE		UNKNOWN		TOTAL
	n	%	n	%	n	%	n	%	
1542–1600	0	–	0	–	0	–	4		4
1601–50	7	50.0	0	–	7	50.0	0	–	14
1651–1700	2	33.3	0	–	4	66.7	1	–	7
1701–50	5	23.8	1	4.8	15	71.4	5	–	26
1751–98	28	42.4	2	3.0	36	54.5	12		78
Total/Avg.	42	39.3	3	2.8	62	57.9	22	n/a	129

a. Source: Etat Civil: Livres des Baptêmes, Mariages et Morts; Procès Criminels; Registres du Conseil. Not included in the percentages are the twenty-two female suicides for whom it is unknown if they left any offspring. Illegitimate children are listed separately because the birth of a bastard could be more a motive for than a deterrent to suicide.

is unknown if any children survived, we find that those who died without heirs made up only 19 percent of the married male suicides. The percentage is virtually identical after 1750: if we exclude the two whose parental status was unknown, we find that only twelve (18.8 percent) of the remaining sixty-four married male suicides died without children. Among the forty-two female suicides who were married, only five definitely left no children, while for eight it is unknown if any children survived. Excluding these eight, we thus find that only 14.7 percent of the married female suicides left no children. Surprisingly, the percentage of married female suicides who died childless dropped after 1750. From 1751 on, only two of the twenty-one (9.5 percent) married female suicides were not survived by children, not counting the four whose parental status is unknown.

[75]Perrenoud, "Comportements démographiques," in *Economie genevoise*, ed. Piuz and Mottu-Weber, 106.

Table 38: Male Suicides Survived by Offspring[a]

DATES	LEGITIMATE		ILLEGITIMATE		NONE		UNKNOWN		TOTAL
	n	%	*n*	%	*n*	%	*n*	%	
1542–1600	2	66.7	0	–	1	33.3	7	–	10
1601–50	5	50.0	0	–	5	50.0	2	–	12
1651–1700	4	40.0	0	–	6	60.0	5	–	15
1701–50	7	28.0	0	–	18	72.0	3	–	28
1751–98	82[b]	42.5	3[b]	1.6	109	56.5	17	–	210
Total/Avg.	100[b]	41.5	3[b]	1.2	139	57.7	34	–	275

a. Source: Etat Civil: Livres des Baptêmes, Mariages et Morts; Procès Criminels; Registres du Conseil.

b. One man was survived by a newborn bastard and two legitimate teenagers. Not included in the percentages are the thirty-four male suicides for whom it is unknown if they left any offspring.

This finding runs directly contrary to Durkheim's contention that motherhood, more than marriage, provided immunity to suicide. If motherhood deterred suicide, then one should find many childless women among married suicides. In reality, after 1750, the proportion of married female suicides who left no children was clearly lower than the percentage of childless families in Geneva; married women with children were thus slightly more likely to kill themselves than married women without children. The corresponding figure for men appears roughly in line with the proportion of families that were childless. Although fathers, to be sure, outnumbered mothers among suicides, the proportion of married suicides who were parents was higher among women. The greater total number of married fathers simply reflected males' greater propensity for suicide in general. That the parental status of some of these married suicides is unknown is offset by the fact that five of these married suicides produced only children who preceded them in death. These five, all men, would not have been included among the childless families. Simply put, this evidence does not support the contention that parenthood provided more immunity to suicide than marriage. In fact, the contrary appears true, especially for women.

In dealing with parenthood, however, we should take into consideration the age of the children. On the one hand, the responsibility of having a small child under one's care might serve as a greater deterrent to suicide than having an adult son or daughter who is living independently. And even if mother-

Table 39: Age of Legitimate Offspring Left
by Male and Female Suicides, 1542–1798[a]

Survived by	Male Suicides		Female Suicides	
	n	%	*n*	%
Children 12 and Under	55	67.9	26	32.1
Children under 18	65	70.7	27	29.3
Adult Offspring Only	35	71.4	14	28.6
Total Suicides Survived by Offspring	100	70.4	42[b]	29.6

a. Source: Etat Civil: Livres des Baptêmes, Mariages et Morts; Procès Criminels; Registres du Conseil.

b. For one case from the early seventeenth century, the age of neither the suicide, an accused witch, nor her daughter can be identified. Many suicides left both minor and adult offspring.

hood in general did not convey a special immunity to suicide, perhaps the considerable responsibilities of child rearing might deter the mothers of small children from taking their lives. On the other hand, many women suffer from postpartum depression, and some parents of young children might feel overwhelmed by their familial duties and emotionally devastated by their inability to fulfill them, making them more prone to suicidal tendencies. As table 39 indicates, of the 142 suicides—be they married, widowed, separated, or divorced—who left legitimate sons or daughters, eighty-one (fifty-five men and twenty-six women) left surviving children who were not yet teenagers, whereas forty-nine (thirty-five men and fourteen women) left only adult offspring eighteen and over.[76] There were thus five-eighths as many suicides whose children were all grown as those who had small children.

Although the number of parents of young children who took their lives is surprisingly high, these figures nonetheless suggest that having small children offered more immunity to suicide than having adult sons or daughters. Although we do not have precise demographic statistics, it stands to reason

[76] I am somewhat arbitrarily dividing minors from majors at the age of eighteen, even though sons and daughters in their early twenties were at times referred to as minors, elsewhere as majors. Even though eighteen-year-olds ordinarily were still legally minors, most were no longer very dependent on their parents. Among artisans, most eighteen-year-old males were advancing in their apprenticeships, often living away from home and earning their own keep. At eighteen, the daughters of many unskilled workers and some artisans worked in domestic service; others made valuable contributions to the household economy, often in various forms of cottage industry. As their children became more economically independent, Genevan parents surely felt less responsible for them than for young children.

that in a society with relatively late marriages and high mortality, there would be far more parents of young children than of adults. As noted above, Genevans tended to marry in their late twenties in the eighteenth century, and people who had survived until the age of ten could expect to live to their early- to mid-fifties.[77] With these demographic trends, it is inconceivable that there were five-eighths as many parents of adult offspring as of preteen children. If we cannot compute the suicide rates for these different types of parents, we can nonetheless be sure that parents with minor children killed themselves less often than those with only adult offspring. In short, any immunity that parenthood provided was concentrated among the parents of minor children.

Among suicides who were parents, regardless of their marital status, women comprised almost exactly the same proportion of those who left legitimate children as of suicides in general. Throughout the early modern period, women comprised 31.9 percent of all suicides and 29.6 percent of those who were survived by children. As table 39 reveals, this proportion between male and female suicides varied little regardless of the ages of their children. Indeed, female suicides who left small children were proportionally slightly more common vis-à-vis their male counterparts than those who left only adult offspring. Significantly, women comprised virtually the same proportion of suicides who left no children as those who left offspring: of the 209 suicides throughout the early modern period who left no children, sixty-six (31.6 percent) were women. The figures for the latter half of the eighteenth century also show that parenthood had no effect on the male/female ratio among suicides. After 1750, women comprised 27.1 percent of all suicides (78 of 288), 26.3 percent of those who left children (30 of 114), and 29 percent (18 of 62) of those who left children twelve and under. Surprisingly, the figure that deviates most from the norm is that for suicides who left no children: from 1751 on, women comprised only 24.8 percent (36 of 145) of such suicides.[78] Although the differences in these percentages are too

---

[77]Perrenoud, "Comportements démographiques," in *Economie genevoise*, ed. Piuz and Mottu-Weber, 86–88, 120–21.

[78]Likewise, for the previous two hundred years, parenthood did not appreciably influence the ratio of women to men among suicides. For 1542–1750, women comprised 43.6 percent of all suicides, 42.9 percent of those who left children, 42.1 percent of suicides who left children twelve and under, and 46.4 percent of those who left no children.

modest to allow for generalizations, at first glance they seem to suggest that being childless provided women more immunity to suicide than motherhood. Statistics alone, however, cannot tell the whole story. Surely a wide range of variables beyond parenthood was behind the increasing numbers of Genevan men and women who chose death in the late eighteenth century. Quite simply, parenthood, like marriage, was not responsible for the gap between the numbers of male and female suicides.

As alluded to in chapter 3, men with dependents stood out among suicides that were motivated directly by poverty. Of the twenty-five men for whom poverty was a motive for suicide, eight were single, nine were married, three were widowers, three were separated from their wives, and two were of unknown marital status. Thus while bachelors comprised 45.9 percent of all suicides whose marital status was known, they made up only 34.8 percent among men who took their lives over poverty. What was the cause of this discrepancy? On the one hand, having a spouse and children to support could in some cases push a person into poverty. More important, while a person may have been able to tolerate emotionally his or her own poverty, the sight of his dependents living in misery could cause greater distress. As they were expected to be the principal breadwinners, men could become quite distraught when they were unable to support their wives and children. For example, in the case of Jean Huguenin, forty-three, an artisan in La Fabrique, desperation over his family's misery, rather than his own, was most likely what drove him to jump to his death from his fifth-story abode—a single room that he shared with his wife and three children. Having lost much of their furniture and the tools of his trade to creditors, Huguenin found himself unable to support his family.[79]

Evidence further shows that four men committed suicide in the turbulent years of 1789–94 because they felt they had failed as providers for their families. A former baker, Jean Marc Champury, thirty-five, tried unsuccessfully to support his wife and four young children by producing silk ornaments. Before shooting himself in his apartment in September 1793,

---

[79]AEG, EC, LM 62: 56, 7 January 1755; PC 10149; RC 255: 6. Moreover, two of the three men who killed themselves because of poverty and were separated from their wives, had dependent children. Testimony specifically reveals that one of them was upset that he was financially unable to help his teen-aged daughter secure employment; PC 15670.

Champury wrote a phonetically spelled letter to his wife and children explaining he could no longer endure seeing them suffer.[80] Similarly, the watchmaker Samuel Megevand, thirty-six, shot himself in December 1791 after suffering from an illness. Married and the father of two young daughters, Megevand wrote in a suicide note to his wife that he feared his disease would cause the financial ruin of the family; his death therefore was in their best interests.[81] Although the sick Megevand may have been rationalizing to justify his action, on the surface this resembles what Durkheim termed altruistic suicide, which includes cases of people killing themselves when stricken with illness to avoid being a burden on others. Under certain circumstances, Durkheim argued, committing suicide becomes a duty.[82] Thus some people who had dependents might have been pushed to kill themselves out of guilt that single people, facing the same dire straits, would not have felt. In general, men who were married and the fathers of dependent children were especially prone to take their lives directly because of poverty. Since married women's labor was intended to supplement their husbands' income, they felt less guilty if their family lived in poverty.[83]

These cases call to mind the stereotype that men generally kill themselves because of mundane reversals, such as financial problems, while female suicide is more often motivated by emotional reasons or family problems.[84] According to this reasoning, suicide for both sexes results from failing to fulfill the culturally assigned roles of breadwinners for men and that of wives

[80]AEG, EC, LM 68: 78, 13 September 1793; PC 17057; RC 302: 956. For a very similar case from France in 1770, see Alain Joblin, "Le suicide à l'époque moderne: Un exemple dans la France du Nord-Ouest: À Boulogne-sur-Mer," *Revue historique* 589 (1994): 102.

[81]AEG, PC 16598; RC 298: 1606.

[82]Durkheim, *Suicide*, 217–40.

[83]Examining suicide in the United States in the 1970s, Steven Stack and Ain Haas, "The Effect of Unemployment Duration on National Suicide Rates: A Time Series Analysis, 1948–1982," *Sociological Focus* 17 (1984): 19, find that unemployed men often felt like failures in providing for their families, and their anxiety and guilt often led to increased marital strife. Peter Sainsbury, *Suicide in London: An Ecological Study* (London: Chapman and Hall, 1955), 80, found that men were more vulnerable to suicide than women because of the "more arduous social role" that males have in supporting their families. For nineteenth-century England, Bailey, *"This Rash Act,"* 206–7, found that suicides that were motivated by job loss were most likely to involve married men, especially those with children, and that financial pressures weighed less heavily on women.

[84]Even in Greco-Roman mythology, female suicides were often depicted as being motivated by unrequited love or family problems; Anton J. L. van Hooff, *From Autothanasia to Suicide: Self-Killing in Classical Antiquity* (London: Routledge, 1990), 26–27.

and mothers for women.[85] In early modern Geneva, however, men made up the large majority, roughly equal to their share of suicides in general, of those suicides that were allegedly motivated by problems related to the family. These suicides—motivated at least in part by the death of a loved one, romantic misadventure, marital breakdown, generational conflict, and unwanted pregnancies or illegitimate births—involved sixty-one men (68.5 percent) and twenty-eight women (31.5 percent). As table 40 reveals, apart from suicides motivated by the shame associated with births or pregnancies conceived outside of marriage, men made up the large majority of those who were pushed to kill themselves by family issues. Since family motives did not affect the proportion of males to females among suicides, we must conclude that the greater emphasis on romantic love, the companionate marriage, and the emotional bonds within the family were mutually desired by men and women. On the whole, personal reversals in courtship and the family weighed equally upon women and men.

To a considerable degree, suicides motivated by concerns related to the family also cut across class lines. After 1750 the affluent were slightly under-represented among suicides motivated by issues related to the family vis-à-vis suicides in general. While the well-to-do comprised 10.5 percent of all sui-cides after 1750, they made up only 8.1 percent of those provoked by mat-ters pertaining to love, marriage, and the family. Overrepresented among all suicides, the poor comprised the same proportion of suicides motivated by family concerns as of suicides in general (40.5 percent and 40.7 percent, respectively, after 1750). In that half century, such motives were most common among those who fell between the rich and the poor: 50.5 percent

---

[85]Maris, *Social Forces*, 95–98. This bias can be seen in the investigations of deaths in Victorian England. Coroners and witnesses closely scrutinized the financial status and the domestic life when exam-ining male and female suicides, respectively; Bailey, *"This Rash Act,"* 49. Howard I. Kushner, "Women and Suicide in Historical Perspective," *Signs: Journal of Women in Culture and Society* 10 (1985): 537–52, dismisses these stereotypes as culturally biased and insists that suicide itself is not "a masculine type of behavior." If one includes unsuccessful suicide attempts, women commit suicidal acts as often as men do. Kushner argues that completion rates are lower for women than men simply because of the methods that have been "culturally and historically available" to women. By the same author, see also "Women and Sui-cidal Behavior: Epidemiology, Gender and Lethality in Historical Perspective," in *Women and Suicidal Behavior*, ed. Silvia Sara Canetto and David Lester (New York: Springer Publishing, 1996), 11–34. Kush-ner does not clarify why cultural differences can explain the varying methods used by men and women but not the varying motives for male and female suicides. More important, it is dangerous to assume that completed and attempted suicide are inspired by the same intentions.

of those who killed themselves because of family matters as opposed to 48.8 percent of all post-1750 suicides. Occupations can be identified for only eleven of twenty women who committed suicide because of motives related to the family. All of them worked in rather humble occupations, five being domestic servants. Among men who killed themselves for these reasons, artisans predominated. Excluding two young males who did not yet have professions and one man whose occupation was not identified, we find that 70.6 percent of these suicides were artisans, who comprised between 60 percent and 65 percent of the active male population in the second half of the eighteenth century. Although a few of these suicides came from the ranks of carpenters, coopers, blacksmiths, and others who produced only for local markets, more prominent were the traditionally more prosperous artisans employed in La Fabrique. Watchmaking employed eighteen (35.3 percent) of the men who were motivated to take their lives because of issues related to love, marriage, and the family. As we have seen, however, only about a fourth of the active male population worked in watchmaking in the late eighteenth century. By contrast, only two merchants—the only males among these suicides who can be described as wealthy—committed suicide because of family motives, even though merchants comprised close to 10 percent of the active male population. At the other extreme, apart from three soldiers, only four men who took their lives for these reasons worked as unskilled laborers. Of

Table 40: Family Motives Cited by Male and Female Suicides, 1542–1798[a]

MOTIVE	MALE SUICIDES		FEMALE SUICIDES		TOTAL
	n	%	*n*	%	
Death of Family Member	15	65.2	8	34.8	23
Romantic Misadventure	12	66.7	6	33.3	18
Generational Conflict	15	83.3	3	16.7	18
Marital Breakdown/ Dispute with Spouse	10	62.5	7	37.5	17
Illegitimate Birth or Pregnancy	2	25.0	6	75.0	8
Failure as Provider	4	100.0	0	–	4
Miscellaneous	8	80.0	2	20.0	10
Total Suicides	61[b]	68.5	28[b]	31.5	89[b]

a. Source: Etat Civil: Livres des Baptêmes, Mariages et Morts; Procès Criminels; Registres du Conseil.

b. Several suicides were motivated by more than one family-related issue. Consequently, although a total of ninety-eight family motives were cited, they involved the suicides of eighty-nine individuals.

these, only one was employed in the manufacture of *indiennes*, even though toward the end of the Republic, over 10 percent of the Genevan workforce was employed in this sector.[86] In short, the men who committed suicide because of family motives generally came from relatively modest backgrounds but certainly not from the bottom of the social ladder. Moreover, most of these suicides who were poor were not from the most humble walks of life but rather were artisans who at one time had enjoyed the prospect of earning a decent living.

Do these findings mean that the emphasis on romantic love and the affective ties within the family were stronger in the artisan class than in any other group? Did the sons and daughters of watchmakers and jewelers enjoy more freedom in the formation of marriage than the children of merchants and bankers? Could it be that parental supervision of courting, through the control of the dowry and inheritance, was so strong as to stifle romantic inclinations among Geneva's wealthy youth? If the marriage of convenience remained the norm among Geneva's elite, then one would think that neither romantic misadventure nor marital breakdown would have been likely motives for suicide among the wealthy. If such is the case, then one could properly speak of the companionate marriage and even the modern family as being popular in origin.

While courtships among the wealthy youth undoubtedly were subject to greater parental scrutiny, these findings nonetheless say more about the impact of wealth on suicidal behavior than on affective ties. The absence of the wealthy among certain types of suicides is not surprising. Closely supervised by their parents, women from affluent Genevan families were not likely to bear children out of wedlock; all those who were pushed to kill themselves by illegitimate births or pregnancies were people of modest means, such as servant-girls. The wealthy were obviously less likely to face financial difficulties that could exacerbate tensions and contribute to marital breakdown. Moreover, the records indicate that younger Genevans of all classes habitually sought their parents' approval before marrying. Most important, for the last half century of this study, wealthy people were represented proportionally among those who took their lives because of love stories that went awry

---

[86]Mottu-Weber, "Activités manufacturières," in *Economie genevoise*, ed. Piuz and Mottu-Weber, 458; Perrenoud, *Population de Genève*, 156, 160–61.

or marriages that had turned sour. The case of Dame Martin certainly shows that the marriage of convenience did not satisfy all wealthy people. Although the wealthy more than others had to balance emotion with interest in choosing mates, Genevan suicide patterns indicate that the growing emphasis on romantic love and sentiment within the nuclear family cut across class lines.

All told, the evidence from Genevan suicides suggests that the companionate marriage was at the core of new attitudes about the family in late-eighteenth-century Geneva. Mutual affection was increasingly becoming the essential factor in forming and sustaining marriages. Consequently, the decrease in the percentage of married people among suicides after 1750 reflected greater satisfaction found in matrimony. The larger increase in the suicide rate among the widowed mirrored the greater emotional ties in marriage and, accordingly, the stronger emotional void when the union ended. Desired by merchants, servants, and artisans, the companionate marriage was attractive to both men and women. Factors unrelated to marriage, love, and the family accounted for the imbalance between male and female suicides.

Simply put, in the late eighteenth century, Geneva in effect experienced a quiet revolution in the family which contributed significantly to the boisterous revolution in suicide. Nevertheless, changes in the family, love, and marriage were not solely responsible for the increase in suicide in the late eighteenth century. As we have seen, the 1780s and 1790s were turbulent years for Geneva both economically and politically, and the peak year for suicide occurred immediately after the end of the Old Regime in December 1792. Be that as it may, suicides resembling Werther's were much more common in Geneva than those resembling Cato's.

5

The Cultural Dimensions of Suicide: Part 2

As shown in chapter 2, during the course of the early modern period, European intellectual leaders modified their views on suicide, and the judicial sentences passed in the Republic of Geneva reflected these changing attitudes. Did popular attitudes toward suicide follow a similar transformation from the Reformation to the Enlightenment periods? Did the piety of Reformed Geneva contribute to religious despair and thus to suicide, or did it serve as a prophylactic against self-murder? More broadly, over the course of these two and a half centuries, did Genevans experience cultural developments and changes in mentality which, even if not directly related to suicide, might have removed some of the brakes on suicidal proclivities and thus contributed to the dramatic growth in voluntary deaths in the late 1700s?

Popular Attitudes Toward Suicide in Reformation Geneva

Like Calvin and Genevan authorities, common folk of the Reformation period, including even some of those who took their lives, clearly associated suicide with demon possession. The belief in the diabolical origins of suicide is evident in the inquest in 1555 of the self-inflicted death of Jean Jourdain, referred to briefly in chapter 2. A humble farmer, Jourdain was upset on three counts: he was distraught that he had contracted venereal disease, for which he could not afford medical treatment; he felt guilty for having passed this illness to his sister (though no evidence suggests that he was guilty of incest); and he was worried about having to appear before the Consistory of Thonon, a village near Geneva, because of his fornication. On a Sunday morning, rather than go to church, Jourdain went into the woods where he stabbed himself. Immediately upon inflicting the wound, however, Jourdain heard the ringing of the church bell. Feeling remorse, he asked forgiveness from God and walked to a nearby village where he languished another eight days before expiring. During these days, the most important question asked of the dying Jourdain was whether he had given himself to the devil or heard a voice in the woods. Jourdain replied that he had indeed asked the devil to come kill him. He heard no voice in the woods, however, and the devil did not put Jourdain out of his misery.[1] Jourdain had so assimilated the belief that the devil was behind suicide that he called out for diabolical intervention to put an end to his days.

Since in Reformation Geneva suicide was so often linked to demon possession, contemporaries surely were not surprised that during this period of intense witch-hunting, four people accused of witchcraft killed themselves while in custody in Geneva. In 1547, for example, Perrod Bouloz, a farmer of about sixty in nearby Avusy, was detained and interrogated because he was suspected of being responsible, through witchcraft, for the deaths of two people and a number of heads of livestock, occurring over several years' time. A rather poor man who was generally disliked and distrusted by his neighbors, Bouloz refused to confess to sorcery even when tortured by means of the strappado. After a torture session, he managed to get hold of a knife and stabbed himself five times, dying a few hours later. Before expiring, Bouloz begged God for mercy and on one occasion screamed, "Devil, get away from me."[2] Though he had emphatically denied under torture that the devil was his master, Bouloz associated self-murder with diabolical possession. Witnesses also voiced suspicions that witchcraft was involved in the suicide of Julienne Berard, the woman who jumped in the Rhône out of fear of going

---

[1] AEG, PC 552; RC 50:23v, 25v, 27–28.

[2] AEG, PC 2e série 745; RC 42: 149, 155. The others who took their lives while imprisoned on suspicion of witchcraft were Genon Chambet (13 November 1567, PC 1441), Jeanne Guarin (6 October 1609, PC 2002, RC 106: 185), and Ayma Pelloux (7 October 1615, PC 2292, RC 114: 259); see E. William Monter, *Witchcraft in France and Switzerland: The Borderlands During the Reformation* (Ithaca, N.Y.: Cornell University Press, 1976), 207–15.

before Calvin's Consistory in 1564. Several people reported rumors that Berard was a witch, and one indicated that she had jumped in the water at the very place where the devil had spoken to Berard's former servant-girl, who had herself been executed for witchcraft.[3]

Even when witnesses mentioned mental illness as the possible cause of suicide, self-murder was not as yet dissociated from demon possession. In fact, far from competing with diabolism, mental illness was often viewed as evidence of demon possession: a host of theologians from the Reformation era, both Protestant and Catholic, saw "melancholy" and other mental infirmities as resulting directly from diabolical possession. Thus Timothy Bright, the author of the first English treatise on melancholy (1586), insisted that suicide was the result of diabolical temptation or divine judgment.[4] The London turner Nehemiah Wallington, who survived several suicide attempts in the early 1600s, believed that his "melancholy" stemmed from Satanic temptation, claiming that the devil had appeared to him on many occasions, either in human or animal form.[5] Richard Napier, a seventeenth-century English astrological physician, also recorded numerous cases of patients who suffered from suicidal tendencies, claiming the devil had appeared personally to tempt them.[6] Insanity could also be a cause rather than a consequence of demon possession since the devil purportedly thrived in the bodies of melancholic people. Wallington advised that one avoid solitariness and melancholy, "for Satan works much upon such."[7] In 1547 Wolfgang Seidl, a Benedictine at the Bavarian court, wrote that "sadness is the devil's best tool for destroying a man and his faith," and prescribed as remedies diversions, prayer, Bible reading, confession, and moderate food,

[3]AEG, PC 1179.

[4]Michael MacDonald and Terence R. Murphy, *Sleepless Souls: Suicide in Early Modern England* (Oxford: Clarendon Press, 1990), 105.

[5]Paul S. Seaver, *Wallington's World: A Puritan Artisan in Seventeenth-Century London* (Stanford: Stanford University Press, 1985), 16, 23–24.

[6]Michael MacDonald, *Mystical Bedlam: Madness, Anxiety, and Healing in Seventeenth-Century England* (Cambridge: Cambridge University Press, 1981), 134.

[7]Seaver, *Wallington's World*, 60. See also Pieter Spierenburg, *The Broken Spell: A Cultural and Anthropological History of Preindustrial Europe* (New Brunswick, N.J.: Rutgers University Press, 1991), 176. In a sermon delivered in Boston in 1682, Increase Mather warned that Satan takes advantage of the afflicted, especially the melancholic, tempting them to reject God. A decade later his son, Cotton Mather, reiterated this message; see Howard I. Kushner, *American Suicide: A Psychocultural Exploration* (New Brunswick, N.J.: Rutgers University Press, 1991), 24–25.

drink, and sleep.[8]

More broadly, some scholars maintain that the sixteenth century saw a great increase in the incidence of melancholy precisely because there was a growing emphasis on demonic powers. Miracle literature of the Middle Ages includes stories of a number of people, almost all of them monks or nuns, who contemplated and, in some cases, committed suicide because of religious melancholy—a form of despair that stemmed from the fear that they were damned.[9] As noted in the introduction, various historians see a dramatic increase in the incidence of melancholy and of suicide during the Reformation, which they attribute to both Protestant and Catholic preachers' obsessive warnings against sin, damnation, and Satanic possession. Supposedly, as Protestants espoused the priesthood of all believers and salvation by faith alone, religious melancholy ceased to be a malady found only in monasteries. Despair seemed to spread in growing numbers of lay people as well.[10] Evidence from German hospitals shows an unprecedented number of patients who were diagnosed as suffering from melancholy or diabolical possession in the last decades of the sixteenth century. While belief in Satan predated the Reformation by centuries, the sixteenth century witnessed the growing "demonization" of the world. Never before had the devil seemed so powerful and menacing, capable of assuming an ever increasing variety of forms. Likewise, Europeans had never before perceived so many demons, which far outnumbered the benevolent angels. This growing obsession with demons can be seen in the appearance in later sixteenth-century Lutheran

---

[8]H. C. Erik Midelfort, *Mad Princes of Renaissance Germany* (Charlottesville: University Press of Virginia, 1994), 21–22.

[9]Alexander Murray, *Suicide in the Middle Ages*, vol. 1, *The Violent Against Themselves* (Oxford: Oxford University Press, 1998), 331–47.

[10]Jean Delumeau, *Sin and Fear: The Emergence of a Western Guilt Culture, Thirteenth to Eighteenth Centuries*, trans. Eric Nicholson (New York: St. Martin's Press, 1990), 168–85, 523–54; H. C. Erik Midelfort, "Sin, Melancholy, Obsession: Insanity and Culture in Sixteenth-Century Germany," in *Understanding Popular Culture: Europe from the Middle Ages to the Nineteenth Century*, ed. Steven L. Kaplan (Berlin: Mouton, 1984), 113–45; Murray, *Suicide*, vol. 1, *Violent Against Themselves*, 376–78. For a contemporary account, see John Sym, *Life's Preservative Against Self-Killing*, edited and with an introduction by Michael MacDonald (London: Routledge, 1989). Studying the treatment of insane German princes, Midelfort finds that references to the devil as a cause of mental disorders were rare prior to 1520, becoming much more common thereafter. Providing a nuanced view on the relationship between insanity and diabolism, Midelfort further asserts that physicians in the sixteenth and seventeenth centuries attributed insanity to demon possession only after physical and medical cures had failed: if no natural cause could be found, then the madness must be of supernatural origin; see *Mad Princes*, 46, 149.

Germany of an entirely new genre of literature, *Teufelbücher*, or devil books, in which moralists attacked a wide range of vices, which they saw as the work of demons. This growing preoccupation with the devil was not limited to the treatises of learned authors. Ample evidence from Germany of the late sixteenth century shows, for example, that many ordinary people associated various forms of mental derangement with demonic possession. Both the learned and the illiterate agreed, moreover, that never before had there been so many cases of demonic possession, which they understood as proof of the approaching end of the world.[11]

If the Genevan laity of the late sixteenth and early seventeenth centuries did not believe that the apocalypse was imminent, many at least saw connections between mental disturbances and suicide, on the one hand, and diabolism, on the other. An example was the case of Elisabeth Paschal, a rather wealthy woman who had been mentally deranged for several weeks before committing suicide in November 1625. Often incoherent, Paschal repeatedly said she felt possessed by demons and was frequently so violent, swearing at and occasionally even biting those around her, that she dared not be left alone. A witness reported that several days before her death Paschal declared that "the evil spirit wanted to make her kill herself and she prayed to God to protect her from it."[12] One evening, after reading from the Bible, Paschal managed to jump out a window to her death, despite the efforts made by her niece and chambermaid to restrain her. The niece revealed that Paschal and her husband previously had some heated arguments over finances. Apparently they had lost some money, and Bertrand held his wife to blame. Nonetheless, both the niece and the chambermaid said that Bertrand did try to console her when she was troubled, talking to her about the word of God and asking her to pray.[13]

The most interesting piece of evidence from this case is the report made by Dr. Dauphin, a physician who made numerous house calls over a period of months. He determined that Paschal's melancholy was caused by her domestic disputes and that she alone could cure it. He exhorted her to accept the remedies available through medicine and through God. Paschal agreed

---

[11]H. C. Erik Midelfort, *A History of Madness in Sixteenth-Century Germany* (Stanford: Stanford University Press, 1999), 51–58, 376–81.

[12]AEG, PC 2681bis.

[13]AEG, PC 2681bis.

with Dauphin's diagnosis. In his later visits, Dauphin resembled more a pastor than a physician, praying with her and asking her to think of God. On one occasion, Dauphin was leading her in reciting the Lord's Prayer, and Paschal had trouble getting past the words "lead us not into temptation." When asked why, she replied that the devil was trying to prevent her from praying.[14] A week before her death, both Dauphin and the pastor Diodati implored the furious and violent Paschal to pray to God for help. In concluding, Dauphin reported he had seen other tragic cases involving people whom God allows to behave in such a bizarre way that one cannot cure the ills of their souls. These cases might be initiated by avarice or some other sin, which later produced a corporal illness as "the melancholy humor took root and through its vapor...took over the brain."[15] Paschal herself was convinced that the devil possessed her; Dauphin at least agreed that sin was the root cause of her mental illness and seemed to imply that it was divinely rather than diabolically inspired. Clearly in Geneva, as elsewhere in Europe, clergy and physicians cooperated when dealing with mental illness. The clergy acknowledged that alienation could stem from natural and humoral sources; physicians affirmed that a well-regulated spiritual life was an important foundation for mental health, and that madness could have unnatural causes, stemming from sin and the devil.[16]

The fear of diabolism can be seen in the suicide of Marie Chioccio, the wife of Jean Prevost, a hardware merchant. She became most upset when someone told her that one of her children, who was away with a wet nurse, was bewitched. Assisting in her husband's shop in August 1647, she excused herself, saying she was going upstairs to their apartment to give their servant some instructions. Ordinarily Prevost never left his wife alone—twice before she had to be restrained from jumping out a window—but he was busy with customers at the time. The servant, however, had left the apartment to fetch some water. Five to ten minutes after leaving the shop, Chioccio jumped

[14]Midelfort, *History of Madness*, 310–11, has found a number of Catholics in Counter-Reformation Germany who bemoaned that they were unable to pray and viewed diabolical temptation as the cause.

[15]AEG, PC 2681bis.

[16]Dauphin's testimony brings to mind the opinions of several physicians who wrote on the melancholy of Albrecht Friedrich of Prussia in the late sixteenth century. They referred to the influence of Satan and to the divine punishment of sin as principal causes of his mental disorders; Midelfort, *Mad Princes*, 82–86, 149–50. For other examples of diabolical temptation and suicide from the Reformation era, see idem, *History of Madness*, 295–98, 310–11; idem, "Religious Melancholy and Suicide," 47–48.

from a garret in the building. Witnesses below saw her leap, crying out "Elisabeth!"—evidently the name of the "bewitched" child. In all likelihood, the fear that Satan possessed the girl's soul disturbed Chioccio more than if her daughter had actually died.[17]

Although the devil is not mentioned in every investigation of suicide in Reformation Geneva, evidence nonetheless shows that authorities and common folk shared the conviction that suicide was of diabolical origin. Accordingly, prayer was viewed as the best medicine, and the criminal proceedings provide palpable evidence that Reformed Christianity permeated the everyday lives of Genevans, playing a fundamentally important role in shaping their mentality. Many of those who took their lives, such as Elisabeth Paschal, desperately sought refuge in religion during the difficult weeks prior to their suicides.

Religious devotions both at church and in the home were also an important part of the daily life of Jean Mermillod, a pastry cook who took his life in February 1644. Mermillod, thirty-five, and evidently a widower, had suffered from melancholy and emotional instability for about a year. Witnesses reported that Mermillod was at times furious, having more than once drawn his sword and threatened to kill people. Physicians and surgeons had been treating him during the previous months for "an extraordinary malady." The day before his death, however, Mermillod appeared most joyous after attending a morning church service. He awoke about five the next morning, sleeping in the same bed with his eldest son, whom he awoke and asked to say the morning prayer. A few minutes later, however, Mermillod shot himself in the chest in his room.[18]

The suicide of a merchant in the late 1670s shows that religion still permeated the daily life of many Genevans at that time. Jacques Rigoumier, forty-five, was a wealthy jewelry merchant who took his life in March 1679 after suffering periodically from an unspecified physical illness. On 14 March, a Friday, Rigoumier went to the morning church service and later asked his servant-girl to let him know when it was time to go to church for afternoon prayers. Testifying to the Auditeur, the servant expressed no surprise at her master's request, thus indicating that it was not unusual for

---

[17]AEG, EC, LM 34: 137, 20 August 1647; PC 2e série 2509; RC 146: 119v–120, 140v.
[18]AEG, EC, LM 34: 39v, 14 February 1644; PC 2e série 2476; RC 143: 23v–24, 28.

Rigoumier to attend church twice on a weekday. Early that afternoon, he went into a room in his apartment where he read aloud from the Bible for half an hour, a habit that he performed every day. When the servant notified him at 3:30 that it was time for the afternoon prayer service, however, Rigoumier went into his room and fatally shot himself in the head.[19]

One may wonder whether these daily devotions and prayers were accompanied by feelings of guilt and helplessness before a judgmental God—one who had from all eternity predestined the fate of everyone. Is there evidence to suggest, as has been argued for Puritan England, that Reformed Protestantism helped stimulate melancholy and that "grief was exacerbated to terror by Calvinist theology"?[20] The suicide of Madeleine Sirau sheds light on this issue. Sirau, thirty-five, the wife of the Citizen goldsmith Pierre Sautier, jumped to her death from her upper-story window in December 1636 after having suffered from alienation of spirit for five months. According to her husband and servant-girl, Sirau actively participated in the daily devotions that her husband led. The night before her death, with their young son present, Sirau's husband read from the Bible and sang Psalms, and she herself said the evening prayer. After the prayer, her husband went to bed, leaving Sirau with the servant-girl and their child. Ignoring the servant's entreaties to go to bed, Sirau complained that she had offended God, and began to ask him for forgiveness. The servant-girl fought to stay awake but finally dozed off while Sirau read from the Bible. This gave Sirau the opportunity to jump. Her body was found at 4:00 A.M. by a man who was on his way to church.[21]

At first glance, this testimony concerning Sirau seems to lend credence to the contention that the Reformed faith nurtured guilt feelings in devout believers, ultimately pushing them to suicide. Among suicides in Reformation Geneva, Sirau came closest to resembling a desperate believer who, aware of her sins, suffered from anxiety and feared that her destiny was reprobation. In no case, however—including those of Sirau and Paschal—is

---

[19]AEG, EC, LM 43: 98, 14 March 1679; PC 4451; RC 179: 82–83, 91, 95–96.

[20]Samuel Ernest Sprott, *The English Debate on Suicide from Donne to Hume* (La Salle, Ill.: Open Court, 1961), 48–49, goes on, "A depressive predestinarian who could not feel in his spirit the movement of grace that signified that he was called to salvation might conclude that he was elected to damnation. Why delay death? If grace were wanting, he could not repent. Further sin, in disobedience to God, heaped up future torments."

[21]AEG, PC 2e série 2425; RC 135: 338.

there any mention of predestination, a tenet that some historians claim contributed strongly to melancholy. No evidence from these suicides suggests that Genevans were bothered by or even thought about the doctrine of predestination. Studying the registers of the Genevan Consistory, Robert Kingdon has aptly shown that religion for common folk was more a matter of rituals than theology; the doctrine of predestination, often portrayed as the very essence of Calvinism, appeared to have only a negligible effect on the rank and file.[22] In short, the doctrine of double predestination does not appear to have been a source of anguish for residents of Reformation Geneva.[23]

What is most striking, however, is the fact that so few people reacted in the manner of Sirau, Paschal, and Mermillod. Since there is no comparable study on suicide for a Catholic area, we unfortunately cannot compare the general frequency of self-inflicted deaths among Genevans with that of their Catholic contemporaries. Moreover, since there is no recorded suicide in pre-Reformation Geneva, we cannot know if the ancestors of Paschal and Rigoumier demonstrated similar proclivities. Elsewhere in Europe suicide appears to have been quite rare in the Middle Ages, though extant records are quite scanty.[24] If we assume that medieval suicide was as rare as the meager sources suggest, then Geneva of the sixteenth and seventeenth centuries would have witnessed, at most, a very modest increase in the frequency of suicide. Such an increase pales, however, when compared to the explosion in self-inflicted deaths of the late 1700s. Simply put, suicide was rare in six-

---

[22]Robert M. Kingdon, "The Geneva Consistory as Established by John Calvin," *On the Way: Occasional Papers of the Wisconsin Conference of the United Church of Christ* 7 (1990): 41. The dispute in 1551 between Calvin and Jerome Bolsec, who attacked the doctrine of predestination, did generate considerable interest among common folk. Though they did not follow the nuances of this theological debate, a few artisans clearly had some idea of the possible implications of the doctrine of predestination, repeating Bolsec's claim that it made God the author of evil. Many of those who sided with Bolsec, however, defended not his theological convictions but rather his character, insisting that he was an "homme de bien" and the victim of a personal vendetta with Calvin; idem, "Popular Reactions to the Debate Between Bolsec and Calvin," in *Calvin: Erbe und Auftrag*, ed. Willem van't Spijker (Kampen, The Netherlands: Kok Pharos, 1991), 138–45.

[23]Kaspar von Greyerz arrived at similar conclusions in examining diaries and autobiographies written by seventeenth-century Puritans. Though they were filled with spiritual concerns, these writings contained very few references to the doctrine of predestination, which apparently did not play a very significant role in Puritan lay piety; see "Biographical Evidence on Predestination, Covenant, and Special Providence," in *Weber's Protestant Ethic: Origins, Evidence, Contexts*, ed. Hartmut Lehmann and Guenther Roth (Cambridge: Cambridge University Press, 1993), 273–84.

[24]Murray, *Suicide*, vol. 1, *Violent Against Themselves*, 348–78.

teenth- and seventeenth-century Geneva. True, diligent private devotions, church attendance, and Scripture readings ultimately did not prevent Sirau, Mermillod, Paschal, and a handful of others from taking their lives. If commonly followed by Genevans in general, however, such practices would have, one would think, a strong deterring effect on suicide. More important, while the widespread belief in diabolical power led to a witchcraft craze in Reformation Europe, the contemporary view that the devil was responsible for suicide (a view expressed, as we have seen, by judicial authorities, witnesses, and even some of the suicides themselves) served as one of the most important deterrents to taking one's life. The Calvinist fear of a judgmental God complemented the fear of the devil in effectively discouraging self-inflicted deaths in Geneva's population at large.

The belief that the devil caused suicide, however, disappeared along with the fear of witchcraft. Geneva's last execution for witchcraft, the diabolical work par excellence, occurred in 1652; its last witchcraft trial took place in 1681,[25] and we still find a couple of references to suicide as diabolical after 1650.[26] Nevertheless, by the 1680s, suicide had in effect been divorced from diabolism. In 1686 two men believed that God, not the devil, had afflicted them with maladies which eventually pushed them to kill themselves. François Cartier, forty-eight and a gardener, took his life in January of that year after suffering from hemorrhoids and, for the past two months, from a fever that left him frequently deranged and paranoid. Pastor Dupan, who served as Cartier's minister, reported having consoled Cartier many times during his illness. He declared that Cartier had "a genuine piety and fear of God, with a constant faith and utter confidence in divine mercy,

---

[25]Michel Porret, *Le crime et ses circonstances: De l'esprit de l'arbitraire au siècle des Lumières selon les réquisitoires des procureurs généraux de Genève* (Geneva: Droz, 1995), 43.

[26]In February 1651, Jacques Sollicoffre, nineteen, the son of an affluent merchant, stabbed himself after suffering from an illness. He survived for several hours, during which time he told the surgeon who treated his wounds that the devil had pushed him to commit this act; AEG, PC 2e série 2534, RC 149: 35. Similarly in August 1669, Claude François Montral, thirty, an agricultural laborer, hanged himself in his home in Geneva. Devastated by his death, his wife told the Auditeur that Montral was not alienated but did occasionally get angry and at times made "winds from his mouth as do possessed people"; she acknowledged that he had a brother and sister who had been possessed by demons. Taking these words quite seriously, the Small Council ordered that his assets be confiscated and that his body be dragged on a hurdle through the streets from his home to Champel where it was to be buried; AEG, PC 4053; RC 169: 311–12.

always...resigning himself to God's will."[27] Because of his illness, Dupan argued, the incoherent Cartier no longer had control of his actions. During lucid moments, Cartier even thanked God for the affliction, always assured of his eternal salvation. Dupan described Cartier as a good, hardworking man who attended church on Sundays and was dedicated to his family. The pastor argued that Cartier had not been abandoned by God but had simply succumbed to his illness. He pleaded that Cartier should receive a good Christian burial, claiming that his physical ills and alienation of spirit were of this world. Dupan insisted that Cartier did not suffer "the rage or despair of the soul."[28] Pastor Dupan was in effect medicalizing this suicide. Not for a moment did he suggest that this suicide could have been diabolical in origin.

Similarly, François Dunand of the rural village of Avully drowned himself in September 1686 after suffering from a serious fever. According to his wife, Dunand had stoically said that he had to accept his illness, as it was God's will. Regardless of whether he said those words, her testimony indicates that the proper attitude of the sick was to resign oneself to the will of God, who was responsible for all illnesses.[29]

Though quite distinct from the view that suicide was diabolical, this belief that suffering is divinely inflicted also served as an effective deterrent to suicide. From Augustine to Calvin and beyond, theologians warned Christians that, like Job, they must bear hardships patiently and never hasten their own end. As noted in chapter 2, Calvin categorically condemned suicide primarily because it was a rebellion against God, a refusal to submit to God's will. Though it did not prevent either Cartier or Dunand from ending their lives, this Calvinist emphasis on the judgmental nature of God, far from nurturing despair, effectively deterred self-inflicted deaths in Geneva's population at large. The fear of God's judgment was enough to discourage most Genevans from voluntarily ending their lives.

Most important, the fact remains that suicide was quite rare through the end of the seventeenth century. People who took their lives in Reforma-

---

[27]AEG, PC 4679.

[28]AEG, PC 4679. The Small Council allowed Cartier to be buried in the regular cemetery, but without honors; RC 186: 23–24.

[29]AEG, Juridiction Civile F 212; PC 4712. Throughout the seventeenth and eighteenth centuries, popular beliefs in rural Anjou continued to view illnesses as of supernatural origin, caused either by demon possession or divine command; François Lebrun, *Les Hommes et la mort en Anjou aux 17e et 18e siècles* (Paris: Mouton, 1971), 393–94.

tion Geneva for the most part were not those who had thoroughly internalized Reformed piety; rather, they were generally on the margins of this tightly integrated society: suspected witches, prisoners, and the violently deranged. In Reformation Geneva there is nothing to suggest that Calvinist piety itself contributed to suicidal behavior. On the contrary, evidence indicates that through the mid-seventeenth century, the religious convictions of Geneva's Reformed Christians served as one of the most important restraints on suicidal proclivities. Since suicide was believed to be diabolical, prayer, regular church attendance, and family devotions were viewed as the best medicine for suicidal tendencies. These practices, tied to Genevans' fear of both God and the devil, fostered a strong abhorrence for suicide. Simply put, the evidence from Geneva does not support the contention of some historians that religious despair was an important cause of suicide in the seventeenth century.[30]

The small number of suicides suggests, moreover, that Durkheim's analysis of Protestantism's impact on the frequency of suicide does not hold true for Geneva through the seventeenth century. Durkheim asserted that Protestantism provided for greater individualism and freer inquiry, maintaining a less rigid church hierarchy than Roman Catholicism. Consequently, he argued, Protestant churches were less strongly integrated and played a less dominant role in the lives of parishioners.[31] While these ideas may have been true for the nineteenth-century Europe in which Durkheim lived, they do not apply to Reformation Geneva.

Throughout the Reformation period, the Republic of Geneva was indeed a very tightly integrated society. As in Roman Catholic areas, the church in Geneva was coterminous with society. The complete integration of church and society is aptly seen in the responsibilities of the *dizeniers*, officers who oversaw the mores of those living in their respective districts of the city. Each *dizenier* sought out residents in his district who were quarreling with each other, and endeavored to reconcile them before they took part in

---

[30]Georges Minois, *Histoire du suicide: La société occidentale face à la mort volontaire* (Paris: Fayard, 1995), 160–61; Markus Schär, *Seelennöte der Untertanen: Selbstmord, Melancholie und Religion im Alten Zürich 1500–1800* (Zurich: Chronos, 1985).

[31]Emile Durkheim, *Suicide: A Study in Sociology,* trans. John A. Spaulding and George Simpson, edited and with an introduction by George Simpson (New York: Free Press, 1951), 152–64.

the Eucharist.[32] Moreover, the Consistory, which enforced Reformed morality, was an intrusive institution that oversaw the everyday lives of Genevans in great detail. Geneva's Consistory, which met every week, regularly summoned people for being truant from church, dancing or playing cards, performing forbidden Catholic practices such as saying prayers to saints, and a host of other forms of behavior deemed immoral. Though it could not impose any secular penalties, Geneva's Consistory was able to intimidate the rank and file by denying them the right to participate in the Eucharist. Particularly during the time of Calvin, excommunication apparently brought with it a form of ostracism, adversely affecting one's daily life and business affairs.[33] Having been denied communion, guilty parties were often readmitted to the community only by doing the humiliating act of public *réparation*. Ironically, by excluding people from the community for violating Reformed morality, the Consistory was reinforcing Geneva's very strong sense of community. The fact that religious devotions in the home supplemented the dozens of church services held weekly increased rather than diminished the degree of religious integration in Geneva, allowing little room for deviation. In the Reformation era, Reformed religiosity thoroughly permeated Genevan society. The high degree of individualism that Durkheim believed made suicide endemic in Protestant areas was absent in Reformation Geneva.[34]

---

[32]Thomas Lambert and Isabella Watt, introduction to *Registres du Consistoire de Genève au temps de Calvin, 1542–1544* (Geneva: Droz, 1996), 1: xvi.

[33]Robert M. Kingdon, "Social Control and Political Control in Calvin's Geneva," *Archive for Reformation History* (special volume, 1993): 523.

[34]Three people, including Jean Jourdain, as previously described, and Julienne Berard, described briefly in chapter 2, took their lives because they were most upset about having to appear before the Consistory. Another woman, Louise Bouphaz, was devastated and feared being sent to jail after Calvin and other members of the Consistory forbade her in 1563 to take communion. They censured her because of the fornication of two servants under her roof and of her utter inability to recite the confession of faith. People appearing before the Consistory were regularly questioned about their knowledge of prayers and the confession of faith even if they had not been summoned directly for their religious practices. Ultimately, however, the Consistory nurtured community ties infinitely more than suicidal proclivities; AEG, PC 2e série 1252; Registres du Consistoire de Genève, 19: 216–17, 28 January 1563. See Robert M. Kingdon, "Calvin and the Establishment of Consistory Discipline in Geneva: The Institution and the Men Who Directed It," *Nederlands Archief voor Kerkgeschiedenes* 70 (1990): 158–72; Jeffrey R. Watt, "Women and the Consistory in Calvin's Geneva," *Sixteenth Century Journal* 24 (1993): 429–39.

The Medical Dimension of Suicide

Like other geographical areas, early modern Geneva eventually experienced the medicalization of suicide. By the late 1700s, physicians, Auditeurs, and witnesses all offered medical explanations as to why people took their lives. This medical concern was not altogether new. As early as the thirteenth century, English court rolls reveal that those who took their lives while in a "frenzy," an involuntary state of mind, were deemed not guilty of criminal conduct. In the later Middle Ages one can find evidence that self-inflicted deaths were associated with madness or "melancholy."[35] Throughout the early modern period, we can find cases of Genevan physicians trying to treat "melancholy," fevers, "alienation," and other ills of people who eventually took their lives. As noted above, the physician Dauphin offered medical assistance to Elisabeth Paschal who, believing herself diabolically possessed, took her life in 1625. Marie Chioccio, the woman who killed herself in 1647 because she feared her baby was bewitched, was also under a physician's care and seemed at first to respond well to his treatment for melancholy.[36]

By the end of the eighteenth century, however, suicide in Geneva had been thoroughly medicalized. Michael MacDonald sees the change in mentality that lay behind the medicalization of suicide in England as a complex phenomenon. Following the political and religious turmoil of the seventeenth century, the English ruling classes had a certain repugnance for religious fanaticism and saw the supernatural as a potentially negative force. At the same time, scientific advances called for natural explanations for phenomena such as suicide. As in Geneva, such explanations had already existed in England, often complementing the view that self-murder stemmed from diabolism or divine judgment. Interestingly, physicians did not deserve much of the credit for the medicalization of suicide in England. By and large, physicians at that time did not have the prestige and organizational strength to be able to influence appreciably public opinion. Attitudes toward mental infirmities were molded not only by the ideas of influential thinkers but even more so by the cultural, social, religious, and political environment. In the eighteenth century, as belief in supernatural causes of suicide and

---

[35]Minois, *Histoire du suicide*, 51; Murray, *Suicide*, vol. 1, *Violent Against Themselves*, 160–65, 318–31.

[36]AEG, PC 2e série 2509.

mental illness waned, only the natural, medical explanations remained.[37]

In Geneva, the medicalization of suicide is aptly seen in the death of Jean-Louis Tronchin in 1773. During the brief illness that preceded his death, the physician Butini had cared for Tronchin. Butini testified that he had visited Tronchin twice a day during the last week of his life, declaring that Tronchin suffered from insomnia and a light, "bilious" fever. On 16 May, the day of his death, Butini found that Tronchin no longer had a fever but was extremely nervous and melancholic. He constantly repeated himself in conversation and wept a great deal. Butini concluded that Tronchin's insomnia and poor diet over the past few days were causing this "vaporous state." Accordingly, Butini prescribed daily carriage rides and tepid baths and exhorted him to eat more. Others testified to Tronchin's altered state during the last week of his life. His valet, Frédéric Gremay, reported that Tronchin said several times the day of his death that his head was spinning. A friend of the family, Gédéon Turrettini, a former Syndic, came to pay Tronchin a visit later in the day, hoping to cheer him up. Tronchin spoke little to Turrettini, though he did complain that he had a fever and had not slept in ten days. Tronchin further insisted that it was really his soul that was suffering. At the encouragement of his wife, Tronchin agreed to eat some toast dipped in wine, the only nourishment he had that day apart from a cup of hot chocolate. This seemed to do some good temporarily, though Tronchin soon began moaning again. He complained about a pain in his abdomen that was tearing him apart, yet also proclaimed, "It's the soul, it's the soul!" Tronchin's wife convinced him to take a bath, as recommended by Butini. After the bath, Tronchin was left alone briefly to dress but soon was not to be found. His wife, mother, and servants began frantically looking for him, then heard

---

[37]Michael MacDonald, "The Medicalization of Suicide in England: Laymen, Physicians, and Cultural Change, 1500–1870," in *Framing Disease: Studies in Cultural History*, ed. Charles E. Rosenberg and Janet Golden (New Brunswick, N.J.: Rutgers University Press, 1992), 97–99; idem, "The Secularization of Suicide in England 1660–1800," *Past and Present* 111 (1986): 50–100; and MacDonald and Murphy, *Sleepless Souls*, 109–216. Michael MacDonald, "Suicide and the Rise of the Popular Press in England," *Representations* 22 (1988): 36–55, also finds that the great expansion in the circulation of newspapers in the eighteenth century reflected and reinforced the secularization of suicide by citing mundane causes, thus sharply restricting the range of phenomena that could be attributed to supernatural forces. For changing attitudes toward and treatment of insanity in eighteenth-century Geneva, see Vincent Barras, "Fers, bains et remèdes: 'La maison des allienez' de Genève," *Revue médicale de la Suisse Romande* 109 (1989): 999–1004; idem, "De quelques individus dangereux à Genève au XVIIIe siècle: Un exemple des rapports entre droit et médecine," *Cahiers de la Faculté de Médecine* 17 (1989): 43–63.

a shot coming from the basement, where he had fired a rifle into his throat. Though neighbors immediately went running to get a surgeon, nothing could be done to save his life.[38]

All witnesses, from servants to the Syndic Turrettini, stressed the medical causes of Tronchin's self-inflicted death. During the difficult days leading up to his death, it was the physician Butini who ministered to Tronchin's welfare. If a minister paid a pastoral visit to Tronchin during these days, witnesses did not deem such a visit as worthy of reporting to the Auditeur. While in the early seventeenth century, the physician Dauphin had deemed Paschal's physical illness to have been caused by sin, Butini attributed Tronchin's mental anguish to physical ailments. Had he lived in the Reformation era, Tronchin's complaints about the ills of his soul would have immediately raised suspicions of demon possession. Those around him, however, encouraged Tronchin to take baths, eat nourishing meals, and get fresh air; they did not mention if they told him to pray and think of God. Nothing in this investigation suggests that Tronchin sought solace through prayer during his last days, nor did he leave a note in which he asked for God's forgiveness. For all involved, the miserable Tronchin was the victim of an illness, not the perpetrator of a sin and certainly not the instrument of the devil.

One may wonder if this medicalization of suicide may have had an impact on the manner in which deaths were reported. The belief, expressed by some eighteenth-century thinkers, that suicide was invariably the result of mental illness tended of course to exculpate those who took their lives. If they were not morally or legally responsible for this action, does that mean that their survivors would have had no reason to hide the cause of death? If so, could that mean that Genevans had successfully covered up family members' suicides in the previous two centuries and simply saw no reason to do so after 1750? On the contrary, this medicalization of suicide provided a further incentive to hide self-inflicted deaths. Fears and prejudices against insanity were quite strong, especially since mental illness was so often assumed to be congenital. Consequently, the insanity of one member of a

[38] AEG, PC 12450.

family might seem to impugn the mental stability of all its members.[39] Thus, apart from the fact that covering up a suicide in Geneva was never easy, the motivation to do so certainly did not diminish in the late 1700s.

Throughout the early modern period, the medical terms for mental and physical maladies lacked precision. Nonetheless, the records are generally clear enough to indicate whether a person's illness had definite physical symptoms. A few suicides had contracted venereal diseases; others were epileptic; and a large number had suffered from illnesses that were vaguely described as fevers, which often left the victims delirious. The terms employed in the Genevan records for mental illnesses were even less precise than those used for physical illnesses. In the Middle Ages, "melancholy" referred to a physical malady, which stemmed from an excess of black bile that disturbed the brain and caused sad moods. Terms such as "frenzy" or "furor" referred to maladies that might involve delirium, hallucinations, violent acts, and so on.[40] The English parson Robert Burton, who acknowledged suffering himself from melancholy, contributed to the use of this term through the publication in 1621 of his influential treatise, *The Anatomy of Melancholy*. In discussing causes of suicide, eighteenth-century French medical writers saw three categories of mental illnesses: *frénésie*, *manie*, and *mélancolie*. They associated the first with feverishness and the second with tensions and the excessive dryness of fibers, particularly in the brain. *Mélancolie*, they believed, resulted from imbalances in the liquids of the brain and the nervous system. Physicians of the eighteenth century thus remained very much tied to traditional notions about the balance of humors.[41]

When used in Geneva's criminal investigations, these terms did not always denote such clear-cut distinctions of these maladies. Geneva's physicians, Auditeurs, and common folk frequently referred to people suffering from "melancholy," describing symptoms that we associate with depression,

---

[39]Henry Romilly Fedden, *Suicide: A Social and Historical Study* (New York: Benjamin Blom, 1972), 260.

[40]Minois, *Histoire du suicide*, 51.¬

[41]John McManners, *Death and the Enlightenment: Changing Attitudes to Death in Eighteenth-Century France* (Oxford: Oxford University Press, 1981), 435. Midelfort, *Mad Princes*, 3–10, found that German physicians used "furor" to describe insanity so severe that one was not responsible for one's actions. "Melancholia" remained tied to black bile, and physicians were very concerned about humoral imbalances as a cause of mental disorders.

which, as modern psychiatric studies suggest, is the mental disorder most likely to end in suicide.[42] Genevans who suffered from "melancholy" were quite sad, listless, and reclusive, enduring frequent bouts of weeping. Some individuals were described as being by nature melancholic, while others' melancholy allegedly resulted from physical illness or an unpleasant experience, such as a love affair gone awry. Other terms were used to describe a higher degree of mental instability, the most common of which was "alienated in spirit." People were also described as demented, delirious, frenetic, feeble-minded, troubled or weak in spirit, or simply sick in the head.[43] People suffering from such mental illnesses might be subject to paranoia or violent and erratic behavior; some were clearly demented.

Although in identifying motives I have listed no one as both "melancholic" and "alienated," the distinction between these mental ailments was quite blurry. Nonetheless, the fact that authorities used different terms may at least tell us something about their prejudices. Authorities were more likely to describe women and the nonwealthy as alienated, whereas men and the wealthy were more likely to be labeled melancholic. Of those described as alienated or mad, women made up the majority (forty-three of seventy-nine), a remarkable finding insofar as women made up a small minority of total suicides. By contrast, the records describe as melancholic fifty men and twenty-one women, roughly in line with the overall male-to-female ratio for suicides.[44] This discrepancy undoubtedly tells us more about the biases of authorities than the actual mental state of these individuals. These male authorities clearly viewed women as less stable and more prone to insanity than men, aptly reflecting the views of contemporary medical authorities.

---

[42]A few studies have attempted to establish suicide rates for different diagnostic groups. These studies suggest that the suicide rate is highest among those afflicted by depressive psychoses. The groups with the next highest rate would be those afflicted by psychoneuroses or alcohol disorders, who killed themselves at roughly the same rate; see David Lester, *Why People Kill Themselves: A Summary of Research Findings on Suicidal Behavior* (Springfield, Ill.: Charles C. Thomas, 1972), 194–98; Seymour Perlin and Chester W. Schmidt, Jr., "Psychiatry," in *Handbook for Study of Suicide*, ed. Seymour Perlin (New York: Oxford University Press, 1975), 154.

[43]Terms included: "aliené d'esprit," "troublé d'esprit," "extravagance d'esprit," "dans le delire," "malade à la tête," "transport de cerveau," "accès de démence," "en démence," "malade d'esprit," "cerveau faible," "faible d'esprit," and "faiblesse de cerveau."

[44]Some modern psychiatric studies find that psychoses are more common among men, while neuroses are more common among women. Moreover, evidence indicates that while neurotics may be more likely to attempt suicide, psychotics are more apt to succeed in killing themselves; Lester, *Why People Kill Themselves*, 194–98.

While physicians had long associated "hysteria" and other mental afflictions with the uterus, eighteenth-century medical writers modified this stance somewhat. Writing in 1758, Joseph Raulin avowed that women's special susceptibility to "vapors"—purportedly the most widespread disease of eighteenth-century France—stemmed not from their physiology but rather from the fact that they were so idle. In his *Système physique et moral de la femme* (1775), Pierre Roussel offered an organic explanation for mental infirmities among women. He claimed that women have an overabundance of nerve fibers, which makes them much more sensitive than men to any stimuli; hence there were far more cases of vapors and other maladies among females.[45]

In Geneva, while the rich made up about an eighth of the suicides described as alienated, they comprised a fourth of the melancholic.[46] The authorities were clearly reluctant to describe as alienated or demented their fellow members of the male Genevan elite. For the entire period, only three wealthy men were described as alienated, and one of them was a foreigner who had just arrived in Geneva.[47] Even though insanity might remove a suicide's culpability, Auditeurs and members of the Small Council were quite reticent to use this term in describing the mental instability of the wealthy and men in general, apparently deeming melancholy less shameful than insanity.

Taken together, the evidence concerning melancholy and alienation provides surprising results with regard to class. The wealthy were definitely overrepresented among suicides for whom mental instability, be it melancholy or alienation, was cited as a major factor. The poor, while present in greater numbers than their proportion of the population would dictate, were under-

[45]Evelyne Berriot-Salvadore, "The Discourse of Medicine and Science," in *History of Women in the West*, ed. Natalie Zemon Davis and Arlette Farge, vol. 3, *Renaissance and Enlightenment Paradoxes* (Cambridge: Harvard University Press, 1993), 348–88. Juliana Schiesari, *The Gendering of Melancholia: Feminism, Psychoanalysis, and the Symbolics of Loss in Renaissance Literature* (Ithaca, N.Y.: Cornell University Press, 1996), maintains that early modern medical writers viewed melancholia as a female illness. Other scholars have found, however, that men were about as likely as women to be diagnosed as melancholic. Moreover, as prominent a writer as Jean Bodin viewed melancholy as a malady that afflicted males exclusively; see Midelfort, *History of Madness*, 6–7, 215.

[46]Of the 79 suicides described as mad or alienated, 8 were wealthy, 34 were modest to comfortable, 25 were poor, and 12 were of unknown financial status. The figures for melancholy were, respectively, 16, 33, 17, and 5.

[47]AEG, EC, LM 62: 266, 16 December 1758; PC 10617.

represented with regard to the percentage of total suicides related to mental instability.[48] Although this may at first appear as if the wealthy were particularly susceptible to depression or insanity, what this really shows is that the poor had many other reasons to kill themselves than did the rich. Needless to say, the rich never killed themselves out of poverty.[49] The poor also had a virtual monopoly on those who committed suicide in prison. The poor included unmarried female servants who were pushed to kill themselves because their masters accused them of stealing or because they were pregnant. In short, the poor faced so many more difficulties that did not affect the affluent; those living in poverty did not have to suffer from depression or insanity to take their lives.

The same largely holds true for physical illness. Among those who killed themselves because of physical maladies, the poor, comprising about a third of the total, were somewhat underrepresented. The well-to-do, at 18 percent, were overrepresented when compared to the overall figures for suicides.[50] Again, the poor were much more likely to have motives other than physical and mental maladies than the wealthy or middling sorts. Nonetheless, if we compare the percentage of suicides who were physically sick to the population at large, then we find that, as with all motives, the poor were indeed overrepresented. The poor comprised much less than a third of Geneva's population. Having a more meager diet and more difficult working conditions, the poor understandably faced greater dangers of falling ill. They also had less access to medical care, but that was not always to their health's disadvantage. While medical practitioners did at times have the right idea— they saw the benefit of fresh air, a calm environment, and regular bathing— their frequent prescriptions of enemas, leeches, and above all bleedings had unfortunate consequences all too often.

Taken together, motives of physical and mental illnesses were present in over half the suicides for which plausible motives can be identified (188 of

---

[48]If we exclude those of unknown financial status, the affluent comprised 18.1 percent of the melancholic and alienated. The poor were 31.6 percent of such suicides, although they made up over 40 percent of all those who took their lives.

[49]While two affluent Genevans did kill themselves because of financial concerns, they also both suffered from melancholy or alienation; AEG, PC 10707 and 13885.

[50]Excluding the seven of unknown financial status, 16 suicides (18 percent) were affluent, 42 (47.2 percent) were of modest to comfortable means, and 31 (34.8 percent) were poor. Men outnumbered women 63 to 25.

359). Interestingly, the vast majority of suicides motivated by physical (73 of 96) and mental (97 of 150) ailments occurred after 1750. The fact that only twenty-seven suicides attributed in part to alienation or melancholy took place before 1701 might lead one to believe that Genevans of the sixteenth and seventeenth centuries enjoyed a certain immunity from depression and insanity that was lost after 1750. Clearly, however, the large numbers of suicides who suffered from mental and physical illnesses in the late eighteenth century were not simply a reflection of the medicalization of suicide. The large number of suicides who were mentally or physically sick cannot be dismissed as simply a change in terminology, as authorities and the rank and file increasingly attributed medical causes to self-inflicted deaths. To begin with, as noted above, the motives that I have assigned to suicides do not always coincide with those alleged in the investigations. Thus, while Elisabeth Paschal believed she was possessed by demons and her physician thought that sin was the source of her mental woes, I have listed alienation and domestic discord, not diabolical possession, as principally responsible for her self-inflicted death of 1625. More important, the low number of suicides before 1700 militates against such an argument. There were considerably more suicides motivated by mental and physical maladies after 1750 than the total number of suicides for the previous two hundred years, including those for which no motive could be established.

Moreover, it is important to note that even though suicides by the ill, the depressed, and the deranged were far more numerous after 1750 than before, the percentage of suicides affected by these factors declined in the second half of the eighteenth century. Through 1750 mental illness appeared as a cause in 51.5 percent of the suicides for which motives can be identified, while representing only 38 percent after that date. Associating suicide with mental illness was not something that appeared suddenly in the late eighteenth century. Excluding suicides of unknown causes, we find that mental and physical maladies together appeared as motives in two-thirds (68 of 103) of self-inflicted deaths through 1750 as opposed to 58.4 percent thereafter.[51]

Nonetheless, one may wonder whether demographic changes, involving decreasing mortality and increasing longevity, might explain the explosion in

---

[51]True, physical illness was a factor in a slightly higher proportion of suicides after 1750 (28.6 percent) than before (22.3 percent).

suicides in late-eighteenth-century Geneva. Sociological studies have consistently shown that suicide rates are higher among older people than among younger folk. Twentieth-century evidence from a host of Western countries shows that preadolescent suicides are quite rare. This evidence also shows that suicide rates continue to increase throughout life for males, while for females they tend to increase until the age of fifty or sixty, declining thereafter.[52] Suicidologists have identified a number of reasons why people are more susceptible to suicide as they age. As people grow older, attacks of melancholy are likely to be more frequent, and the elderly are more apt to be afflicted with painful and incurable illnesses. The effects of alcoholism usually get stronger with age, and the elderly often have fewer contacts with others, resulting in greater social isolation. Retirement often brings a decline in social status, and material hardship is more likely in old age.[53]

If often fatal diseases, such as the plague and smallpox, disappeared or declined, then Genevans should have lived longer than their ancestors. If the population in general was getting older, then perhaps Genevans were facing this wide array of geriatric woes. Most notably, an aging population may have suffered more bouts with physical and mental ailments which, even if not fatal, could make their lives miserable. If so, greater longevity and declining mortality might have been decisive factors in the explosion in suicides in the late eighteenth century.

Geneva did indeed experience a decrease in mortality and an increase in longevity during the course of the early modern period. Geneva endured frequent bouts with the plague in the sixteenth and early seventeenth centuries, but the plague's last appearance in Geneva occurred in 1636–40.[54] More-

[52]Anthony Giddens, "The Statistics of Suicide," in *The Sociology of Suicide: A Selection of Readings*, ed. Anthony Giddens (London: Frank Cass, 1971), 422; Ronald W. Maris, *Social Forces in Urban Suicide* (Homewood, Ill.: Dorsey Press, 1969), 92–93. See also Durkheim, *Suicide*, 73, 100–3. Jean-Claude Chesnais, "History of Violence: Homicide and Suicide Through the Ages," *International Social Science Journal* 44 (1992): 227, suggests that suicide rates are higher in contemporary Europe than in past centuries in part because of greater longevity. With the disappearance of natural selection, there are growing numbers of people "who are delicate in their constitution, both physical and psychological," and accordingly more prone to suicide.

[53]Jean Baechler, *Suicides*, trans. Barry Cooper (New York: Basic Books, 1979), 284–85. See also Arlette Moullembé et al., "Conduites suicidaires, approche théorique et clinique," *Bulletin de Psychologie* 27 (1973–74): 872; Perlin and Schmidt, "Psychiatry," in *Handbook for Study of Suicide*, ed. Perlin, 153.

[54]Alfred Perrenoud, "Comportements démographiques," in *L'economie genevoise de la Réforme à la fin de l'Ancien Régime XVIe–XVIIIe siècles*, ed. Anne-Marie Piuz and Liliane Mottu-Weber (Geneva: Société d'histoire et d'archéologie de Genève, 1990), 111–13.

over, even before inoculation was introduced in the eighteenth century, smallpox, a disease that mainly killed young children, was less deadly than before.[55] Among Genevans, life expectancy at birth rose from 23.6 years for the period 1625–49 to 27.1 for 1675–99, reaching a plateau of 33 to 34 years from 1725 to 1790. Less spectacular was the increase in life expectancy at the age of ten. In 1625–49 ten-year-olds in Geneva could expect to live another 39.5 years, increasing to 42 years in the early eighteenth century and 46.3 years for the period 1770–90. The proportion of Geneva's population that was over 55 increased steadily from the late sixteenth to the end of the eighteenth centuries.[56] In short, the late eighteenth century showed an increase, albeit a rather modest one, in life expectancy for adults.

Did this increase in longevity play a role in the growing number of individuals who killed themselves because of illnesses? We can find examples of suicides involving older people who took their lives to put an end to physical or emotional misery. As noted above in chapter 2, in November 1768 "Noble" Marc Pictet, seventy-five, a former Syndic and friend of Voltaire, drowned himself after suffering for months from acute abdominal pains.[57] Pierre Grenus, an attorney and former member of the Council of Two Hundred, was long afflicted with severe migraines, terrible abdominal pains, and worst of all, acute urine retention. He drowned himself in June 1775 at the age of seventy-eight.[58] Another member of Geneva's elite, "Noble" Robert Dunant—a church elder, member of the Consistory and of the Small Council, and a former Syndic—had suffered from "black melancholy" before stabbing himself to death at the age of seventy-one in November 1770.[59]

While these men belonged to wealthy families and probably enjoyed

---

[55]Perrenoud, "Comportements démographiques," in *Economie genevoise*, ed. Piuz and Mottu-Weber, 114.

[56]These figures for life expectancy were quite high by eighteenth-century standards and were roughly in line with those for contemporary England, the most advanced country with regard to health and longevity. While life expectancy at birth in France was only twenty-eight in the second quarter of the eighteenth century, contemporary Geneva enjoyed a life expectancy of 33.8 years; Perrenoud, "Comportements démographiques," in *Economie genevoise*, ed. Piuz and Mottu-Weber, 120–21; idem, *La population de Genève XVIe–XIXe siècles* (Geneva: Société d'histoire et d'archéologie de Genève), 427–28. See also Liliane Mottu-Weber, "Etre vieux à Genève," in *Le poids des ans: Une histoire de la vieillesse en Suisse Romande,* ed. Geneviève Heller (Lausanne, Switzerland: Editions d'en Bas et Société d'histoire de la Suisse Romande, 1994), 50–51.

[57]AEG, EC, LM 64: 51, 27 November 1768; PC 11794; RC 269: 646–47.

[58]AEG, EC, LM 65: 25, 9 June 1775; PC 12742; RC 276: 278.

[59]AEG, EC, LM 64: 150, 12 November 1770; PC 12092; RC 271: 707, 709, 712.

longer life expectancy than poorer folk, some people of very modest means also committed suicide because of problems associated with old age. In December 1774 the Swiss Jean Daniel Anet, age seventy, received an honorable discharge after serving the Republic for many years as a corporal in the garrison. Unable to serve any longer because of his failing eyesight, the bachelor Anet received a modest pension and moved in with his sergeant, Louis Bavot, and his wife. Bavot spoke very highly of Anet, saying that his military service had been exemplary, but added, "Ever since the first day he left the service, Anet repeatedly said that he regretted leaving it and was bored to death. The boredom even prevented him entirely from sleeping. He was devastated after retiring and wanted desperately to return to the service of the Republic."[60] Anet took his life by shooting himself in January 1775, just a month after he had retired. Although a poor man, Anet killed himself not out of poverty but out of boredom; not used to having leisure time at his disposal, he simply did not know what to do with himself. Retirement, particularly for members of the lower classes, was generally unknown in early modern Geneva.[61]

Notwithstanding these examples, there is a fundamental problem with the theory that greater longevity played a major role in the explosion in suicides after 1750. The average age of all suicides, regardless of motives, did not increase substantially in the second half of the eighteenth century. Although the average age of suicides was higher in the eighteenth century than in the seventeenth, there was virtually no change from the first to the second half of the eighteenth century. For 1701–50, the average age of suicides was 42.5 years (42.7 for men and 42.3 for women).[62] After 1750 people took their lives at the average age of 42.8 (43.5 for men and 41 for women).[63] The average age of suicides for the entire early modern period was 42.2 (42.9 for men and 40.6 for women).[64]

---

[60]AEG, PC 12679.

[61]AEG, PC 12679; RC 276: 6; Mottu-Weber, "Etre vieux à Genève," in *Poids des ans*, ed. Heller, 58–59.

[62]These figures are based on forty-six suicides, as the age of eight suicides (five men and three women) was unknown.

[63]The age cannot be identified for eight (again, three women and five men) of the 288 suicides in this half century.

[64]For the period 1542–1650 the average age for all suicides was 35.5 (35.6 for men and 35.4 for women). Those figures are not trustworthy, however, as the age remains unknown for fully twenty of the forty-one suicides from this century. For the second half of the seventeenth century, suicides took their lives on the average at 37.4 years (38.9 for men and 34 for women). For the peak years 1781–1798, the average age of suicides was 43 (43.3 for men and 42 for women).

Moreover, people who were motivated to take their lives in part by physical and mental illnesses were not appreciably older than other suicides. For the entire early modern period, the average age of those who took their lives because of physical illness was 44.3 years. If we look at men and women separately, the average age of ill suicides among men (47) was slightly higher than that of male suicides in general. Conversely, women who took their lives because of illness (38.6 years) were younger than the average female suicide. True, physically ill suicides did become a bit older in the late eighteenth century. Through 1750, the average age of ill suicides was 39.5 years (41.5 for men and 35.6 for women). After 1750, this figure increased to 45.3 (48.1 for men and 39.5 for women). Similar figures apply for suicides motivated by alienation or melancholy. For the entire early modern period, suicides motivated by these factors averaged 43.4 years (43.5 for men and 43.3 for women). The average age of suicides motivated by melancholy or alienation was slightly higher after 1750 than before: respectively, 45 (45.7 for men and 43.9 for women) and 40 (37.9 for men and 42.2 for women). But an increase of five or six years in the average age of ill suicides cannot begin to explain why two-thirds of mentally infirm suicides and three-fourths of physically ill suicides occurred after 1750.[65]

In short, the increase in longevity was at most a minor contributing factor to the huge late-eighteenth-century increase in suicides, even among those motivated by physical or mental illnesses. The suicide explosion in general cannot be attributed to a growing population of infirm elderly people who longed to be put out of their misery. Genevans living in the second half of the eighteenth century were not more prone to illness than their ancestors. Indeed, with their improved diet, they generally enjoyed both better health and slightly longer lives.[66]

[65]There was no appreciable difference in the average age of melancholic and alienated suicides. For the entire early modern period, those described as alienated were on the average 43.6 when they took their lives (42.3 for men, 44.6 for women). The melancholic were 43.2 (44.2 for men, 40.4 for women). I could not determine the ages of twelve (six men and six women) of the 150 suicides motivated by mental illness; nine of these twelve occurred before 1750.

[66]According to some psychological theories, a decline in mortality could effect a drop in the suicide rate. Among factors that allegedly predispose people to suicide is the disruption of relationships in childhood. Studies have suggested that people who endure disrupted relationships in childhood, especially the mother/child relationship, experience difficulty in making lasting relationships later in life, increasing the likelihood of antisocial behavior, and, one assumes, of suicide; see Perlin and Schmidt, "Psychiatry," in *Handbook for Study of Suicide*, ed. Perlin, 152–53; Steve Taylor, *Durkheim and the Study of Suicide* (New

RATIONALISM AND SECULARISM IN THE EIGHTEENTH CENTURY

The medicalization of suicide, as seen in Geneva and elsewhere in the eighteenth century, implies the secularization of suicide, whereby natural explanations supersede supernatural interpretations of voluntary death. What were the engines of this change? More broadly, could greater secularization in general have been a fundamental cause of the increase in suicides in late-eighteenth-century Geneva? Could it be that Genevans of the late 1700s, perhaps influenced by "Enlightened" mores, were more secular in orientation than ever before? Did Geneva witness a decline in religious beliefs and practices, and did religion's influence in shaping mentality decline? Sociologists have long recognized the protection against suicide that strong religious beliefs provide. Religion can offer both social integration and regulation of behavior, serving as a source of both authority and comfort.[67] The sociologist Louis Dublin has said, for example, "Religious teaching has always provided positive support for those who are troubled. The consolations of religious faith and a belief in the efficacy of prayer have proved a solace to many people. To the sincere believer, faith elevates life and gives it joy, confidence, and strength. One who has this emotional attitude has usually a sense of security. He has a feeling of oneness with the cosmic process. We can well understand why those who have a strong religious faith rarely commit suicide."[68]

Similarly, Thomas Masaryk, the future first president of the Czech state, wrote about suicide in 1881, anticipating the work of Durkheim. Masaryk believed the decline in religious faith was the most fundamental cause of the moral malaise that was in turn responsible for the increasing numbers of suicides in his day. For Masaryk the solution was obvious: a

York: St. Martin's Press, 1982), 127–28, citing John Bowlby, *Child Care and the Growth of Love* (Baltimore: Penguin, 1965). Such theories cannot apply to early modern Geneva, however. Throughout the life of the Republic, mortality rates were quite high by modern standards. Although it was very common for children to lose a parent throughout the early modern period, suicide rates were extremely low through the late seventeenth century. The high rates of self-inflicted deaths of the late eighteenth century coincided with a period of increased longevity and, undoubtedly, a perceptible though not dramatic decline in the number of children who lost their mothers or fathers.

[67] Bernice A. Pescolido and Sharon Georgianna, "Durkheim, Suicide, and Religion: Toward a Network Theory of Suicide," *American Sociological Review* 54 (1989): 33–48.

[68] Louis I. Dublin, *Suicide: A Sociological and Statistical Study* (New York: Ronald Press, 1963), 189.

return to the Christian faith.[69]

One deficiency with many sociological studies on the impact of religion on suicide is that they pay scant attention to the content of religious beliefs. Durkheim generally believed that religion deterred suicide more as a means of integrating individuals through shared beliefs than as a source of life-sustaining ideas. He viewed excessive individualism, which he traced back to the philosophes of the Enlightenment, as principally responsible for the isolation of individuals in modern European society, which in turn resulted in high suicide rates. In developed societies where the individual is considered quite significant, people who fail to realize their goals and aspirations may feel like failures, blame themselves, and view suicide as a viable choice.[70] Religion, however, may serve as an important means of subordinating the individual to a community united through faith. Durkheim claimed, moreover, that Catholics committed suicide less often than Protestants not because of doctrinal differences but because Catholics formed a much more tightly integrated religious community.[71] Religion, like family life, promotes self-sacrifice for a broader social purpose and nurtures a sense of duty and caring for other members. Religion, like marriage and parenthood, can thus reduce suicide through subordination of the individual to a collective body.[72]

The content of religious faith, however, can also be very important with regard to suicide. A belief in an afterlife can effectively serve as a safeguard against suicide. Like the biblical Job, the believer may suffer hardships in this life, such as unemployment or poor health, yet persevere out of the belief that these afflictions are part of a divine plan and that eternal happiness awaits those who endure adversity. Moreover, as Christianity has often glorified poverty, religion can provide a certain moral status to rival mundane prestige: a person who lives in misery can take solace in being morally

---

[69]Thomas G. Masaryk, *Suicide and the Meaning of Civilization*, trans. William B. Weist and Robert G. Batson (Chicago: University of Chicago Press, 1970).

[70]Richard Quinney, "Suicide, Homicide, and Economic Development," *Social Forces* 43 (1965): 405.

[71]Durkheim, *Suicide*, 152–164. Cf. Steven Stack, "Suicide and Religion: A Comparative Analysis," *Sociological Focus* 14 (1981): 207–20.

[72]Steven Stack, "The Effect of Domestic/Religious Individualism on Suicide, 1954–1978," *Journal of Marriage and the Family* 47 (1985): 431–47.

rich.[73] Perhaps most important, as previously discussed, is the belief that suicides were condemned to eternal damnation—a belief that served as a most effective restraint on suicidal impulses.

While Genevans of the eighteenth century were generally not rejecting religion, their religious beliefs were changing in important ways. The issue of secularization is a complex one, especially when applying it to early modern society. Secularization may refer to institutional changes, whereby the church loses influence in government or sees its role declining in areas such as education or poor relief. Secularization can also be construed to mean the decline of religion in the area of thought, meaning that growing numbers of people reject various traditional religious tenets and embrace deism, agnosticism, or even atheism. Concomitantly, religious institutions and beliefs may see their roles declining in areas such as political thought, economic theory, diplomacy, and the natural sciences. Secularization may further refer to a decline not in belief but in practice, as witnessed by decreasing church attendance. Finally, secularization may refer to a certain "desacralization" of society, whereby people begin downplaying the importance of the supernatural in this world, seeking rather rational or scientific explanations in human affairs and natural phenomena.[74] As we shall see, while Geneva experienced to various degrees elements of all these forms of secularization, it is this last cultural change, the desacralization of mentality, that was most important in eighteenth-century Geneva.[75]

That European intellectuals became more secular in orientation in the 1700s is beyond question. Due to the advances of the Scientific Revolution, the traditional Christian worldview was threatened. Following the publica-

---

[73]Stack, "Effect of Domestic/Religious Individualism," 431–47.

[74]See Michael Heyd, *Between Orthodoxy and the Enlightenment: Jean-Robert Chouet and the Introduction of Cartesian Science in the Academy of Geneva* (The Hague: Martinus Nijhoff; Jerusalem: Magnes Press, 1982), 9–10.

[75]There were limits to secularization in Geneva. Even during the Revolutionary period, the preamble to the new constitution (1794) forbade Genevans to practice any religion other than Protestantism; see Lucien Fulpius, "Institutions politiques de Genève dès origines à la fin de l'ancienne république," *Actes de l'Institut National Genevois*, nouvelle série 3 (1965): 26–27. Unlike their French counterparts, Genevan revolutionaries were not anticlerical. Although the revolutionary movement was on the whole indifferent to religion, a number of pastors themselves came out in favor of democracy; see Eric Golay, "1792–1798: Révolution genevoise et Révolution française: Similitudes et contrastes," in *Regards sur la Révolution genevoise 1792–1798*, ed. Louis Binz and others (Geneva: Société d'histoire et d'archéologie de Genève, 1992): 34–35.

tion of Newton's *Principia* in 1687, European intellectuals increasingly viewed the universe in mechanistic and materialistic terms, and sought knowledge and truth not through revelation and tradition but through observation and experimentation. Even for those who continued to embrace Christianity, religion tended to become separated from the sciences, which were increasingly viewed as the source of real knowledge.[76]

One obvious change is that eighteenth-century intellectuals in effect killed Satan. While everyone believed in Satan in the Reformation era, the devil was on the defensive already in the late seventeenth century in certain educated circles. The violence associated with the witch-hunts, for example, caused many to reconsider the traditional belief in Satan.[77] Among the various tenets of Christianity, the belief in the devil (whose existence could not be verified through sense experience) and in eternal damnation was surely among the most difficult to reconcile with the new scientific mentality. In England latitudinarians stressed the harmony between Christianity and reason, views that were eloquently expressed in John Locke's *Reasonableness of Christianity* (1696). Drawing inspiration from nature and the Scientific Revolution, Locke and others viewed the harmony of the universe as ample proof of God's omnipotence and benevolence. Concerns about original sin, redemption, and the devil, were viewed as counterproductive theological baggage. In the later seventeenth century, intellectuals such as Locke, Newton, and Pierre Bayle rejected or at least questioned the existence of an eternal hell, though many recognized the social utility of this belief as a deterrent to sin and crime.[78]

Eighteenth-century thinkers were much more willing to challenge many Christian traditions. By the mid-1700s, deism held sway among many intellectual circles both in England and the continent. Some deists still called themselves Christians while others flatly rejected Christianity. In either case, however, deists believed that God showed himself through nature and that the best way to worship God was to lead good moral lives. Promoters of such

---

[76]It has been argued that Protestantism, especially Calvinism, was more receptive than Catholicism to the discoveries of the Scientific Revolution; see Reijer Hooykaas, *Religion and the Rise of Modern Science* (Edinburgh: Scottish Academic Press, 1973).

[77]Jeffrey Burton Russell, *Mephistopheles: The Devil in the Modern World* (Ithaca, N.Y.: Cornell University Press, 1986), 128, 149.

[78]Russell, *Mephistopheles*, 130; D. P. Walker, *The Decline of Hell: Seventeenth-Century Discussions of Eternal Torment* (Chicago: University of Chicago Press, 1964).

a natural religion tended to maintain only a few ethical ties to Christian tradition. Certainly there was no place for the devil in such a worldview.[79]

The philosophes, admirers of Locke's rationalism and Newton's universe, viewed the notion of the devil with such contempt that they had little to say about it, calling it a superstition that was too silly to bother ridiculing. Although Voltaire did once characterize the devil as "disgusting fantasy," the philosophes in general saw little need to attack the notion of Satan since few educated Christians defended the existence of the devil.[80] The *Encyclopédie's* entry for the "devil" was limited to one column, in which the author ironically noted that "Ethiopians, who are black, paint the devil white, in order to contradict Europeans, who represent him as black: the one view is as well founded as the other."[81] As for the problem of evil, Voltaire, among other philosophes, denied divine revelation but believed that nature prescribed and proscribed various forms of behavior; through reason, humans can identify the eternal laws of nature. But while Voltaire in effect deified nature, other eighteenth-century thinkers went well beyond that. Atheists among the philosophes included Denis Diderot (1713–84), Claude-Adrien Helvétius (1715–71), and Paul-Thierry, Baron d'Holbach (1723–89), who all believed that the universe is material and infinite and was formed purely by chance, leaving no role for God or the devil. The skeptical empiricism of David Hume provided a philosophical justification for atheism. Hume argued that the existence of evil, all too evident in this universe, militates against the existence of a benevolent and omnipotent God. Since nature is imperfect, one cannot argue from it to a perfect cause (God); by the same token, one cannot use God, the allegedly perfect cause, to explain the existence of this universe, which is blatantly imperfect. Thus, far from displaying the wonders of God the creator, nature shows rather that God does not exist. Hume's argument thus attacked not only Christianity but also deism. In providing one of the most potent philosophical attacks against Christianity, Hume did

---

[79]Russell, *Mephistopheles*, 128–31, 149.

[80]Jeffrey Burton Russell, *The Prince of Darkness: Radical Evil and the Power of Good in History* (Ithaca, N.Y.: Cornell University Press, 1988), 208. One exception from the early eighteenth century was the English theologian Isaac Watts (1674–1748), who insisted that the increasing number of suicides in Britain was the result of diabolical temptation; MacDonald and Murphy, *Sleepless Souls*, 311.

[81]Denis Diderot and Jean Le Rond d'Alembert, eds., *Encyclopédie, ou Dictionnaire raisonné des sciences, des arts et des métiers*, 28 vols. (Paris: Briasson, David, Le Breton, and Durand, 1751–72), s.v. "Diable" and "Démon"; see also Russell, *Mephistopheles*, 146.

not deign to attack the concept of the devil. In short, while many educated Europeans still accepted the traditional Christian belief in the devil in 1700, few did so by 1800.[82]

Conservatives of course rushed to the defense of various Christian traditions under attack by philosophes and deists. One reaction was fideism, which held that Christian truths cannot be proven rationally and must be accepted as mysteries of faith. Probably the most dynamic group of fideists in the eighteenth century were the Pietists, with their unfailing insistence upon the importance of Scripture. Fearing that rational philosophy would likely lead to atheism, Pietists emphasized the emotions, insisting that an inner rebirth was most essential for salvation. Downplaying the need for secular learning, this evangelical movement was little affected by the intellectual changes associated with the Enlightenment. Among all eighteenth-century religious movements, Pietism was among the few that strongly embraced the traditional belief in the devil; though its stronghold was in Lutheran Germany, Pietism nonetheless enjoyed a certain following in Geneva in the first half of the eighteenth century.[83] In England, the Methodists still laid considerable emphasis on the devil and damnation, as evidenced by numerous accounts of diabolical temptation in John Wesley's *Arminian Magazine*. Methodists in fact still affirmed that Satan was responsible for suicide.[84] Conservatives, however, did not speak with one voice. In late-eighteenth-century France, Abbé Bergier, a fierce critic of the philosophes, made no mention of the devil or hell even while condemning suicide as a sin.[85]

By contrast, various liberal Christian thinkers tried to accommodate their faith with the rational, scientific atmosphere of the eighteenth century, rejecting certain beliefs that they deemed were not in accord with reason. Viewing the Bible as a historical document, some were embarrassed by the fact that Jesus believed in the devil. Liberal theologians by the end of the

---

[82]By the end of the eighteenth century, the devil began to reappear in literature, having been largely absent since the witchcraft craze. Often, however, the devil in literature bore little resemblance to the traditional Christian image of the personification of evil. The most important diabolical character of the early nineteenth century was Mephistopheles in Goethe's *Faust*. But while Goethe willingly borrowed ideas about the Christian devil, that character was much more complex. Moreover, Goethe himself vehemently denied the actual existence of Christianity's Satan; see Russell, *Mephistopheles*, 136–45, 157–67.

[83]Anne-Marie Piuz, "Genève des Lumières," in *Histoire de Genève*, ed. Paul Guichonnet (Toulouse: Edouard Privat, 1974), 245; Russell, *Mephistopheles*, 131–32.

[84]MacDonald, "Medicalization of Suicide," 95; Minois, *Histoire du suicide*, 255.

[85]Minois, *Histoire du suicide*, 251–52.

eighteenth century defended their faith with historical arguments, declaring that Jesus himself was a product of his time, a simple man who reflected the superstitions of his day. Many also abandoned the notion of original sin, preferring to remain silent on the issue of the problem of evil.[86]

The rationalism of Descartes, Locke, and Bacon obviously influenced theologians in Geneva in the early eighteenth century. The Academy, the precursor to the University of Geneva, and the Company of Pastors, had been bastions of Calvinist orthodoxy throughout most of the seventeenth century. From the late seventeenth into the early eighteenth centuries, however, these institutions changed in important ways under the influence of the rationalism associated with the Scientific Revolution. Throughout the seventeenth century, the Company of Pastors remained very much tied to Calvinist traditions, resisting all attempts to push the church in a more liberal direction. In order to reinforce Calvinism, the Company of Pastors embraced the Helvetic Consensus Formula, which reaffirmed the doctrines outlined in the canons of the Synod of Dort (1618–19). Approved in 1675 by the Swiss Confederation, this Formula was accepted in Geneva four years later. This was due in large part to the efforts of François Turrettini (d. 1687), professor of theology at the Academy and one of the principal architects of the Formula, who sought strict adherence to Calvinist orthodoxy. Thereafter, all Genevan pastors were required to take an oath to subscribe to the Helvetic Consensus Formula, leaving very little room for deviation.[87]

For its part, Geneva's Academy was also strongly attached to Calvinist orthodoxy throughout most of the seventeenth century. Founded by Calvin in 1559, the Academy was divided into two sections: the *Collège*, consisting of seven grades that offered secondary education for local Genevans, and the Academy proper, which offered higher learning in theology. Since its inception until the late seventeenth century, the Academy's raison d'être was to train pastors, and most of the theology students were foreign, a large proportion of whom came from France. In the mid-seventeenth century, for example, foreigners made up almost three-fourths of the Academy's student body,

[86]Russell, *Mephistopheles*, 152–53.
[87]Martin I. Klauber, *Between Reformed Scholasticism and Pan-Protestantism: Jean-Alphonse Turretin (1671–1737) and Enlightened Orthodoxy at the Academy of Geneva* (Selinsgrove, Penn.: Susquehanna University Press, 1994), 25–29; Anne-Marie Piuz, "De la Réforme aux Lumières (XVIIe–XVIIIe siècles)," in *Histoire de Genève*, ed. Guichonnet, 218–19.

and about 70 percent went on to become pastors. Through the mid-seventeenth century, philosophy was viewed as merely the handmaiden to theology; ever since the late sixteenth century, the Academy embraced a form of Reformed scholasticism, viewing Aristotelianism as the philosophy that was the least dangerous for theology. Since the Academy's ultimate mission was to train Calvinist ministers, Geneva's Company of Pastors had the right to elect the Rector (the superintendent of the Academy and the *Collège*), the professors, and the Principal and teachers of the *Collège*.[88]

Jean-Robert Chouet (1641–1731) was a principal player in the changes that occurred in the Academy beginning in the last decades of the seventeenth century. In 1669 Chouet was named professor of philosophy at the Academy. Although a devout Reformed Christian, Chouet's intellectual pursuits were entirely secular and included a strong interest in the physical sciences. As a professor, his most important contribution was the introduction of Cartesian natural philosophy into his courses. By the 1670s and 1680s, thanks to the popular teaching of Chouet, many foreign students came to Geneva to study philosophy for its own sake, having no intention of studying theology or pursuing a career in the ministry. The introduction of Cartesian natural philosophy thus contributed to a more secular atmosphere in terms of the subjects taught and the makeup of the student body.[89]

Chouet's impact on the Academy was more significant after he stepped down as professor in 1686 to become a town magistrate, serving as a member of the Small Council and six times as Syndic. Following the Revocation of the Edict of Nantes in 1685, the Academy experienced a significant drop in enrollment, which was exacerbated by the economic crisis in the 1690s. To deal with the problem of declining enrollment, members of the Council of Two Hundred called for further changes in the curriculum, involving more emphasis on the sciences and mathematics. The Council of Two Hundred represented the interests of merchants, lawyers, and other professionals who wanted to secularize the Academy entirely, cutting its ties to the Company of Pastors. Ultimately, although the Company of Pastors retained the right to approve appointments, an assembly of professors and

---

[88]Heyd, *Between Orthodoxy and Enlightenment*, 14–15, 147–51. All these appointments were subject, however, to confirmation by the Small Council. See also Louis Binz, "Coup d'oeil sur l'histoire du Collège," in *Le Collège de Genève 1559–1959* (Geneva: Jullien, 1959), 13–33.

[89]Heyd, *Between Orthodoxy and Enlightenment*, 146–64.

selected members of the Small Council began determining policy for the Academy in the early eighteenth century. Thus the Academy experienced a degree of institutional secularization as lay authorities enjoyed an increasing role in its governance.[90]

More important, the curriculum became still more secularly oriented in the early 1700s. Ironically, along with Chouet, one of the principal movers and shakers behind these changes was Jean-Alphonse Turrettini (1637–1737), the son of François. The younger Turrettini served as Rector (1701–11) and professor of theology at the Academy and was the most influential theologian of his generation. Together, J.-A. Turrettini and Chouet stressed the importance of the natural sciences and mathematics, promoting the scientific method based on induction and experimentation. With the support of the Company of Pastors in 1703, the Small Council agreed to the creation of a chair of mathematics at the Academy. In a speech to the Small Council in favor of the establishment of this chair, Turrettini called for more empirical, scientific studies. He downplayed the "scholastic" method, with its emphasis on logic and syllogistic reasoning, which had long been the mainstay at the Academy:

> A last area of progress would be the abandoning or at least the reduction of the strict requirements of the scholastic heritage. We should pay more attention to natural history. We should conduct more experiments and learn more about the vault of heaven, the kingdom of the animals, the properties of minerals and plants. The entire laboratory of nature would be opened to our investigations.... And because all these things are beginning to be better and more exactly known today, I think, without better advice, that they should be taught more fully in our schools.[91]

In the 1720s, the Academy's law faculty was reorganized with the introduction into the curriculum of Natural Law, which was taught by the eminent jurist Jean-Jacques Burlamaqui (1694–1748). Like earlier jurists, such as Hugo Grotius of Holland (1582–1645) and Samuel Pufendorf (1632–94) of Germany, Burlamaqui insisted that reason, not revelation, was the ulti-

---

[90]Heyd, *Between Orthodoxy and Enlightenment*, 51–52, 174–202.
[91]Jean-Alphonse Turrettini, "De studiis emendandis et promovendis," quoted in Klauber, *Reformed Scholasticism*, 145.

mate ground on which laws were to be based. In his *Principes du droit naturel* (1747), Burlamaqui described Natural Law as "the rules that reason prescribes for men in order to lead them… to true and secure happiness."[92] These curricular alterations were accompanied by important changes in the Academy's student body. By the 1720s, Genevans comprised about half the students at the Academy, and only 40 percent of the Academy's students eventually became pastors. As the sons of merchants increasingly filled the Academy's lecture halls, more and more alumni went into business, law, the military, and the sciences rather than the ministry. The Academy had thus been transformed from an international seminary into an institution of higher learning to train Geneva's political, economic, military, as well as ecclesiastical elite.[93]

As a theologian and pastor, J.-A. Turrettini promoted a form of "enlightened orthodoxy" or "natural theology" in which reason was made the principal arbiter in theological matters. Concerned about the growth in deism and atheism, Turrettini believed that the orthodoxy of his father was out of touch with current intellectual developments. Desiring to find harmony between the "new philosophy" and the Christian faith, Turrettini affirmed a strong belief in Natural Law, which he believed supported rather than undercut Christian doctrine. He insisted, for example, that the Copernican universe, governed by mechanistic laws, reflected divine providence.[94] While acknowledging the Bible as the sole source of religious truth, he did not insist that Scripture is inerrant. He believed rather that the general doctrines outlined in Scripture were true but that many details, particularly in the Old Testament, might be erroneous. Accordingly, he favored the reduction of the fundamentals of religion to a very few doctrines he deemed necessary for salvation. Moreover, while he affirmed a strong belief in the Incarnation and the Trinity—which he considered mysteries that could not be proven by rational argument—he deemed it counterproductive to argue about the physical presence of Christ in the Eucharist or the doctrine of predestina-

---

[92]Quoted by Jean de Senarclens, "Les écrivains politiques," in *Encyclopédie de Genève,* ed. Bernard Lescaze and Françoise Hirsch, vol. 4, *Les institutions politiques, judiciaires et militaires* (Geneva: Association de l'Encyclopédie de Genève, 1985), 190. See also Bernard Gagnebin, *Burlamaqui et le droit naturel* (Geneva: Editions de la Frégate, 1944); André-Luc Poncet, "La renaissance des études juridiques au début du XVIII siècle et l'introduction du droit naturel à l'Académie," *Revue de Vieux Genève* 8 (1978): 77–84.

[93]Heyd, *Between Orthodoxy and Enlightenment,* 230–35.

[94]Heyd, *Between Orthodoxy and Enlightenment,* 200–201.

tion, preferring to emphasize morality over theology.[95]

J.-A. Turrettini understandably blamed creeds, such as the Helvetic Consensus Formula, for the disunity among Christians, and campaigned just as aggressively to abrogate the Formula as his father had crusaded to adopt it. His vision was aptly summed up in words delivered in a speech to the Academy on 1 January 1700: "The century of the Reformation caused division and schism; the century that we have just finished consecrated these divisions by the formulas of discord; now that we have woken up to a new century, we ought to start it by covering the errors of our fathers with a coat of love, and in seeking to unite all churches in the same spirit by the bonds of peace."[96] A majority of the Company of Pastors agreed with Turrettini to stop requiring pastors to sign the Formula, a decision that was ratified by the Council of Two Hundred in 1706. In 1725 the Company went even further and agreed to do away with the Formula altogether. Thereafter, pastors upon ordination were simply instructed to keep the doctrines of the prophets and the apostles, as found in the Old and New Testaments and as summarized in the catechism. The Genevan church had in effect become "confessionless." Ultimately, Turrettini hoped to convince deists and atheists, through the common ground of reason, that the Christian faith was indeed reasonable.[97] In short, by the early eighteenth century, the intellectual atmosphere in Geneva had changed dramatically within the span of a generation or two. The Company of Pastors became much more tolerant, and the Academy became much more secular.[98]

---

[95]Heyd, *Between Orthodoxy and Enlightenment*, 240.

[96]Quoted in Klauber, *Reformed Scholasticism*, 144.

[97]Klauber, *Reformed Scholasticism*, 143–48.

[98]It should be noted that in the early eighteenth century, one could still get in trouble in Geneva for denying the divinity of Jesus. In 1707 the Consistory referred the Citizen André-Robert Vaudenet to the Small Council because he had doubts about certain tenets of Christianity. Vaudenet admitted these doubts and was unwilling to affirm anything beyond his belief in one God who created and governed the world. The Council revoked his citizenship and banished him from the city. Vaudenet then went to Savoy where Catholic authorities also questioned him about his faith. There Vaudenet explicitly rejected the existence of hell and proclaimed that the only revelation he accepted was that which "natural reason dictated." Vaudenet claimed, however, that he was banished from Geneva not for his religious beliefs but because of his criticism of political authorities; see Henri Fazy, "Procès et condamnation d'un Déiste genevois en 1707," *Mémoires de l'Institut National Genevois* 13 (1877): 3–11. The *Procès Criminels* do suggest that Vaudenet had a combative personality and clashed with Genevan leaders. In 1706 Vaudenet was imprisoned and censured for having slandered the former Syndic Gautier, accusing him of misdeeds and telling him he ought to be hanged; AEG, PC 5725. Vaudenet was allowed to return to Geneva and reclaim his citizenship, but he continued to have run-ins with the powers that be. In 1712 the Small

This rejection of a precise confession of faith in and of itself contributed to the loosening of communal ties in Geneva. In discussing the role of religion in fostering an integrated society, Durkheim wrote:

> A religious society cannot exist without a collective *credo,* and the more extensive the *credo* the more unified and strong is the society. For it does not unite men by an exchange and reciprocity of services, a temporal bond of union which permits and even presupposes differences, but which a religious society cannot form. It socializes men only by attaching them completely to an identical body of doctrine and socializes them in proportion as this body of doctrine is extensive and firm.... Inversely, the greater concessions a confessional group makes to individual judgment, the less it dominates lives, the less its cohesion and vitality.[99]

If Durkheim is correct in this regard, then J.-A. Turrettini and other religious leaders, by extending the parameters for religious beliefs and expression, were unintentionally weakening religious society itself in Geneva. And as Genevans were less integrated religiously, they became more susceptible to suicide than before.

The influence of rationalism and the process of secularization accelerated in the second half of the eighteenth century, when Genevans killed themselves in unprecedented numbers. Geneva was of course the birthplace of Jean-Jacques Rousseau, and Voltaire resided near Geneva for decades. In the late 1700s, Geneva was known more as a center of Enlightened than of Reformed thought. Though late-eighteenth-century Geneva was still very much a Reformed republic, Calvinism's influence continued to weaken in shaping the mentality of all classes, including religious and intellectual leaders of the city. During this "Age of Reason," Genevan intellectuals, including prominent theologians and pastors, were more influenced by Enlightened than Calvinist thought. Turrettini's successor as professor of theology at the

---

Council required him to apologize to the former Syndic J. P. Trembley for calling him a thief; PC 6149. In light of his personal conflicts, perhaps his deistic beliefs were not primarily responsible for his banishment.

[99]Durkheim, *Suicide,* 159.

Genevan Academy was his former student, Jacob Vernet (1698–1789), who gave even freer rein to reason in the formation of his religious views, insisting that revelation never contradicts natural reason. Embracing a form of natural theology, Vernet argued, for example, that God might save the "heathen of Africa" who had never been exposed to Christian revelation, if they responded favorably to the revelation that God provided through nature and conscience.[100] Vernet had a strong interest in Natural Law, as evidenced by his editing Burlamaqui's *Principes du droit politique*, published in 1751, three years after Burlamaqui's death. For Vernet, an "Enlightened" theologian, God was entirely transcendent, and postbiblical miracles violated the order of the universe. Having spent time in Paris, Vernet was on familiar, if not always friendly, terms with Voltaire, Rousseau, and Montesquieu. Vernet and other Genevan pastors had a bitter disagreement with Voltaire and other philosophes following the publication in 1757 of d'Alembert's article, "Genève," in the seventh volume of the *Encyclopédie*. In an effort to compliment Geneva's pastors and, no doubt, to encourage the French clergy to emulate them, d'Alembert portrayed Genevan pastors as freethinkers, declaring that many of them were Socinians, or deists who did not believe in the divinity of Jesus Christ. These same pastors, d'Alembert averred, did not believe in hell in the traditional sense, viewing eternal damnation as incompatible with an all-loving God. Rather, they believed that punishments in the afterlife for misdeeds in this world were temporary rather than eternal, which, d'Alembert rightly pointed out, resembled the Catholic conception of purgatory. Though Vernet and other pastors vehemently denied this description and reasserted their own orthodoxy, there was plenty of justification for d'Alembert's appraisal of Genevan ministers. Vernet himself had indeed been rather evasive on the divinity of Jesus and did suggest that an eternal hell was irreconcilable with the benevolence of God. Moreover, as d'Alembert aptly observed in the midst of this controversy, if the Genevan clergy really wanted to prove their orthodoxy, all they had to do was sign a confession of faith declaring they believed that infernal punishments were eternal and that Jesus Christ was divine and entirely equal to God the Father.

[100]Martin I. Klauber, "The Eclipse of Reformed Scholasticism in Eighteenth-Century Geneva: Natural Theology from Jean-Alphonse Turretin to Jacob Vernet," in *The Identity of Geneva: The Christian Commonwealth, 1564–1864*, ed. John B. Roney and Martin I. Klauber (Westport, Conn.: Greenwood, 1998), 134.

At no time, however, did the pastors issue such a statement.[101]

Though he complained about the unbelief of his contemporaries (for which he held the philosophes partly responsible), Vernet, by equivocating on the divinity of Jesus and rejecting postbiblical miracles, continued the unintentional movement toward deism that had begun in Geneva with J.-A. Turrettini. Another pastor, Jacob Vernes (1728–91), who has often been confused with Vernet, also had close contacts with several philosophes and edited the journal *Choix littéraire*, which catered to those with Enlightened, though Christian, tastes.[102] The pastor Paul Moultou also demonstrated how little importance he and others gave to theological conformity; in a letter in 1761, Moultou reassured Rousseau, whom he greatly admired, that he had little concern for the church's teachings, so long as it respected those beliefs that were essential for maintaining moral order.[103] By the late eighteenth century, theologians at the Genevan Academy went so far as to deny the Trinity and Incarnation, views that would have landed them at the stake in Calvin's time. In short, views associated with modern liberal Protestantism were flourishing among pastors and theologians in eighteenth-century Geneva.[104]

All told, the views espoused by Turrettini, Vernet, and other Genevan pastors were in vivid contrast to those of Calvin and Beza; these new ideas reflected the growing secularization of mentality in the eighteenth century. While many of the most influential thinkers of the sixteenth century were theologians, theology was pushed to the fringe of European thought in the 1700s. Whereas Geneva had been the city of Calvin in the Reformation era, it was the city of Rousseau and Voltaire in the Enlightenment. Themselves imbued with the rationalism of the era, many religious leaders willingly rejected certain Christian traditions that conflicted with reason. Most important with regard to suicide was rationalism's relationship with the

---

[101]Diderot and d'Alembert, *Encyclopédie*, s.v. "Genève," by d'Alembert; see also Graham Gargett, *Jacob Vernet, Geneva, and the Philosophes* (Oxford: Voltaire Foundation, 1994), 144–51.

[102]Published in Geneva during the years 1755–60, *Choix littéraire* published the works of both Protestant and Catholic authors, rejecting the atheism associated with some philosophes; see Michel Porret, "Mourir l'âme angoissée: Les 'réflexions sur le suicide' de l'horloger genevois J.-J. Mellaret (1769)," *Revue d'histoire moderne et contemporaine* 42 (1995): 81, n. 46.

[103]Linda Kirk, "'Going Soft,'" in *Identity of Geneva*, ed. Roney and Klauber, 149.

[104]Gargett, *Jacob Vernet*, 144–51; Klauber, *Reformed Scholasticism*; idem, "Eclipse of Reformed Scholasticism," in *Identity of Geneva*, ed. Roney and Klauber, 129–42.

devil. While Calvin viewed the devil as responsible for suicide, Turrettini, Vernet, and others tacitly rejected the very existence of Satan. Indeed, while Calvin delivered few sermons without referring to Satan, the devil in effect disappeared from the sermons of eighteenth-century Genevan pastors. [105] Also absent in their theology is the fear of God (so prevalent in Calvinist thought) as Vernet and other pastors stressed the benevolent as opposed to the judgmental side of God. As Vernet and others questioned the traditional belief in an eternal hell, the fear of damnation obviously declined. Quite simply, Geneva's eighteenth-century church leaders promoted religious values that seemed better suited than Calvin's for the more secular world in which they lived. The question remains, however, to what degree the rank and file reflected these new religious trends.

Michel Vovelle has found a decisive change in mentality, what he refers to as de-Christianization, among Catholics in Provence in the second half of the eighteenth century. Studying wills and testaments written over the course of the eighteenth century, Vovelle found a dramatic decrease in the number of wills that bequeathed sums to religious institutions, called for elaborate funerary processions, and, most important, requested masses for the testator after his or her death. According to Vovelle, this trend was apparent among all social strata. In the mid-eighteenth century the overwhelming majority of wills for merchants and other middle-class professionals showed a strong interest in "baroque Catholicism." That proportion, however, had decreased by half in the 1780s, and testaments for artisans and small shopkeepers revealed similar contemporaneous declines. During the same period, wills and testaments suggest that the wage laborers of Marseilles became almost entirely secularized. Vovelle's evidence further indicates that women remained more tied to religious traditions than men. He questions, however, if this decline in the importance that people gave to religion can be attributed directly to the influence of the philosophes. He sees similar patterns in both rural and urban areas and notes that there was no direct correlation between increases in literacy and decreases in requests for masses for the

---

[105]Geneva's *Liturgy* of 1543 warned of the great risk that the devil might seize the souls of sick people during their last miserable hours. By contrast, official prayers of the eighteenth century besought God to heal the afflicted, if that be his [God's] will, or to accept his or her soul into eternal paradise. No mention at all is made of the devil; see Kirk, "'Going Soft,'" in *Identity of Geneva*, ed. Roney and Klauber, 148.

dead. In short, Vovelle finds a dramatic decline in religiosity and a much more secular mentality in Provence in the late eighteenth century.[106]

On the basis of Parisian wills, Pierre Chaunu has reached very similar conclusions, finding that the "Christian discourse" virtually disappeared from testaments about 1770. Religious invocations, present in nearly all testaments of the late seventeenth century, were largely absent in the late 1700s as were requests for prayers for the dead. Donations to religious institutions, almost *de rigueur* a century earlier, were present in only a minority of wills and had less and less financial value.[107]

Is there evidence for a similar decline in religiosity in Geneva? Barbara Roth-Lochner has studied holograph testaments written by Genevan women, virtually all of whom were upper class, from the first decade of the eighteenth century and from the 1780s. She has found that women who wrote their wills at the end of the century dedicated less space to religion than had their predecessors. Even in the 1780s, however, the expression of religious convictions was invariably present and did not appear to be formulaic. Since Protestants of course never made arrangements for prayers to be said after their deaths, the differences in the religious tenor of the testaments from the beginning and end of the eighteenth century were less obvious than those for Catholics. The emphasis, however, seems to have evolved somewhat. In the earlier group of testaments, the large majority of authors asked for forgiveness for their sins, many of them specifically begging for God's mercy. By the 1780s, only a third of the authors expressed such sentiments. By contrast, testaments from the latter period demonstrated unprecedented prayers for survivors.[108]

Moreover, in the second half of the eighteenth century, Reformed

---

[106]Michel Vovelle, *Piété baroque et déchristianisation en Provence au XVIIIe siècle: Les attitudes devant la mort d'après les clauses de testaments* (Paris: Plon, 1973).

[107]Pierre Chaunu, *La mort à Paris: XVIe, XVIIe et XVIIIe siècles* (Paris: Fayard, 1978). François Lebrun, *Les hommes et la mort en Anjou aux 17e et 18e siècles* (Paris: Mouton, 1971), 452–53, finds that the discourse of testaments in Anjou also became almost entirely secular in the late eighteenth century. He too found a decisive reduction in the number of religious donations and requests for masses for the dead in wills, noting a significant decline in the importance of religious sentiment.

[108]Barbara Roth-Lochner, "'Il m'est doux de penser que je vivrai toujours dans leur coeur': Quelques testaments olographes féminins à Genève au XVIIIe siècle," in *Des archives à la mémoire: Mélanges d'histoire politique, religieuse et sociale offerts à Louis Binz*, ed. Barbara Roth-Lochner, Marc Neuenschwander, and Françoise Walter (Geneva: Société d'histoire et d'archéologie de Genève, 1995), 267–72.

authors published works for the religious education of children which made no mention of the devil and emphasized God's love over his wrath.[109] An examination of Genevan sermons pertaining to childhood shows important changes in attitudes beginning about 1750. Pastors traditionally insisted that children were naturally prone to sin and that parents therefore must be strict disciplinarians, leading their young down the straight and narrow path. After 1750 Genevan pastors preached rather against the excesses of corporal punishment, and Vernet and other pastors insisted that humans are born with a natural inclination to do good, an emphatic rejection of the Calvinist view that children are hopelessly tainted by sin.[110] These findings indicate that Genevans of the late eighteenth century had considerably less fear of God and damnation than those living at the beginning of the century. As Chaunu observes, the judgmental side of Christianity, central to Tridentine Catholicism, was no longer intimidating by the late eighteenth century. By the late 1700s, Christian pedagogy "had so exorcized the fear of death" and the belief in divine judgment that one was left with nothing but "a pale survival of the soul" as reflected in the religiously empty discourse of testaments.[111]

---

[109]In the 1770s the Zuricher Johann Rudolf Schellenberg published two volumes of illustrated Bible stories intended for young children, which were immediately translated into French. These volumes showed a change in focus from earlier pedagogical religious works. There was still an element of the fear of God (most notable were examples from the Old Testament of the punishment of those who abandoned God), but more evident was God's love, aptly portrayed in a picture of Jesus blessing children. Significantly, neither volume contained any image of or reference to the devil, a reflection of the influence of rationalism. Moreover, in this work, Schellenberg exhibited a new sensitivity toward children, in whom he sought to nurture a Christian conscience. In his selection and treatment of biblical stories, Schellenberg avoided depicting scenes from the Bible of bad parenting or violence, evidently deeming such images as inappropriate for young eyes. One most interesting exception was the illustration of the suicide of Saul, who was shown falling on his sword. Even though the Bible does not condemn this suicide, Schellenberg described this suicide as the result of Saul's abandoning God. One cannot help but wonder if Schellenberg chose to depict this act of self-destruction out of hopes of deterring suicides, which were occurring at unprecedented rates at this time; see Max Engammare, "De la peur à la crainte: Un jeu subtil dans le premier recueil d'images bibliques composé à l'usage de jeunes enfants (1774–1779)," in *La peur au XVIIIe siècle: Discours, représentations, pratiques*, ed. Jacques Berchtold and Michel Porret (Geneva: Droz, 1994), 19–43.

[110]Philippe Rieder, "Discipline ecclésiastique et relations familiales à Genève au XVIIIe siècle," *Equinoxe: Revue Romande de Sciences Humaines* 11 (1994): 93–110.

[111]According to Chaunu, *Mort à Paris*, 455–56, many among the educated leisure class identified with Diderot's character, Jacques le Fataliste, who neither believed, nor disbelieved, nor even thought about the existence of an afterlife. Lebrun, *Hommes et mort*, 436–50, however, finds that even as late as 1748, catechisms in Anjou placed considerable importance on the fear of damnation. Interestingly, catechisms produced in the Protestant center of Saumur placed more emphasis on the hopes and rewards of those who would be saved than on the fear of hell. Patricia Jalland, *Death in the Victorian Family* (Oxford:

For a variety of reasons, Genevans' mentality of the late 1700s was surely even more desacralized than that of their French contemporaries. To begin with, the Genevan population was quite literate and therefore less apt to be attracted to religious beliefs that were increasingly viewed as superstitions among educated circles. From its inception, Protestantism stressed much more than Catholicism God's transcendence, a tendency that was further accentuated by the end of the early modern period. The natural theology of Vernet and others was an almost predictable outgrowth of a faith that allegedly championed not only Scripture over tradition but also reason over superstition. For centuries Reformed Protestants had ridiculed the concept of transubstantiation and tales of "bowing, speaking, or bleeding statues." Jean-Alphonse Turrettini declared that one of the most reprehensible characteristics of Roman Catholicism is that it required its followers to reject "the clear light of common sense."[112] Protestants did not witness apparitions of the Virgin Mary, nor did God work miracles through Protestant saints. Christ was not physically present in the Reformed Eucharist, nor did Protestants make the sign of the cross when they passed in front of the altar. While post-Tridentine Catholic leaders had tried to eliminate some of the excesses associated with the veneration of saints, they still insisted that one could pray to saints and especially to the Virgin Mary as a mediator to God. In the eighteenth century and beyond, peasants in France and elsewhere shared a strong belief in "healing saints," each of whom had the power to cure certain illnesses. In Anjou, for example, Saint Sebastian was believed to have a miraculous cure for the plague and other epidemics. While Protestants believed that God was not swayed by pilgrimages or fasts, Catholics in France regularly went to fountains and sanctuaries where saints were said to provide these miraculous cures.[113] Quite simply, while the French undoubtedly experi-

---

Oxford University Press, 1996), 59–61, 70–71, sees a decline in the fear of hell in nineteenth-century England and notes its impact on changing attitudes toward suicide.

[112]Kirk, "'Going Soft,'" in *Identity of Geneva*, ed. Roney and Klauber, 148.

[113]Lebrun, *Hommes et mort*, 395–415, further adds that in the eighteenth century there was still plenty of confusion between magic and religion in rural Anjou as people consulted diviners and conjurers who might cast out evil spirits by saying incantations and making the sign of the cross. Though ecclesiastical authorities condemned in 1710 the consulting of diviners, astrologers, and magicians, such practices persisted.

enced a noticeable desacralization of mentality, the persistence of these prac- tices, which had been forbidden to Genevans ever since the time of Calvin, all testified to God's continued active presence in this world. Even if God seemed less judgmental to Catholics of the late eighteenth century than ever before, these acts of popular piety ought to have served as a greater deterrent to suicide than did the Reformed faith. By the late 1700s the religious world of the liberal Protestants of Geneva had been stripped of almost all mysteries.

A desacralized mentality is evident in Genevans' increasingly skeptical attitudes toward magic and the occult, as seen in court records. In 1716, Louise Chartier, the wife of the printer Jacques Odel, was investigated for selling books on magic. Interestingly, none of the people who bought these works from her were Genevans; her clientele for magic books consisted entirely of Savoyards. The Auditeur in charge of the investigation confiscated two copies of a book which described the nature of the devil and how he wished to be served. Having perused the pamphlet, the Auditeur believed that this work posed no danger of corrupting the hearts and souls of anyone but the feebleminded; nevertheless, he did believe that the availability of such a work could place Geneva in a bad light. Accordingly, the Small Coun- cil demonstrated restraint in handling this case, censuring Chartier and for- bidding her to sell any literature other than books of piety.[114]

Similar skepticism can be seen in the case against the printer Moise Morié, an Habitant originally from Château d'Oex, accused in 1767 of sell- ing a book of magic to a gullible, illiterate Savoyard. Pierre Briffon reported having been robbed in Sardinia of 1,000 écus four years earlier. Though Brif- fon was unable to read or write, Morié claimed to have a book that would enable him to find the money. Briffon purchased the book as well as a plant's root and some pieces of paper that supposedly possessed magical qualities. Morié explained that Briffon had to return to Sardinia and burn the root and paper along with some vine branches, which he and three other men were to beat with four hazel sticks. The next day he would find the stolen money at his door, which the robbers had returned. On one of these pieces of paper was a request written to Beelzebub, written in black ink and spelled horren- dously, to send a spirit to assist in finding the money. Beelzebub responded

---

[114]AEG, PC 6456; RC 215: 249, 282. This and the following two cases concerning magic came to my attention through Waldemar Deonna, "Superstitions à Genève aux XVIIe et XVIIIe siècles," *Archives suisses des traditions populaires* 43 (1946): 343–90.

in red ink, demonstrating a similar ineptitude in spelling, proclaiming that the bearer of this note would receive the money provided he served the devil.[115] When Briffon spoke to some friends about this deal, they were immediately convinced that he had been duped, even though they, like Briffon, were illiterate. The Small Council convicted Morié of swindling and claiming to have magical and divining powers in order to take advantage of "the credulity of a foreigner."[116]

Morié, however, did not cease to try to sell books of magic to credulous foreigners. In 1773 he again stood trial, this time for having sold to Vincent Carret, a humble Savoyard who eked out a living selling marcasite. When Morié offered to sell him a book that would enable him to make his fortune, Carret jumped at the chance, even heeding Morié's warning that he must not open the book until he reached his abode. After parting with Morié, Carret encountered his friend Gaspard Roget, another Savoyard who worked at the inn where Carret was staying in Carouge. When Carret described what had just happened, Roget exclaimed, "You silly devil, you have been tricked!" When they reached the inn, Roget opened the book in the dining room and began reading aloud in the presence of several people. The book in question—which may have been the same one Morié peddled six years earlier—purportedly contained all the secrets of King Solomon. The knowledge of these secrets supposedly enabled Christians to force rebellious spirits, such as Lucifer, to assist in finding treasures, winning the affection of women, uncovering all secrets, and so on.[117] After Roget had read just one page, everyone present roared with laughter and made fun of Carret for having

---

[115]The invocation to Beelzebub read: "Par la permission du grand metre et prinse de Bellezebu ge te prie de manvoieyer un des tes espris"; Beelzebub responded, "Je t'a corde tout se que tu mes desmande pour vu que tu tangage tu ara des covet des lagante." The root was wrapped in a printed cartoon that depicted "le diable d'argent," showing the devil covered and filled with gold coins who was surrounded by people of different walks of life who got money from him; AEG, PC 11664.

[116]AEG, RC 268: 414. Morié was sentenced to be censured severely, to ask on bended knee for forgiveness from God and the state, to return the money he had received from Briffon, to spend fifteen days in jail (in addition to those already spent) on bread and water, and to pay for court costs.

[117]The book was entitled, *Le Grand Grimoire avec la Grande Clavicule et la Magie Noire, où* [sic] *les forces infernales du grand Agrippa, pour découvrir tous les Trésors cachés, et se faire obéir toutes sortes d'Esprits;* AEG, PC 12420. The title page includes no publisher or place of publication but lists its date of publication as 1583, though as Deonna notes, this clearly was published in the eighteenth century. The "grand Agrippa" referred to in the title was the occult philosopher Agrippa de Nettesheim (1487–1535). He was author of magical works who came to Geneva in 1521 and was admitted to the Bourgeoisie the following year, though left the city shortly thereafter; see Deonna, "Superstitions à Genève," 383–85.

been so easily misled. Carret immediately recognized his mistake and returned to ask for his money back from Morié. Morié then said that if Carret was not satisfied with the book, perhaps he would be interested in a small tin box which, Morié swore, miraculously produced a coin (a *louis d'or neuf*) every day. Carret, however, would not be fooled again; he pressed charges when Morié still refused to return his money.[118]

In summing up his arguments in this later case, the prosecutor Galiffe was most distraught that there were still some people who were "so ignorant and superstitious" as to believe in magic. Even more, Galiffe was indignant that there were other people who nurtured such superstitions in order to take advantage of the naiveté of simple folk and deprive them of their goods. Noting that Morié had already been convicted of a similar crime and that he admitted to all the principal allegations, Galiffe insisted that these actions differed little from theft. He added, "Formerly, those who indulged in sorcery were punished very severely. But now that the reign of superstition has passed, we punish them only for the real wrong that they inflict on society and the harm that they cause individuals."[119] For having taken advantage of the credulity of a person and for being a recidivist, the Small Council condemned Morié to be censured, to ask forgiveness publicly on his knees for his wrongs, to return the money he received from the victim, and to spend five months in prison beyond the time he had already been incarcerated.[120]

Although the magistrates' skeptical attitude toward magic in these cases is predictable, more impressive is the fact that so many people of very humble backgrounds—some of whom were even illiterate—obviously disbelieved the efficacy of such practices. Interestingly, all the victims and their close associates in these cases were foreigners and, almost certainly, Catholics. By the 1770s the Citizens and Natifs of Geneva were for the most part literate and not likely to be duped by swindlers such as Morié. The religious ambience in Geneva of the late eighteenth century did not lend itself to superstitious beliefs of this nature. Although a few poor foreigners, probably of peasant origin, could still be tricked by the schemes of Morié, the incredulity of most of their friends and compatriots demonstrates the extent to

[118]AEG, PC 12420.
[119]AEG, PC 12420.
[120]AEG, RC 274: 221–22. The Council declined to impose a life banishment from the Republic, as recommended by Galiffe.

which the role of the supernatural had declined in their mentalities. By the late eighteenth century, cases of this nature were quite rare, as Morié and others like him were hard-pressed to find such ingenuous people.

If Catholics were more likely to see the supernatural playing an active role in their lives, they were also less likely to take their lives for the same reason. Some telling figures are available for Protestant and Catholic suicides in the canton of Geneva in the early nineteenth century. Concerned about the frequency of self-inflicted deaths, a Genevan judge, Guillaume Prevost, compiled statistics on suicide in 1835 for the previous ten years. He found that Catholics, who then made up 42.1 percent of the population of the canton, committed only 19.5 percent of the suicides, while Protestants comprised 57.9 percent of the population but 80.5 percent of the suicides. The figures Prevost cited corresponded to suicide rates of 11.7 per 100,000 for Catholics and 34.8 per 100,000 for Protestants.[121] Though only a third the rate of the Protestants, the suicide rate for Catholics living in the canton was nonetheless more than double the rate that the overwhelmingly Protestant Republic of Geneva had experienced in the first half of the eighteenth century. How do we explain, though, this dramatic difference in the rates with which Genevan Protestants and Catholics killed themselves in the early nineteenth century? To a degree, this may have been a difference between the propensity for suicide among urban and rural dwellers. Catholics were especially concentrated in the rural villages surrounding Geneva rather than in the city itself, and those involved in agriculture comprised a third of the canton's population but committed only 9 percent of the suicides.[122] While rural Catholics probably had a more tightly integrated community than did Protestants in the city, another key factor is that the supernatural remained much more evident in the faith and everyday lives of Catholic peasants who were, to be sure, less educated than Protestants in the neighboring city.

The Impact of Rationalism and Secularism on Suicides

Chaunu is rightly convinced that the change in mentality in eighteenth-century France allowed to resurface certain forms of behavior—most notably,

---

[121]Guillaume Prevost, "Extrait d'une note statistique sur le suicide," *Bibliothèque universelle* (June 1835): 1–20, recorded 133 suicides in the canton of Geneva for the period 1825–34, during which time the average population was 53,000.

[122]Prevost, "Note statistique sur le suicide," 5–7, 16.

suicide—that Christianity had largely succeeded in eliminating. In spite of the paucity of records for some periods and the unreliability of official statistics, Chaunu believes there is abundant evidence of an increase in self-inflicted deaths in the eighteenth century, contemporaneous to the waning of the Christian horror for suicide which had prevailed into the seventeenth century.[123] The question remains to what extent the amply documented increase in suicide in eighteenth-century Geneva was related to an increasingly secular mentality. As noted in chapter 3, the increase in suicide began modestly in the first half of the century, affecting above all affluent people. Since they were not killing themselves for financial reasons, we should examine whether these merchants were more secular in orientation than other segments of the population and, consequently, less impeded by Christian mores from committing suicide.

A postmortem inventory of the assets of Jacques Rigoumier, the previously described merchant who took his life in 1679, provides insight as to how he and future merchants differed from most Genevans. Rigoumier not only devoutly read the Bible every day but also had been exposed to some literature that was not religious in nature. Possessing thirteen published works, Rigoumier owned five religious books, including a Bible and two books of Psalms. In addition to these, he possessed three works by Descartes and Tacitus's *Annales*.[124] Although this library seems very modest, it would have surpassed those of almost all contemporaries. Merchants were among the most educated and wealthiest of Genevans; at this time, they were more likely than others to have both the inclination and the means to read something other than Scripture. The fact that the Bible shared shelf space with nonreligious publications in Rigoumier's library foreshadowed growing secular interests that probably appeared among merchants before other sectors of the population, such as artisans.

Perhaps the mentality of merchants of the next generation was less dominated by religion. At the time of Rigoumier's death, the devil, like witchcraft, though much less visible than in the Reformation era, had not been expunged from popular religious culture. As previously noted, Geneva's last witchcraft trial occurred in 1681, two years after Rigoumier's death. By

---

[123]Chaunu, *Mort à Paris*, 463–65.

[124]Works by Descartes included *Un discours de la méthode pour bien conduire sa raison*, *Les principes de la philosophie*, and *Les passions de l'âme*; AEG, Juridiction Civile F b 10.

1715—the date of the next suicide by a merchant—the cultural ambience had changed noticeably. By then witchcraft had been consigned to the dustbins of Genevan history, and just as Turrettini and other theologians ignored the devil, so did Geneva's rank and file. Apart from an isolated remark by a person described as demented, witnesses interrogated about the 342 recorded suicides for eighteenth-century Geneva made no references to the devil.[125] By the early eighteenth century, perhaps merchants were less diligent in their religious practices than Rigoumier had been. If we can ascertain a decline in the role of religion in shaping the *Weltanschauung* of merchants, then we may be on our way to explaining why merchants were the first to begin killing themselves in greater numbers after 1700. As educated people developed more cultural interests that were unrelated to religion, one would expect the degree of control religion had over behavior to decline. Merchants were not more likely to fall ill or to suffer from depression than artisans or unskilled laborers. But if religion played less of a role in shaping their mentality, then it was less likely to serve as a deterrent to suicide, as it had in the Reformation period.

The suicide of the Auditeur Antoine Mallet in December 1715, described at length in chapter 2, lends support to the theory that merchants had developed more secular interests. Well respected in Geneva, Mallet was quite wealthy; and through his service as Auditeur, he could foresee enjoying increased political responsibilities in the future, perhaps becoming a member of one of the small councils. All testimony reveals that he had a stable family life, enjoying a good rapport with his wife and young daughter. The only hint of a motive for the suicide was contained in an anonymous note which alleged that Mallet feared the calumnies of a French woman, who purportedly was going to denounce him to the duke of Orléans, the regent of France. The note does not specify the nature of the feared libel, but one cannot help but wonder whether an adulterous affair was at issue. Whether real or fabricated, the accusations supposedly would have seriously damaged

---

[125]The sole reference to the devil involved Suzanne Lesage, forty-eight, André Chatel's divorced wife, who jumped to her death from her fourth-floor window in February 1778. Described as having been alienated for a number of years, Lesage had recently been quite agitated, crying profusely and suffering from insomnia and occasional convulsions. According to her brother, on the day of her death Lesage had cried out, "I have Satan in my body!" The Small Council simply ordered that she be buried without prayers; AEG, EC, LM 65: 194, 3 February 1778; PC 13079; RC 279: 69.

his reputation. As noted above, just before he jumped in the Rhône, a woman saw Mallet standing on a bridge overlooking the river, his hat under his arm, and his hands folded in prayer.[126]

At first glance, this case may seem to show anything but a secular world-view. But saying a prayer at the hour of one's death is quite different from attending sermons a few times a week and leading family devotions in the home, as people in Reformation Geneva were expected to do. Even if Mallet attended church regularly and led prayers in his home (there is no evidence one way or the other on either of these practices) Mallet clearly had varied interests. The postmortem inventory reveals that Mallet had an impressive library which included over one hundred fifty titles. Only about 10 percent of these works were related to religion. These included a New Testament in German (the only edition of Scripture that he owned), one collection of ser-mons, and a few theological works such as the Genevan pastor Pictet's *Traité de la verité de la religion crestienne.* Also included were translations of the early medieval apocalyptical *Sibylline Oracles* and of *The Imitation of Christ,* the most important literary expression of the late medieval lay piety move-ment known as the *devotio moderna.* The presence of works such as these reflected Mallet's strong interest in history, further testified to by works on Church history, including histories of the Council of Trent and the papacy. More numerous were works on secular history, particularly on the recent past. Mallet owned a translation of Machiavelli's *History of Florence* and numerous biographies, including works on the lives of Richelieu, Cardinal Ximenes, Descartes, and William of Orange. Almost totally absent were clas-sics, although he did possess a translation of Suetonius's *The First Twelve Emperors* and a work on the history of ancient Greece. Although history was most prevalent, Mallet also had an interest in travel literature and possessed a few masterpieces of modern literature, including Boccaccio's *Decameron, Cyrano de Bergerac,* and works by Molière. He also obviously had an interest in law, as witnessed by his owning a copy of Justinian's *Institutes* and works on Natural Law by Grotius and Domat.[127]

The inventory of Mallet's books suggests that while religion was impor-

---

[126]AEG, PC 6430.

[127]AEG, Juridiction Civile F 478. Evidence on personal libraries from the early eighteenth century shows that lawyers had a strong interest in the sciences, the "new philosophy," and Natural Law. Theolog-ical works made up a small percentage of their libraries. Pierre Fatio, the leader of a rebellion in1707, pos

tant to him, it was not at the center of his life as it had been for Rigoumier. While Rigoumier dedicated a half hour every day to reading the Bible, Mallet owned only one New Testament which was not in his native language. Mallet obviously spent much more time reading fully secularized history than religious literature. The prayer made just before jumping in the river was uttered by a man who, though clearly a self-affirmed Christian, had enjoyed intellectual pursuits that were overwhelmingly secular.

Though in a less obvious way, the suicide of the Habitant François Dupuget lends credence to the notion of increasingly secular interests among merchants. Although not as wealthy as Mallet, Dupuget, forty, was a rather affluent merchant who jumped off his roof in August 1722 after suffering from a fever for a brief period. The postmortem inventory revealed that his library was not as impressive as Mallet's: Dupuget owned twenty-three published works, many of which were in multivolume sets. Although he did not possess a Bible or New Testament (but he did own the Psalms), religious works were the most common. Eight titles were books about Christianity, including two collections of sermons. Like Mallet, Dupuget had a certain interest in history as witnessed by the presence on his bookshelf of a three-volume history of the Roman Republic and a biography of Mohammed. He also owned some works on geography and law. His holdings included a few titles on philosophy, and creative literature was present in the form of collections of fairy tales and of Molière comedies.[128] As he did not own a Bible, Dupuget obviously did not read daily from Scripture. The variety of reading material, only a third of which was religious in nature, testifies to varied intellectual pursuits.

To be sure, there were other merchants who committed suicide whose very modest libraries were stocked mainly with religious publications. Even in such cases, however, we find evidence to suggest that religion, at least for the better-educated Genevans, had become simply a part of Genevan culture rather than its very basis. The Habitant David Gérard, seventy, a rather wealthy clothing merchant, drowned himself in January 1749 after becom-

---

sessed 615 titles, of which only 15 percent were theological; see Heyd, *Between Orthodoxy and Enlightenment*, 184–85.

[128]AEG, Juridiction Civile Fd 15.

ing insanely upset following his wife's death. According to all reports, however, he was devastated not because he had lost his beloved companion, but because his wife had not, as promised, left him half of her estate. The postmortem inventory revealed that he was fairly well off even without his wife's inheritance. His clothing merchandise and real estate holdings (four substantial buildings) were worth tens of thousands of florins. His book collection, however, was very modest. Religious literature was prominent, including two Bibles, Jean-Frédéric Ostervald's *Réflexions sur la Bible*, and a work entitled *La morale chrestienne*. He also owned, however, books such as *Le parfait jardinier, Dictionnaire de commerce*, and a two-volume *Histoire de Genève*.[129] Likewise, the tiny library of the wealthy Bourgeois textile merchant Jean Liotard, who committed suicide at thirty-six in November 1720, was not limited to religious literature. Of the half-dozen titles, only three, including a Bible and a New Testament, pertained to religion.[130]

Later in the century, the young attorney Jean-Louis Tronchin showed increasingly secular interests. Referred to briefly in chapters 2 and 3, Tronchin took his life in May 1773 after a brief illness. Because of the conflict between his father, Jean-Robert, and Rousseau, the very name Tronchin has often been associated with reactionary conservatism, a reputation that is quite unwarranted. Having studied under Burlamaqui, the elder Tronchin, who outlived his son by twenty years, was strongly influenced by Natural Law and admired Montesquieu. He was a most articulate spokesman for attenuating harsh penalties for many crimes; like Beccaria, he stressed the importance of crime prevention and preferred correcting and rehabilitating criminals to punishing them. The attitudes that he shared with other prominent contemporary jurists explain why authorities in eighteenth-century Geneva, like those in many other European states, abolished judicial torture and imposed the death penalty much less frequently than ever before. In spite of their quarrels, even Rousseau himself described Jean-Robert Tronchin as an "enlightened man."[131]

[129]AEG, EC, LM 61: 87, 19 January 1749; Juridiction Civile F 359; PC 9545; RC 249: 28, 31.

[130]Married and the father of young children, Liotard was quite wealthy. He and his wife had three live-in servants, and the postmortem inventory revealed considerable wealth; AEG, EC, LM 56: 13, 4 November 1720; Juridiction Civile F 420; PC 6854.

[131]Porret, *Crime et ses circonstances*, 57–58, 92–96, 353–56, 382–83.

Jean-Louis Tronchin, Jean-Robert's only child, was also very much a part of the Enlightenment. The postmortem inventory revealed that the younger Tronchin not only enjoyed great wealth but also was a very cultivated man. He owned three violins and two upright basses and, more important, had a most impressive library. At a time when books were still beyond the means of many people, Tronchin had a library consisting of 376 titles, many of which were multivolume works, such as the fourteen-volume *Théâtre français*, published in Geneva in 1767. His library had a wide variety of works, the majority of which were in French, though a significant minority was in Latin and eight were in Italian. Books by classical authors, be they in Latin or in French translation, were well represented, including works by Julius Caesar, Cicero, Homer, Horace, Lucretius, Ovid, Plato, Plautus, Virgil, and a host of others. Numerous works reveal that Tronchin had a keen interest in history. As an attorney, Tronchin not surprisingly had some works on law, including two editions—both apparently abridgments—of the *Corpus Juris Civilis* and three editions of Justinian's *Institutionum*. He also was in tune with works by seventeenth- and eighteenth-century theorists on Natural Law, possessing works by Samuel Ostervald, Emer de Vattel, Hugo Grotius, Samuel Pufendorf (including *Le droit de la nature et des gens*), and Jean-Jacques Burlamaqui *(Principes du droit naturel)*. Conspicuous by their scarcity, however, were religious works. Out of 376 titles, only seven were traditional religious works: two Bibles, an *Histoire de la Bible*, two published sermons, and two New Testaments in the original Greek with parallel Latin translations. Much more common were works by various Enlightenment writers, including publications by Diderot, Montesquieu, Voltaire, and David Hume. Locke's *Essay Concerning Human Understanding*—one of the most important precursors to Enlightenment thought—could be found on Tronchin's shelves. In spite of his father's feud, Tronchin owned several works by Jean-Jacques Rousseau, including the *Discourse on the Origins of Inequality* and, most ironically, two copies of the *Social Contract*, which his father had advocated burning a decade earlier.

Simply put, Tronchin's library was overwhelmingly secular and revealed interests that were typical of intellectuals of the Enlightenment. Nevertheless, because of his father's conflict with Rousseau, the very name Tronchin has unjustly been associated with rigid conservatism and even religious obscurantism.[132]

While affluent merchants and lawyers may have been the first to exhibit this secularization of reading material, a study suggests that this pattern of change was not limited to Geneva's elite. Research on five hundred postmortem inventories shows an evolution in the libraries of Genevans during the course of the eighteenth century. Among the inventories studied, many individuals left only one book. In those cases, the book most commonly owned was the Bible or, by the end of the century, simply the Psalms. Excluding those, we find changes in the reading material owned by people who possessed more than one book. At the beginning of the century, more than a third of the titles in these personal libraries were religious in nature, the Bible easily being the most popular book. Among smaller libraries, which generally belonged to artisans, religious works were even more pronounced. These works represented 57 percent of the titles, suggesting that religion was probably of greater interest to artisans than to merchants and lawyers. By the 1780s, when personal libraries were more common, religious works had fallen to only 8 percent of all titles in personal libraries, a trend that was even more pronounced among the smaller libraries. While religious literature declined in importance (as did the classics), books on "arts and sciences" and "les belles lettres" enjoyed growing popularity, especially among artisanal households. While Calvin and Locke were among the authors whose works were most commonly found on Genevans' shelves in the early eighteenth century, they had been replaced by the end by Rousseau, Voltaire, and Montesquieu.[133] Rousseau had considerable praise for the cultural level of Gene-

---

[132]Even works on music outnumbered religious literature eleven to seven; AEG, Juridiction Civile F 747. Without referring to Jean-Robert Tronchin by name, an author has written, "[Rousseau's] most important books, *Emile* and *The Social Contract*, were burned...in his native Switzerland [sic], whose religious fanatics forced him to take refuge for a year in England under the protection of David Hume"; Matthew Josephson, introduction to *The Essential Rousseau*, trans. Lowell Bair (New York: Penguin, 1975), xv. Such an appraisal fails to take into account that the controversy was overwhelmingly political rather than religious.

[133]In 1700–1715, works by the following authors could be found in the personal libraries: Calvin (15 works), La Fontaine (11), Beza (7), Machiavelli (5), and Racine (5). In 1775–95, libraries included works by Jean-Jacques Rousseau (99), Voltaire (57), Montesquieu (37), La Fontaine (32), Fénelon (23), Locke (22), Molière (17), Racine (15), the *Encyclopédie* (13). Among the writings of Rousseau, the most common were the following: his *Oeuvres* (21), *Lettres écrites de la montagne* (18), *Emile* (15), and *Social Contract* (12). The dispute with Tronchin was followed very closely in Geneva; see François Grounauer, "Livre et Société à Genève au XVIIIe siècle à partir des inventaires après décès" (Mémoire de licence,

van watchmakers, and evidence indeed suggests that at least some of them were quite well read. The watchmaker Jacques Argaud (d. 1782) had a very impressive personal library, which included many volumes of the classics and works on mathematics and music. He was most interested in the works of the philosophes. He owned Bayle's *Dictionary*, a complete set of the *Encyclo-pédie*, works by Voltaire, and twenty-four volumes of works by Rousseau, of whom Argaud was a "fanatic disciple."[134]

Simply put, evidence from the postmortem inventories suggests growing secular interests among people of a variety of classes in the eighteenth century. This is not to say that those who killed themselves were necessarily reading arguments in defense of suicide in their personal libraries. While such defenses could be found in Tronchin's impressive library, in the first half of the century, Dupuget and Mallet probably could not have found justifications for committing suicide in any of the books they owned.[135] Nevertheless it stands to reason that if the Christian religion was having to share shelf space with philosophy, history, geography, and creative literature, then its role in shaping mentality would have been reduced. Since it was Christian thinkers, beginning especially with Augustine, who emphatically denied that suicide was ever acceptable, the deterring effect of Christianity against suicide also likely declined. More important, even if people attended church regularly and maintained and actively practiced the Reformed faith, their world was less permeated by the supernatural.

Other evidence aptly shows that Genevans were letting go of the strict

Université de Genève, 1969), 24. See also Barbara Roth-Lochner, *De la banche à l'étude: Une histoire insti-tutionnelle, professionnelle et sociale du notariat genevois sous l'Ancien Régime* (Geneva: Société d'histoire et d'archéologie de Genève, 1997), 493–96.

[134]Patrick O'Mara, "Geneva in the Eighteenth Century: A Socio-Economic Study of the Bourgeois City-State During Its Golden Age" (Ph.D. diss., University of California, Berkeley, 1954), 352–53.

[135]Tronchin could have read Montesquieu's defense of suicide in his *Oeuvres*, for example. Tronchin clearly had an interest in the work of the empiricist and radical skeptic David Hume, owning the follow-ing translations of the Scottish author's works: *Discours politiques*, 2 vols. (Amsterdam, 1754); *Essais moraux et politiques*, 4 vols. (Amsterdam, 1764); *Exposé de la contestation entre Hume et Rousseau* (London, 1766); *Histoire d'Angleterre*, 18 vols.; AEG, Juridiction Civile F 747. Tronchin did not, however, possess a copy of Hume's "On Suicide" which, though written in the mid-1750s, was not officially published until after Tronchin's death. Prior to its first official publication in 1777, however, Hume's treatise had circu-lated clandestinely, including in French translation beginning in 1770; Sprott, *English Debate on Suicide*, 128. Nonetheless, it is unlikely Tronchin ever cast his eyes upon this treatise.

Calvinist morality they had embraced for much of the early modern period. Theatrical productions, for example, had long been forbidden in Geneva, considered by many as nothing but pleasure-seeking decadence. And while Jean-Jacques Rousseau approved of this ban, Voltaire vigorously condemned it. Voltaire himself had theatrical productions staged on his nearby estate, and a significant number of Geneva's ruling elite were attracted to the idea of having a theater in the city itself. In January 1768 a theater that was under construction in Geneva was destroyed by fire, perhaps the result of arson. Interest continued, however, and a theater was constructed just outside the city walls in 1784. Theatrical productions, once anathema in the city of Calvin, now attracted large Genevan audiences. Similar changes can be seen in attitudes toward dancing, long forbidden among Genevan Calvinists. Though authorities reaffirmed the ban on balls and dancing in 1749, in 1772 they simply declared that dancing must stop at 10 P.M., pushed back to midnight in 1785. In 1786 the pendulum had gone full swing from prohibition to institutionalization: city magistrates claimed the exclusive right to license dancing masters. In a similar fashion, while cardplaying had been forbidden from Calvin's day into the early eighteenth century, by the end of the century authorities mandated that playing cards bear the stamp indicating that the appropriate tax had been paid.[136]

Religion was no longer the essential glue that held Genevan society together. Long gone were the days when the Consistory, armed only with censures and excommunications, could regulate the everyday lives of Genevans in great detail, fostering a strong sense of community and stifling deviation. By the eighteenth century, the formerly intrusive Consistory no longer had much clout and had long given up trying to make all Genevans attend church. The greater freedom accorded individuals could lead to growing feelings of isolation and alienation, feelings that could nurture suicidal behavior. More broadly, like contemporary England, early modern Geneva witnessed the transformation from a religious culture to a religious faith. By the eighteenth century, religion had become one aspect of Genevan society's culture rather than the very basis of its culture, as had been the case in Calvin's Geneva.[137]

---

[136]Kirk, "'Going Soft,'" in *Identity of Geneva*, ed. Roney and Klauber, 146–47.

[137]See C. John Sommerville, *The Secularization of Early Modern England: From Religious Culture to Religious Faith* (New York: Oxford University Press, 1992), 9, 16–17.

Caution of course must be used in discussing the issue of secularization. This was an issue of degrees. Throughout the early modern period, the most commonly cited printed work for all postmortem inventories was the Bible (or simply the New Testament or Psalms). Moreover, the wealthy business-man and publisher, Jean Antoine Pelissari, who drowned himself in 1738 (see chapter 2) displayed behavior that was anything but secular. Although his employees expressed shock at this suicide, some acquaintances men-tioned that Pelissari, a thirty-five-year-old bachelor, had clearly been most upset for an extended period. His neighbors who lived above him, for exam-ple, reported having heard over a period of several years, Pelissari lamenting and weeping during the middle of the night in his abode. Often he was up virtually all night sighing, crying, screaming to himself, and kicking and pounding things in desperation. He frequently screamed out that he was a terrible sinner, begging God for forgiveness. The neighbors noted that his lamentations were particularly intense during a period in which he was having some business conflicts with a certain Sieur Bousquet, another pub-lisher in Geneva. Concerned about his well-being, they asked a pastor to visit him.[138]

His former servant, Susanne Matthieu, reported similar nocturnal scenes. Having worked for Pelissari from 1734 until April 1738, Matthieu also observed that he was most upset about disagreements with Bousquet, pacing in the night, praying to God, and complaining violently about his own sins. In the middle of one such night, Matthieu was so concerned about Pelissari's lamentations that she entered his room to see what was the matter. Furious, Pelissari screamed at her, demanded what she was doing there, and even tried to strike her with a pickax. Fortunately, she avoided the blow by jumping out of the way and hastened out of the room. A few moments later she returned, finding a more sedate Pelissari. She asked him to come drink some milk flavored with almonds which she had prepared. He went with her to the kitchen and as he drank the milk, began weeping and begging Mat-thieu forgiveness for his violence. Asked why he was so upset, Pelissari said that he had committed a number of sins and feared that God would not for-give him. Asked if his business dealings were the cause of his chagrin, Pelis-sari first said no, but then acknowledged that perhaps they were. Pelissari

[138]AEG, PC 8581.

further told Matthieu that he wanted to go to the church of St. Pierre to make a public confession of his sins. Matthieu warned him, however, that his enemies would take advantage of such a public spectacle to ridicule him. She suggested that it would be more prudent to confide in someone he could trust such as the pastor Vernet, referring to the professor and promoter of liberal theological views. Early the next morning, Matthieu brought Vernet to Pelissari who, weeping, embraced the pastor and then had a private two-hour conversation with him. Thereafter Pelissari seemed somewhat less tense, although he still got up at times in the middle of the night to curse himself. During the past year, he was often still sad, although less violent.[139]

Obviously Pelissari's mind-set was strongly shaped by religion. Plagued by feelings of guilt, Pelissari desperately sought forgiveness from God for unspecified sins. As a publisher, Pelissari undoubtedly was exposed to secular literature; but as no postmortem inventory was made, we know nothing about his personal library. Yet the tearful prayers, the rueful confessions, and the consoling pastoral visits all point to a man for whom religion was very much internalized. From the testimony it appears that the Reformed faith was for him more a source of guilt than consolation. The angst that Pelissari suffered, like that described by Schär, was apparently the result of spiritual unrest, based on intense feelings of guilt for sins that could not be forgiven. Of the 404 self-inflicted deaths in early modern Geneva, Pelissari was the best—and virtually the only—example of a suicide that may have been religiously inspired.

The case of Pelissari notwithstanding, the unusually high proportion of merchants among suicides in the first half of the eighteenth century attests to growing secularization. True, the arrival a half century before of large numbers of Huguenots in the wake of the Revocation of the Edict of Nantes testified to the strong religious convictions of many.[140] Be that as it may, although Genevans were still very much tied to the Reformed faith, religion did not permeate everyday life as it had during the sixteenth and much of the seventeenth centuries. Since merchants were better educated and had more access to printed material than most people, they were among the first

---

[139]AEG, PC 8581. Vernet himself was not questioned; pastoral visits were evidently recognized as confidential.

[140]See Olivier Reverdin and others, *Genève au temps de la Révocation de l'Edit de Nantes 1680–1705* (Geneva: Droz, 1985).

to drift away from the traditional Reformed mentality. After 1750 the desacralization of mentality increasingly affected Genevans of lower socioeconomic status, who in effect caught up with and even surpassed the merchants in exhibiting the growing penchant for suicide.

Since all these examples involved men, one may wonder if increasingly secular attitudes also help explain the gender gap with regard to suicide. Perhaps Protestant Geneva experienced a feminization of religion similar to that found in nineteenth-century Catholic France, the seeds of which were sown in the eighteenth century.[141] Could it be, as some scholars have suggested for other periods, that the gender gap in suicide was directly related to the gender gap in education? Denied equal access to education, were women less disturbed by "the unsettling influence of independence of thought, the weight of abstract problems of life and death"?[142] As previously noted in chapter 1, sociologists see higher suicide rates among the more educated. According to Durkheim, suicide is higher among the better educated because intellectual development contributes to "the weakening of traditional beliefs" and, concomitantly, to "the state of moral individualism."[143]

Genevan men certainly were better educated than their female counterparts. An institution, the Collège de Rive, provided secondary education for boys from affluent Genevan families already in the 1530s.[144] By contrast, secondary education was not available for girls until the nineteenth century. Although beginning in 1736, all girls and boys in Geneva were to receive some primary education associated with the mandatory catechism classes, throughout the eighteenth century men continued to have higher literacy rates and to be better read than women.[145] True, female literacy was extraor-

[141]Chaunu, *Mort à Paris*, 434–36; Suzanne Desan, *Reclaiming the Sacred: Lay Religion and Popular Politics in Revolutionary France* (Ithaca, N.Y.: Cornell University Press, 1992), 210–16; Philip T. Hoffman, *Church and Community in the Diocese of Lyon, 1500–1789* (New Haven, Conn.: Yale University Press, 1984), 144–45; Kathryn Norberg, *Rich and Poor in Grenoble, 1600–1814* (Berkeley: University of California Press, 1985), 250–52; Bonnie Smith, *Ladies of Leisure: The Bourgeoises of the Nord* (Princeton: Princeton University Press, 1982); Vovelle, *Piété baroque*, 322.

[142]Fedden, *Suicide*, 326.

[143]Durkheim, *Suicide*, 168.

[144]Louis Binz, "Coup d'oeil sur l'histoire du Collège," in *Le Collège de Genève 1559–1959* (Geneva: Jullien, 1959), 14–20.

[145]Josiane Ferrari-Clément, "From Household to School, From School to Household," in *Forgotten Women of Geneva*, trans. Rebecca Zorac, ed. Anne-Marie Käppeli (Geneva: Metropolis, 1993), 78–97. For information on literacy rates, based on the ability to sign one's name, see Roger Girod, "Le recul de l'

dinarily high by the late eighteenth century, and by 1798 a third of Geneva's primary school teachers were women. Still, a considerable cultural gap existed between Genevan men and women. From the conversion to Protestantism until the nineteenth century, there were no works published by a female author who was both born and raised in Geneva. Unlike their contemporaries in France, Genevan women did not organize any important salons for eloquent conversation and poetry readings. In short, the Enlightenment did little to alter the "cultural marginality" of Genevan women.[146] Records further reveal that of those who took their lives, a few men, but no women, expressed religious sentiments that bordered on the deism of many philosophes.[147]

A case in point was the suicide of Jean-Jacques Aimé Mellaret, a twenty-two-year-old employed in the watchmaking industry, who shot himself in the head in his room in July 1769. Although he apparently felt quite alone following the deaths of both parents, Mellaret seems to have suffered from a general unhappiness which did not stem from any one cause.[148] Mellaret certainly was a very religious young man and an avid reader, as evidenced by

---

analphabétisme dans la région de Genève, de la fin du XVIIIe au milieu du XIXe siècle," in *Mélanges d'histoire économique et sociale en hommage au professeur Antony Babel*, vol. 2 (Geneva, 1963), 179–89; Laurent Haeberli, "Le taux d'alphabétisation à Genève au XVIIIe siècle," *Revue du Vieux Genève* 12 (1984): 59–64. For the growing personal libraries of Genevans of the late eighteenth century, see Grounauer, "Livre et société à Genève."

[146]E. William Monter, "Women in Calvinist Geneva (1550–1800)," *Signs* 6 (1980): 205–7.

[147]The evidence from suicide further suggests that male artisans were better read than their female counterparts in contemporary popular literature. As noted in chapter 4, in the late 1700s, three male apprentices in their late teens, but no females, were inspired to take their lives after reading Goethe's *Werther*. To be sure, a male reader would have been more likely than a female to identify with the character of Werther; AEG, PC 13346, 14170, 17092.

[148]Mellaret had certainly experienced more than his share of sorrow. His mother, Marthe Robin, died of a fever at the age of thirty-four on 6 November 1751; AEG, EC, LM 61: 285. Six years later, his father, the master writer Samuel Mellaret, remarried (Registres de Mariages et Baptêmes, St. Pierre: 2 August 1757) but died himself from a chest infection in July 1765; EC, LM 63: 249, 13 July 1765. The first marriage produced four children while six children were born of the second marriage. Five of these children—his only full brother and four half brothers and sisters—died before Jean-Jacques Aimé; Registres de Mariages et Baptêmes, Temple Neuf: 9 September 1741, 1 October 1742, 23 September 1743, 27 May 1764; Registres de Mariages et Baptêmes, St. Pierre: 17 April 1758, 15 February 1759, 22 February 1762, 15 June 1763. EC, LM 62: 123, 11 May 1756; 233, 26 April 1758; 391, 12 February 1761; EC, LM 63: 37, 5 March 1762; 177, 8 June 1764. In a note to his two surviving full sisters, Jean-Jacques Aimé asked that his meager assets go toward the education of the last "rejeton" of their family, a veiled reference to his six-year-old half brother, Jean.

the number of printed works which the Auditeur found on his desk. These
included a number of books of devotion but also works that showed a keen
interest in the Enlightenment. Found among his reading material was a
French translation of poetry by Albrecht von Haller (1708–77), a physician
and native of Bern. Well known among Swiss Enlightenment thinkers,
Haller wrote, among other creative works, an epic poem in which he celebrated the natural beauty of Switzerland, which he described as the home of
liberty.[149] Also present was an issue of Verne's journal, *Choix littéraire*. In
that particular issue was an article by Voltaire ("Sur l'esprit," taken from the
Encyclopédie) and another article appropriately titled, "Philosophical Reflections on the Moment of Death," by the French naturalist Buffon.[150]

Of greatest interest, however, is a fifteen-page manuscript that Mellaret
himself wrote just before pulling the trigger. More a treatise than a suicide
note, his "Reflections on Suicide" is fascinating and, though a bit rambling,
even eloquent. A strong religious theme runs throughout this treatise, in
which Mellaret defended the taking of one's life. He admitted that at first
glance suicide seems revolting and contrary to nature and reason, avowing
that the desire to live is divinely inspired, stemming from the incertitude the
individual faces with regard to his or her destiny:

> The creator acted very wisely by imprinting in our hearts the love of
> life, hiding from us the book of destinies. As a result, we cling to life
> and, ignoring what will be our destiny when we leave this world, we
> prefer to put up with pains and chagrins.... We have countless
> examples before us. Regardless of how bitter life can be, humans are
> so attached to it that even when in the middle of suffering, an old
> man in the face of death still desires to prolong his life at any price.
> Where does this come from? It is a result... of the incertitude of our
> fate, which always causes people to tremble when faced with the
> prospect of leaving this world.[151]

[149]AEG, PC 11902; Porret, "Mourir l'âme angoissée," 81, n. 45.
[150]In Buffon's article, Mellaret could have read that death "is not as terrible as we imagine it. It
seems awful from afar. It is a specter that terrifies us from a certain distance, but this fear disappears when
we draw near to it"; *Choix littéraire* 4 (1755): 200; cited in Porret, "Mourir l'âme angoissée," 81, nn. 46–
47.
[151]AEG, PC 11902.

Though acknowledging the natural instinct of survival, Mellaret asked why suicide is considered a crime. He concluded that the criminal nature of suicide stems from the fact that we do not give ourselves life. Many argue therefore that we are no more masters of our lives than of those of our neighbors; killing oneself is therefore just as bad as killing another person. But where does this logic come from? Mellaret rightly insisted that one cannot find this antagonism to suicide in either the Old or New Testaments. Life, he argued, is simply one of the many favors that God has bestowed upon us. As God created us free and made us the masters of nature, life is one of the myriad things over which God has given us dominion.[152]

Mellaret asked rhetorically whether God would punish someone for being too sensitive to "life's calamities." If experiencing excruciating pain from a certain part of the body, would not a sensible person amputate that limb in order to be rid of the pain? According to Mellaret, the same applies to the body and the soul if one becomes unbearable to the other. The forced separation of the soul from the body must not obliterate the former because the body is simply the recipient in which the soul is placed. The soul will survive the death of the body if its sentiments are pure, its inclination noble and kind, and if "one of the causes of its anxiety was not being able to use its noble faculties for itself or for others."[153] Surely God would not condemn that soul to more punishment than it deserves; he [God] would not place such a soul in the same class as the degraded soul of a totally wicked person.

Needless to say, Mellaret did not believe that God always approved of self-inflicted deaths. He wrote that humans, though sublime as far as the soul is concerned, are base from the point of view of carnal desires. Accordingly, he spoke very disparagingly of the "sensual man" who is totally dominated by sordid desires. Such a man pursues only frivolous things, which, once attained, leave his heart no more fulfilled than before, ultimately ruining his health and his character. Having enjoyed hedonistic pleasures, he will experience great pain once his senses are exhausted. In such a state, he cannot even delude himself into thinking that he can find peace and deliver himself from his evils by taking his life. Repose after death can come only to those who have a clear conscience. Mellaret thus clearly believed that God

[152]AEG, PC 11902.
[153]AEG, PC 11902.

still had a judgmental side.[154]

The religious Mellaret also revealed an affinity for Enlightened thought in his celebration of nature. With religious passion, he sang the praises of nature and, like the philosophes, of God as creator of an ordered, beautiful universe. According to Mellaret, a person who is dominated by the intellect, rather than by animal-like passions, has a real appreciation of nature:

> He is enraptured in considering the magnificent spectacle of nature.... In getting closer and closer to nature, he feels rejuvenated; his soul acquires a more noble taste than when he pursues vain objects which are the perpetual occupation of the sensual man. He begins to broaden his view. He discovers the beautiful things which until now he has been unaware of. He delves deeper into the secrets of nature. He discovers everywhere the power and infinite goodness of the creator who displays before his eyes the harmonious vastness of the world; the laughing greenness of meadows, flecked with flowers; the healthy and abundant food that is everywhere available.... Transported with admiration and full of love for his creator, he cries out [with joy].[155]

The sensitive person "lifts up his eyes to the immense azure sky." There he sees the sun, "the most beautiful ornament, whose warmth gives life to plants and revives all of nature and whose splendid light cheers up and revitalizes all beings."[156]

Appropriately, this young watchmaker praised God as the author of order in the universe, much as Enlightenment thinkers likened God to a clockmaker. For Mellaret, the sensitive person admires the "regular, constant, and unvarying" movements of the planets, stars, heavens, and the earth. These planets and stars are worthy of admiration as they are "faithfully following their orbits, without ever straying from them, continually announc[ing] to the intelligent man, the boundless power, the admirable wisdom, and the immense goodness of a God creator." Reflective people will be "overjoyed to the point of ecstasy by seeing this beautiful order of creation," their hearts flooded with inexpressible happiness, their souls enno-

---

[154]AEG, PC 11902.
[155]AEG, PC 11902.
[156]AEG, PC 11902.

bled. Constantly meditating on the wonders of creation, such people endeavor to perfect their "noble faculties" by imitating the "perfect Being."[157]

All told, Mellaret was inspired by Enlightenment thought which was strongly tempered by Christianity. The young artisan ended his "Reflections on Suicide" with a lengthy prayer. Invoking the name of Jesus Christ, Mellaret asked for God's compassion, acknowledging his faults and also his fears concerning the life to come. Begging for mercy, Mellaret besought God "to efface my transgressions and my hidden faults with the blood that cries for grace for us." In begging for mercy, however, Mellaret also reminded God of his good side: "Lord, if the extent of my loathing of life pushes me to this point, you know, Lord,... the integrity of my heart.... Oh, Lord, will your goodness be offended by the great desire that I have to leave this world? I do this not out of scorn for life. On the contrary, I thank you for giving me a soul that was capable of knowing you and of lifting itself up to you." Mellaret celebrated above all God as creator of nature and the universe, emphasizing his goodness over his power:

> It is your goodness that has guided your power. It is you who keeps the sun, that blazing star, to stay at the center and orders it not to stray from it. You determine the limits of the waves of the sea, preventing them from passing beyond. From the shores of the Tagus to the banks of the Ganges, from one end of the universe to the other, is manifest the greatness of your marvelous deeds which shine everywhere to the eyes of the attentive man.[158]

Begging God not to be angry since he is a "tender father," Mellaret wrote his last words: "My Lord, I submit to your judgment.... Lord, forgive me; Lord, have mercy. Let yourself be swayed by my prayer that the blood of your son cleanse me of all sins, that he be my intercessor—hear my prayer!—and servant of almighty God! It is in throwing myself in the arms of Jesus, my savior, that I implore your mercy."[159]

Simply put, the religious convictions expressed in this treatise were a far cry from those of John Calvin. Though there is a trace of the fear of God in

---

[157]AEG, PC 11902.
[158]AEG, PC 11902.
[159]AEG, PC 11902.

these words, Mellaret concentrated much more on the benevolent than the judgmental side of God. Though not exactly depicted as the remote clock-maker described by some philosophes, God appears as the compassionate creator of a beautiful world and the author of natural order. With some mis-givings about the afterlife, Mellaret convinced himself that God's love was greater than his wrath. In short, although Mellaret's values can hardly be described as entirely secular, his religious convictions were quite different from those of earlier generations. His religion—and that of his contemporar-ies—did not offer much of a deterrent to suicide.[160]

Another watchmaker with strong literary interests was Pierre Dombre, forty-seven, mentioned above in chapters 3 and 4, who committed suicide in 1787 because he was the victim of technological change and was bitter toward his adulterous wife from whom he was separated. An amateur poet, Dombre was, like Mellaret, a very cultivated man. Although Dombre, unlike Mellaret, was more absorbed with mundane concerns than religion, he nonetheless composed a prayer shortly before pulling the trigger. In words that resonated with Enlightened themes, Dombre wrote:

> God or Heavenly Being, creator and preserver of all things, have mercy on this soul that is burdened with worries and stifled by the miseries of this life. I have broken the tower in which it has been held captive. In doing this, have I offended you, as people of little faith allege? As you know, how many times have my eyes, filled with tears, eager to see your glory, asked you for death as an act of grace? Today it will all come to an end. And may I be assured that my arm is merely the instrument that carries out your will? The power that animates my soul and moves it is a spirit that emanates from you. If I have not dishonored [this spirit], it will recover its rights.[161]

---

[160]In some ways, Mellaret's treatise resembled that associated with an infamous double suicide that occurred in France a few years later. Two young dragoons shot themselves on Christmas Day 1773 at Saint-Denis and left a "philosophic testament." In that treatise, they did not beg for mercy from God. They simply said that, having exhausted all pleasures, they had grown weary of life. Confident that there would be no punishment for thus voluntarily ending their lives prematurely, they promised that if there were some penalty after death they would do their best to warn others. If nothing was heard of them, they suggested that unhappy people follow their example. This suicide proved most unsettling; the religiously devout blamed the philosophes while the philosophes held the government responsible; see McManners, *Death and Enlightenment*, 431.

[161]AEG, PC 15188.

There is nothing decidedly Christian about this prayer, and the fear of God is all but absent. His generic reference to "God or Heavenly Being" sounds vaguely similar to the Cult of the Supreme Being, celebrated a few years later during the French Revolution. The religious sentiments expressed in this last appeal surely offered little restraint to suicidal tendencies.

Mellaret and Dombre at least clearly believed in an afterlife, whereas another man who took his life obviously had his doubts. Charles Dalloz, thirty-five, was the aide-de-camp described in chapter 3, who shot himself in 1793 because he was upset about the direction the French Revolution had taken during the Reign of Terror. Just before shooting himself, he ended a letter to a friend with the following words: "If there is anything after death, I will try to inform you about it."[162] Quite simply, the religious convictions of neither Mellaret, Dombre, nor Dalloz would have offered much of a deterrent to suicide. Their experiences show a considerable degree of desacralization, proving that a more secular mentality was not limited to an educated elite.

True, most Genevans were not as well read and, most likely, not as imbued with Enlightened mentality as were these men. For the most part, however, Genevans who committed suicide in the late 1700s were not drawing inspiration directly from Enlightened apologists for suicide, nor were they little philosophes in their own right. In Geneva, as in France and elsewhere, suicide notes first became common in the late 1700s. Minois suggests this represented the culmination of the secularization of suicide; in justifying the act, the note served to reinforce the belief that suicide was a rational act. It also represented the affirmation of the freedom of the individual vis-à-vis society and, as such, exemplified the spirit of the Enlightenment.[163] While notes surely did bolster the contention that suicide had mundane rather than demoniacal causes, in Geneva, as in France, suicide notes that were "enlightened" in tone, such as those of Mellaret and Dombre, were in the minority.[164] Moreover, even in the cases of Mellaret and Dombre, Genevans were

---

[162]AEG, PC 17079.

[163]Minois, *Histoire du suicide*, 333.

[164]Though the bookseller Hardy complained about irreligion of his day as a factor behind suicide, more suicides made religious gestures before killing themselves than left evidence of "philosophic convictions"; see Jeffrey Merrick, "Patterns and Prosecution of Suicide in Eighteenth-Century Paris," *Historical*

not killing themselves to make a statement about human freedom, a subject so dear to the philosophes in general. Rather, they took their lives because of financial reversals, unrequited love, the death of a loved one, and, the most common motives of all, because of physical and mental illness.[165]

Mental disorders may of course be related to these other mundane reversals. Modern psychologists might perceive elements of "inadequate reinforcement" in many of these cases of suicide. According to this theory, depression can result when a person's actions, which were formally rewarded in one way or another, no longer generate emotional reinforcement because the source of rewards is gone. Such a void may occur through the death of a spouse, the loss of a job, the departure of children from the household, and other similar changes. Bereft of these positive reinforcers, a person may cease performing those actions that were formerly rewarded and become passive and withdrawn.[166]

Earlier generations of Genevans, however, had stoically borne similar afflictions without taking their lives. The greater importance given to the affective ties within marriage and the family in the eighteenth century surely increased the feelings of emptiness when certain "positive reinforcers" were withdrawn. But the most important reason that their descendants of the late eighteenth century were more prone to give in to suicidal impulses is tied to religious change. By the late eighteenth century, the faith of common folk, like that of Turrettini, Vernet, and Vernes, had clearly deviated considerably from the traditions of Calvin. Far from nurturing suicidal proclivities, the

---

Reflections 16 (1989): 19–22. Modern psychological studies suggest that there are no significant differences between the causes and situations of suicides who left notes and those who did not; see Lester, *Why People Kill Themselves*, 242–58. See also Jerry Jacobs, "A Phenomenological Study of Suicide Notes," *Social Problems* 15 (1967): 60–72.

[165]Baechler, *Suicides*, 59–204, identifies four types of suicide: (1)escapist, fleeing an intolerable situation; (2)aggressive, aimed at harming or taking vengeance against another; (3)oblative, a sacrifice effected for a higher objective; (4)ludic, gambling with life as an ordeal or game. These four categories are not very useful at all when applied to early modern Genevan suicides. Apart from a handful of individuals who killed themselves to get revenge or to avoid being a burden on others, all were escapist, reacting against illness, melancholy, grief, or financial reversals. Taylor, *Durkheim*, 197, rightly criticizes these types because they lump together suicides which are quite different; the suicides of a terminally ill person and of someone who has been shunned by all others have little in common, though both would fall under the rubric of escapist.

[166]David Lester, *Suicide as Learned Behavior* (Springfield, Ill.: Charles C. Thomas, 1987), 13.

traditional Reformed emphases on the fear of God, the devil, and damnation, served as most effective deterrents to self-murder. But when intellectuals, judicial authorities, and common folk alike lost their fear of divine wrath and dissociated killing oneself from demon possession, the abhorrence for suicide waned. As Genevans largely forgot about the devil, and God became for them increasingly transcendent and removed from mortals, voluntary death seemed less terrible, even though religious leaders and magistrates continued to deplore it. The content of religious beliefs and practices, especially with regard to divine judgment and damnation, was thus fundamentally important in determining the degree to which religion diverted suicidal proclivities.[167]

Moreover, a feminization of religion was at most a minor factor behind the suicide gender gap. True, a cultural gap between men and women clearly persisted in the late eighteenth century, and no women left suicide notes expressing "Enlightened" religious sentiments similar to those of Mellaret or Dalloz. Be that as it may, the desacralization of Genevan society in the eighteenth century affected everyone, male and female. Even if women were not as well read as men, they were no more apt to see the devil or God behind suicide than were men. Men were more likely to succumb to suicidal tendencies not so much because they were less religious than women; rather, the decline of religious deterrents to suicide simply made them more vulnerable to the wider range of motives they faced. Thus while three-fourths of female suicides were motivated by mental or physical infirmities, less than half the men who took their lives were motivated by poor health.[168] While men had many more opportunities in pursuit of wealth, education, knowledge, and power, they also, as we have seen, were much more apt to fail in measuring up to the standards that society set for them.

[167]Pescolido and Georgianna, "Durkheim, Suicide, and Religion," 33–48, observe that in the contemporary United States, the suicide rate is much lower among Roman Catholics and evangelical Protestants than among mainline Protestants churches, such as Presbyterianism, the United Church of Christ, and Episcopalianism. Since all these groups disapprove of suicide, the authors claim that dogma is not responsible for the different rates, asserting rather that the groups that provide the stronger social "networks" have the lower suicide rates. The evidence from early modern Geneva suggests that the degree to which a faith stresses the fear of God, the devil, and damnation determines to a considerable extent religion's deterrence to suicide.

[168]From 1781 on, twenty-five (75.8 percent) of the thirty-three women who took their lives (and for whom motives can be established) were motivated at least in part by mental or physical illness. Among male suicides, the corresponding figure is forty-four (44.4 percent) of ninety-nine.

In short, the political and economic crises of the late eighteenth century may have been more immediately responsible for both the explosion in suicides and the growing disparity between the numbers of male and female suicides. But the cultural change involving a more secular mentality ultimately played a most decisive role in forming modern attitudes toward and patterns of suicide. The findings from Geneva show that suicide is more common when custom and tradition show a grudging toleration of it; it was much rarer when church, state, and popular mores aggressively condemned it.[169] Most important, the restricting of the domain of the supernatural was a vitally important factor behind the dramatic increase in suicides in the late 1700s. This evidence on suicide and the different experiences of men and women in early modern Geneva reveals an important conjunction among social, cultural, intellectual, political, and economic history.

[169]See also Dublin, *Suicide*, 13.

Epilogue

EARLY MODERN GENEVA experienced most dramatic changes with regard to suicide. One can even say that Geneva, by the late eighteenth century, had witnessed the birth of modern suicide, both in terms of attitudes toward it—fully secularized, medicalized, and stripped of diabolical overtones—and in the frequency of it. This explosion in suicides was not simply a fluke that one can attribute to the political and economic crises of the 1780s and 1790s. As noted above, the suicide rate in the canton of Geneva was still high in the years 1825–34, a calm period that experienced moderate economic growth and was free of political crisis.[1] True, the frequency with which Genevans took their lives in that decade was lower than in the turbulent years of 1781–1798. Nonetheless, the figures for the early nineteenth century are almost five times the suicide rate for the first half of the eighteenth century. We can confidently say, therefore, that the high rate during the 1820s and 1830s reflected a permanent change in suicide patterns.

How do these findings for early modern Geneva compare with modern theories on suicide? In American sociology, the "Chicago School" was in the vanguard in research on suicide in the 1920s and its influence is still felt strongly. Studying social disorders, the Chicago School consisted of urban sociologists who used local surveys and became convinced that urbanization, with its rampant social disintegration, was the crucial factor in the growing incidence of suicide. This "urban thesis" has gone virtually unchal-

---

[1]Guillaume Prevost, "Extrait d'une note statistique sur le suicide," *Bibliothèque universelle* (June 1835): 13–14. The period 1814–41 was justifiably described as "vingt-sept années de bonheur"; see Paul Guichonnet and Paul Waeber, "Révolutions et restauration (1782–1846)," in *Histoire de Genève*, ed. Paul Guichonnet (Toulouse: Edouard Privat, 1974), 286–88.

lenged among sociologists since the 1920s.[2]

One can hardly argue, however, that urbanization or—as Morselli avowed for nineteenth-century Europe—industrialization was to blame for the growing number of suicides in early modern Geneva. Though tiny when compared to modern cities, Geneva of course was an urban setting throughout the early modern period; at no time were its residents closely tied to the supposedly timeless traditions of rural Europe. Though its size increased perceptibly during the course of these two and a half centuries, it did not experience the rapid demographic growth characteristic of many modern cities. The city of Geneva numbered about 13,100 people at the beginning of this study and reached a peak of about 29,000 in 1790.[3] It was a small city throughout this period, but the frequency with which Genevans killed themselves changed most dramatically.[4] Although the *indienneurs* can be likened to industrial workers—and as we have seen, they were not prone to commit suicide—Geneva witnessed a very high suicide rate without experiencing either industrialization or very rapid demographic expansion.

What explanations might psychiatrists offer for the huge increase in suicides in Geneva in the eighteenth century? Since the 1950s, psychiatric research has paid special attention to the biochemical dimension of suicide, an aspect which of course cannot be studied for early modern Europe. Considerable research has focused on the role of neurotransmitters, chemical messengers in the brain. A number of studies have found that low levels of a particular neurotransmitter, serotonin, are associated with both depression

[2]Among the few to challenge the urban thesis is the historian Olive Anderson who, as we have seen, found suicides more common among rural villagers than residents of industrial cities; see *Suicide in Victorian and Edwardian England* (Oxford: Clarendon Press, 1987). That finding nonetheless does not necessarily undercut the urban thesis: industrialization tends to have a strong and disruptive impact on the everyday life of rural areas surrounding industrial cities. Roger Lane, *Violent Death in the City: Suicide, Accident, and Murder in Nineteenth-Century Philadelphia* (Cambridge: Harvard University Press, 1979), 33–34, 115–34, denies that social disintegration causes suicide. He argues that, unlike murderers, those who take their own lives have internalized social regulation. Like adherents to the Chicago School, Lane nonetheless affirms that urbanization ultimately was responsible for the rise in suicide rates. See also Howard I. Kushner, *American Suicide: A Psychocultural Exploration* (New Brunswick, N.J.: Rutgers University Press, 1991), 64–65.

[3]Alfred Perrenoud, *La population de Genève XVIe–XIXe siècles* (Geneva: Société d'histoire et d'archéologie de Genève, 1979), 37.

[4]Evidence also suggests that the enormous growth of the city of London in Stuart times did not spawn a large number of suicides, in spite of the incredible disruption this process of urbanization caused in people's lives; Peter Laslett, *The World We Have Lost: England Before the Industrial Age*, 3d ed. (New York: Scribner's, 1984), 175–77.

and suicide. This evidence of course suggests that depression and, ultimately, suicide, has a biochemical rather than a social or even psychological etiology. These findings should be used with a degree of caution, however. Generally based on a small number of patients, these studies must focus on people who made unsuccessful suicide attempts rather than completed suicides, and it is dangerous to base conclusions about people who kill themselves on findings for those who merely made attempts on their lives. Moreover, depression is far and away the mental disorder that is most often associated with suicide, but only a small percentage of the depressed take their own lives. Currently in the United States, an estimated 17 million people suffer from depression, and about forty thousand people take their lives annually. What causes this small minority of depressed people to take the fatal step? Most important, the biochemical explanation alone neglects entirely the cultural and psychological elements.[5]

If suicide were reduced entirely to physiological causes, how do we explain the changes in suicide rates in early modern Geneva? Were an unprecedented number of Genevans born with chemical deficiencies in the eighteenth century? Or did a large number of Genevans suddenly experience dramatic drops in their serotonin levels in the mid-1700s? Must we assume that this affected first merchants and then watchmakers and that women maintained much higher levels of that neurotransmitter than men? As we have seen, industrial contamination was not a likely cause. Among those at greatest risk of mercury poisoning were gilders, who were usually women, while the sizeable majority of those who took their lives were men.

How might modern researchers evaluate specific cases of suicide from early modern Geneva? Let us consider one more time the case of Pierre Dombre, the unemployed watchmaker who shot himself in 1787 after suffering from poverty, marital breakdown, and unrequited love.[6] Reading the various letters that he left behind, a psychiatrist might concentrate on one written to the married woman with whom he was in love. In that missive, Dombre talked about going days without eating and drinking, but not because he did not have the means to do so. For a psychiatrist, that descrip-

---

[5]Kushner, *American Suicide*, 82–88. For a summary of research trends on the physiological dimension of suicide, see David Lester, *The Biochemical Basis of Suicide* (Springfield, Ill.: Charles C. Thomas, 1988).

[6]AEG, PC 15188.

tion might imply an organic disorder, and a chemical imbalance might indeed have been behind Dombre's unhappy mental state and his suicide. A psychologist with a Freudian bent, however, would likely concentrate on some apparent intrapsychic conflicts. His unpleasant experiences with women, for example, surely must have left an emotional void. Dombre might have concentrated his libido entirely on one object, investing all his romantic and sexual interests first in his wife and then in the other woman. When both relationships failed, ending with the wife's departure and the other woman's rejection, the void may have been so great that life no longer seemed worth living. A sociologist, on the other hand, might view Dombre's social isolation and the economic crisis as the culprits. Separated from his wife and child, Dombre lived alone in a small room and had no close relatives in Geneva. Moreover, as noted above, sociologists see an important correlation between work failure and suicide among males. Dombre's failed marriage, isolated lifestyle, and unemployment all testified to very weak social integration, placing him at very high risk for suicide.

Are these explanations contradictory or complementary? Although the link between abnormal levels of serotonin and suicide remains rather tentative, let us assume that Dombre did have a low level of that neurotransmitter. Does that mean, however, that there were no external causes to his emotional malaise and his suicide? We must beware of the danger of confusing cause and effect. A depressed person may indeed have a low level of serotonin, but personal experiences, such as job loss or marital breakdown, may quite plausibly affect one's chemical balance. Traumatic experiences may excite the nervous system, causing an abnormally high depletion in the supply of serotonin.[7] Thus both the psychiatrist and the psychologist may be right in citing, respectively, chemical imbalance and failed love as causes of this suicide. Dombre's woes could well have been both organic and psychological.

Sociologists, however, are also right. To a large extent, behavior is culture bound. If Dombre had lived in a society that put little emphasis on romantic love or the companionate marriage, his lack of success with women would not have been so emotionally devastating. If he attended church several times a week, hearing sermons filled with warnings of fire and brimstone, Dombre surely would have hesitated before pulling the trigger and would

[7]Kushner, *American Suicide*, 174.

not have addressed his last prayer, in a generic fashion, to "God or Heavenly Being." Unlike Jean Jourdain, who took his life in 1555, Dombre did not cry out to the devil to come put an end to his days. Social mores changed considerably from the Reformation to the Enlightenment. Genevan attitudes toward marriage and the family, material wealth, political rights, medicine and science, religion, and the supernatural all underwent substantial transformations during these two and a half centuries. These changes quite reasonably may have contributed to rising numbers of biochemical imbalances and psychoses among Genevans; they certainly made some Genevans, when faced with ills and failures, more willing to jump in the Rhône or shoot themselves.

Most psychologists and psychiatrists now agree that social factors, such as popular values, contribute in an important way to suicide—a phenomenon that is not simply a product of mental illness or physiology. Most scholars now believe that physiological characteristics do not determine suicidal behavior: they simply mean that some people are more susceptible to suicidal impulses than others. A noted psychiatrist asserts, "Suicide is a three-dimensional problem involving psychology, sociology, and biology. Given a state of increased suicidality, the reasons why one picks up a gun, another takes a pill, and another suppresses the intention are very much caused by that person's personality and what kind of environment he lives in."[8]

For a wide variety of reasons, the early modern period was a turning point in the history of suicide and, more broadly, the history of mentality in Geneva. When suicide became secularized, medicalized, and decriminalized, exhortations alone proved inadequate in dissuading people from taking their lives. While Morselli may have been right in identifying cultural confusion as the ultimate source of high suicide rates, the evidence from Geneva suggests he was wrong to attribute normative confusion to industrialization or urbanization. In a broad European context, how representative was Geneva of these social and cultural trends? Future research will determine how typical these patterns of change were. An important next step is to examine a

---

[8]Herman van Praag, psychiatrist at Albert Einstein College of Medicine in New York City, quoted in George Howe Colt, *The Enigma of Suicide* (New York: Summit Books, 1991), 204–5. See also David Lester, *Why People Kill Themselves: A Summary of Research Findings on Suicidal Behavior* (Springfield, Ill.: Charles C. Thomas, 1972), 33–34, 194; Steve Taylor, *Durkheim and the Study of Suicide* (New York: St. Martin's Press, 1982), 36–37.

similar early modern urban society in a Catholic setting. Though there is already evidence to suggest rising suicide rates in Paris, for example, Catholics were probably less likely to show the same dramatic rise in suicidal proclivities that we have seen for Geneva. This, I would argue, is less because religious integration was stronger among Catholics than because a host of Catholic rituals continued to testify to the divine presence in this world. If the world was less desacralized for Catholics than Protestants, they were apt to be more restrained from succumbing to suicidal impulses. To be sure, any change in suicide rates in Catholic areas, as in early modern Geneva, almost certainly cannot be reduced to monocausal explanations. Geneva's explosion in suicide in the late eighteenth century resulted from a combination of social, economic, political, legal, and above all cultural factors. Surely Geneva was not unique among early modern cities in experiencing these developments.

About the Author

Throughout his research, Jeffrey R. Watt has focused on the intersection between the history of religion and everyday life, studying court records as a window to the popular culture of early modern Europe. His scholarship thus far has concentrated on the impact of the Reformed faith, examining its influence on various aspects of daily life in an attempt to uncover the conjunction of religious, cultural, and social history. His first book, *The Making of Modern Marriage: Matrimonial Control and the Rise of Sentiment in Neuchâtel, 1550–1800* (Ithaca, N.Y.: Cornell University Press, 1992), analyzes the impact of the Reformation on marriage and traces changes in the control of matrimony and in popular attitudes toward marriage during the course of the early modern period. Watt has also published articles on the registers of Geneva's Consistory during the time of Calvin, examining the Reformed faith's impact on women, popular religion, and the institutions of marriage and the family. Currently he is editing a book on suicide in early modern Europe and has begun research on the Inquisition in Modena, Italy. Watt received his A.B. from Grove City College in 1980, his M.A. from Ohio University in 1982, and his Ph.D. from the University of Wisconsin–Madison in 1987. He is associate professor of history at the University of Mississippi, where he has taught since 1988.

Bibliography

ARCHIVAL SOURCES

Archives d'Etat de Genève, Geneva, Switzerland
  Etat Civil: Livres des Baptêmes, Mariages et Morts
  Juridiction Civile (Selected Inventaires après Décès)
  Juridiction Pénale B, C, D, Lc 59
  Manuscrit Historique 133ter
  Procès Criminels (1e et 2e séries)
  Registres du Conseil
  Registres du Consistoire de Genève

PRINTED SOURCES

Abray, Jane. "Feminism in the French Revolution." *American Historical Review* 80 (1975): 43–62.

Adler, Jeffrey S. "'If We Can't Live in Peace, We Might as Well Die': Homicide-Suicide in Chicago, 1875–1910." *Journal of Urban History* 26 (1999): 3–21.

Ahlburg, Dennis A., and Morton Owen Schapiro. "Socioeconomic Ramifications of Changing Cohort Size: An Analysis of U.S. Postwar Suicide Rates by Age and Sex." *Demography* 21 (1984): 97–108.

Anderson, Olive. "Did Suicide Increase with Industrialization in Victorian England?" *Past and Present* 86 (1980): 149–73.

———. *Suicide in Victorian and Edwardian England.* Oxford: Clarendon Press, 1987.

Aquillon, Daniel. "'Celui qui se cache bien vit heureux' ou l'exposition d'enfant à Genève entre 1765 et 1785." *Revue de Vieux Genève* 13 (1983): 22–27.

Aquinas, Thomas. *Summa Theologica.* Translated by Fathers of the English Dominican Province. 22 vols. London: R. and T. Washbourne, 1911–24.

Ariès, Philippe. *Centuries of Childhood: A Social History of Family Life.* Translated by Robert Baldick. London: Jonathan Cape, 1962.

Aristotle. *The Nicomachean Ethics.* Translated by H. Rackham. Cambridge: Harvard University Press; London: William Heinemann, 1982.

Atkinson, J. Maxwell. *Discovering Suicide: Studies in the Social Organization of Sudden Death.* Pittsburgh: University of Pittsburgh Press, 1978.

Augustine. *The City of God.* Translated by George E. McCracken, William M. Green,

David S. Wiesen, Philip Levine, Eva Matthews Sanford, William McAllen Green, and William Chase Greene. 7 vols. Cambridge: Harvard University Press; London: William Heinemann, 1957–72.

Babel, Antony. *Histoire corporative de l'horlogerie, de l'orfèvrerie et des industries annexes.* Geneva: A. Kundig, 1916.

Baechler, Jean. *Suicides.* With a foreword by Raymond Aron. Translated by Barry Cooper. New York: Basic Books, 1979.

Bailey, Victor. *"This Rash Act": Suicide Across the Life Cycle in the Victorian City.* Stanford: Stanford University Press, 1998.

Barbone, Steven, and Lee Rice. "Spinoza and the Problem of Suicide." *International Philosophical Quarterly* 34 (1994): 229–41.

Barras, Vincent. "De quelques individus dangereux à Genève au XVIIIe siècle: Un exemple des rapports entre droit et médecine." *Cahiers de la Faculté de Médecine* 17 (1989): 43–63.

———. "Fers, bains et remèdes: 'La maison des allienez' de Genève." *Revue médicale de la Suisse Romande* 109 (1989): 999–1004.

Bartel, Roland. "Suicide in Eighteenth-Century England: The Myth of a Reputation." *Huntington Library Quarterly* 23 (1959): 145–58.

Baulant, Micheline, Anton Schuurman, and Paul Servais, eds. *Inventaires après décès et vente de meubles: Apports à une histoire de la vie économique et quotidienne (XIVe–XIXe siècle).* Louvain-La-Neuve: Academia, 1987.

Bayard, Françoise. "Régions et morts subites en Lyonnais et Beaujolais aux XVIIe et XVIIIe siècles." In *Du provincialisme au régionalisme XVIIIe–XXe siècle,* 211–22. Montbrison, France: Ville de Montbrison, 1989.

Bayet, Albert. *Le suicide et la morale.* Paris: Félix Alcan, 1922. Reprint, New York: Arno Press, 1975.

Beccaria, Cesare. *On Crimes and Punishments.* Translated by Henry Paolucci. Indianapolis: Bobbs-Merrill, 1963.

Bédé, Joseph-Albert. "Madame de Staël, Rousseau, et le suicide." *Revue d'histoire littéraire de la France* 66 (1966): 52–70.

Bennett, Judith M. *Ale, Beer, and Brewsters in England: Women's Work in a Changing World, 1300–1600.* New York: Oxford University Press, 1996.

Berardino, Angelo Di, ed. *Encyclopedia of the Early Church.* New York: Oxford University Press, 1992.

Berchtold, Jacques, and Michel Porret, eds. *Etre riche au siècle de Voltaire.* Geneva: Droz, 1996.

Bernardini, Paolo. "Dal suicidio come crimine al suicidio come malattia: Appunti sulla questione suicidologica nell'etica e nella giurisprudenza europea tra Sei e Settecento." *Materiali per una storia della cultura giuridica* 24 (1994): 81–101.

———. "Solitudine malinconia e loro esiti 'esiziali' nel Settecento tedesco: Alcune linee di ricerca." *Atti dell'Accademia Ligure di Scienze e Lettere* 51 (1994): 321–41.

———. *Literature on Suicide, 1516–1815: A Bibliographical Essay.* Lewiston, N.Y.: Edwin Mellen Press, 1996.

Besnard, Philippe. "Durkheim et les femmes ou le *Suicide* inachevé." *Revue française de sociologie* 14 (1973): 27–61.

Bèze, Théodore de. *Correspondance de Théodore de Bèze.* Assembled by Hippolyte Aubert.

Edited by Henri Meylan and Alain Dufour. Vol. 3. Geneva: Droz, 1963.

Binz, Louis. "Coup d'oeil sur l'histoire du Collège." In *Le Collège de Genève 1559–1959*, 13–33. Geneva: Jullien, 1959.

———. *Vie religieuse et réforme ecclésiastique dans le diocèse de Genève pendant le Grand Schisme et la crise conciliaire (1378–1450)*. Geneva: Jullien, 1973.

Binz, Louis, Bronislaw Baczko, Marc Neuenschwander, Olivier Labarthe, and Roger Durand, eds. *Regards sur la Révolution genevoise 1792–1798*. Geneva: Société d'histoire et d'archéologie de Genève, 1992.

Blanc, Hermann. *La Chambre des Blés de Genève 1628–1798*. Geneva: Georg, 1941.

Blesch, Werner. "'Sich selbsten leibloß gemacht und aus Verzweiflung erhenkt': Selbsttötungen im 16. Jahrhundert im Raum Mosbach-Eberbach-Sinsheim." *Beiträge zur Volkskunde in Baden-Württemberg* 5 (1993): 311–31.

Bowersock, G. W. *Martyrdom and Rome*. Cambridge: Cambridge University Press, 1995.

Bowlby, John. *Child Care and the Growth of Love*. Baltimore: Penguin, 1965.

Braun, Rudolf. *Industrialisation and Everyday Life*. Translated by Sarah Hanbury Tenison. Cambridge: Cambridge University Press; Paris: Editions de la Maison des Sciences de L'Homme, 1990.

Breault, K. D. "Suicide in America: A Test of Durkheim's Theory of Religious and Family Integration, 1933–1980." *American Journal of Sociology* 92 (1986): 628–56.

Breed, Warren. "Occupational Mobility and Suicide Among White Males." *American Sociological Review* 28 (1963): 179–88.

Brennan, Thomas. *Public Drinking and Popular Culture in Eighteenth-Century Paris*. Princeton: Princeton University Press, 1988.

Brunschwig, Henri. *Enlightenment and Romanticism in Eighteenth-Century Prussia*. Translated by Frank Jellinek. Chicago: University of Chicago Press, 1974.

Byman, Seymour. "Suicide and Alienation: Martyrdom in Tudor England." *Psychoanalytic Review* 61 (1974): 355–73.

Cahier-Buccelli, Gabriella. "L'Hôpital général de Genève entre 1675 et 1685." *Revue du Vieux Genève* 15 (1985): 12–17.

———. "Dans l'ombre de la Réforme: Les membres de l'ancien clergé demeurés à Genève." *Bulletin de la Société d'histoire et d'archéologie de Genève* 18 (1987): 367–89.

Calvin, John. *Ioannis Calvini Opera Quae Supersunt Omnia*. Edited by Gulielmus Baum, Eduardus Cunitz, and Eduardus Reus. Brunswick: C. A. Schwetschke and Sons, 1834–1968.

———. *Supplementa Calviniana*. Edited by Hanns Rückert. Neukirchen, Germany: Neukirchen Verlag, 1961.

Canetto, Silvia Sara, and David Lester, eds. *Women and Suicidal Behavior*. New York: Springer Publishing, 1996.

Chapuisat, Édouard. *La prise d'armes de 1782 à Genève*. Geneva: Jullien, 1932.

Charron, Pierre. *De la sagesse*. Bordeaux: Simon Millanges, 1601.

Chaunu, Pierre. *La mort à Paris: XVIe, XVIIe et XVIIIe siècles*. Paris: Fayard, 1978.

Chesnais, Jean-Claude. "The History of Violence: Homicide and Suicide Through the Ages." *International Social Science Journal* 44 (1992): 217–34.

———. "Géographie du suicide." *Histoire* 189 (1995): 30.

Cicero, Marcus Tullius. *De Officiis*. Translated by Walter Miller. London: William Heinemann; New York: MacMillan, 1921.

———. *Tusculan Disputations.* Translated by J. E. King. London: William Heinemann; New York: G. P. Putnam's Sons, 1927.

———. *M. Tulli Ciceronis Scripta Quae Manserunt Omnia. De Re Publica.* Edited by K. Ziegler. Leipzig: B. G. Teubner, 1958.

The Civil Law. Edited and translated by Samuel P. Scott. 17 vols. Cincinnati: Central Trust, 1932. Reprint, New York: AMS Press, 1973.

Cobb, Richard. *Death in Paris: The Records of the Basse-Geôle de la Seine, October 1795–September 1801, Vendémiaire Year IV–Fructidor Year IX.* New York: Oxford University Press, 1978.

Cockburn, J. S., ed. *Crime in England 1550–1800.* Princeton: Princeton University Press, 1977.

Colt, George Howe. *The Enigma of Suicide.* New York: Summit Books, 1991.

Corpus Iuris Canonici. Edited by Emil Friedberg. 2 vols. Leipzig: Bernhard Tauchnitz, 1879–81.

Crocker, Lester G. "The Discussion of Suicide in the Eighteenth Century." *Journal of the History of Ideas* 13 (1952): 47–72.

———. *An Age of Crisis: Man and World in Eighteenth-Century French Thought.* Baltimore: Johns Hopkins Press, 1959.

Crouzet, Denis. *Les guerriers de Dieu.* 2 vols. Seyssel, France: Champ Vallon, 1990.

Dallinge, Jean-David. "Dépôts de bilans et papiers de faillites à Genève durant la seconde moitié du XVIIIe siècle." Mémoire de licence, Université de Genève, 1992.

Daneau, Lambert. *Ethices Christianea: Libri tres.* Geneva: Eustathius Vignon, 1579.

Danigelis, Nick, and Whitney Pope. "Durkheim's Theory of Suicide as Applied to the Family: An Empirical Test." *Social Forces* 57 (1979): 1081–106.

Darnton, Robert. *The Business of the Enlightenment: A Publishing History of the "Encyclopédie" 1775–1800.* Cambridge: Harvard University Press, 1979.

Davis, Natalie Zemon. *Society and Culture in Early Modern France.* Stanford: Stanford University Press, 1975.

Davis, Natalie Zemon, and Arlette Farge, eds. *A History of Women in the West.* Vol. 3. In *Renaissance and Enlightenment Paradoxes.* Cambridge: Harvard University Press, 1993.

Delumeau, Jean. *La peur en occident (XIVe–XVIIIe siècles).* Paris: Fayard, 1978.

———. *Sin and Fear: The Emergence of a Western Guilt Culture, Thirteenth to Eighteenth Centuries.* Translated by Eric Nicholson. New York: St. Martin's Press, 1990.

Deonna, Waldemar. "Superstitions à Genève aux XVIIe et XVIIIe siècles." *Archives suisses des traditions populaires* 43 (1946): 343–90.

Desan, Suzanne. *Reclaiming the Sacred: Lay Religion and Popular Politics in Revolutionary France.* Ithaca, N.Y.: Cornell University Press, 1992.

Deshoulières, Antoinette du Ligier de la Garde. *Oeuvres.* 2 vols. Paris, 1770.

Diderot, Denis, and Jean Le Rond d'Alembert, eds. *Encyclopédie, ou Dictionnaire raisonné des sciences, des arts et des métiers.* 28 vols. Paris: Briasson, David, Le Breton, and Durand, 1751–72. [Volumes 8–17 were published in 1765 under the imprint of Neuchâtel: Samuel Faulché.]

Dieselhorst, Jürsten. "Die Bestrafung der Selbstmörder im Territorium der Reichsstadt Nürnberg." *Mitteilungen des Vereins Geschichte der Stadt Nürnberg* 44 (1953): 58–

230.

Donne, John. *Biathanatos: A Declaration of that Paradox or Thesis that Self-Homicide Is Not So Naturally a Sin that It May Never Be Otherwise.* London: John Dawson, 1647. Reprint, New York: Facsimile Text Society, 1930.

Douglas, Jack D. *The Social Meanings of Suicide.* Princeton: Princeton University Press, 1967.

Droge, Arthur J., and James D. Tabor. *A Noble Death: Suicide and Martyrdom Among Christians and Jews of Antiquity.* San Francisco: Harper San Francisco, 1992.

Dublin, Louis I. *Suicide: A Sociological and Statistical Study.* New York: Ronald Press, 1963.

Du Bois-Melly, Charles. *Des usages funèbres et des cimetières à Genève.* Geneva: Jules Carey, 1888.

Dufour, Alfred. *Le mariage dans l'école romande du droit naturel au XVIIIe siècle.* Geneva: Librairie de l'Université, 1976.

Durkheim, Emile. *Suicide: A Study in Sociology.* Translated by John A. Spaulding and George Simpson. Edited and with an introduction by George Simpson. New York: Free Press, 1951.

Egli, Myriam. "La paillardise à Genève dans la première moitié du XVIIIe siècle." *Revue du Vieux Genève* 14 (1984): 39–44.

Elias, Norbert. *The History of Manners.* Translated by Edmund Jephcott. New York: Pantheon Books, 1982.

———. *Power and Civility.* Translated by Edmund Jephcott. New York: Pantheon Books, 1982.

Emch-Dériaz, Antoinette. *Tissot: Physician of the Enlightenment.* New York: Peter Lang, 1992.

Engammare, Max. "De la peur à la crainte: Un jeu subtil dans le premier recueil d'images bibliques composé à l'usage de jeunes enfants (1774–1779)." In *La peur au XVIIIe siècle: Discours, représentations, pratiques,* ed. Jacques Berchtold and Michel Porret, 19–43. Geneva: Droz, 1994.

Esquirol, Etienne. *Des maladies mentales: Considerées sous les rapports médical, hygiénique et médico-légal.* 3 vols. Paris: J. S. Chaude, 1838.

Farge, Arlette. *Le cours ordinaire des choses dans la cité du XVIIIe siècle.* Paris: Seuil, 1994.

Fatio, Olivier. *Lambert Daneau et les débuts de la scolastique réformée.* Geneva: Droz, 1976.

Favre, Robert. *La mort dans la littérature et la pensée françaises au siècle des Lumières.* Lyon: Presses Universitaires de Lyon, 1978.

Fazy, Henri. "Procès et condamnation d'un Déiste genevois en 1707." *Mémoires de l'Institut National Genevois* 13 (1877): 3–11.

Fedden, Henry Romilly. *Suicide: A Social and Historical Study.* New York: Benjamin Blom, 1972.

Ferrier, Jean-Pierre. *Drames et comédies judiciaires de la Genève d'autrefois.* Geneva: Payot, 1930.

Flandrin, Jean-Louis. *Families in Former Times: Kinship, Household and Sexuality.* Translated by Richard Southern. Cambridge: Cambridge University Press, 1979.

Fulpius, Lucien. "Les institutions politiques de Genève dès origines à la fin de l'ancienne république." *Actes de l'Institut National Genevois, nouvelle série* 3 (1965): 3–36.

Gagnebin, Bernard. *Burlamaqui et le droit naturel.* Geneva: Editions de la Frégate, 1944.

Galiffe, Jaques Augustin. *Notices généalogiques sur les familles genevoises, depuis les premiers temps jusqu'à nos jours.* Vol. 3. Geneva: Gruaz, 1836.

Galland, Jean-Paul. *Dictionnaire des rues de Genève.* 3d ed. Geneva: Promoédition, 1988.

Gargett, Graham. *Jacob Vernet, Geneva, and the Philosophes.* Oxford: Voltaire Foundation, 1994.

Gates, Barbara T. *Victorian Suicides: Mad Crimes and Sad Histories.* Princeton: Princeton University Press, 1988.

The Geneva Bible: A Facsimile of the 1560 Edition. Madison: University of Wisconsin Press, 1969.

Gennep, Arnold Van. *The Rites of Passage.* Translated by Monika B. Vizedom and Gabrielle L. Caffee. Chicago: University of Chicago Press, 1960.

Gibbs, Jack P. "Marital Status and Suicide in the United States: A Special Test of the Status Integration Theory." *American Journal of Sociology* 74 (1969): 521–33.

Gibbs, Jack P., and Walter T. Martin. *Status Integration and Suicide: A Sociological Study.* Eugene: University of Oregon Books, 1964.

Giddens, Anthony, ed. *The Sociology of Suicide: A Selection of Readings.* London: Frank Cass, 1971.

Girod, Roger. "Le recul de l'analphabétisme dans la région de Genève, de la fin du XVIIIe au milieu du XIXe siècle." In *Mélanges d'histoire économique et sociale en hommage au professeur Antony Babel,* 2 vols., 2: 179–89. Geneva, 1963.

Glenn, Gary D. "Inalienable Rights and Locke's Argument for Limited Government: Political Implications of a Right to Suicide." *Journal of Politics* 46 (1984): 80–105.

Gold, Martin. "Suicide, Homicide, and the Socialization of Aggression." *American Journal of Sociology* 53 (1958): 651–61.

Goubert, Pierre. *Louis XIV and Twenty Million Frenchmen.* Translated by Anne Carter. New York: Vintage Books, 1970.

Grande Encyclopédie Larousse. Paris: Larousse, 1983.

Green, Paul D. "Suicide, Martyrdom, and Thomas More." *Studies in the Renaissance* 19 (1972): 135–55.

Greyerz, Kaspar von. "Biographical Evidence on Predestination, Covenant, and Special Providence." In *Weber's Protestant Ethic: Origins, Evidence, Contexts,* ed. Hartmut Lehmann and Guenther Roth, 273–84. Cambridge: Cambridge University Press, 1993.

Griffin, Miriam. "Philosophy, Cato, and Roman Suicide." *Greece and Rome* 33 (1986): 64–77, 192–202.

Grisé, Yolande. *Le suicide dans la Rome antique.* Montreal: Bellarmin; Paris: Les Belles Lettres, 1982.

Grounauer, François. "Livre et société à Genève au XVIIIe siècle: Essai d'étude socio-culturelle à partir des inventaires après décès." Mémoire de licence, Université de Genève, 1969.

Guichonnet, Paul, ed. *Histoire de Genève.* Toulouse: Edouard Privat, 1974.

Haeberli, Laurent. "Le suicide à Genève au XVIIIe siècle." In *Pour une Histoire Qualitative: Etudes offertes à Sven Stelling-Michaud,* 115–29. Geneva: Presses Universitaires Romandes, 1975.

———. "Le taux d'alphabétisation à Genève au XVIIIe siècle." *Revue de Vieux Genève*

12 (1984): 59–64.

Hair, P. E. H. "Deaths from Violence in Britain: A Tentative Secular Survey." *Population Studies* 25 (1971): 5–23.

Halbwachs, Maurice. *Les causes du suicide.* Foreword by Marcel Mauss. Paris: Félix Alcan, 1930.

Hanawalt, Barbara. *Crime and Conflict in English Communities 1300–1348.* Cambridge: Harvard University Press, 1979.

———, ed. *Women and Work in Preindustrial Europe.* Bloomington: Indiana University Press, 1986.

Heller, Geneviève, ed. *Le poids des ans: Une histoire de la vieillesse en Suisse Romande.* Lausanne, Switzerland: Editions d'en Bas et Société d'histoire de la Suisse Romande, 1994.

Henry, Andrew F., and James F. Short, Jr. *Suicide and Homicide: Some Economic, Sociological, and Psychological Aspects of Aggression.* Glencoe, Ill.: Free Press, 1954.

Henry, Patrick. "The Dialectic of Suicide in Montaigne's 'Coutume de l'Isle de Cea.'" *Modern Language Review* 79 (1984): 278–89.

Henry, Philippe. *Crime, justice et société dans la principauté de Neuchâtel au XVIIIe siècle (1707–1806).* Neuchâtel, Switzerland: Baconnière, 1984.

Heyd, Michael. *Between Orthodoxy and the Enlightenment: Jean-Robert Chouet and the Introduction of Cartesian Science in the Academy of Geneva.* The Hague: Martinus Nijhoff; Jerusalem: Magnes Press, 1982.

Higonnet, Patrice. "Du suicide sentimental au suicide politique." In *La Révolution et la mort,* ed. Elisabeth Liris and Jean-Maurice Bizière, 137–50. Toulouse: Presses Universitaires du Mirail, 1991.

———. "Joint Suicide in Eighteenth-Century French Literature and Revolutionary Politics." In *Fictions of the French Revolution,* ed. Bernadette Fort, 87–110. Evanston, Ill.: Northwestern University Press, 1991.

Hiler, David. "Fiscalité, conjoncture et consommation à Genève au XVIIIe siècle." *Bulletin du Département d'histoire économique: Université de Genève* 13 (1982–83): 24–51.

———. "Permanences et innovations alimentaires: L'évolution de la consommation des Genevois pendant le XVIIIe siècle." *Bulletin de la Société d'histoire et d'archéologie de Genève* 18 (1984): 23–48.

Hiler, David, and Laurence Wiedmer. "Notes sur le prix du pain et les budgets populaires à Genève dans la première moitié du XVIIIe siècle." *Bulletin du Département d'histoire économique: Université de Genève* 15 (1984–85): 37–46.

Hoffman, Philip T. *Church and Community in the Diocese of Lyon, 1500–1789.* New Haven, Conn.: Yale University Press, 1984.

Holbach, Paul Henri Thiery d'. *The System of Nature.* Translated by Samuel Wilkinson. 3 vols. London: Thomas Davison, 1820. Reprint, New York: Garland, 1984.

Hooff, Anton J. L. van. *From Autothanasia to Suicide: Self-Killing in Classical Antiquity.* London: Routledge, 1990.

Hooykaas, Reijer. *Religion and the Rise of Modern Science.* Edinburgh: Scottish Academic Press, 1973.

Houlbrooke, Ralph A. "Women's Social Life and Common Action in England from the Fifteenth Century to the Eve of the Civil War." *Continuity and Change* 1 (1986):

171–89.

Hufton, Olwen. "Women in Revolution, 1789–1796." *Past and Present* 53 (1971): 90–108.

Jacobs, Jerry. "A Phenomenological Study of Suicide Notes." *Social Problems* 15 (1967): 60–72.

Jalland, Patricia. *Death in the Victorian Family.* Oxford: Oxford University Press, 1996.

Jansson, Arne. *From Swords to Sorrow: Homicide and Suicide in Early Modern Stockholm.* Stockholm: Almqvist and Wiksell, 1998.

Joblin, Alain. "Le suicide à l'époque moderne: Un exemple dans la France du Nord-Ouest: À Boulogne-sur-Mer." *Revue historique* 589 (1994): 85–119.

Kaden, Erich Hans. *Le jurisconsulte Germain Colladon, ami de Jean Calvin et de Théodore de Bèze.* Geneva: Georg, 1974.

Käppeli, Anne-Marie, ed. *Forgotten Women of Geneva.* Translated by Rebecca Zorach. Geneva: Metropolis, 1993.

Kelly, Linda. *Women of the French Revolution.* London: Hamish Hamilton, 1987.

Kingdon, Robert M. "Calvinism and Democracy: Some Political Implications and Debates on French Reformed Church Government, 1562–1572." *American Historical Review* 69 (1964): 393–401.

———. "Calvin and the Government of Geneva." In *Calvinus Ecclesiae Genevensis Custos,* ed. W. H. Neuser, 167–80. Frankfurt: Lang, 1984.

———. "Calvin and the Establishment of Consistory Discipline in Geneva: The Institution and the Men Who Directed It." *Nederlands Archief voor Kerkgeschiedenes* 70 (1990): 158–72.

———. "The Geneva Consistory as Established by John Calvin." *On the Way: Occasional Papers of the Wisconsin Conference of the United Church of Christ* 7 (1990): 30–44.

———. "Popular Reactions to the Debate Between Bolsec and Calvin." In *Calvin: Erbe und Auftrag,* ed. Willem van't Spijker, 138–45. Kampen, The Netherlands: Kok Pharos, 1991.

———. "Social Control and Political Control in Calvin's Geneva." *Archive for Reformation History* (special volume, 1993): 521–32.

Klauber, Martin I. *Between Reformed Scholasticism and Pan-Protestantism: Jean-Alphonse Turretin (1671–1737) and Enlightened Orthodoxy at the Academy of Geneva.* Selinsgrove, Penn.: Susquehanna University Press, 1994.

Koslofsky, Craig. "Suicide and the Secularization of the Body in Early Modern Saxony." *Continuity and Change.* Forthcoming.

Kushner, Howard I. "Women and Suicide in Historical Perspective." *Signs: Journal of Women in Culture and Society* 10 (1985): 537–52.

———. *American Suicide: A Psychocultural Exploration.* New Brunswick, N.J.: Rutgers University Press, 1991.

Lambert, Thomas A., and Isabella M. Watt, eds. *Registres du Consistoire de Genève au temps de Calvin, 1542–1544.* Under the supervision of Robert M. Kingdon, with the assistance of Jeffrey R. Watt. Geneva: Droz, 1996.

Landes, David S. *Revolution in Time: Clocks and the Making of the Modern World.* Cambridge: Harvard University Press, 1983.

Lane, Roger. *Violent Death in the City: Suicide, Accident, and Murder in Nineteenth-Cen-*

tury Philadelphia. Cambridge: Harvard University Press, 1979.

Langbein, John H. *Torture and the Law of Proof: Europe and England in the Ancien Régime.* Chicago: University of Chicago Press, 1977.

Laslett, Peter. *The World We Have Lost: England Before the Industrial Age.* 3d ed. New York: Scribner's, 1984.

Lebrun, François. *Les hommes et la mort en Anjou aux 17e et 18e siècles.* Paris: Mouton, 1971.

Lescaze, Bernard. "Crimes et Lumières, l'oeuvre du pénaliste Julien Dentand (1736–1817)." *Bulletin de la Société d'histoire et d'archéologie de Genève* 16 (1977): 163–85.

Lescaze, Bernard, and Françoise Hirsch, eds. *Encyclopédie de Genève.* In *Les institutions politiques, judiciaires et militaires,* vol. 4. Geneva: Association de l'Encyclopédie de Genève, 1985.

Lester, David. *Why People Kill Themselves: A Summary of Research Findings on Suicidal Behavior.* Springfield, Ill.: Charles C. Thomas, 1972.

———. "The Association Between the Quality of Life and Suicide and Homicide Rates." *Journal of Social Psychology* 124 (1984): 247–48.

———. *Suicide as Learned Behavior.* Springfield, Ill.: Charles C. Thomas, 1987.

———. *The Biochemical Basis of Suicide.* Springfield, Ill.: Charles C. Thomas, 1988.

Levi, Ken. "Homicide and Suicide: Structure and Process." *Deviant Behavior* 3 (1982): 91–115.

Levy, Darline, Harriet Applewhite, and Mary Johnson, eds. and trans. *Women in Revolutionary Paris.* Urbana: University of Illinois Press, 1979.

Lieberman, Lisa. "Romanticism and the Culture of Suicide in Nineteenth-Century France." *Comparative Studies in Society and History* 33 (1991): 611–29.

———. "Crimes of Reason, Crimes of Passion: Suicide and the Adulterous Woman in Nineteenth-Century France." *Journal of Family History* 24 (1999): 131–47.

Locke, John. *Political Writings of John Locke.* Edited and with an introduction by David Wootton. New York: Mentor, 1993.

Lüthy, Herbert. *La banque protestante en France de la Révocation de l'Edit de Nantes à la Révolution.* 2 vols. Paris: Service d'Edition et de Vente des Publications d'Education Nationale, 1959–61.

MacDonald, Michael. *Mystical Bedlam: Madness, Anxiety, and Healing in Seventeenth-Century England.* Cambridge: Cambridge University Press, 1981.

———. "The Secularization of Suicide in England 1660–1800." *Past and Present* 111 (1986): 50–100.

———. "Suicide and the Rise of the Popular Press in England." *Representations* 22 (1988): 36–55.

———. "'The Fearful Estate of Francis Spiera': Narrative, Identity and Emotion in Early Modern England." *Journal of British Studies* 31 (1990): 32–61.

———. "The Medicalization of Suicide in England: Laymen, Physicians, and Cultural Change, 1500–1870." In *Framing Disease: Studies in Cultural History,* ed. Charles E. Rosenberg and Janet Golden, 86–103. New Brunswick, N.J.: Rutgers University Press, 1992.

MacDonald, Michael, and Terence R. Murphy. *Sleepless Souls: Suicide in Early Modern England.* Oxford: Clarendon Press, 1990.

Mallet, Alfredo. "Structure et évolution des fortunes à Genève au XVIIIe siècle (d'après les inventaires après décès)." Mémoire de licence, Université de Genève, 1981.

Maris, Ronald W. *Social Forces in Urban Suicide.* Homewood, Ill.: Dorsey Press, 1969.

Martial. *Epigrams.* Edited and translated by D. R. Shackleton Bailey. 3 vols. Cambridge: Harvard University Press, 1993.

Masaryk, Thomas G. *Suicide and the Meaning of Civilization.* Translated by William B. Weist and Robert G. Batson. With an introduction by Anthony Giddens. Chicago: University of Chicago Press, 1970.

Mauzi, Robert. *L'idée du bonheur dans la littérature et la pensée françaises au XVIIIe siècle.* Paris: Armand Colin, 1969.

May, Gita. "Staël and the Fascination of Suicide: The Eighteenth-Century Background." In *Germaine de Staël: Crossing the Borders,* ed. Madelyn Gutwirth, Avriel Goldberger, and Karyna Szmurlo, 168–76. New Brunswick, N.J.: Rutgers University Press, 1991.

McManners, John. *Death and the Enlightenment: Changing Attitudes to Death in Eighteenth-Century France.* Oxford: Oxford University Press, 1981.

Merrick, Jeffrey. "Patterns and Prosecution of Suicide in Eighteenth-Century Paris." *Historical Reflections* 16 (1989): 1–53.

Midelfort, H. C. Erik. "Sin, Melancholy, Obsession: Insanity and Culture in Sixteenth-Century Germany." In *Understanding Popular Culture: Europe from the Middle Ages to the Nineteenth Century,* ed. Steven L. Kaplan, 113–45. Berlin: Mouton, 1984.

———. *Mad Princes of Renaissance Germany.* Charlottesville: University Press of Virginia, 1994.

———. "Religious Melancholy and Suicide: On the Reformation Origins of a Sociological Stereotype." In *Madness, Melancholy, and the Limits of the Self,* ed. Andrew D. Weiner and Leonard V. Kaplan, 41–56. Vol. 3 of *Graven Images: Studies in Culture, Law, and the Sacred.* Madison: University of Wisconsin Law School, 1996.

———. *A History of Madness in Sixteenth-Century Germany.* Stanford: Stanford University Press, 1999.

Miller, Emily. "*Biathanatos:* The Question of Audience." *Mid-Hudson Language Studies* 10 (1987): 7–14.

Minois, Georges. *Histoire du suicide: La société occidentale face à la mort volontaire.* Paris: Fayard, 1995.

——— "L'historien et la question du suicide." *Histoire* 189 (1995). 24–31.

Mitterauer, Michael, and Reinhard Sieder. *The European Family: Patriarchy to Partnership from the Middle Ages to the Present.* Translated by Karla Oosterveen and Manfred Hörzinger. Foreword by Peter Laslett. Chicago: University of Chicago Press, 1982.

Montaigne, Michel de. *Essays.* Translated by George B. Ives. With an introduction by André Gide. 3 vols. New York: Heritage Press, 1947.

Monter, E. William. *Studies in Genevan Government (1536–1605).* Geneva: Droz, 1964.

———. *Calvin's Geneva.* New York: Robert E. Krieger, 1975.

———. "The Consistory of Geneva, 1559–1569." *Bibliothèque d'humanisme et renaissance* 38 (1976): 467–84.

———. *Witchcraft in France and Switzerland: The Borderlands During the Reformation.* Ithaca, N.Y.: Cornell University Press, 1976.

———. "Historical Demography and Religious History in Sixteenth-Century Geneva." *Journal of Interdisciplinary History* 9 (1979): 399–427.

————. "Women in Calvinist Geneva (1550–1800)." *Signs* 6 (1980): 189–209.

Montesquieu, Charles de Secondat de. *Considérations sur les causes de la grandeur des Romains et de leur décadence.* In *Oeuvres complètes de Montesquieu,* ed. Edouard Laboulaye, vol. 2: 115–326. Paris: Garnier Frères, 1876.

————. *De l'esprit des lois.* Paris: Garnier Frères, 1927.

————. *Lettres Persanes.* Edited by Antoine Adam. Geneva: Droz, 1965.

More, Thomas. *Utopia.* Translated and with an introduction by Paul Turner. London: Penguin, 1965.

Moron, Pierre. *Le suicide.* Paris: Presses Universitaires de France, 1975.

Morselli, Enrico. *Il Suicidio: Saggio di statistica morale comparata.* Milan: Dumolard, 1879.

Mottu-Weber, Liliane. "Les femmes dans la vie économique de Genève, XVIe–XVIIe siècles." *Bulletin de la Société d'histoire et d'archéologie de Genève* 16 (1979): 381–401.

————. *Genève au siècle de la Réforme: Economie et Refuge.* Geneva: Société d'histoire et d'archéologie de Genève, 1987.

————. "Les 'Halles du Molard' du XVIe au XVIIIe siècle: Contribution à l'histoire du commerce et de la politique douanière de Genève." *Revue suisse d'histoire* 39 (1989): 371–421.

————. "L'évolution des activités professionnelles des femmes à Genève du XVIe au XVIIIe siècle." In *La Donna nell'economia, secc. XVIII–XVIII,* ed. Simonetta Cavaciocchi, 345–57. Florence: Le Monnier, 1990.

————. "A propos de la crise de 1586–1587 à Genève: Du devoir des magistrats de nourrir le peuple et du droit des pasteurs de leur résister." In *Quand la Montagne aussi a une Histoire: Mélanges offerts à Jean-François Bergier,* ed. Martin Körner and François Walter, 151–65. Bern: Paul Haupt, 1996.

————. "Le statut des étrangers et de leurs descendants à Genève (XVIe–XVIIIe siècles)." In *Les immigrants et la ville: Insertion, intégration, discrimination (XIIe–XXe siècles),* ed. Denis Menjot and Jean-Luc Pinol, 27–42. Paris: L'Harmattan, 1996.

————. "Des ordonnances ecclésiastiques au Code civil (1804): Jalons pour une étude du divorce à Genève de la Réformation à la Restauration." In *Dossier Helvetik–Dossier Helvétique,* ed. Christian Simon, vol. 2. *Structures sociales et économiques: Histoire des femmes,* 167–185. Basel: Helbing; Frankfurt am Main: Lichtenhahn, 1997.

Mottu-Weber, Liliane, and Dominique Zumkeller, eds. *Mélanges d'histoire économique offerts au Professeur Anne-Marie Piuz.* Geneva: Istec, 1989.

Moullembé, Arlette, Florence Tiano, Gérard Anavi, Claude Anavi, and Jean-Marc Parichon. "Conduites suicidaires, approche théorique et clinique." *Bulletin de Psychologie* 27 (1973–74): 801–944.

Murphy, Terence R. "'Woful Childe of Parents Rage': Suicide of Children and Adolescents in Early Modern England, 1507–1710." *Sixteenth Century Journal* 17 (1986): 259–70.

Murray, Alexander. *Suicide in the Middle Ages.* Vol. 1. *The Violent Against Themselves.* Oxford: Oxford University Press, 1998.

Norberg, Kathryn. *Rich and Poor in Grenoble, 1600–1814.* Berkeley: University of California Press, 1985.

Olson, Jeannine E. *Calvin and Social Welfare: Deacons and the Bourse Française.* Selinsgrove, Penn.: Susquehanna University Press; London: Associated University Press, 1989.

O'Mara, Patrick. "Geneva in the Eighteenth Century: A Socio-Economic Study of the Bourgeois City-State During Its Golden Age." Ph.D. dissertation, University of California, Berkeley, 1954.

Ordonnances somptuaires. Geneva: Pierre Aubert, 1631.

Outram, Dorinda. *The Body and the French Revolution: Sex, Class, and Political Culture.* New Haven, Conn.: Yale University Press, 1989.

Overell, M. A. "The Exploitation of Francesco Spiera." *Sixteenth Century Journal* 26 (1995): 619–37.

Paulin, Bernard. *Du couteau à la plume: Le suicide dans la littérature anglaise de la Renaissance (1580–1625).* Lyon: L'Hermès, 1977.

Perlin, Seymour, ed. *A Handbook for the Study of Suicide.* New York: Oxford University Press, 1975.

Perrenoud, Alfred. *La population de Genève XVIe–XIXe siècles.* Geneva: Société d'histoire et d'archéologie de Genève, 1979.

Pescolido, Bernice A., and Sharon Georgianna. "Durkheim, Suicide, and Religion: Toward a Network Theory of Suicide." *American Sociological Review* 54 (1989): 33–48.

Peter, Marc. *Genève et la Révolution: Le gouvernement constitutionnel, l'annexation, la société économique.* Geneva: Jullien, 1950.

Pierce, Albert. "The Economic Cycle and the Social Suicide Rate." *American Sociological Review* 32 (1967): 457–62.

Pittard, Thérèse. *Femmes de Genève aux jours d'autrefois.* Geneva: Labor et Fides, 1946.

Piuz, Anne-Marie. *Affaires et politique: Recherches sur le commerce de Genève au XVIIe siècle.* Geneva: Jullien, 1964.

———. "Note sur les rapports entre le prix du pain et le prix de la viande à Genève au XVIIIe siècle." *Bulletin du Département d'histoire économique: Université de Genève* 15 (1984–1985): 47–51.

———. *A Genève et autour de Genève aux XVIIe et XVIIIe siècles: Etudes d'histoire économique.* Lausanne, Switzerland: Payot, 1985.

Piuz, Anne-Marie, and Liliane Mottu-Weber. *L'économie genevoise de la Réforme à la fin de l'Ancien Régime XVIe–XVIIIe siècles.* Geneva: Société d'histoire et d'archéologie de Genève, 1990.

Plato. *The Laws.* Translated and with an introduction by Trevor J. Saunders. Middlesex, England: Penguin, 1970.

———. *Phaedo.* Translated by David Gallop. Oxford: Clarendon Press, 1990.

Poncet, André-Luc. *Châtelains et sujets dans la campagne genevoise (1536–1792).* Geneva: Presses Universitaires Romandes, 1973.

———. "La renaissance des études juridiques au début du XVIII siècle et l'introduction du droit naturel à l'Académie." *Revue de Vieux Genève* 8 (1978): 77–84.

Porret, Michel. "La 'mort de la belle jeunesse' ou le suicide juvénile à Genève au XVIIIe siècle." *Gesnerus: Revue suisse d'histoire de la médecine et des sciences naturelles* 49 (1992): 351–69.

———. "'Je suis bien criminel de vous quitter ainsi,' ou l'adieu des suicidés: L'exemple de Genève au XVIIIe siècle." In *Savoir mourir,* ed. Christiane Montandon-Binet and Alain Montandon, 38–63. Paris: L'Harmattan, 1993.

———. "Solitude, mélancolie, souffrance: Le suicide à Genève durant l'Ancien Régime (XVIIe–XVIIIe siècles)." *Cahiers Psychiatriques Genevois* 16 (1994): 9–21.

———. *Le crime et ses circonstances: De l'esprit de l'arbitraire au siècle des Lumières selon les réquisitoires des procureurs généraux de Genève.* Geneva: Droz, 1995.

———. "Mourir l'âme angoissée: Les 'réflexions sur le suicide' de l'horloger genevois J.-J. Mellaret (1769)." *Revue d'histoire moderne et contemporaine* 42 (1995): 71–90.

Powell, Elwin H. "Occupation, Status, and Suicide: Toward a Redefinition of Anomie." *American Sociological Review* 23 (1958): 131–39.

Prevost, Guillaume. "Extrait d'une note statistique sur le suicide." *Bibliothèque universelle* (June 1835): 1–20.

Pufendorf, Samuel. *De Jure Naturae et Gentium Libri Octo.* Translated by C. H. Oldfather and W. A. Oldfather. 2 vols. Oxford: Clarendon Press, 1934.

Quinney, Richard. "Suicide, Homicide, and Economic Development." *Social Forces* 43 (1965): 401–6.

Reverdin, Olivier, Jérôme Sautier, Olivier Fatio, Louise Martin, Liliane Mottu-Weber, Michel Grandjean, and Cécile Holtz. *Genève au temps de la Révocation de l'Edit de Nantes 1680–1705.* Geneva: Droz, 1985.

Rieder, Philippe. "Discipline ecclésiastique et relations familiales à Genève au XVIIIe siècle." *Equinoxe: Revue Romande de Sciences Humaines* 11 (1994): 93–110.

Rivoire, Emile, and Victor Van Berchem, eds. *Les sources du droit du canton de Genève.* 4 vols. Aarau, Switzerland: Sauerländer, 1927–35.

Roget, Amédée. *Histoire du peuple de Genève depuis la Réforme jusqu'à l'Escalade.* 7 vols. Geneva: John Jullien, 1873.

Roney, John B., and Martin I. Klauber, eds. *The Identity of Geneva: The Christian Commonwealth, 1564–1864.* Westport, Conn.: Greenwood, 1998.

Rosa, Annette. *Citoyennes: Les femmes et la Révolution française.* Paris: Messidor, 1988.

Roth, Robert. "Juges et médecins face à l'infanticide à Genève au XIXe siècle." *Gesnerus: Histoire de la médecine et des sciences naturelles à Genève* 34 (1977): 113–28.

———. *Pratiques pénitentiaires et théorie sociale: L'exemple de la prison de Genève (1825–1862).* Geneva: Droz, 1981.

Roth-Lochner, Barbara. *De la banche à l'étude: Une histoire institutionnelle, professionnelle et sociale du notariat genevois sous l'Ancien Régime.* Geneva: Société d'histoire et d'archéologie de Genève, 1997.

———. *Messieurs de la Justice et leur greffe: Aspects de la législation, de l'administration de la justice civile genevoise et du monde de la pratique sous l'Ancien Régime.* Geneva: Société d'histoire et d'archéologie de Genève, 1992.

Roth-Lochner, Barbara, Marc Neuenschwander, and François Walter, eds. *Des archives à la mémoire: Mélanges d'histoire politique, religieuse et sociale offerts à Louis Binz.* Geneva: Société d'histoire et d'archéologie de Genève, 1995.

Rousseau, Jean-Jacques. *Julie ou la nouvelle Héloïse.* Edited by René Pomeau. Paris: Garnier Frères, 1960.

———. *The Essential Rousseau.* Translated by Lowell Bair. With an introduction by Matthew Josephson. New York: Penguin, 1975.

Russell, Jeffrey Burton. *Mephistopheles: The Devil in the Modern World.* Ithaca, N.Y.: Cornell University Press, 1986.

————. *The Prince of Darkness: Radical Evil and the Power of Good in History.* Ithaca, N.Y.: Cornell University Press, 1988.

Sainsbury, Peter. *Suicide in London: An Ecological Study.* London: Chapman and Hall, 1955.

Schama, Simon. *The Embarrassment of Riches: An Interpretation of Dutch Culture in the Golden Age.* Berkeley: University of California Press, 1988.

Schär, Markus. *Seelennöte der Untertanen: Selbstmord, Melancholie und Religion im Alten Zürich 1500–1800.* Zurich: Chronos, 1985.

Schiesari, Juliana. *The Gendering of Melancholia: Feminism, Psychoanalysis, and the Symbolics of Loss in Renaissance Literature.* Ithaca, N.Y.: Cornell University Press, 1996.

Schmitt, Jean-Claude. "Le suicide au Moyen Age." *Annales: E.S.C.* 31 (1976): 3–28.

Schnegg, Alfred. "Justice et suicide sous l'Ancien Régime." *Musée Neuchâtelois* (1982): 73–94.

Seaver, Paul S. *Wallington's World: A Puritan Artisan in Seventeenth-Century London.* Stanford: Stanford University Press, 1985.

Seidler, Michael J. "Kant and the Stoics on Suicide." *Journal of the History of Ideas* 44 (1983): 429–53.

Seneca, Lucius Annaeus. *Moral Essays.* Translated by John W. Basore. Includes *On Anger,* 1: 106–355; *On Providence,* 1: 2–47. 3 vols. London: William Heinemann; New York: G. P. Putnam's Sons, 1928.

Shorter, Edward. *The Making of the Modern Family.* New York: Basic Books, 1975.

Signori, Gabriela, ed. *Trauer, Verzweiflung und Anfechtung: Selbstmord und Selbstmordversuche in mittelalterlichen und früheneuzeitlichen Gesellschaften.* In *Forum Psychohistorie,* ed. Hedwig Röckelein, vol. 3. Tübingen: Diskord, 1994.

Smith, Bonnie. *Ladies of Leisure: The Bourgeoises of the Nord.* Princeton: Princeton University Press, 1982.

Soman, Alfred. "Anatomy of an Infanticide Trial: The Case of Marie-Jeanne Bartonnet (1742)." In *Changing Identities in Early Modern France,* ed. Michael Wolfe, 248–72. Durham, N.C.: Duke University Press, 1997.

Sommerville, C. John. *The Secularization of Early Modern England: From Religious Culture to Religious Faith.* New York: Oxford University Press, 1992.

Sonnaillon, Bernard. "Etude des divorces à Genève dans la seconde moitié du XVIIIe siècle." Mémoire de licence, Université de Genève, 1975.

Spierenburg, Pieter. *The Broken Spell: A Cultural and Anthropological History of Preindustrial Europe.* New Brunswick, N.J.: Rutgers University Press, 1991.

Sprott, Samuel Ernest. *The English Debate on Suicide from Donne to Hume.* La Salle, Ill.: Open Court, 1961.

Stack, Steven. "The Effects of Marital Dissolution on Suicide." *Journal of Marriage and the Family* 42 (1980): 83–92.

————. "Religion and Suicide: A Reanalysis." *Social Psychiatry* 15 (1980): 65–70.

————. "Divorce and Suicide: A Time Series Analysis, 1933–1970." *Journal of Family Issues* 2 (1981): 77–90.

————. "Suicide and Religion: A Comparative Analysis." *Sociological Focus* 14 (1981): 207–20.

————. "The Effect of Domestic/Religious Individualism on Suicide, 1954–1978." *Journal of Marriage and the Family* 47 (1985): 431–47.

Stack, Steven, and Ain Haas. "The Effect of Unemployment Duration on National Suicide Rates: A Time Series Analysis, 1948–1982." *Sociological Focus* 17 (1984): 17–29.

Stelling-Michaud, Suzanne, ed. *Le livre du recteur de l'Académie de Genève (1559–1878).* 6 vols. Geneva: Droz, 1959–80.

Stepczynski, Marian, ed. *Genève et la Suisse: Un mariage d'amour et de raison.* Geneva: Bourse de Genève, 1992.

Stevenson, S. J. "The Rise of Suicide Verdicts in South-East England, 1530–1590: The Legal Process." *Continuity and Change* 2 (1987): 37–75.

———. "Social and Economic Contributions to the Pattern of 'Suicide' in South-East England, 1530–1590." *Continuity and Change* 2 (1987): 225–62.

Stone, Lawrence. *The Family, Sex and Marriage in England 1500–1800.* London: Weidenfeld and Nicolson, 1977.

Sym, John. *Life's Preservative Against Self-Killing.* Edited and with an introduction by Michael MacDonald. London: Routledge, 1989.

Tadic-Gilloteaux, Nicole. "Sénèque face au suicide." *L'antiquité classique* 32 (1963): 541–51.

Taylor, Steve. *Durkheim and the Study of Suicide.* New York: St. Martin's Press, 1982.

Terré, François, ed. *Le suicide.* Paris: Presses Universitaires de France, 1994.

Trainor, Stephen L. "Suicide and Seneca in Two Eighteenth-Century Tragedies." In *Drama and the Classical Heritage,* ed. Clifford Davidson, Rand Johnson, and John H. Stroupe, 227–40. New York: AMS Press, 1993.

Trumbach, Randolph. *The Rise of the Egalitarian Family: Aristocratic Kinship and Domestic Relations in Eighteenth-Century England.* New York: Academic Press, 1978.

U.S. Bureau of the Census. *Statistical Abstract of the United States: 1997.* 117th ed. Washington, D.C.: U.S. Bureau of the Census, 1997.

Virgil. *Aeneid.* In *Virgil.* Translated by H. Rushton Fairclough. 2 vols. Cambridge: Harvard University Press; London: William Heinemann, 1969.

Voltaire, François Marie Arouet de. "De Caton, du suicide." In *Dictionnaire philosophique.* From *Oeuvres complètes de Voltaire,* vol. 38: 390–404. Basel: Jean-Jacques Tourneisen, 1786.

———. *Candide, Zadig and Selected Stories.* Translated by Donald M. Frame. New York: Signet Classic, 1961.

———. *Correspondence and Related Documents.* Edited by Theodore Besterman. Definitive ed. 51 vols. Banbury, U.K.: Voltaire Foundation, 1968–77.

Vovelle, Michel. *Piété baroque et déchristianisation en Provence au XVIIIe siècle: Les attitudes devant la mort d'après les clauses des testaments.* Paris: Plon, 1973.

Walker, Corinne. "Images du luxe à Genève: Douze années de répression par la Chambre de la Réformation (1646–1658)." *Revue du Vieux Genève* 17 (1987): 21–26.

———. "Esquisse pour une histoire de la vie nocturne: Genève au XVIIIe siècle." *Revue de Vieux Genève* 19 (1989): 73–85.

———. "Les lois somptuaires ou le rêve d'un ordre social: Evolution et enjeux de la politique somptuaire à Genève (XVIe–XVIIIe siècles)." *Equinoxe: Revue Romande de Sciences Humaines* 11 (1994): 111–27.

Walker, Corinne, and Micheline Louis-Courvoisier. *Dictionnaire des communes genevoises: Rues, chemins, lieux-dits.* Geneva: Promoédition, 1985.

Walker, D. P. *The Decline of Hell: Seventeenth-Century Discussions of Eternal Torment.* Chicago: University of Chicago Press, 1964.

Watt, Jeffrey R. *The Making of Modern Marriage: Matrimonial Control and the Rise of Sentiment in Neuchâtel, 1550–1800.* Ithaca, N.Y.: Cornell University Press, 1992.

———. "Women and the Consistory in Calvin's Geneva." *Sixteenth Century Journal* 24 (1993): 429–39.

———. "The Marriage Laws Calvin Drafted for Geneva." In *Calvinus Sacrae Scripturae Professor,* ed. W. H. Neuser, 245–55. Grand Rapids, Mich.: Eerdman's, 1994.

———. "The Family, Love, and Suicide in Early Modern Geneva." *Journal of Family History* 21 (1996): 63–86.

———. "Calvin on Suicide." *Church History* 66 (1997): 463–76.

———. "Suicide in Reformation Geneva." *Archive for Reformation History* 89 (1998): 227–46.

Wegert, Karl. *Popular Culture, Crime, and Social Control in Eighteenth-Century Württemberg.* Stuttgart: Franz Steiner, 1994.

Wiedmer, Laurence. "Le cadre de vie matériel dans la campagne genevoise au XVIIIe siècle." *Revue du Vieux Genève* 12 (1982): 50–58.

———. *Pain quotidien et pain de disette: Meuniers, boulangers et Etat nourricier à Genève (XVIIe–XVIIIe siècles).* Geneva: Editions Passé Présent, 1993.

Zell, Michael. "Suicide in Pre-Industrial England." *Social History* 11 (1986): 303–17.

Zumkeller, Dominique. *Le paysan et la terre: Agriculture et structure agraire à Genève au XVIIIe siècle.* Geneva: Editions Passé Présent, 1992.

Index